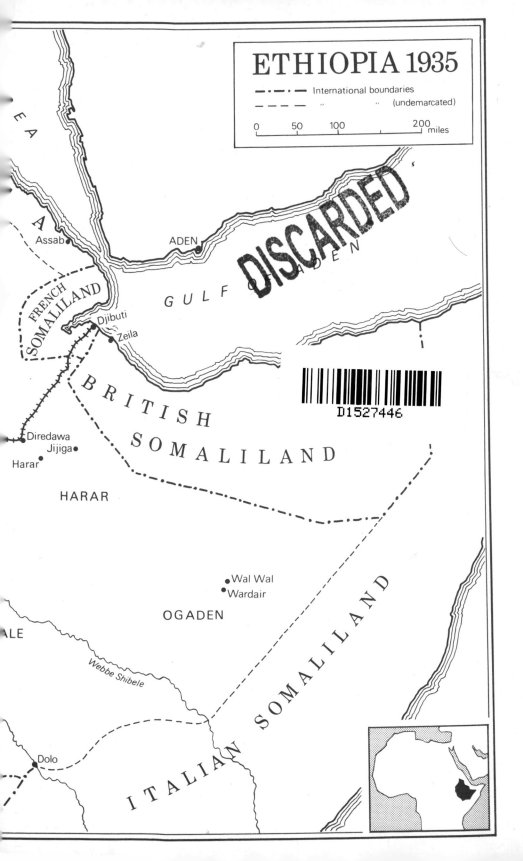

ETHIOPIA 1935

International boundaries —·—·—
" " (undemarcated) —————

0   50   100   200 miles

E A

A

Assab

FRENCH SOMALILAND

Djibuti
Zeila

ADEN

GULF OF ADEN

DISCARDED

B R I T I S H
S O M A L I L A N D

Diredawa
Jijiga
Harar

HARAR

Wal Wal
Wardair

OGADEN

Webbe Shibele

I T A L I A N   S O M A L I L A N D

ALE

Dolo

LION BY THE TAIL

Also by Thomas M. Coffey

AGONY AT EASTER
IMPERIAL TRAGEDY

LION BY THE TAIL

The Story of the
Italian–Ethiopian War

by

Thomas M. Coffey

THE VIKING PRESS

New York

Acknowledgment is made to the following
for permission to quote:

Casa Editrice G. C. Sansoni, for material from *Anno XIII*
by Emilio DeBono.

Curtis Brown Ltd., for material from *Nine Troubled Years*
by Sir Samuel Hoare.

Houghton Mifflin Company and Times Newspaper Limited
for material from *The Eden Memoirs: Facing The Dictators*
by Anthony Eden.

CONTENTS

ILLUSTRATIONS

between pages 178 *and* 179

FOREWORD

ITALIANS and Ethiopians met for the first time on a battlefield in 1887 when the Italians, having occupied the strip of Red Sea coast which was later to be called Eritrea, decided they were ready to move inland. It was an ill-advised decision. On January 26, 1887, a force of five hundred Italians met an estimated twenty thousand Ethiopians at a place called Dogali. The Ethiopians, under the aegis of their Emperor Yohannis IV, virtually wiped out the Italian force, thus persuading Italy to delay for several years its territorial aspirations.

When Emperor Yohannis died in 1889, his successor, Menelik II, found it useful to establish friendly relations with the Italians, even signing a pact (the Treaty of Uccialli) in which he recognized their right to Eritrea and agreed that he might conduct some Ethiopian foreign affairs through the good offices of the Italian government. To seal the agreement, Italy, in the name of its King Umberto, rather foolishly gave Menelik twenty-eight cannon and thirty-eight thousand rifles. Menelik's friendship with Italy soon faded when the Italians chose to interpret this document as an acknowledgment that Ethiopia had become a protectorate of Italy. In an effort to soothe him, and to demonstrate the benefits of protectorate status, the Italians compounded their earlier foolishness by offering him in 1893 two million cartridges for the thirty-eight thousand rifles they had already given him. Menelik, after receiving the cartridges, promptly denounced the Treaty of Uccialli and began using the threat of Italian encroachment to unite the Ethiopian chiefs behind him. The Italians then very obligingly fostered his efforts to develop Ethiopian nationalism and solidify his own power. Using his treaty denunciation as a pretext, they organized, under the leadership of General Oreste Baratieri, the Governor of Eritrea, an expeditionary force of 17,700 men, a considerably larger force than other colonialist European countries were accustomed to using, and marched south into Ethiopia.

Unfortunately for the Italians, the area they were invading included the Holy City of Axum, by tradition the spiritual center of the Christian

ix

Orthodox Church, which was the official religion of Ethiopia. The possible loss of Axum was a rallying argument which no Ethiopian chief could ignore. In 1895, Menelik was able to lead northward an army of more than a hundred thousand fierce and united men, armed with cannon and rifles the Italians themselves had provided. Though he believed he could defeat the Italians, it eventually became apparent that he might not get an opportunity to do so. By late February 1896, his army was so short of food and provisions he was at the point of being forced to withdraw southward, leaving the invader unchallenged.

Once again, the Italians themselves proved helpful to him. General Baratieri, whose army was encamped in a well-fortified, virtually impregnable position at Sauria, sixteen miles northeast of Adowa, decided to finish his campaign quickly by taking the Ethiopians by surprise. The ideal day would be Sunday, March 1, 1896, an Ethiopian religious feast day on which, he hoped, a large part of the enemy force would be worshiping in Axum, twenty miles away. He had not bothered to learn the size of the army facing him, nor did he know that the Ethiopians were beginning to suffer acutely from hunger, although he could easily have acquired such information by sending a few native spies into the enemy camps. He hadn't even bothered to check the accuracy of the area maps on which his strategy depended.

Dividing his army into three columns, each of which was to occupy a specified hill commanding the plain of Adowa, General Baratieri broke camp at nightfall, Saturday, February 29, and began the twelve-to-fifteen-mile march toward their assigned positions. But the column on the left, commanded by an unfortunate major general named Matteo Albertone, soon lost its way on the dark, ill-defined Ethiopian trails which were now obscured by several hours of rainfall. Albertone's men, attempting to correct their route, then found themselves crossing in front of the other two columns, thus costing the entire Italian army a delay of almost two hours.

After disengaging themselves from their comrades, Albertone's troops finally reached the hill to which his map indicated they were assigned, but as soon as they were installed upon it, their native guides pointed out that they were on the wrong hill, and that they were four or five miles from the right one. Though dawn was now approaching, General Albertone decided to correct his mistake. In doing so, he made a more serious one. The Ethiopians, whose spies had discovered the Italian movements, were waiting for Albertone's column as it approached its destination and proceeded virtually to obliterate it.

At dawn, the Italian center and right columns entered battle against other Ethiopian forces unaware that their entire left wing was unprotected. Outflanked and eventually surrounded thanks to the peculiar leadership of their generals, the Italian soldiers soon found themselves in a mael-strom from which they could not escape. Though they fought bravely, twelve thousand of them had fallen by the end of the day, and the four or five thousand survivors were saved only by the Ethiopian tradition of ending every battle at nightfall. As the sun set, Emperor Menelik called off his army to make ready for another Ethiopian tradition, the all-night victory celebration.

The 1896 Battle of Adowa solidified Ethiopian nationalism and exposed Italian militarism to ridicule. Not until thirty-nine years later had the Italians recovered sufficiently from the humiliating catastrophe to try their luck again in Ethiopia. When they did so, in 1935, the invasion they launched was felt not only in Africa but throughout the world. Benito Mussolini's Italian conquest of Ethiopia was destined to become the most important single factor in the destruction of the League of Nations and the failure of collective security against aggression. His bluffing, bullying conduct of foreign relations exposed the flabbiness and cynicism of the western European and American democracies and demonstrated to his junior colleague, Adolf Hitler, an ideal *modus operandi* for the manipulation and intimidation of those countries during the three years that followed. The conquest of Ethiopia was not, of course, the primary cause of World War II, but more than any other single event, it opened the route toward that cataclysm.

At the same time, Mussolini's Italian aggression created an oppressive challenge to Ethiopia's Emperor Haile Selassie I and demanded of him a kind of heroism few men are ever called upon to exhibit. In the years since the World War II defeat of Italy and the restoration of the Emperor to his throne, some of his policies in dealing with Ethiopia's problems have brought criticism upon him. No one can doubt, however, his epic heroism in the years of his country's greatest travail. Largely because of his conduct during the troubles with Italy, the story of the Ethiopian-Italian War achieves the proportions of classic tragedy.

That story is the story of *Lion by the Tail*. In pursuing its details, the author has visited Ethiopia, Italy, France, and England, and has received assistance from many institutions and many people in those countries and in the United States. Because several individuals still wish to remain anonymous, the following is only a partial list of those who have been most helpful: Fred Abel, retired Addis Ababa banker; Miss Sara Andreassian, United Nations librarian; John Baker, Executive Assistant, Research Libraries, New York Public Library; Benvenuto Bonassisa and Nevio Del Medico, librarians at Biblioteca Comunale, Milan; Patrick T. Coffey, who translated and interpreted many Italian documents, books, and interviews; Miss Naomi Cohen, Argosy Book Store, New York, for the pursuit of rare items; Dr. Stetson Conn, Miss Hanna Zeidlik, and Ditmar

Finke of the United States Army Military History Department, Washington, D.C.; Sir Duncan Cumming, retired British Chief Administrator of Eritrea and Deputy Civil Secretary, Government of Anglo-Egyptian Sudan; Dr. George Dassios, medical adviser to the Ethiopian Ministry of Public Health and a Red Cross doctor in Ethiopia during the Italian invasion; Angelo Del Boca, editor, *Il Giorno*, Milan, and author of *The Ethiopian War*; Dusan Djonovich, New York University law librarian, and Philip Cohen, president of Oceana Publishing Company, for assistance in procuring League of Nations documents; Patrick Gilkes, onetime lecturer at Haile Selassie I University in Addis Ababa and researcher into Ethiopian history and customs; Librarian Stanley G. Gillan and the staff of London Library, one of the world's most congenial institutions; Antranig Gocherian, General Manager, Serafian & Company, Ethiopia, who provided great assistance in Addis Ababa; Mrs. Olga Henkel, CBS News, United Nations Bureau; Sasha and Josephina Kandare, who offered expert guidance through the Ethiopian countryside; Arthur Kogan, Special Assistant to the Director, Historical Office, United States Department of State; Dr. Robert Krauskopf and John E. Taylor, Modern Military Records Division, United States National Archives; Dr. Antonio Enrico Leva, L'Istituto Italiano per l'Africa, Rome; Hans W. Lockot, adviser, National Library of Ethiopia, Addis Ababa; Roger Machell, Hamish Hamilton Ltd.; His Excellency Lij Endalkachew Makonnen, Ethiopian Minister of Communications; Terere Makonnen, who translated many Ethiopian documents; Dr. W. Don McClure, Manager, American Evangelical Presbyterian Mission in Ethiopia; Paolo Molaioli, for his guidance through the Palazzo Venezia in Rome; L. Quincy Mumford, Librarian of Congress, and his staff; Charles Miller, author of *Lunatic Express*, for valuable information about Africa; Miss Anne Mullins, for research assistance; Dr. Richard Pankhurst, Director, Institute of Ethiopian Studies, Addis Ababa; Mrs. Rita Pankhurst, Chief Librarian, Haile Selassie I University; Krikor Pogharian, long-time Addis Ababa resident, for his recollections of the city's past; Miss Mary Regan, New York Public Library; Dr. Giorgio Rochat, Istituto Nazionale per la Storia del Movimento di Liberazione in Italia, Milan, for research guidance; Hagop Sarafian, a member of the Ethiopian Air Force during the Italian invasion; Richard Sawyer and Miss Nicola Edwards of Chas. Sawyer Ltd., Booksellers, London, for the pursuit of rare items; Jane F. Smith, Director, Civil Archives Division, United States National Archives; Gunther Stuhlmann, author's agent and instigator; Graham Tayar, British Broadcasting Corporation producer, Ethiopian resident for several years, and writer on Ethiopian affairs; Miss Tsehai Berhane Selassie, who translated Ethiopian books and documents; Alan D. Williams, The Viking Press; Dr. Neville Williams, Deputy

Keeper of the Public Records Office of Great Britain; and Robert Wolfe, Chief of the Captured Records Branch, Military Archives Division, United States National Archives.

The institutions which helped were the British Museum, the British Public Records Office, the Istituto Italiano per l'Africa in Rome, the London Library, the New York Public Library, the National Library of Ethiopia in Addis Ababa, the University of California Library at Berkeley, the United States Army Military History Section, the Library of Congress, and the United States National Archives.

Note concerning usage : In the spelling of Ethiopian place names, the text adheres to modern consensus. Ethiopian citizens mentioned in the book are designated by their first names as is customary, except in the case of Dejasmatch Haile Selassie Gugsa, who is sometimes referred to by his last name to avoid confusing him in the reader's mind with Emperor Haile Selassie.

PART ONE

CHAPTER ONE

THE sun had been up for two hours and the Italian native sentries were perched as usual on a platform of branches and boughs near the wells at Wal Wal, a hot, scrubby watering place for nomadic tribes in the low-lying East African desert seven degrees above the Equator and about two hundred and fifty miles from the shore of the Indian Ocean. The date was November 22, 1934. From the brush some distance to the northwest, far beyond the wells, one of the sentries suddenly saw a group of men emerge, then move circumspectly closer.

The sentry quickly leaped down from his roost and ran the hundred and twenty yards back to the small outpost of native troops the Italians had maintained at Wal Wal for several years. No white officer was present; the sentry reported what he had seen to the black in command, a non-commissioned officer named Ali Uelie.[1] At the age of thirty, Ali Uelie, small in stature but unquestionably brave, had spent fifteen years in the Italian army.

Gathering a force of about sixty troops from their round, thatch-roofed quarters inside the fortification, he led them out to meet the invaders. After marching more than a mile to the northwest, through the extensive zone of wells, his detail had still encountered no one, but trusting the report of his sentry, he decided to take precautionary measures. Returning part way to camp, he spread his men in a thin, wide arc around the wells and waited. Though his force was ridiculously small for an area several hundred yards wide, he had confidence in these men. The Italians had trained them rigorously and armed them with modern rifles.

Uelie and his troops did not have long to wait. Out of the thorny brush came a small group of men, some wearing khaki uniforms with wide-brimmed gray hats, some wearing the graceful, flowing, toga-like *shamma* which was the traditional costume of Ethiopians. All were armed with rifles and wore full cartridge belts. Stopping just a few yards short of the Italian line, they neither attacked nor entered into conversation. Within a few minutes, more of them arrived, followed by still more, until, as

3

midday approached, Ali Uelie's force of sixty was facing a force of six hundred.

The last group to arrive, shortly before noon, was led by three Ethiopian officers dressed in elegant khaki uniforms of European style. Assuming these three to be in command, Ali Uelie walked up to them and asked them for what reason they had approached the Italian post.

The highest in rank of the three, identifying himself as Fitaurari (Vanguard Commander) Balchi Shiferra, Governor of the eastern Ethiopian provinces of Ogaden and Jijiga, announced that he was in charge of a military escort for an Anglo-Ethiopian border-delimitation commission which was soon to arrive, and that he and his men intended to use the wells.

Ali Uelie, under standing instructions from the white officers in command of the nearest Italian installation at Wardair, about twenty miles distant, informed Fitaurari Shiferra that the Ethiopians were not authorized to use the wells.

Shiferra insisted that the Italians could not exclude the Ethiopians from the wells because Wal Wal was within the borders of Ethiopia, and the Italians had no right to be there.

Ali Uelie, without bothering to argue this point, threatened that his men would open fire if the Ethiopians continued to advance.

Fitaurari Shiferra decided now to break off the discussion, perhaps because his superior Ethiopian force had by this time pushed back the thin Italian line far enough to gain access to some of the wells. After talking for a while to the two officers accompanying him, he approached the black Italian N.C.O. again and said he would like to confer with a white Italian officer. Ali Uelie, who had already sent one runner to Wardair informing his superiors of the unexpected developments, agreed now to send another with Shiferra's request. The danger of a bloody conflict temporarily averted, the troops on both sides of the line, separated by only a few yards of ground, began to settle down, digging trenches, pitching tents, watering camels, and building hedges of thorny brush more formidable than barbed wire.

When the Anglo-Ethiopian Border Commission, transported across the hot desert by camels and trucks, arrived at Wal Wal the next morning half an hour before noon, the five commissioners found the two armed camps menacing each other across a hedge of piled-up thorn.[2] The Italian contingent, having been reinforced overnight from Wardair, now comprised about two hundred fifty native troops, still under the command of Ali Uelie. The two English and three Ethiopian commissioners, led by a tall, blond, experienced British lieutenant colonel named E.H.M. Clifford, approached the rifle-pointing Italian troops and asked Ali Uelie to move his men back far enough so that their men could pitch camp close to the wells.

4

Again the black Italian N.C.O. refused, but again, during the discussion, the superior Ethiopian force was able to nudge the Italians back another three hundred fifty yards without a shot being fired.

After establishing their camps side by side about five hundred yards from the camp of the Ethiopian soldiers, the five commissioners met and composed a letter to the Italians in Wardair, stating the reason for their visit to Wal Wal ("to study the question of pasturage") and protesting against their unfriendly reception as well as the disappearance of one member of the Ethiopian escort, a Somal N.C.O. who the Ethiopians said had been forcibly dragged away during the night by the Italian troops.

The next morning, November 24, at six a.m., Colonel Clifford received a visiting card from Captain Roberto Cimmaruta, the ranking white Italian officer in the area and a man with whom Clifford had dealt cordially on previous occasions. Cimmaruta acknowledged receipt of the commission's protest and inquired whether Clifford wished to see him. Clifford and the ranking Ethiopian commissioner, Tessama Bantie, replied jointly, asking the Italian officer to come to the British camp that morning at ten a.m.

When Cimmaruta arrived from Wardair, his automobile had to drive through an unsettling crowd of Ethiopian soldiers to reach the British camp.[3] At the entrance to the compound, now surrounded by a hedge of thorn (Ethiopians usually built such hedges to keep out night-prowling hyenas), a squadron of camel corpsmen stood at present arms in his honor. Alighting from his car, he was welcomed by Colonel Clifford, the British civilian commissioner Alex T. Curle, and two junior officers. While he was exchanging pleasantries with them, the three Ethiopian commissioners, Bantie, Zaude Balaineh, and Dr. Lorenzo Taezaz, emerged from a nearby tent and joined the group. They were as cordial as the British. Cimmaruta and the five commissioners went into the tent of the British mission, an imposingly large structure with a veranda and, inside, a full set of wood and fabric armchairs, nicely arranged around a camp table. A servant brought beer, and the discussion, which began with a few jokes from Cimmaruta, proceeded smoothly until the British and Ethiopians raised the subject of their protest.

Wal Wal, the Ethiopians said, was very clearly in Ethiopia. It was not, as the Italians claimed, in Italian Somaliland. Therefore, the Italians had no right to be here.

Captain Cimmaruta had no doubts about Italy's right to occupy the area. The Italians had been here for several years. He himself had been here for several years. Wal Wal was most certainly a part of Italian Somaliland, despite several Ethiopian efforts to drive the Italians away. Yet he had no intention of engaging in a pointless argument about this, especially since it was a political rather than a military question.

5

He said simply, "Why did you approach our presidio without warning, and with so many and such aggressive troops? If you had let my government know your intention of carrying out projects here, I myself would have come out to meet you, and we would have celebrated with a dinner under a tent or in one of the forts."

The Ethiopians, claiming the territory was theirs, refused to acknowledge any need to inform the Italians of their intention to visit it.

Captain Cimmaruta turned the discussion to the subject of the Ethiopian N.C.O. who had disappeared during the night. This man had simply deserted the Ethiopians, he said, and had presented himself at the Italian post. If the commissioners wished to meet and question him, they were welcome to do so. He also proposed that since the Ethiopians and native Italian troops were confronting each other at such close quarters, some provisional arrangements should be made to prevent incidents between them. When the Ethiopian commissioners said that, subject to reservations, they were willing to discuss his suggestion with him on the spot, the six men left the tent and walked to where the two forces faced each other.

Lines could be drawn separating the two sides, Cimmaruta said, by putting marks on tree trunks.

Although the Ethiopian commissioners acknowledged that his suggestion was sincere and opportune, they decided they could not accept it because it might imply recognition of Italian territorial rights. They asked him instead to withdraw his troops far enough so that their men would have access to more water.

Cimmaruta refused this request but offered to let the Ethiopians draw water under Italian supervision from wells behind the Italian line. The Ethiopians rejected this offer because it would imply Italian ownership of the wells.

Cimmaruta, becoming impatient, said, "Take it or leave it." And when the Ethiopians continued to decline what he considered a very generous offer, he suggested that in such case, he would send for several hundred more men.

At about this time, four p.m., two Italian military airplanes, appearing from the south, began flying low over the commissioners and over the British and Ethiopian camps. From one of these planes, Colonel Clifford and other members of the party saw what they were certain was a machine gun, aimed at them.

Colonel Clifford, ordinarily mild-mannered, became indignant at what he regarded as a provocative demonstration and announced that, to avoid complicating the situation for the Abyssinian government, the British mission would retire to the town of Ado as soon as possible. (Most Europeans used the Latinized Arabic word "Abyssinia," although the country's inhabitants preferred to call it "Ethiopia," the ancient Greek word for peoples living south of Egypt.)

The Ethiopian commissioners, also indignant, said that such a gesture by agents of a government with which Ethiopia had concluded a treaty of friendship was hardly in keeping with international usage.

Captain Cimmaruta withdrew in anger and the two armed camps settled down for another uneasy night in which epithets and insults were continually hurled across the line.

It was late that evening when Haile Selassie I, Emperor of Ethiopia, learned through a telephone call to the Imperial Palace in Addis Ababa that a dangerous situation had arisen at Wal Wal.[4] He had known when he sent the six-hundred-man military escort to protect the Anglo-Ethiopian Border Commission that they would find the Italians entrenched at Wal Wal and Wardair. In recent years he had failed in several attempts to dislodge them. Perhaps he had hoped that this time, accompanied by an official British mission, his troops might be more successful in persuading the Italians to relinquish the area. Such a hope now seemed unrealistic, since the British, after the unpleasant confrontation with the Italians, had already announced their prudent intention to retire. That being the case, it would be pointless for the Ethiopian commissioners to remain, for they could do nothing without their British colleagues. But what about the Ethiopian military escort? If Fitaurari Shiferra and his men were to retire, would it not be tantamount to recognition of Italian sovereignty over the wells and over the entire area? Recent discussions with England had raised the possibility of a land exchange which would give Ethiopia a seaport, probably at Zeila on the Gulf of Aden in British Somaliland, in return for a tract which would include the Wal Wal area. The British would hardly be inclined to conclude such an exchange if they were not satisfied that this land was Ethiopia's to give. After consulting his advisers, the Emperor decided his troops should remain at Wal Wal.

On the following morning, November 25, Colonel Clifford carried out his intention to remove the British mission to Ado and await the Italian government's reply to the border commission's protest. The Ethiopian commissioners accompanied the British to Ado. The Ethiopian military detail held its place, confronting the Italians.

For ten days, during which reinforcements arrived to augment both sides, they maintained their relative positions without a clash, despite

7

minor provocations, several accidental rifle bursts, and increasingly hostile correspondence between the commanders.

Shortly after noon, December 5, Fitaurari Shiferra received a letter from Captain Cimmaruta dated the previous day in Wardair, addressed to both Shiferra and Bantie. As it was written in Italian, a language which neither Shiferra nor any of his men could read, he sent it on by truck to Ado for translation, as he had done with other letters. He might have been better prepared for subsequent events had he been able immediately to read the letter, which said:

> I have the honor to communicate to you the following:
> I have reliable news that a very strong concentration of men is taking place on the Abyssinian line opposite Wal Wal. I also have news that aggressive intentions are entertained against our line.
> These armed men endeavoured last night to force the line and to carry off the branches marking it. I consider it my duty as a soldier to warn any of you who receive this letter that I shall be obliged to regard any act of violence aimed at forcing the line at any point or at outflanking it, or at taking other places occupied by us, as directed against the territory of His Majesty the King of Italy, and shall forthwith take steps to prevent it. . . .

At three-thirty that afternoon, while the truck was carrying this letter to Ado for translation, Fitaurari Shiferra, in the camp behind his men, heard an order being shouted on the Italian side of the line, followed by the sound of a whistle. Turning to one of his aides he said, "What was that order?"

The aide said, "'*A terra!*' ['Get down!'] and '*Fuoco!*' ['Fire!']."

There was no opportunity to determine whether the aide had heard the commands correctly. Within a very short time a shot rang out (from which side it was impossible to say), followed by heavy fusillades from both sides.

In the first exchanges, a large number of Ethiopians standing in the open were hit. Their second-in-command, Fitaurari Alemayehu, was wounded in the left shoulder when he emerged from his tent. Despite the wound, he took his position and began directing the attack.

Those who had survived the first burst were now dug into their shelters, returning the Italian fire. They were somewhat handicapped because their most formidable weapons, a pair of machine guns, had been placed in an unfortunate location, between Shiferra's tent and the ammunition storage tent, from which position they could not be fired. In any case, they had not been uncovered and prepared for action. Yet for the first ten minutes the battle seemed fairly even and the outcome was in doubt.

At this point, three Italian airplanes appeared from the south and two armored cars moved ominously through the hedge of thorns into the

8

midst of the Ethiopians, spraying machine-gun fire in all directions. Alemayehu fell dead with a bullet hole in his forehead. All around him, other men were falling. Their rifle bullets bounced off the armored cars, and the holes they had dug provided them no shelter from machine guns whose muzzles could be depressed. Though the bombs and machine-gun barrages from the airplanes were so inaccurate they could be ignored, the armored cars proved overwhelming. The battle was no longer in doubt. Fitaurari Shiferra, a man with only limited experience in war and even less taste for it, looked at the carnage around him and decided the most useful, or at least the most prudent, thing he could do would be to gather up the wounded and withdraw. Yet even after Shiferra had retired with a large company of his men, the remaining Ethiopians, accepting the command of a Mohammedan named Ali Nur who had once been an interpreter for the British consular service, continued the fight far into the night, breaking their spears against the armored cars, or falling victim to the machine-gun fire when they tried to rush the vehicles and tip them over. It was after midnight when Ali Nur and his surviving companions broke contact with the Italians and followed Shiferra northward on the route to Ado.

The defeated Ethiopians had left 107 men dead on the field; 45 were wounded. The victorious Italians had suffered 30 deaths; 100 were wounded. All the Italian casualties were native troops.

It was a measure of Ethiopia's woefully inadequate communications system that Emperor Haile Selassie worked through most of the day, December 6, in his English country-style palace at Addis Ababa totally unaware that a serious battle had taken place the previous day at Wal Wal.[5] Ironically, he had, two days earlier, invited British minister Sir Sidney Barton to his palace for a discussion of the Wal Wal situation. A messenger from the Anglo-Ethiopian Boundary Commission had arrived that morning, after two days of traveling as fast as possible from Ado (about five hundred miles), with a full account of the Wal Wal confrontation. The Emperor had asked for Sir Sidney's advice on several points, including the need for immediate demarcation of the Ethiopian-Somali border and the dangers arising from the proximity of Ethiopian and Italian troops in that area. It would be difficult to withdraw his troops, the Emperor had said, unless the Italians would also agree to withdraw, pending demarcation.

Sir Sidney was never reticent in the presence of His Imperial Majesty. It was he, more than any other man, who had taught Haile Selassie how to conduct himself like an emperor. A career diplomat with a background

9

of colonial service in the Far East, Barton had strongly and effectively pursued, as British Consul General in Shanghai, his country's policy of separating Chiang Kai-shek's Kuomintang from the emerging Chinese Communist Party. After arriving in Addis Ababa in 1932, he had quickly become the Emperor's unofficial mentor in matters of court etiquette and procedure as well as international relations. On this occasion he had seemed less than sympathetic to the Emperor's complaint against the Italians.[6] The sooner His Majesty's government got in touch with the Italian legation in Addis Ababa and worked out a *modus vivendi*, he said, the better it would be for both sides.

The Emperor mentioned that he was considering the possibility of approaching the League of Nations about the situation at the same time as he approached the Italians.

Such a course would be ill-advised, Sir Sidney warned. Before doing anything else, he should exhaust every means of direct settlement.

The Emperor had then shown concern about the make-up of the Ethiopian contingent encamped at Wal Wal. Would it appear provocative, he asked, if he were to replace those troops with others?

Sir Sidney's answer had been so sharp and pointed as to end the audience. It was more important, he told the Emperor, that he supply his troops properly instead of allowing them to live off surrounding tribes, including some under British protection, as they were doing at present.

After this less than satisfactory discussion with the testy British minister on the fourth, the Emperor had summoned to his palace, early on the morning of the fifth, his three most trusted foreign advisers— Everett Colson of the United States, General Eric Virgin of Sweden, and Raymonde Auberson of Switzerland—to discuss with them the continuing armed confrontation which was then in its thirteenth day.[7]

Virgin pointed out, perhaps superfluously, that at any moment a shot might be fired, and that general fighting would then break out. The Emperor had assured Virgin he understood very clearly the gravity of the situation, but he insisted that the Italians had no right to be at Wal Wal.

With the aid of his three advisers, and with Sir Sidney Barton's admonition in mind, he had drawn up a protest against Italian occupation of the area, to be delivered at the Italian legation in Addis Ababa, first orally, then in writing, by the Ethiopian Foreign Minister, Blattengeta Herouy Wolde Selassie. Though Herouy signed the note, the words were not his.

In the leisurely tradition of his government, the foreign minister had not delivered the spoken protest until midday of the sixth and the written protest until later in the afternoon. This Ethiopian note simply set forth what was known to have happened so far in the course of the confrontation at Wal Wal, and after protesting against the "occupation by armed troops under the command of Italian officers, of various portions of Ethiopian territory, and in particular the places known as Wal Wal and Wardair," went on to state that "such armed occupation, and proceedings of this kind . . . conflict with the fundamental principles of the League of Nations Covenant as well as with those solemnly proclaimed in the Italo-Ethiopian Treaty of Amity, Conciliation and Arbitration of August 2nd, 1928. Being desirous that the incident briefly described in this note shall be settled in accordance with law and without any resort to force, my Government is anxious, in view of the gravity of the dispute, that a prompt reply should be made to the present note."

By the time Herouy delivered the note, the incident had already been settled by a resort to force twelve hours earlier. Only after he had presented the note did the Italians, who depended on their own wireless communication system, let him know a clash had taken place at Wal Wal. This was the Ethiopian government's first information about the incident. It was not until the afternoon of December 7 that the Foreign Ministry received a telegram from Tessama Bantie of the border commission at Ado confirming the bare facts of the bloody battle.

> Today, the 26th of Hedar [December 5], at 3:30 P.M., the Italians unexpectedly attacked our men who are at Wal Wal, employing aircraft, bombs, tanks, guns, and machine guns. Many men have been killed but the exact number is not known.

This telegram was immediately transmitted to the Emperor, who had now to call his foreign advisers together once more and ask their help in deciding what to do next. Ethiopia's relations with Italy were uncomfortable at best. Despite the Italo-Ethiopian Treaty of Amity, Conciliation and Arbitration of August 2, 1928, which was mentioned in the note to the Italian minister, the two countries had been viewing each other with reservations since 1896, when Emperor Menelik II wiped out the Italian army at Adowa, thus making Italy the only European nation that had ever been repelled successfully by Africans in an attempt at colonization. The Italians had never forgotten that insult to their national pride. In 1906, Italy, England, and France, without consulting Emperor Menelik, discreetly got together and signed an agreement in which England and France acknowledged Italy's priority in Ethiopia, with the stipulation that Italy would never hinder the operation of the French-owned railway from Addis Ababa to Djibuti, or the flow of Blue Nile water from Ethiopia's Lake Tana into the White Nile, which fed England's dependencies, Egypt and the Sudan.

When Emperor Menelik died in 1913, he was succeeded by his seventeen-year-old grandson, Lidj Yasu, a dissolute prince whose control was soon eroded by his personal habits, by his politically imprudent conversion to the Moslem religion, and by his poor international judgment in supporting Germany during the European War. In 1916, Lidj Yasu was relieved of his throne by a group of powerful chiefs whose enterprise was not discouraged by England and France. He was replaced by a daughter of Menelik, the placid but sometimes stubborn Princess Zauditu. Among the chiefs most influential in the downfall of Lidj Yasu was the twenty-four-year-old governor of Harar Province, Ras Tafari Makonnen, a man so small of stature (five feet four inches tall, 110 pounds) he might easily have become a figure of fun in the eyes of his fellow warrior chiefs had it not been for his penetrating intelligence, his grasp of European culture including the French language, and the compelling determination which was evident in the controlled features of his face. He understood Europe and had become fluent in French because his father, Emperor Menelik's cousin, the old Ras Makonnen, who had also been governor of Harar province and had always maintained the highest possible aspirations for his son, made certain he received a thorough European training from French clerics at their missionary school in Harar.

Upon the ascendancy of Zauditu as Empress, Ras Tafari, who would one day become Emperor Haile Selassie, assumed virtual control of the Ethiopian government after his appointment as Prince Regent.

Three years of civil disruption during the reign of Lidj Yasu had dissipated the central government's power, carefully developed by Menelik. Ras Tafari's efforts to re-establish it in the name of Empress Zauditu were hampered by the very intelligence and enlightened outlook which had won him his position as Prince Regent. His familiarity with European civilization convinced him that if Ethiopia were ever to be strong, it would have to adopt some of the progressive technological and social measures which made European nations strong. But when he began trying to introduce such measures, he met opposition from the country's most powerful conservative elements—the Church and the wealthy chiefs. During his first years as Prince Regent, Ethiopia was so unstable internally that Italy might have had an excellent opportunity to appropriate it if the Italians had not been so occupied by their futile participation in World War I.

Postwar Italy was in no condition to appropriate anything, and after Benito Mussolini assumed power in 1922, his early gestures toward Ethiopia were conciliatory. When the Ethiopian government, at Tafari's instigation, applied for League of Nations membership in 1923, Mussolini supported the application because he didn't think he could defeat it, even though England opposed it. The British argued that Ethiopia should not be admitted into a society of civilized nations because Ethiopians still practiced slavery. The argument was somewhat weakened by the discovery that the British minister in Addis Ababa at the time was maintaining several slaves, perhaps inadvertently, on his domestic staff. In addition, Ras Tafari had already taken steps, not always effective, toward abolishing slavery. His application prevailed and Ethiopia became a League of Nations Member.

In the summer of 1924, Ras Tafari and Mussolini met for the first and last time when Tafari took his wife to Rome for a visit. Though this visit was amicable, it was marred by the fact that Mussolini, not yet an all-powerful dictator, was currently embarrassed by the highly publicized disappearance of his most outspoken political enemy, Giacomo Matteotti. While it was quite likely that Matteotti had been murdered by Mussolini's henchmen, his body had not yet been found at the time of Ras Tafari's visit. A cartoon in a Roman periodical, depicting the Ethiopian Prince Regent as a black cannibal, showed him whispering to the Italian Chief of Police, "You can tell me in all confidence, did you eat him?"

Despite such lighthearted Italian insults, and despite further alarms over Italian diplomatic arrangements with England in 1925 and 1926, Ras Tafari welcomed an opportunity to sign the Treaty of Amity with Italy in August 1928. Two years later, when Empress Zauditu died, Tafari's political strength in Ethiopia was so impressive that he could proclaim himself Emperor without opposition. And as Emperor, he had continued his efforts to get along with Italy, but Mussolini became less conciliatory.

Now, in the afternoon of December 7, 1934, after receiving the telegram from Tessama Bantie, the Emperor immediately sent another note, over Herouy's signature, to the Italian legation, reaffirming the previous day's Ethiopian protest.

The same afternoon in Rome, the Italian government, having received the news from Wal Wal a full day earlier, was releasing it to the government-controlled Stefani News Agency. The Associated Press bureau in Rome, taking its information from Stefani, wired to America that evening a dispatch which was published the following day, December 8, 1934, in *The New York Times* and most other American newspapers. The *Times* cable editors considered the story so limited in importance that it appeared on page 11:

ITALY AGAIN FIGHTS
ABYSSINIAN ATTACK

ROME, Dec. 7 AP—A strongly worded Italian protest—the second in two months—was made to the Abyssinian Government today, after armed bodies of Abyssinians attacked Ualual [Wal Wal] in Italian Somaliland.

The assault, Stefani News Agency dispatches reported, took place December 5, and the attackers, said to have had machine guns and artillery, were driven off only after reinforcements had been rushed to the isolated Italian garrison at the wells of Ualual. . . .

13

This story from Rome was contradicted on page 20 of *The New York Times* the following day by an Associated Press dispatch from Addis Ababa:

ABYSSINIA ACCUSES
ITALIANS OF ATTACK

ADDIS ABABA, Abyssinia, Dec. 8 AP—The Abyssinian Government today denied Rome reports that armed Ethiopians attacked an Italian outpost Wednesday, asserted the Italians took the initiative, and ordered its Chargé d'Affaires at Rome to file a vigorous protest.

Native forces from the Italian Somaliland started the clash, Emperor Haile Selassie's Government charged, adding that these forces now have advanced 75 miles into Abyssinian territory. . . .

Below this rebuttal was another rebuttal from Rome, dated December 8, which said:

An official communiqué issued tonight declared "false" dispatches from Addis Ababa asserting Italian forces were the aggressors in an affray between Italians and Ethiopians Dec. 5. The communiqué pointed out that the Italians were defenders in their own territory. . . .

Between December 6 and December 10, the Italian notes to the Ethiopian government were generally accusatory but tentative, technical, and unspecific. The first concrete proposal for settling the incident came on December 9 in an Ethiopian note, signed by Herouy, which said, ". . . The Imperial Ethiopian Government is sincerely desirous of reaching a settlement in accordance with law as rapidly as possible, and I have therefore the honor, on behalf of my Government, to invoke Article 5 of the Treaty of Amity, Conciliation and Arbitration concluded on August 2nd, 1928, between our two Governments, and beg you to transmit this proposal to your Government."

On December 11, the Italians delivered to the Ethiopian Foreign Ministry in Addis Ababa a communication so demanding it could be regarded as nothing less than an ultimatum. It enumerated specifically the Italian government's attitudes and expectations:

(1) There can be no doubt that Wal Wal and Wardair belong to Italian Somaliland, as the Italian Government will show in due course;

(2) Consequently, Captain Cimmaruta's conduct was quite correct, as all that he did was: (a) to point out to the members of the Anglo-Abyssinian Commission that, as is self-evident, armed Abyssinians could not enter Italian territory; (b) to take in advance defensive and precautionary measures, including air reconnaissances; (c) lastly, to forward to the Government of Somaliland the statements made to him by the members of the above-mentioned Commission;

(3) Armed Abyssinians, without any provocation from the Italian side,

14

took the initiative of launching an unexpected attack in force upon our post at Wal Wal;

(4) Consequently, the responsibility for this sanguinary incident lies entirely with the Abyssinian Government, whose attention had already been drawn on many occasions by Count [Luigi] Vinci, the Italian Minister, to the deplorable consequences likely to follow upon the known movements of "shefta" [bandits] in the Ogaden;

(5) The Italian Government therefore requires the Abyssinian Government to tender a formal apology and to make reparations commensurate with the seriousness of the losses and damage we have sustained.

Accordingly, I have the honor, on behalf of the Italian Government, to demand from the Abyssinian Government the following apologies and reparations:

(1) The Degiac [commander of a province] Gabre Mariam, Governor of the Harrar [he was actually deputy governor], will proceed to Wal Wal, where he will present, on behalf of the Abyssinian Government, a formal apology to the commander of the Italian post, while an Abyssinian detachment will render the honors to the Italian flag;

(2) The Abyssinian Government will pay to the Royal Italian Legation at Addis Ababa a sum of two hundred thousand (200,000) T.M.T. [Maria Theresa thalers, the Ethiopian medium of exchange] as compensation for the heavy losses in dead and wounded sustained by our troops, as reparation for the damage caused to our fortified posts and as a refund of the expenditure which the Government of Somaliland has had to incur as a result of the act of aggression committed against it;

(3) The persons responsible for the attack must be arrested and deprived of their respective commands; after having been present at the honors rendered to the Italian flag in accordance with local usage, they must as soon as possible undergo suitable punishment. . . .

Even more importtant than the rude severity of the note was the emphasis the Italians placed on what had to be the essential issue in the Wal Wal incident—the location of Wal Wal. If it was in Italian Somaliland, then the Italians had a prima-facie case against Ethiopia. If it was in Ethiopia, the reverse was true. But would the Italians keep raising this issue so prominently if they were not certain of it?

The tone of the message and the punitive demands, while they were so humiliating and insulting that it is difficult to imagine one nation addressing itself thus to another, were nevertheless not unusual in colonial affairs. Other European governments, the British and the French in particular, had made comparable demands against African and Asian peoples after incidents of violence, and some even dispatched punitive expeditions with instructions to reciprocate the violence. Ethiopia was quite familiar with these procedures. Emperor Haile Selassie had already agreed to make amends to Italy for a minor incident which had taken place two weeks earlier at the Italian Consulate in the northwestern city of Gondar.

15

Now again he invited to the palace the man who knew more about punitive colonial measures than anyone else in Addis Ababa—His Britannic Majesty's Minister, Sir Sidney Barton. It was quite common those days to see the proud, forbidding figure of Sir Sidney, mounted on his horse and followed by a troop of the British cavalry he kept at his legation, making his way to and from the Imperial Palace.

Sir Sidney had become almost as concerned about the Wal Wal matter as the Emperor himself. Three days earlier, on December 8, he had received a telegram on the subject from British Foreign Secretary Sir John Simon, who was now also aware of the Wal Wal implications and fearful that this trivial border clash in Africa might disturb a delicate international balance in Europe.[8] Sir John indicated to Sir Sidney the British government's eagerness to avoid complications with Italy. "It will be clearly appreciated," he wired from London, "that incidents [in Europe] emphasize necessity for a definite settlement [by the Ethiopians] with the Italians."

Bearing this suggestion in mind, Sir Sidney, even after reading Italy's demeaning ultimatum, advised the Emperor to find some way of accepting it to settle the controversy.

Haile Selassie listened politely but did not commit himself. He was also listening each day now to a succession of Ethiopian chiefs, some of them arriving at the palace on bejeweled donkeys and followed by great retinues of shamma-clad retainers. Many of these chiefs, descended from proud warrior tribes, favored an immediate attack against the Italians, who, they felt, needed another lesson of the kind Emperor Menelik had given them in 1896.

Haile Selassie's own view of the Italians was not so simple. He did not delude himself that he faced the same Italy against which his father had helped Menelik fight at Adowa. It would take more than rifles, swords, and spears to defeat Mussolini, whose behavior was becoming daily more worrisome. The Italian dictator had recently installed consular representatives in all the principal Ethiopian cities. Why? Few of those cities conducted any appreciable business with Italy. His representatives had begun to pursue, almost openly, a policy of bribing and suborning any Ethiopian chiefs they found susceptible. And he had enlarged Italy's military establishments both in Eritrea, on Ethiopia's northern borders, and Somaliland, on Ethiopia's southeastern border. These garrisons had been reinforced, the Italian government announced to the press, because Ethiopia had territorial ambitions (desiring especially a seaport, of which the Italian colonies had several), and because the Ethiopian army was now so modern, well trained, and well equipped it might be prompted at any time to carry out those ambitions. The Italians were so effusive in their assessment of the Ethiopian army and so free with their information about its increasing power that several newspapers in Europe and America had published stories

about the strength of Emperor Haile Selassie's forces. He and General Virgin both wished that these forces were half as formidable as the Italians advertised them to be.

Despite its apparent thoroughness, the Italian ultimatum of December 11 did neglect to mention one matter of prime importance—the proposal by Ethiopia two days earlier that the Wal Wal incident be arbitrated in accordance with the 1928 treaty between the two countries. Rather than answer the demands in the Italian ultimatum, the Emperor and his advisers decided to remind the Italians of this prior proposal, which they did, in a note dispatched December 13.

The Italian answer came quickly the morning of December 14. Over the signature of G. Mombelli, the chargé d'affaires in Addis Ababa, it said:

> ... The Wal Wal incident of the 5th instant occurred in circumstances so definite and clear that there can be no doubt as to its nature. It was a surprise attack carried out by Abyssinians against the Italian post without any provocation.
>
> In view of the foregoing, the Italian Government does not see how the settlement of an incident of that kind can be submitted to arbitration procedure as requested by the Abyssinian Government. It must therefore insist that the reparation and apologies due to it by reason of this incident be made as soon as possible, and in that connection renews the demands it has already formulated.

Emperor Haile Selassie had now to reach one of the most important decisions of his life. The morning of the fourteenth, he again called his three principal foreign advisers to his new palace, a mile and a half up the slope from Emperor Menelik's Grand Palace, for a grave and portentous all-day session. Of these three men whom the Emperor had recruited to help him cope with the great white European powers, the most useful was the American, Everett Colson. General Eric Virgin, the tall, handsome Swede, was expert only in military matters, though his advice was heard on other affairs of state. Raymonde Auberson, the elderly Swiss, was scholarly and thoughtful but lacked dynamism, perhaps because of his delicate health. His mastery of the French language and the precise style in which he wrote it made him especially valuable in preparing diplomatic communications.

Colson, who also wrote fluently in French, was the most influential and effective of the three in formulating policy. An American career diplomat, he had served his own country during two tours of duty (1904–1911 and 1916–1917) as an administrative officer in the Philippines, and had also spent a short time in the China Consular Service. He had already retired when Haile Selassie, at the time of his coronation as Emperor in 1930, asked the United States government to recommend a financial adviser for Ethiopia. The State Department chose Colson, a

17

plain, sometimes blunt Scotch-Irish New Englander from Maine, Presbyterian in religion and a Wilsonian Democrat in politics. Despite, or perhaps because of, his service in the Philippines, he was opposed to colonialism and viewed suspiciously the motives of the three colonial powers whose possessions surrounded Ethiopia—Italy, France, and Great Britain.

The Emperor discussed with these three men all the divergent advice which had been pouring in on him during the last several days. The admonitions of the English could not be taken lightly. Great Britain was still considered the most powerful nation in the world and it was the only European nation from which Ethiopia had any hope of receiving help in case of crisis. Neither could the contrary advice of the great chiefs be ignored, because it was from their support that the Emperor derived his power, and some of them were noticeably restive.

After studying these considerations throughout the day of the fourteenth, the Emperor decided finally to reject the appeasement pleas of Great Britain as well as the warlike demands of his chiefs, and to adopt instead a course which his three advisers, Colson in particular, pressed upon him. It was a course not likely to be received with favor in Europe, because it could involve the whole world in what most people might regard as an insignificant quarrel between Ethiopia and Italy. To comply with the Italian ultimatum, to give honors to the Italian flag on what Haile Selassie regarded as Ethiopian territory, would be to surrender sovereignty and invite whatever depredations Italy chose to practice thereafter. Since the Italians refused arbitration, Ethiopia had only one hope of countering the demands against it: The Emperor would lay his case before the League of Nations and, using that body as a forum, try to convince the world that his country was the victim of Italian aggression.

Haile Selassie and his advisers having settled on this course, Colson and Auberson sat down and composed a telegram which was remarkably comprehensive despite its brevity. It was dispatched that night, December 14, to League of Nations Secretary-General Joseph Avenol in Geneva:

> Imperial Government has the honour to inform you, for communication to the Council and States Members, that, on November 23rd last, Anglo-Abyssinian Commission investigating pasture-lands in Abyssinian province of Ogaden was prevented by Italian military force from continuing its work upon its arrival at Wal Wal, situated about 100 kilometres within the frontier. On December 5th Italian troops with tanks and military aeroplanes suddenly and without provocation attacked Abyssinian escort of the Commission. Abyssinian Government protested by note of December 6th. Despite protest, Italian military aeroplanes three days later bombarded Ado and Gerlogubi in the same province. In response to protest of December 6th and request for arbitration of December 9th

18

under Article 5 of the Italo-Abyssinian Treaty of August 2nd, 1928, Italian Chargé d'Affaires, disregarding the protest, demanded indemnity and moral reparation in note of December 11th and declared in note of December 14th that his Government does not see how the solution of an incident of this character can be submitted to arbitral decision. In presence of Italian aggression Abyssinian Government diaws Council's attention to gravity of situation. Detailed confirmation and documents follow.
—HEROUY, Minister Foreign Affairs

The only surprising contention in the Ethiopian communication to the League was the claim that Wal Wal could be found "about 100 kilometres within the frontier." If this was true, it meant that Italy had actually established a military garrison sixty miles inside another country's territory. European and American newspapers, finding such a charge incredible, pointed out that the boundary between Ethiopia and Italy had never been officially demarcated, although it had been fixed definitely by treaty. Despite a few rumors that Wal Wal might actually be in Ethiopia, most newspapers accepted the Italian assertion that it was in Somaliland, especially after Italy sent a note to the League December 16 renewing the assertion and decrying Ethiopia's charges.

Eventually, a correspondent in the press room of the League of Nations Permanent Secretariat Building at Geneva, on or about December 20, did something no one else had thought to do. He looked up at a map on the wall in front of him. It was a map of Africa, issued by the Italian Geographical Institute at Bergamo, which showed that Wal Wal was indeed at least sixty miles inside Ethiopia according to terms of the 1897 treaty which settled the 1896 war between the two countries.

The Italian delegation, apprised of this evidence, reacted immediately. Baron Pompeo Aloisi, Rome's slender, elegant, and aristocratic representative in Geneva, demanded that the map be removed from the press room because it was obsolete. It took no account of certain modifications of the 1897 treaty which were made in 1908.

No sooner had the map been removed than the correspondents, now full of enterprise, went all the way to the League library in the north wing of the main building, where they found an Italian government map of Ethiopia, issued by the Colonial Office in 1925. This map also showed that Wal Wal was at least sixty miles inside Ethiopia.

Such incontrovertible evidence was surely enough to settle the matter. If any reparations were to be made, Italy should make them. But the Ethiopian government had not demanded reparations. African nations were unaccustomed to demanding reparations from European nations. Ethiopia hadn't even asked for an apology. It would no doubt be sufficient if Italy's dictator, Benito Mussolini, were simply to let the matter rest. Mussolini, however, had no such intention.

CHAPTER TWO

Two weeks after the Wal Wal clash, on December 20, 1934, Benito Mussolini sat at the rosewood desk in the far corner of his huge Palazzo Venezia office, composing a memorandum he would show to no one for ten days, and then to only a handful of his most trusted associates. It was a document which envisioned much more from Ethiopia than monetary reparations and honors to the Italian flag at a dreary desert outpost.

At the age of fifty-one, the squarely built, rock-faced blacksmith's son, now in his thirteenth year as Italy's Fascist dictator, had developed so much personal power within the country that he thought the time opportune to expand his reach abroad. His own people had already given him so much they had little left to offer. The Italians seemed to revere him more than they revered the Pope. In official proclamations, his name stood out more prominently than that of King Victor Emmanuel III. In the Italian Senate and Chamber of Deputies, his words were never controverted and no other laws than his were passed. In the administration of government, his commands were supreme and even his most outrageous whims were immediately obeyed. Finding that he couldn't quite see the ancient Roman Colosseum from his office, he had ordered that a wide new street, the Via dei Fori Imperiale, be cut just to give him an unobstructed view.

When he first discovered this now-famous Palazzo Venezia office of his, the Sala Mappamondo, it was in such dreadful condition that it took three years, 1925 to 1928, to restore it. The beautiful yellow, Venetian-style *palazzo* had been built by Pope Paul II in the years 1464–1471, and the Sala had been decorated originally by Andrea Mantegna at the behest of Innocent VIII, the project being completed the year Columbus discovered America.

Among Mussolini's decorative additions was a floor mosaic of the ancient symbol of Roman authority, the fascis (a bundle of rods bound around a long-handled ax), which had given Fascism its name and which he had

20

revived as a symbol of the movement. To reach his desk in the far corner of the room, a visitor had to endure, under his fearsome gaze, the long walk across this mosaicked floor, and unless the visitor was a special personage or an important representative of the foreign press, he would then find himself standing uncomfortably in front of the desk during the whole interview, like a defendant in front of a judge, with no chair offered. Near the front door of the room, at the far end from Mussolini's desk, was the double door opening onto the famous little (eight-by-three-foot) balcony from which he harangued the frenzied multitudes in the Piazza Venezia below. His recent words, here and in other parts of Italy, had been increasingly warlike in tone.

Speaking to the second quinquennial assembly of Fascists the previous March 18, he had proclaimed "a natural expansion which ought to lead to a collaboration between Italy and the peoples of Africa and the East." He also proclaimed that Italy could "civilize Africa, and her position in the Mediterranean gave her this right and imposed this duty on her." Then as a warning to other colonial powers he said Italy did not "want earlier arrivals to block her spiritual, political, and economic expansion."

In August, he had said privately to Austrian Chancellor Kurt von Schuschnigg, "Italy cannot ignore the constant and continuous provocation on the part of Abyssinia: it will perhaps be necessary for us to engage ourselves for awhile in East Africa."[1] Then within a few days he told an audience of soldiers at an army maneuver:

> It is necessary to prepare for war. . . . Not tomorrow but today. We are becoming, and shall become increasingly—because this is our desire—a military nation. A militaristic nation, I will add, since I am not afraid of words.

Though some people considered Mussolini a cowardly man who concealed his lack of valor by indulging in loud and frequent bombast (only with difficulty had his followers persuaded him to take part in the ludicrous but dangerous march on Rome which brought him to power in 1922), the plan he was now formulating in the privacy of his grandiose office would have to entail, if it were to succeed, enough courage to cover an outrageous and protracted bluff against the world's greatest powers.

The memorandum he was composing bore the title "Directive and Plan of Action for the Resolution of the Italian-Abyssinian Question."[2] It was a lengthy document divided into fourteen sections, all pointing toward one end: the defeat and complete subjugation of Ethiopia. Beginning with the statement that it was too late for diplomacy to solve what he called the "problem" of Ethiopia, he justified this assumption by describing the power of the new Ethiopian army, trained by European officers, and the sophistication of the Ethiopian government under the direction of Emperor Haile Selassie. For Italy this meant it was necessary to "resolve the problem as soon as possible." And that could be accomplished in only one way: "The destruction of the Abyssinian armed forces and the total conquest of Ethiopia."

Having thus determined Italy's course, he turned his attention to what was certain to be the most perilous complicating factor—the attitudes of the other great European powers, and of the League of Nations. He knew he couldn't launch a campaign in East Africa if Britain and France forbade him to do so. As his memorandum acknowledged, he would need at least a hundred thousand white European troops in addition to a native corps that large or perhaps larger. And in his view these men would have to be provided at the earliest possible moment, because an unconquered Ethiopia would become a dire threat to the Italian African colonies on the expected day when Italy would take up arms in the military struggle for control of Europe. That struggle, he calculated, would not occur until at least 1937, by which time Germany might be strong enough to grasp the initiative. But 1937 was only a little more than two years away, which meant the Ethiopian campaign would have to begin during the coming year. Since it could not begin until after the heavy Ethiopian rains subsided in late September, the elected month was October. Between now and October, therefore, the entire campaign would have to be planned, installations built, and strategy developed. An endless line of ships carrying men and supplies would have to file through the Suez Canal to Eritrea and Somaliland. Therein lay the greatest potential danger. What would he do if Britain, France, the League of Nations were to say no? The League couldn't stop him. He felt certain of that. But Britain and France, or Britain alone, could simply close the Canal to Italian ships. He decided he would be able to forestall that possibility. "The more rapid our military action," he wrote in the memorandum, "the less will be the danger of diplomatic complications. No one in Europe will raise any difficulties for us if the conduct of military operations rapidly creates an accomplished fact. It will be enough to declare to England and France that their interests will be recognized."

At least he could hope so. His dreams of colonial glory and his bitter boyhood memories of Italy's defeat at Adowa forced him to hope so. "This problem has existed since 1885," he concluded in his secret memorandum. "Ethiopia is the last part of Africa that is now owned by Europeans. The Gordian knot of Italo-Abyssinian relations is going to become increasingly entangled. It is necessary to cut it before it is too late." But he was not so confident of the inertia of Britain and France that he could leave to chance the likelihood of their standing idly by while he solved the Ethiopian problem. He had a plan for handling these two formidable countries—a strategy he had already put into action by suggesting in a speech October 6 that "an entente with France would be very useful," and by opening negotiations November 1 in Rome for the settlement of certain long-standing differences between France and Italy. These negotiations were apparently bogging down now in December, but he could be confident that a few timely concessions on his part would revive them because France, after several years of cool relations with Italy, now needed his friendship as the shadow of Adolf Hitler's Nazi Germany grew daily more ominous. Pierre Laval (France's foreign minister since October) had expressed in the Chamber of Deputies December 18 his continuing faith in an eventual accord between the two countries.

"We don't propose to regulate only Franco-Italian questions with the government of Rome," Laval had said. "With his contribution to the collective work of Geneva, Mussolini has shown us the measure of his attachment to the conditions of international understanding. With the same feeling, I intend to express my faith to him. The task of France is not one of mediation. Mussolini has, as we have, friendships to which he intends to remain faithful. There cannot be between our countries any problems whose particulars are unresolvable." Mussolini, in light of his cynicism about "the collective work of Geneva," must have been amused by this reference in Laval's speech.

The Wal Wal incident, meanwhile, became more vexing every day as a result of Haile Selassie's decision to seek League of Nations sympathy. Ethiopia's League membership might prove unfortunate now if it were to give the Emperor a forum from which he could complain to the world that he was the victim of aggression. This was another danger which would have to be neutralized if Italy was to avoid bad publicity for doing what other European powers had already done with impunity.

On December 18, the Ethiopian government sent another note to the League contending that the night before the clash three Italian officers reconnoitered the Ethiopian camp, and pointing out that the Italian airplanes and "tanks" (armored cars) had arrived, dropping bombs and firing machine guns, at the beginning of the battle, which would indicate that their arrival was timed in advance. The Ethiopian note also mentioned that "the only two Ethiopian machine guns were still in their covers, and were not in their battle positions."

If the Ethiopians intended to keep up a stream of such embarrassing communications to the League, and thereby to the whole world, the Italian government would simply have to match them until the whole affair became clouded by charges and countercharges. On Christmas Eve, Italy's Undersecretary for Foreign Affairs Fulvio Suvich sent the League a seven-paragraph telegram about Ethiopian encroachment. The same day, Ethiopian Foreign Minister Herouy sent a telegram about

Italian encroachment. Suvich sent another December 28, and Herouy sent two more, December 31 and January 3, claiming now that Italian troops were advancing toward the town of Gerlogubi, about thirty miles southwest of Wal Wal. But the January 3 telegram was significantly different from and much more disturbing than the others. For the first time, the Ethiopians asked that the League take some kind of action. They requested "application of Article 2 of the [League] Covenant."

The opening paragraph of Article 2 stated: "Any war or threat of war, whether immediately affecting any of the Members of the League or not, is hereby declared a matter of concern to the whole League, and the League shall take any action that may be deemed wise and effectual to safeguard the peace of nations."

The League might feel strong pressure now to do something more than note with interest such an appeal by one of its members. Mussolini, confronted by Ethiopia's aggressive insistence on being heard and protected, began to realize that French Foreign Minister Laval could be quite useful to him in Geneva during the weeks ahead.

Pierre Laval, a squat and swarthy man who looked more like an Algerian merchant than a French statesman, was quite surprised to be boarding the Paris-Rome express on the evening of January 3, 1935, with his helpful and beloved daughter Josée. Until just a few days earlier the negotiations with Italy which were proceeding in Rome at a secondary level had seemed destined to break down because of Mussolini's stubborn attitude about some matters France could not concede. On the last day of the old year the talks had come to a virtual stop, and on January 2, the day before Laval's departure for Rome, he had indicated secretly to the Council of Ministers that the hope of an accord with Italy had just about elapsed.[3] Mussolini had reacted so quickly after Laval's confidential remarks that one might almost have concluded he had sources of information within the French Cabinet. Indeed, there were some people who believed he did have such sources. A few hours after Laval's pessimistic report to his fellow ministers, Mussolini sent him an invitation to come to Rome the next day, assuring him that when the two sat down together, all the outstanding differences would be resolved.

With this assurance in his pocket, Laval addressed the reporters who had gathered to hear him explain, before he boarded the train, his sudden, unexpected decision to go to Rome. "I shall defend the interests of France and Premier Mussolini will defend the interests of Italy," he said, "and because we have the same understanding of the grave difficulties at this time, we shall defend together the interests of peace."

24

For Pierre Laval it was quite a communicative statement. He did not believe in forcing upon the public any more information than necessary about the workings of government or diplomacy. As Laval and his party passed through the station, the newspapers on sale were announcing in prominent headlines the Ethiopian telegram demanding that the League take some kind of action to contain Italy. It is doubtful that Laval gave more than passing thought to this latest Ethiopian move. Ethiopia was a concept barely within his consciousness. When the country was mentioned to him at the time of the Wal Wal incident, he was reputed to have asked where it was. His mind was on more important countries. Chiefly Germany. He bore the traditional French distrust of the Germans, coupled with a growing fear of Adolf Hitler, who, after less than two years in power, was already expanding his army and air force at an alarming rate. Laval, envisioning the possibility of what he called a "conjunction" between the German and Italian dictators, believed he could prevent it by winning for France the friendship of Mussolini.[4]

The lack of friendship between France and Italy in recent years had stemmed first of all from the Versailles Treaty, which had given Italy fewer of the spoils of the 1914–1918 war than she had been led to expect. In 1915, when France and England were desperately eager to bring Italy into the war against Germany, they had stipulated in the tripartite Treaty of London that if they should increase their African colonies at Germany's expense, "an appropriate agreement shall be made to secure to Italy some corresponding and equitable compensation, and that specifically in the regulation in her favor of the boundary questions between colonies of Eritrea, Somaliland and Libya [all Italian], and the contiguous French and English colonies."

For sixteen years, since the end of the Great War, the Italians had been awaiting in vain this "equitable compensation," especially in Tunisia, where a hundred thousand Italian nationals, encouraged by Mussolini, clamored for freedom from France and annexation by the Italian colony of Libya. The Italians, perhaps irritated at themselves because they had let slip an opportunity to grasp Tunisia and other North African lands ahead of the French, demanded also an extension of Libya southward a thousand miles to Lake Chad—a concession the French were quite disinclined to make, inasmuch as it would divide in the middle their enormous tract of uninterrupted colonies stretching from the Mediterranean all the way south to Portuguese Angola. In addition, the Italians wanted to add a piece of French Somaliland (they would gladly accept all of it) to their neighboring colony of Eritrea, along the northeastern borders of Ethiopia.

The friction between France and Italy caused by all these Italian demands in Africa was further intensified by the system of alliances which had developed on the European continent. France, always mindful of the possibility of a resurgent Germany, had signed defensive pacts with three middle-European countries, Czechoslovakia, Yugoslavia, and Rumania; while Italy, also wary of Germany and eager, under Mussolini, to assume the role of a great power, had declared itself the protector of Austria, Hungary, Albania, and Bulgaria. The Yugoslavs, after one look at the map, saw with some apprehension the possibility of Italy's almost surrounding them. It was to their protector France that they voiced their complaints. At the same time, they, as well as the Czechs, Slovaks, and Rumanians, never let the French forget that they had disliked Austria and Hungary ever since the days of the Austro-Hungarian Empire. The French and Italians, having chosen sides among these squabbling little countries, found themselves squabbling with each other. Pierre Laval felt such a need to end all this that he only partially realized Mussolini's eagerness to do likewise.

The French foreign minister must have sensed Mussolini's eagerness shortly after his train reached the Italian border. Everyone along his route acted as if his arrival were the greatest boon to Italy since Mussolini himself descended on Rome, twelve years earlier. At fifty-yard intervals all the way from the border to the capital there were Fascist militiamen beside the track to salute the passing Laval. At Turin, Genoa, and many smaller cities the Fascist organization had recruited large crowds to cheer him.

As he emerged from the train in Rome the evening of January 4, Mussolini in person stepped up to shake his hand and kiss him on both cheeks. After Mussolini said a few words in French which could not be heard above the cheers of the multitude jammed into the station, Laval presented his daughter, Josée, and his staff of experts. Italian Undersecretary for Foreign Affairs Fulvio Suvich gave the young lady a bouquet of roses in Mussolini's name. The entire party followed the course of a red plush carpet into a reception room usually reserved for royalty, and after pausing to pose for the government-disciplined press photographers, Laval made a characteristically short statement to the reporters.

"I value extremely," he said, "the growing *rapprochement* between Italy and France which is of such value for peace on the Danube and throughout the world."

The following day, January 5, when Mussolini and Laval talked twice at the Palazzo Venezia and their staffs talked at the Foreign Ministry in the Palazzo Chigi, questions about Austria and the Danube countries dominated the conversations. Both sides were so agreeable that in the late afternoon they announced full accord on matters pertaining to Europe, though they did not announce either the nature of these matters or the scope of the accord. There was reason enough for not elaborating. After all the talk, they had arrived at no more than a hopeful resolution that Austria's neighbors, meaning Germany more than any others, should be prevailed upon to leave that country alone.

Agreement on the African matters, which promised to be more vexing, was yet to come. This did not, however, dampen the gaiety of the banquet Mussolini staged that night at the Palazzo Venezia. Laval stood up and said, "The peace of Europe remains precarious and requires the attentive care of statesmen." After declaring to the bemusement of his listeners that the people of Europe were "not willing to wait any longer for peace" (they had been at peace now for more than sixteen years), he made a solemn promise: "We have given rise to great hopes. We will not deceive them." Then, before sitting down, he called Mussolini "the writer of the most beautiful page in the history of modern Italy."

When Mussolini arose he spoke of "a consecration of the ideals which came from our community of origin, and of which people have the greatest need in times of uneasiness and incertitude like the present." He did not speak about peace, perhaps because he had in mind an article he had recently written for a Carnegie Foundation magazine, *International Conciliation*. In this article, which was due to be published five days later, on January 10, Mussolini said,

> Fascism . . . believes neither in the possibility nor the utility of perpetual peace. It thus repudiates the doctrine of pacifism. . . . War alone brings up to its highest tension all human energy and puts the stamp of nobility upon the peoples who have the courage to meet it. . . . Thus a doctrine which is founded upon this harmful postulate of peace is hostile to Fascism; and thus [also] harmful to the spirit of Fascism (though accepted for what use they can be in dealing with particular political situations) are all the international leagues and societies which, as history will show, can be scattered to the winds when once strong feeling is aroused by any motive—sentimental, ideal, practical.

Rumors were now circulating to the effect that Laval was prepared to give Mussolini a "free hand" for an intended war against Ethiopia. The rumors had in fact spread as far as Paris. One of Laval's aides at the French Foreign Ministry in Paris, on this very evening, had to tell the press it was "absurd" to think Laval would consent to such a thing, as France, Great Britain, and Italy were pledged to respect Abyssinian territorial rights. Earlier in the day, while Mussolini was talking to Laval, Italy's King Victor Emmanuel received Ethiopian Chargé d'Affaires Yesus Negradas and, in the words of the official communiqué which followed, "told him that Italy had no aggressive intentions against his country."

While Mussolini and Laval held conversations both in the morning and afternoon of the sixth, the detailed negotiations proceeded at the

Palazzo Chigi—and they proceeded slowly, to the chagrin of French Ambassador Charles de Chambrun, a strong advocate of friendship with Italy who had been trying since November to secure the agreement and who had scheduled for this evening a lavish party at which he hoped Rome's entire diplomatic corps would celebrate its completion. Chambrun himself was no longer conducting the negotiations since the arrival, with Laval, of France's two foremost African experts, Alexis Léger, Secretary-General of the Foreign Ministry, and René Comte de Saint-Quentin, chief of the Ministry's African Department. Léger, believing that Laval after only two months as Foreign Secretary was not yet well enough prepared to understand the issues involved in a pact with Italy, had strongly opposed this trip to Rome.[5] It seemed to him it was the trip itself, with all the attendant fanfare, that had seduced Laval into coming. Nevertheless, he and his aides worked diligently throughout the day of the sixth with Suvich and his Italian staff. By late afternoon, they were able to reach a tentative agreement, which, however, was hedged by crucial reservations, the most crucial being that both Mussolini and Laval had to ratify it. Though this might seem simple, it was complicated by the question of French willingness to make an essential commitment about Ethiopia—a commitment so secretive it might not even be put on paper. Only Laval and Mussolini themselves could thrash out this matter, which, as the French now saw, was the key to the whole bargain.

When the dinner began that evening at the French Embassy in the beautiful Palazzo Farnese, a mood of apprehension hung over those close enough to the negotiations to realize the uncertainty still clouding them. After the dinner, to which only a select group had been invited, most of the guests removed to the great hall of the building, now swarming with international diplomats and their ladies, who had been invited only to a reception. These people were disappointed to notice that the most notable personages at the dinner did not follow the others into the great hall. Laval with Léger and Chambrun, and Mussolini with Suvich and Baron Pompeo Aloisi, the Italian League of Nations envoy, had retired to the Ambassador's study, where the pivotal discussions of the Laval visit were now in progress.[6]

Despite Léger's concern, Pierre Laval was in no way out of his depths during these discussions. Like Mussolini himself, he had come from tough, shrewd peasant stock and during a long career, first as a socialist labor lawyer then as a very successful parliamentarian and Cabinet minister (he had also been Minister of Labor and Minister of the Interior), had often proven himself an intelligent, persistent, and above all clever negotiator. A onetime associate said of him that he had "always retained the bitterness, the meanness, the cunning, the mistrustfulness of his peasant origin," and that he was "a past-master at promising a great deal and giving very little."[7] He had never been a popular man, nor did he seek popularity. He didn't seem to worry about his lack of grace. In his invariable costume—black suit, white tie, gray vest—he was said to resemble a chestnut vendor in his Sunday best. His black hair was unruly even though oily, and his discolored teeth showed an appalling need of dental work. At the table he used his fork for a toothpick and his hand for a fork. He was not even a good speaker. His political power had developed neither from winning voters with charm nor from dazzling them with words; indeed, the voters seemed of secondary interest to him. He gave his primary attention to the men with whom he had to deal in public life, and when he dealt with a man on a personal basis he was difficult to outwit.

After two days in Rome, he knew this evening, if he hadn't already known, exactly what it was Mussolini wanted. Though Mussolini was asking for a chunk of Tunisia and a thousand-mile strip connecting Libya with Lake Chad, both men knew he wasn't going to get either.

Finally, Laval said to him, "You are the undisputed chief of Italy. I am a French minister. If you want these negotiations to come to a happy conclusion, it is you who will have to concede."[8]

Ethiopia, which had already been discussed obliquely, now became the principal subject of concern. Laval was happy to stipulate that, aside from the French-owned Addis Ababa–Djibuti railroad and a few business enterprises near the border of French Somaliland, France had absolutely no economic interest in Ethiopia.

Could it be agreed, then, that France would give Italy a free hand in Ethiopia?

It was because the expression "a free hand" had already been bruited about so widely in public that the French Foreign Office had tried, the previous night, to dissociate Laval from it. He had no desire tonight to reassociate himself with it. He said later that, although the expression was used, he had not agreed to Italian military operations in Africa.[9] Did this mean he had offered an economic "free hand" which Mussolini might have interpreted as a military free hand? Neither man, nor any of their aides, ever reported the exact sentences that passed between them. Léger said later he had no idea of the extent of Laval's private concessions to Mussolini—but that he was sure they existed.[10] Both Mussolini and Laval had expressive faces. With or without words, each knew what the other meant, and each was convinced he had got what he wanted.

A plain-clothes man on duty in the hall when Mussolini emerged from the meeting reported to the Assistant Chief of Police that the Duce was "visibly radiant with joy."[11] No one else had the opportunity to observe this. He departed quickly through a side door without granting even a glimpse of himself to the party guests in the great hall.

Next day, when those parts of the agreement which could be made public were announced, Mussolini's popularity dropped among the Italians and his reputation for shrewdness dropped throughout the world. It appeared from the joint communiqué issued at the Palazzo Venezia on the evening of January 7 that Laval had bested him badly.

Concerning Africa, the agreement included three clauses. The first gave Italy forty-four thousand square miles to be annexed to Libya (all desert land, and none of it close to Lake Chad), plus three hundred nine square miles, equally useless, to be transferred from French Somaliland to Eritrea. The second clause provided for the solution of the Tunisian question entirely in favor of France, including even the cancellation of Italian citizenship for the hundred thousand Italian nationals who lived there. And the third clause gave Italy twenty-five hundred shares (only about seven per cent) of the Addis Ababa–Djibuti railroad.

Mussolini, wearing striped pants and cutaway with a winged collar, stood at the end of the table looking down with an expression of theatrical ferocity as Laval signed the document. Then the two men punctuated it by making a few remarks to the press. Laval assured the world that France and Italy had only the friendliest intentions toward everyone. Mussolini echoed him. "As M. Laval has said, the Franco-Italian general agreements don't have a single point directed against anyone, but are made in and with the hope that they might serve, not to restrain but to enlarge the horizon of European life, to bring us out of the painful situation in which the people have found themselves for such a long time."

The whole world was startled by the publicized terms of the pact. If Laval had not given Mussolini Abyssinia, then he had given him practically nothing. In the two tracts of land which Italy gained, the population totaled sixty-nine. Would the race-proud dictator, for this scattering of blacks, have surrendered a hundred thousand ardent, patriotic Italians in Tunisia plus all of Italy's claims to Tunisian territory? He was not popular among Italians in North Africa during the days ahead. The French governor of Tunisia reported to Laval that at the Italian schools there the teachers were removing pictures of Mussolini from the walls and throwing them on the ground, where the children were invited to spit upon them.

In Naples, January 7, Italian General Emilio De Bono, an elderly, slender man with a white goatee, was boarding, without fanfare, the regular monthly steamer for Eritrea, where he maintained his headquarters as Minister for the Colonies.[12] He had been home in Italy for a month, and it was a highly satisfying month. On December 30, he had been one of a handful of Italian officials who received from Mussolini that most secret memorandum written in the strictest privacy ten days earlier—"Directive and Plan of Action for the Resolution of the Italian-Abyssinian Question." It was a document which promised De Bono the realization of hopes he had harbored and fostered for several years. A few days later, at a time when all the complications of the Laval visit were swirling in Mussolini's head, he had nevertheless managed to fit in a long meeting with De Bono from which the old general emerged in a state of euphoric anticipation. He could now envision a glorious climax to a career in which glory had always escaped him.

Though De Bono had served in Eritrea as a young lieutenant in 1888, he had been back in Italy in 1896 when the cataclysmic Battle of Adowa took place. In the 1914–1918 war he did not distinguish himself, and while there were few Italian military men in a position to reproach him for that, he was nevertheless unpopular with his colleagues, especially after he embraced Fascism in its early days, when it was still unacceptable to the military establishment. In 1922, he was already such an open and prominent Fascist that he became one of the triumvirate (with Italo Balbo and Cesare De Vecchi) in command of the march on Rome. When the march succeeded and Mussolini became premier, De Bono's future appeared secure. Then came the Matteotti murder in 1924, after which it began to look as if he had no future. At that time, Mussolini, not yet a dictator, was still consolidating his power by intimidating his opponents with threats, beatings, castor oil, and other torture treatments, and in cases where nothing else availed, murder. Giacomo Matteotti, a member of Parliament, who was his loudest critic and who refused to be intimidated, was finally ambushed and killed by a special squad of Fascists whose training for such assignments Mussolini had arranged. Unfortunately for these men, they hadn't been trained well enough. They left such a sloppy trail they were soon caught by law-enforcement agents not yet under Fascist influence. Mussolini then publicly denounced them. But as the investigation of the affair progressed, the Director of Public Safety in Mussolini's government was strongly implicated because it was he, although under Mussolini's orders, who had actually organized the torture and execution squad. This Director of Public Safety was Emilio De Bono. As soon as his involvement in the Matteotti scandal became evident to everyone, Mussolini summarily dismissed him. He was subjected to a lengthy trial and his career seemed to be at an end. But fortunately for him, while he was on trial, Mussolini continued consolidating his power. De Bono was eventually acquitted, and when Fascist control became so nearly absolute that public opinion was no longer an important factor in Italy, Mussolini restored him to favor, then sent him to Africa in 1932 as a special emissary to inspect the colonies there, which were stagnating. When De Bono returned, he reported to his Duce that "the possibilities of our colonial future must be sought in East Africa"— which was to say Ethiopia, because every other inch of land in East Africa was controlled by either France or England. It was not until the following year, in autumn 1933, that Mussolini gave him definite encouragement. One day in conversation with the Duce, De Bono said, "If there is war down there, and if you think me worthy of it and capable, you ought to grant me the honor of conducting the campaign."[13]

Mussolini, looking at him hard, said, "Surely."

De Bono said, "You don't think me too old?" He was then sixty-seven.

Mussolini said, "No, because we mustn't lose time." Even then he was convinced, as he told De Bono, that the Abyssinian solution had to come no later than 1936.

De Bono was delighted but still not fully certain of Mussolini's determination. He said, "Money will be needed, Chief. Lots of money."

"There will be no lack of money," Mussolini assured him.

Early in 1934, the money began to flow from Rome to Eritrea, first for roads, then for water development, military bases, and airfields. All the roads from Massawa on the Red Sea coast up to Asmara on the high plateau, plus those from Asmara to the Ethiopian border south of it, had to be completely rebuilt. In the beginning, De Bono had relied on black laborers of whom he said, "their output was low but they were cheap. And in any case, in 1934, given the secrecy which we wished to maintain, it was out of the question to think of sending Italian workers." By December 1934, when De Bono returned to Italy after escorting King Victor Emmanuel on a tour of Somaliland, he had already done much to convert Eritrea into a base for military operations, but he still had much more to do.

In his long interview with Mussolini just before he embarked again for Africa on January 7, he learned that when he arrived there he was to assume a new and higher title than Minister for the Colonies. Henceforth he would be High Commissioner for East Africa, although it would not be announced immediately.

"You leave with the olive-bough in your pocket," Mussolini instructed him. "We shall see how the Wal Wal affair turns out. If it suits us to accept the conditions offered us in consequence of the award [which Italy was expecting as compensation] you will inform the Emperor of your assumption of the post of High Commissioner, telling him that you have been sent out to clear up any misunderstandings and to collaborate in establishing friendly relations in the moral and material interests of the two States. In the meantime, continue to make active preparations such as you would make in view of the more difficult and adverse outcome of the affair. If no solution of the incident is offered, or if it is not such as to satisfy us, we shall follow subsequent events exclusively in accordance with our own standpoint."

So far, the Wal Wal clash had been very useful to De Bono in forwarding his plans. If the Ethiopians continued to hold out against the Italian settlement demands, he might yet win an opportunity to crown his career with military glory.

CHAPTER THREE

As diplomats from all over the world gathered in Geneva for the January 11, 1935, meeting of the League of Nations Council, the respect with which men of other nations approached and sought the guidance of the British and French representatives demonstrated the transcendent power of England and France within the organization. Of the two, England was the more influential by far, being still considered at that time the mightiest nation in the entire world. Unfortunately for the League, English politicians and statesmen (like their counterparts in many other countries) tended to think in national rather than supernational terms, and therefore to use the League more as an instrument of British foreign policy than of world governance.

The vision upon which the League was conceived at the end of the Great War by United States President Woodrow Wilson, whose own country then refused to join it, grew out of the notion of collective security through unified action to maintain universal peace and order. This notion was still to be fully tested because it had not been invoked on the one occasion so far when it might have prevailed—before Japan's 1931 invasion of China. The League had declined to try it at that time, partly because China was too far away to concern most of the League members and partly because there was uncertainty as to whether collective security would actually work.

The men of Great Britain's ruling class, while willing to operate within the League, were reserved almost to the point of cynicism about its potential powers. Stanley Baldwin, Conservative Party leader who was virtually Acting Prime Minister in the coalition government of aging and tired Ramsay MacDonald and who was himself an old and tired man so reassuringly placid most of his countrymen considered him thoughtfully solid, had declared in Glasgow the previous year that the League's collective-peace system was "perfectly impracticable." Another Conservative statesman, Sir Samuel Hoare, after attending a League Council meeting in 1932, had referred to the atmosphere in Geneva as "curiously artificial and neurotic" and said of Britain's Commonwealth representative there, J.H.Thomas, that he was doing his job excellently, "and as long as he does not get it into his head that he and Geneva are necessarily moving the world, he will continue to do it excellently."[1]

The League had just gained an apparent supporter, however, in another Conservative statesman, the young (thirty-eight-year-old) Lord Privy Seal, Anthony Eden, who was now Britain's chief delegate in Geneva. Only three days before the January 11 Council meeting, Eden, who had not previously shown any strong tendency to champion the League, said in an Edinburgh speech that "balance of power is no longer British policy. Ours is League policy." It is difficult to determine what put this idea into his head.

Eden was such a handsome, well-dressed man, was endowed with such a pleasant personality, and was so moderate in his views that he had become a Baldwin protégé and had risen quickly within the Conservative Party, which at that time suffered from a shortage of attractive young members. The son of a moderately wealthy country gentleman, he had studied at Eton and Oxford and had won a Military Cross for heroism in the Great War. He had entered politics not because of any burning passion to improve the world but because government was a responsibility which upper-class people had a duty to accept. He was so impressive in appearance and got along so well with his associates that he soon found himself rising more rapidly than anyone else in his age group. His appointment as Privy Seal and as League of Nations delegate gave him his first opportunity to deal with diplomats of other countries, and he seemed to get along as well with most of them as with his British colleagues.

The business of the League was conducted in a complex of large, stately, neoclassical buildings located on the broad, green lawns of Ariana Park, from which the delegates could enjoy a glorious view of Lake Geneva and the Alps, including Mount Blanc. The League Council, with representatives from fourteen of the more influential Member States, met in a chamber of the three-wing main building, which housed also the two-thousand-seat hall of the Assembly. The more than fifty Members of the Assembly (the number varied as some nations joined or withdrew) convened infrequently, leaving the essential workings of the League to the Council, which exercised virtual control over the organization. The Council, and therefore the entire League, was dominated by Europe's two foremost powers, Great Britain and France.

Perhaps not the most important but surely the most annoying piece of business the League Council had to consider in the meeting which opened January 11 was Ethiopia's appeal, first expressed in its note of January 3, for League action to settle the Wal Wal dispute. The only thing certain about the fate of Ethiopia's appeal as the Council session

35

began was the fact that it would be decided not in the Council chamber but in the corridors, the meeting rooms, and the hotels where the English and French representatives were already cajoling the Italians and cautioning the Ethiopians. On the French side, Foreign Minister Pierre Laval showed such apparent sympathy for the Italian viewpoint that he was quite ineffective in dealing with the Ethiopians. When in December he and Eden had first heard about the Wal Wal incident from Ethiopian League delegate P. Tecle Hawariate, Laval had shown himself more interested in the name of Ethiopia's capital, Addis Ababa, which he seemed never to have heard of, than in the account of this apparently trivial frontier clash. The words "Addis Ababa"—or "Addis Abeba," as they were spelled in French—sounded so delightful to him that he kept repeating, "*A-be-ba. Que c'est chic, ça. A-be-ba.*"[2] His concern about Ethiopia since December had not noticeably increased. The celebrated days he had just spent in Rome and his public embrace of Mussolini were not likely to recommend him to the Ethiopians as a champion of their cause.

Eden was more persuasive with them, though handicapped for the first two days by the presence of his chief, the British Foreign Secretary himself, Sir John Simon, who had come along to be helpful. Simon, a distinguished lawyer who had been for more than three years an undistinguished and unpopular foreign secretary, had little concern for the League (his opposition had been a strong factor in preventing collective action against Japan's 1931 China venture) and less for Ethiopia, of which he had taken public notice only once before in his life, when he wrote a preface to a book by his wife[3] exposing the horrors of slavery there. He agreed with Laval that the continuing friendship of Italy was more important than the fate of a black nation in Africa. Unfortunately for Ethiopia, the English and French ruling classes found more in common with white Europeans than with black Africans. But Simon was more subtle than Laval and he had the additional advantage that Ethiopia's Emperor trusted the British more than the French. The traditional British reputation for fair play still impressed people in some parts of the world.

Simon and Eden, when they spoke to Baron Pompeo Aloisi, the suave, aristocratic but powerless Italian delegate, concluded from his remarks that his chief, Dictator Mussolini, was exceedingly eager to prevent a public hearing of Ethiopia's complaints on the floor of the Council chamber. Though this might seem to create an opportunity to press the Italians for concessions, Simon saw it instead as an opportunity to press the Ethiopians for concessions, especially after talking to Ethiopian delegate Tecle Hawariate, a tiny old man, crippled with rheumatism, who had been away from his wife and his large farm in Harar province for two

36

years, and who wished devoutly that he were back there rather than here in Geneva, facing the world's most formidable diplomats. Tecle Hawariate had in hand a fully detailed bill of particulars against Italian conduct at Wal Wal which he had been instructed by Emperor Haile Selassie to submit to the League Council as an elaboration of previous communications on the subject. He made it clear to Simon and Eden, however, that the Emperor was in a conciliatory mood and very eager to settle the dispute peacefully.

On the second day of the Council meeting, January 12, Simon, having worked out a proposal which asked little of Italy and much of Ethiopia, telegraphed it to his minister in Addis Ababa, Sir Sidney Barton, and his ambassador in Rome, Sir Eric Drummond. His message to Barton suggested that if the Emperor wanted to reach a settlement, he, rather than Mussolini, should make the concessions, including one which would tacitly admit Ethiopia's guilt.

"If the Emperor could take the initiative," Simon wrote,

> by a note to the Italian government in which he would first express in general terms his regret that lives should have been lost in an encounter between Ethiopian and Italian forces, and that relations between the two countries should have become strained, and secondly undertake to pay into a bank in neutral territory (not Geneva) 200,000 [Ethiopian] dollars on the understanding that it would be the first task of an Italian-Ethiopian boundary commission, proposed to be set up in the note, to distribute the sum for the relief of sufferers from the encounter of 5th December and/or in making good to that extent any special expenditures (e.g., on troop movements) necessitated thereby, and assuming such note also contained a definite assurance pending delimitation of the frontier that every endeavour would be made by Ethiopian forces to avoid contact with the Italian (on the understanding of course that the latter do not attempt to advance) then I think it might be possible to persuade the Italian Government to take favorable note of such communication. . . .

While Sir John didn't think the Italians should advance any farther, neither did he seem to think they should retreat back to their own border; nor did he suggest that Italy also put up the equivalent of Ethiopia's contribution to the relief of the Wal Wal victims. As the British Foreign Secretary busied himself launching this curious attempt at mediation, his League delegate, Eden, pleaded successfully with Tecle Hawariate to withhold Ethiopia's detailed complaint for two more days while secret conciliation efforts continued. Eden listened so patiently to the Ethiopians he rapidly earned for his troubles the enmity of the Italians, who did not believe, as Mussolini said, that Ethiopia should be treated as an equal of Italy, even in a dispute between the two countries.

When Eden saw Baron Aloisi on the fourteenth, he found the Italian diplomat polite but less than friendly. After considerable discussion, Aloisi finally remarked that he had some complaints to make against British behavior. "The impression is current in the lobby," he said, "that the Ethiopians can count on British sympathy."

Before Eden could answer this, one of Aloisi's aides began talking about a consignment of arms for Ethiopia, apparently supplied by British firms, which had passed through the port of Aden. Inasmuch as Aden was a British protected port, it was surprising that the Italians could or would claim to know so much about operations there. Aloisi's aide did not explain how he had come upon such information. In another instance, he said, cartons marked MACHINERY, but which he insisted were weapons bound for Ethiopia by rail, had also been unloaded at Djibuti, a French port. He didn't explain his knowledge of this, either.

Eden, too startled by the charges to question Italy's apparent espionage, answered nevertheless with righteous anger. "I have no knowledge of these details," he said, "but it is of course fantastic to suppose that British authorities anywhere are abetting Ethiopians."

While Mussolini's representatives pursued this hard line against Great Britain's delegate in Geneva, Mussolini himself prepared a few aggressive thrusts for Great Britain's ambassador in Rome, Sir Eric Drummond, whom he was granting an audience that same afternoon of the fourteenth, after making him wait two weeks for an appointment.[4]

Drummond, who was quite sensitive to Mussolini's combative manner and eager to get along with him, began by explaining to him Sir John Simon's suggestion to the Emperor.

Mussolini did not appear impressed. He had made, he reminded Drummond, four important demands: a letter of apology, two hundred thousand dollars in reparations, a salute to the Italian flag at Wal Wal, and punishment of the guilty Ethiopian commanders. He was willing to abandon his demand for punishment of the guilty, but he must insist on the other three. And as for Simon's suggestion about reparations, he said, "I cannot admit that the money should be paid to a bank in neutral territory. It must be paid to a bank in Eritrea."

Sir Eric said he feared that such conditions could hardly be accepted by the Emperor, who, after all, had stated that he was ready to submit the whole question to an impartial tribunal. "It seems to me," he remarked probingly, "that the matter may have to go before the League."

Mussolini shrugged his shoulders. "If it does," he said, "the consequences might be very serious."

Since he did not seem inclined to explain this warning, Sir Eric went on to point out that if the Emperor were to meet the Italian demands it might endanger his own position in Ethiopia.

"If this is so," Mussolini declared, "it only shows that the Emperor

38

is not firmly established. As for myself, I don't really care whether this emperor rules Ethiopia, or another one, as long as he is strong."

"The present Emperor," Drummond said, "is the most stable element in Ethiopia."

"What constitutes stability in Ethiopia?" Mussolini asked. "Is it the number of slaves?" Whereupon he quoted a figure on the number of slaves in Ethiopia—a figure which he said had come from the book on the subject by Sir John Simon's wife.

Drummond tried to speak of conciliation, but to no avail. The Ethiopian chiefs had got out of hand, Mussolini declared, and were refusing to follow the Emperor. It was essential that they be brought to reason. If Italy were to yield, they would think it was because of the Ethiopian troops near Wal Wal and frontier incidents would multiply. He had personal knowledge of the Ethiopian troop concentrations—perhaps more than a hundred thousand men with machine guns and some artillery—and if this sort of thing did not cease, Italy would have to take action. It was not a question of prestige but a matter which must be settled along the lines he had already detailed in the interest of future quiet on the frontiers.

"There is no doubt at all that a wanton attack was made upon Italian forces," Mussolini insisted. "I've made a great sacrifice in withdrawing my demand for punishment of the guilty. The Emperor could therefore quite well give way on the three points about which I must insist. In return, he would receive definite assurances that the frontier would be delimited and all future incidents thus avoided."

Though Mussolini did not say where the new frontier limits would be placed, it had to be assumed that if the Ethiopians agreed to honor the Italian flag at Wal Wal, the boundary would be moved at least that far east. Mussolini's offer to drop one small demand in exchange for the Emperor's acceptance of the three big ones might have seemed laughable, but the British government treated it seriously. In Addis Ababa, Sir Sidney Barton, who had already transmitted Simon's January 12 suggestion to the Emperor and urged him to act upon it, now submitted to him the revision on which Mussolini had insisted, that Ethiopia was to pay the indemnity to an Eritrean bank rather than a neutral one.

On the evening of the fifteenth, Ethiopian delegate Tecle Hawariate paid a visit to Anthony Eden's hotel in Geneva, but not with the purpose of accepting the latest British proposal. He had come to inform Eden he could no longer withhold his country's demand that the dispute with Italy be discussed at this session of the Council.

"I've given the matter careful consideration," the old man declared uneasily. "I've sent two telegrams to His Imperial Majesty explaining the fact that I was holding back the application, but I've had no reply from him. I can't defer action any longer."

39

While the Emperor's silence might be attributable to the vagaries of the communication system in Addis Ababa, it was more likely to be an indication of his disapproval of the delay. Tecle Hawariate's decision to end the delay was quite understandable. But Eden, who had spent the last four days, at the behest of Sir John Simon and Pierre Laval, trying to prevent the public embarrassment of Mussolini—whom he thoroughly disliked—now proved once more his loyalty to the policies of the Foreign Secretary by trying again to delay Tecle Hawariate.

"Could you not perhaps consider postponing action for another twenty-four hours?" he suggested.

This time Eden was unable to prevail. Tecle Hawariate's resolve was firm. An hour later, Ethiopia's application for a hearing at the current Council session was officially lodged with the League's Secretary-General, Joseph Avenol.

This application was so completely in accord with the League Covenant and rules of procedure it appeared to end all possibility that Italy could avoid a public debate of the Wal Wal dispute and a detailed disclosure of what had actually happened there. But so strong was the British and French desire to retain Mussolini's friendship that they continued their efforts in his behalf even though Eden and Laval, after more meetings with Aloisi, still found their favors unattractive. Aloisi refused to modify Italy's demands, for a reason which became increasingly obvious: he had no authority to do so. His decisions were made in Rome, just as Eden's were made in London.

Finally, on the sixteenth, Eden informed London by telephone of his continuing frustration and suggested that he be authorized to tell the Italians there was nothing more he could do. Proceedings would have to take their course in the Council. He was pleased and perhaps somewhat surprised to find Sir John Simon agreeing with him.

Shortly after Aloisi was informed of the British decision to let the matter come before the Council, the Italian position suddenly seemed to soften. Eden and Laval both argued that if Italy didn't want the affair handled by the League, they would have to agree to handle it themselves in direct negotiations with Ethiopia under the terms of the 1928 treaty between the two countries. Aloisi now began interrupting their meetings at frequent intervals to make telephone calls to Rome.

In Addis Ababa, on the evening of January 17, Sir Sidney Barton visited the Emperor's palace to hear his reaction to Sir John Simon's suggestion for settling the dispute.[5] The Emperor, who had not hastened his consideration of the proposal or of its subsequent modification, discussed it now with what some might describe as "composed features" and others might call "a straight face." Was this latest suggestion of Simon's, he asked, the same as the one he had made on the twelfth with the exception that the money be paid into an Eritrean bank? Or was Simon making a completely new proposal which envisioned Ethiopia's paying indemnities to injured Italians without even so much as an investigation by a joint commission to determine what happened at Wal Wal?

If the latter proved true, a very substantive change had taken place in Simon's proposal, a change of such magnitude it could hardly have been made unconsciously. Sir Sidney professed his own uncertainty about it. "I'll have to telegraph London for an explanation," he said. "But I must urge Your Imperial Majesty," he added, "to take a decision on the matter as soon as possible, without necessarily waiting for a reply from London."

To help hasten the Emperor's decision, Sir Sidney finished with one more argument which contained just a slight suggestion of a threat. "If you fail to settle the dispute," he said, "it might give rise to differences within the League of Nations, in which case the League's power to deal with your appeal will be diminished."

Emperor Haile Selassie showed no fear of this ominous possibility. He respectfully declined the British proposal.

By January 18, the day before the Ethiopians were scheduled to take their complaint to the floor of the Council chamber, Baron Aloisi had made enough Geneva-Rome telephone calls to assure himself it would be permissible to attend a meeting with Eden, Laval, and Tecle Hawariate in the office of Secretary-General Avenol, who was also present. At this meeting two conciliatory letters were drafted, one to be sent by Ethiopia, the other by Italy to the Council. When Tecle Hawariate studied the Ethiopian letter he pronounced it satisfactory. When Aloisi studied the Italian letter he made another phone call to Rome after which he demanded some revisions. Eventually, each man signed his letter and the embarrassing confrontation in the Council was at least temporarily averted. Anthony Eden could congratulate himself for his adroitness in making the Italians acknowledge that the Ethiopians deserved at least some kind of attention. Benito Mussolini, however, would not soon forgive Eden for this.

Each letter stipulated that the two countries would accept the arbitration procedure set forth in Article 5 of the 1928 Italo-Ethiopian Treaty. Aside from this stipulation, the Ethiopian letter simply reaffirmed a willingness to arbitrate and, in the hope that the arbitration would proceed with dispatch, agreed to postpone to the next Council session its demand to be heard.

The Italian letter noted mellowly that "it is in conformity with the spirit of the Covenant and the tradition of the League of Nations to encourage direct negotiations concerning disputes that may arise between two State Members." It did not mention the ease with which a dispute could be prolonged when there was no third party to referee the negotiations and make sure they were conducted with reasonable promptness and sincerity. The letter ended with the friendly, soothing assertion that "Italy does not regard [the incident] as likely to affect the peaceful relations between the two countries."

On February 13, Mussolini, now full of plans and enthusiasm for his Ethiopian enterprise, received some disappointing news from Africa. He had intended to launch the campaign there, as he had outlined to General De Bono several months earlier, with a procedure which he called "the defensive-counteroffensive," a self-descriptive designation. He and De Bono, from what they knew or had heard about the Ethiopian mentality, traditions, and fighting style, felt confident that their chosen enemy could be counted upon to provide, at the proper moment, the kind of border incident that might be answered by a massive "defensive" offensive. But on the thirteenth, an aide handed Mussolini a disconcerting telegram from De Bono in Eritrea:

> At present the Negus Neghesti [Haile Selassie] is ordering too many prayers and fasts to give us reason to think that he wishes to attack us; however, it would be criminal not to be on our guard; the more so as one cannot exclude the possibility of some act of rashness on the part of excited subordinate chieftains.

If De Bono's assessment was correct, it would be unfortunate because in other respects the project was moving smoothly. On February 5, Mussolini had ordered the mobilization of one of Italy's best divisions, the Gavinana, composed mostly of Florentines; and on the eleventh, he had called up another division, the Peloritana. These two units together totaled about thirty-five thousand men. The railroad station in Rome was developing a smart military atmosphere as trains filled with officers had begun arriving from Milan on their way south. Troop centers had been opened in Piacenza, Florence, Bari, and Messina. Civilian employers of all mobilized men had been instructed to continue paying them full wages for the first three months and half wages for the next three months, and to assure them they would lose neither jobs nor seniority during their service. Naples, in the meantime, was being converted into a huge embarkation depot for both troops and supplies.

42

The government was filtering enough information about these developments through the rigid censorship apparatus to make everyone aware that big events were in the making. On February 11, another incident which had happened in Africa January 29 was finally reported in the Italian newspapers. At a tiny place called Afdub, five Italian native troops were killed in a clash against Ethiopians. The Italian public, already incensed about the Wal Wal clash, was further aroused by this one, especially when Ethiopian Chargé d'Affaires Yesus Negradas, claiming the Italian troops had launched the attack, announced that his government would pay no indemnity for it.

The Afdub incident, while useful to Mussolini in stirring domestic wrath against Ethiopia, had very little effect outside Italy and could hardly be described as the kind of border incident for which he and De Bono were hoping: Afdub, thirty-five miles south of Wal Wal, was just as unquestionably inside Ethiopia.

There was, however, some promising news February 13 from outside Italy. London correspondents reported a surprising sympathy for Italy in British government circles. British Foreign Office officials that day, ignoring the fact that Wal Wal and Afdub were well inside Ethiopia, told newsmen they were convinced the Italians had sufficient cause to demand indemnification for the deaths of their soldiers at Wal Wal and they went almost as far as to admit that Sir Sidney Barton in Addis Ababa had suggested the Emperor make some kind of payment.

Even more comforting to Mussolini were some remarks British Foreign Secretary Simon made the same day to the House of Commons. Simon began by explaining that the Italian government had "as a precautionary defensive measure mobilized in Italy two divisions," which he said aggregated "some seven thousand men." (His ambassador in Rome had reported to him two days earlier that the total was thirty thousand men.)[6] This, he assured the members of Parliament, in no way implied that Italy had abandoned amicable intentions. Naturally, in making its protests, the Italian government had reserved the right to seek reparations, but the Abyssinian government insisted it had lived up to the undertaking it had given to the League of Nations and that strict orders had been given to avoid further incidents.

Sir John was evidently saying that while the Ethiopians claimed they didn't do it, they also promised not to do it again. Having thus judged them and found them guilty, he finished with a declaration of his government's admirable impartiality. "Our position in the matter," he said, "is that we stand in friendly relations with both countries and we naturally wish to do all we can to insure a peaceful settlement."

Simon's words about Italy's amicable intentions must have seemed curious to the Foreign Office's expert on Ethiopia, Geoffrey Thompson, to whom Sir John had said a month earlier, "You realize, don't you, that the Italians intend to take Abyssinia?" And his words about the British government's impartiality must have puzzled the nation's ill and aging King George V, to whom Simon had recently said that his overriding concern in the Italian-Ethiopian dispute was to handle it "in a way which will not affect adversely Anglo-Italian relations."

If Anglo-Italian relations were adversely affected by Simon's conduct in the matter it could only be because Mussolini was a difficult man to please. He could not be displeased, however, at this tacit public approval of his plans by the British Foreign Minister.

On February 16, three days after Sir John Simon's comforting remarks to the House of Commons, Mussolini drove to the Grenadiers' Barracks in Rome to address the first troops embarking for East Africa—three battalions of Fascist militia, three thousand men, who were leaving that afternoon. He reviewed their ranks, addressed them confidentially with no newsmen present, accepted their cheers, and hurried back to his office while they piled into trucks and busses for the railway station, where thousands of wives, relatives, and girl friends had gathered to bid them farewell. When they boarded their trains, many had flowers fastened to their helmets; one officer was carrying a single rose in his gloved hand.

Italian military preparations had now become so open and public that Drummond, Britain's ambassador in Rome, felt compelled to take notice of them. On February 17, in a telegram to Simon, he wrote:

> The military preparations are questions of fact and speak for themselves. What has disquieted me particularly has been the disparity between official explanation that military measures taken are purely defensive and indications I and members of my staff have received unofficially regarding possible ultimate aims of Italian policy in Abyssinia. ... As regards disparity between official explanations and unofficial indications my military attaché informs me that in his view preparations for dispatch of army corps can hardly be regarded as less than "eventually aggressive," though he points out that the time available before the spring rains would only permit at present of local and preparatory action. My growing suspicion that explanations of Italian Ministry for Foreign Affairs cannot be taken entirely at their face value and that ultimate Italian intentions are more far-reaching were today confirmed by long confidential conversation I had with a particularly well-placed and reliable source. ...

From this moment forward, the British government can hardly be said to have been unaware of Mussolini's eventual intentions. He was no longer bothering to cover them. His worries about British reaction to the

African venture were fading away. On February 26, he wrote De Bono with confidence and enthusiasm, telling him exactly how they would meet the difficulty if the Ethiopians proved too cunning to provoke them.

He began by agreeing with De Bono's earlier alarm:

> ... the bulk of the indications and the messages intercepted allow us to suppose that the Negus does not wish to take the initiative of the encounter. In case the Negus should have no intention of attacking us, we ourselves must take the initiative. This is not possible unless by the end of September you have at your disposal, besides the blacks, at least 100,000 white soldiers, who will have to be rapidly increased to 200,000.

Despite the "bulk of indications" that the Ethiopians didn't want to make war, it might nevertheless be useful to Mussolini to foster in the world quite a different impression. On February 28, a spokesman at the Foreign Ministry in Rome shared with the international press his estimate that ninety thousand Ethiopian troops were massing on the border of Italian Somaliland. The enormity of this information was not sufficient for some of the newsmen. One American correspondent, feeling compelled to augment it, added, "It is believed here that even greater forces are being mobilized."

When Mussolini wrote again to De Bono, March 8, his plans had become precise and explicit:

> It is my profound conviction that, we being obliged to take the initiative of operations at the end of October or September, you ought to have a combined force of 300,000 men (including about 100,000 black troops in the two colonies) plus 300–500 aeroplanes and 300 rapid vehicles—for without these forces to feed the offensive penetration the operations will not have the vigorous rhythm which we desire. You ask for 3 Divisions by the end of October; I mean to send you 10, I say ten: five Divisions of the regular Army; five of volunteer formations of Black Shirts who will be carefully selected and trained.
>
> These Divisions of Black Shirts will be the guarantee that the undertaking will obtain the popular approbation.
>
> Even in view of possible international controversies (League of Nations, etc.) it is as well to hasten our tempo. For the lack of a few thousand men we lost the day at Adowa! We shall never make that mistake. I am willing to commit a sin of excess but never a sin of deficiency.

In Addis Ababa, life continued for most people as if there were no Italian armies growing on Ethiopia's borders. The nation's capital was considered a new city. Though its site had been inhabited since Biblical times, it had not actually become a city until after the 1896 Battle of

Adowa, when Emperor Menelik, triumphant over the Italians, failed, however, to surmount the wishes of his strong-willed Empress who disliked living in his remote mountain stronghold at Ankober. Under her influence, he came here and made it the seat of his government. As soon as Menelik chose the site for his palace, or *gibbi*, on a sunny hill eight thousand feet above sea level at the foot of the Entoto Mountains, the other great Ethiopian rases (chieftains) hurried to build more modest gibbis of their own on the more modest hills around him. When Addis Ababa's first roads, or more precisely mule tracks, were built, it was to connect these gibbis, which explained the apparently random pattern of the city's streets.

Even now, almost all of these streets were unpaved, still little more than mule tracks, along which a new generation of chiefs and aristocrats could be seen riding, some in automobiles, but most on expensively adorned mules, from gibbi to gibbi, followed by rabble-like shamma-clad retinues of anything from a few retainers to several thousand. The highest employment to which most men could aspire in Ethiopia was attachment to one of these feudal lords. A young man with no occupation—which description embraced the majority—would hang around the gate of one of the gibbis, doing for the master's servants whatever jobs they found too odious, exhibiting his eagerness to please in the hope of being noticed and eventually retained. An aristocrat who aspired to any prestige would take on as many such young men as he could possibly afford because the size of his retinue indicated the extent of his power and importance.

Descending into Addis Ababa from Mount Entoto to the north, one approached first, among the eucalyptus trees which Menelik had imported from Australia and which now dotted the landscape in many parts of the country, a scattering of the round, thatch-roofed, picturesque huts called tukuls, the traditional houses of the Ethiopians for many centuries. Inside the fringes of the city, these tukuls, which blended harmoniously with the countryside, became increasingly scarce, giving way to the ugly, tin-roofed mud-and-manure–walled shacks which now provided most of the housing in Ethiopian towns and cities. In the extensive, odd-shaped sectors between the rambling streets, these shacks were so closely crowded together among the eucalyptus that only the residents could possibly find their way through the maze.

Swinging southeastward past the park-like grounds of the Emperor's new gibbi, one reached eventually, by a circuitous route, the Cathedral of St. George, Ethiopia's patron saint, and the equestrian statue of Menelik II, Ethiopia's most renowned ruler—unless one were to include King Solomon and the Queen of Sheba, from whom both Menelik and Haile Selassie claimed descent.

Though the cathedral was relatively new, like the rest of Addis Ababa,

46

and less interesting architecturally or historically than the ancient churches in the northern religious centers of Axum and Lalibela, it was nevertheless the most imposing edifice of the Ethiopian Orthodox Church in the capital, and the site of the nation's most important official religious ceremonies.

Christianity had been brought to Ethiopia midway through the fourth century by a bishop named Frumentius, who was the hero of a bemusingly romantic story related by Roman historian Rufinus Tyrranus. According to Rufinus, Frumentius, as a small boy, had been taken along, together with another boy named Aedesius, on a voyage of a merchant ship from Tyre to "further India." During the return trip, this ship was boarded by hostile warriors from Axum who put to the sword everyone except the two boys. Frumentius and Aedesius they took to their king, Elle Amida, and queen, Candace, who held court at Axum. As the boys grew to manhood, they became so beloved by the royal couple that when the king died, Queen Candace asked them to remain and help her govern until her young son, Aeizanas, was old enough to assume power. For several years, until Aeizanas reached manhood, Frumentius virtually ruled the country as regent. During this time, he learned about Christianity from visiting merchants and encouraged the propagation of Christian ideals among the people. "God stirred his heart," Rufinus wrote, "and he began to search out Roman merchants who were Christians and to give them great influence and urge them to establish conventicles to which they might resort for prayer in the Roman manner."

When Aeizanas assumed his duties as king, Frumentius and Aedesius returned home, Aedesius to Tyre (where he later told this story to Rufinus), and Frumentius to Alexandria, where the famous Athanasius, who was then patriarch, consecrated him a bishop and asked him to return to Axum as a missionary. Since Frumentius had already laid the foundation for Christianity there, he was able within a short time after his return to baptize King Aeizanas and the Queen Mother Candace, thereby assuring the conversion of the populace.

Ethiopian religious historians agree in general with this account by Rufinus except that they believe Frumentius, whom they call Abba Salama (The Father of Peace), had been a eunuch belonging to Queen Candace. The Ethiopian Orthodox Church acknowledges him as the first Bishop of Axum, and, because he was consecrated by the Patriarch of Alexandria, the Egyptian Church has always exercised strong influence over the Ethiopian Church. Through the centuries until very recent years, the chief bishop of Ethiopia (the Abuna) has been invariably the nominee of the Patriarch of Alexandria. Because the Egyptian Church is Coptic in doctrine, the Ethiopian Church also supports the Monophysite doctrine that Christ had not a dual but a single nature, combining the

47

human and the divine. The Ethiopians use the Coptic calendar, which divides the year into twelve months of thirty days each, plus five (or six) extra days, and runs eight years behind the Gregorian calendar. Like the Copts, they also observe ten extra days of Lent plus many long fasts. They differ from the Copts, however, in several respects, including the use of their own liturgical language and the use of several pagan customs in their rituals. While the Ethiopian Orthodox was the nation's official church, it was not the only recognized religion. A large part of the population was Moslem, and Emperor Haile Selassie, though devoutly Orthodox himself, had never discouraged religious freedom.

Two blocks south of the Menelik statue was Addis Ababa's main square with a cluster of shoddy stores and cinemas which constituted the city's business center. Another block south of this was the Greek-owned Imperial Hotel, one of the few in the entire country which offered even an approximation of European-style accommodations. From the business district down the long slope to the imposing French-built railway station ran a stretch of asphalt which was Addis Ababa's one completely paved street. It had been surfaced in 1930 for Haile Selassie's coronation ceremonies, at which time several triumphal arches had also been built—of papier-mâché. These arches had not endured without damage the sun and the rains of the last five years, but it was remarkable that they had endured at all.

In all of Addis Ababa there was no sewage system. Garbage and waste were simply dumped into the streets, where vultures and crows fed during the day, jackals and hyenas at night. The rivers carried away some of the waste; the same rivers supplied the water for the city's 130,000 inhabitants. There was only one electric generator; it provided just enough light and power for the Emperor's gibbi. Thus the city's night life was limited.

But Addis Ababa did have a night life. For Westerners there were the hotels and smaller hostelries, each with bars and some with a few girls to offer. There was also one night club, owned by a Greek, with several girls to offer, mostly White Russian, Hungarian, and Rumanian, girls, some of them quite pretty, who had found it expedient to forgo Europe. They were not, however, the city's only available girls. In a society so impoverished that many of its young men could survive only as virtually idle retainers for the wealthy landowning minority, the young women faced an even narrower choice. One estimate placed the number of prostitutes in Addis Ababa at twenty thousand. Their houses had traditionally borne red crosses to signify what could be found inside, but because representatives of the International Red Cross had pointed out to the Emperor the embarrassing coincidence of symbols, he had ordered that the locals surrender their red crosses in deference to the foreigners. This worked no hardship because the girls didn't really need any symbols.

They stood in their doorways, often with their parents, brothers, and sisters concealed in a back room, using whatever attractions they possessed to lure passers-by into the front room. But while many of these girls were attractive and some were spectacularly beautiful, business was not always good. In a country where the average wage was equivalent to three and a half dollars per year, most men found food more important than love.

In Ethiopia there was also a still sizable group who earned no wages at all—the slaves. The Emperor had taken measures against slavery and a League of Nations report on the subject then in preparation praised him for his efforts.[7] (The report also pointed out that in the Italian colony of Eritrea there were still people living in virtual slavery.) But it would be ludicrous to pretend that slavery had ceased to exist. The Emperor's chief difficulty in eliminating it arose from the fact that the majority of the slaves were owned by the Church and by the most powerful rases.

For many centuries Ethiopian traders had been exporting to the Arabian and Persian markets slaves who were captured in raids on neighboring countries. The British had tried for over a century to stop the transport of such slaves, but even in recent years they sometimes found that the victims themselves were not reluctant to be enslaved. One British naval officer reported that when his ship approached a dhow carrying slaves, the crew of the dhow gave guns to their captives, who immediately joined the battle against their British saviors. Haile Selassie, aided by the British and by the decline of the Mediterranean slave markets, had, however, brought an end to the slave export business.

The internal slave trade had long depended on a chain of markets centered in Jimma province, about a hundred miles southwest of Addis Ababa. Here the business had been so highly organized that slaves were carefully bred, sometimes with whites because it was thought this made their offspring more attractive and salable. The slaves were kept on openly operated farms, like chickens or goats, and their children raised like a crop for sale. Special diets and supposed aphrodisiacs were provided for the stud males and they were kept in contentment by the lubricity of the atmosphere.

While Haile Selassie may not yet have managed to eliminate completely the Jimma slave markets, he had at least suppressed them and damaged their business. He had also issued a decree designed to end all slavery. It provided that a woman slave who bore a child by her master was free, if she wished it, from the time of the birth; that any slave sold or sent as a gift was automatically free; that if a man died without a proper will his slaves were to be freed; and that all children of slaves were automatically free although the master had to support them until the age of fifteen. While this law would seem to fall far short of complete abolition, its gradual aspects took into account two social problems which America's

49

abolition of slavery in 1863 had ignored—the extreme reluctance of owners to part with economically valuable property and the freed slave's difficulty in supporting himself. By phasing out slavery rather than banning it completely, the Emperor had hoped to avoid revolt both by the masters and the slaves themselves, who often complained when they were freed that they had worsened their condition because now there was no one to feed them.

Haile Selassie, in his attempt to modernize Ethiopia's feudal society and to make it more acceptable to other countries in the League of Nations, had modified many of the harsh practices of previous emperors. He had repealed the laws by which liars were deprived of their tongues and thieves of their hands. He had also reduced the number of hangings and had forbidden the practice of leaving hanged men to rot in their nooses while vultures ate them. He had now even begun the construction of a model prison on the edge of town, near the Akaki airport, where his eleven-plane air force was centered. Despite all he had done, however, the administration of justice remained primitive.

Hungarian journalist Ladislas Farago, who arrived in Addis Ababa in February 1935, witnessed several examples of Ethiopian judicial procedure.[8] The first was a street scene in which two quarreling men took their dispute to a policeman. In such instances the police were authorized to act as judges on the spot.

The plaintiff cried out to the officer, "May God open your eyes, sir, and enable you to see the truth of my case. I swear by the life of Haile Selassie that this man stole from me. He took two thalers [seventy cents] and he will not return them. Give judgment to the best of your conscience, sir."

The policeman, turning to the accused, said, "Did you take the money?"

"No, sir," he said, "the money belonged to me. I swear it by the life of Haile Selassie."

The policeman, disbelieving him, pronounced what was still a common sentence in Ethiopia. "The thief," he said, "must be chained to the plaintiff."

The chains were brought; the two men walked away, affixed to each other by the wrists and destined to remain thus until the convictee paid the two thalers.

Farago was allowed to witness, in the Imperial Palace, a session of the nation's highest court, the *Shilot*, or Court of Blood, nominally presided over by the Emperor himself but actually, on this occasion, by the Minister of Justice who passed instant judgment. He decreed that a liar should have his ankles chained together for the period of sentence and the chains were immediately clamped in place. He decreed twenty-five lashes for a swindler, who was bound hand and foot on the floor while a bailiff cut into him with a hippopotamus whip. And he decreed branding for a thief, who was held still while a glowing iron was pressed to his forehead.

The Emperor himself would preside over the Shilot only in extremely important cases, and even then very rarely these days when his mind was occupied by the bewildering crisis with Italy. He spent hours each day with his American financial adviser, Everett Colson, who was now also his chief foreign-affairs adviser. Reactions in Geneva at the January League Council session, when Ethiopia was stalled in its attempt to be heard, made it apparent that if the Emperor was to ward off the danger from Italy, he must make his case as clear as possible to the entire world. The most expedient means at his disposal was the foreign press corps in Addis Ababa. On February 28, he began a series of interview audiences by inviting to his gibbi Harold Pemberton, a writer for *The New York Times*.[9]

Dressed completely in black and wearing no jewels or decorations, he welcomed Pemberton into his private study, held out his hand, then motioned to one of the Louis Seize chairs near his huge desk. Pemberton was impressed immediately by the Emperor's large melancholy eyes, which seemed to gaze directly through him. After seating himself comfortably and glancing around the book-lined room, Pemberton went directly to the most important question in his mind.

"Does your country sincerely desire peace?" he asked in French.

"Ethiopia earnestly desires peace," the Emperor answered in fluent French, choosing not to avail himself of his interpreter. It was his usual custom in audiences with foreigners to have their questions translated into Ethiopia's official language, Amharic, and to answer them in Amharic, even though he was fluent in French and quite conversant in English. By waiting for the Amharic translations, he gained time to frame his answers carefully. But today his emotions were so high and he knew the answers so well that he had no desire to wait. "Ethiopia is not reluctant to make reparation if reparation is found to be due," he continued, "but she is determined to seek a solution of the trouble by other methods than supinely admitting responsibility for the conflict at Wal Wal. Nor does she intend to admit the legality of encroachment on her southeastern frontier without exhausting all means of obtaining an impartial, just, peaceful decision of the entire question."

Pemberton wanted to know how he was working for peace, which prompted the Emperor to review all the steps taken so far: the invocation of the 1928 Treaty of Amity with Italy, the various appeals to the League of Nations, and now his appeal to world opinion in an effort to get an impartial hearing. It was because he relied on League of Nations intentions that he had accepted the postponement of a hearing by the Council.

He was also continuing direct negotiations with the Italian legation in Addis Ababa, but this had not so far accomplished much. "Meanwhile, the Italian military preparations continue," he said. "If this attitude persists, we shall return to Geneva and shall not again consent to adjournment."

Rumors that Ethiopian troops were massing on the borders of Italian Somaliland and Eritrea prompted Pemberton to ask, "Have you mobilized your army?"

Haile Selassie answered emphatically. "Ethiopia has not mobilized a single soldier since the Wal Wal incident. Reports of important concentrations of Ethiopian troops in the [southeastern] province of Ogaden or elsewhere never had the slightest basis. On the contrary, when we received news of the Italian attack at Wal Wal, the Ethiopian troops were ordered immediately to retire, except those considered indispensable to hold existing posts."

Pemberton asked him what it was he wanted in the disputed areas.

"Ethiopia's only desire," the Emperor said, "is to conserve the territory she owns and to regain that to which she is entitled under treaty and private agreements with Italy, and of which she has been deprived through progressive encroachment. We demand simply an impartial hearing by a disinterested party for determination of the facts and the fixing of responsibilities. We shall loyally and unreservedly carry out the decision of such a party."

When this interview was published March 4, it became evident to interested people that the opponent Mussolini had chosen possessed the kind of fierce determination and incisive quality of mind which might make him difficult to handle.

A few days later, the Emperor extended an invitation to Farago, who at that time was representing a Berlin newspaper. Farago was driven up to his gibbi past the great, sprawling wall-enclosed gibbi of Menelik, which was still the official Imperial Palace, and where throngs of shamma-clad Ethiopians waited patiently every day in the hope of a glimpse at their ruler. At the gate of the Emperor's new palace, another mile and a half up the slope toward Mount Entoto, soldiers of the Imperial Guard, dressed in European-style uniforms, except that many of them were barefooted, brought themselves to a smart present arms with rifles of various origins and ages. A few of these weapons looked old enough to be 1870 models.

After passing the guard, Farago found himself traveling up a curved road through extensive gardens, somewhat formal in the European manner but not quite so precisely laid out—perhaps because precision is not an Ethiopian characteristic. Because Addis Ababa had no water system, these gardens were irrigated during the dry season by a staff of two hundred men who carried buckets from the nearest springs. At the door of the seven-month-old not-quite-finished palace, Farago was met by an aide who escorted him through the building toward the Emperor's study.

There were autographed pictures of several European monarchs in the great hall, including one of Italy's King Victor Emmanuel. The furnishings were English and tasteful. All the chairs bore the Imperial Ethiopian monogram in Amharic lettering.

In the study, where Farago was taken to await the Emperor, he looked at the books lining the walls. Most of them were in French but many were also in English and Latin—in all, an impressive library. Careful examination gave him the impression that many of the volumes were well used.[10]

Glancing out the window in one direction, he saw a body of troops being drilled by officers he knew to be Swedish. (General Virgin, who was trying to bring the Ethiopian army up to European standards, had several officers from his own country working under him.) Glancing in another direction, he was surprised to see Haile Selassie himself walking in the garden, apparently lost in deep thought, with two lion cubs frolicking at his heels. The Emperor, like his many predecessors, kept several lions (in cages that were sometimes allowed to get slightly rusty) as symbols of the power of the "all-conquering Lion of Judah." He had on some occasions in the past allowed full-grown lions to sprawl on the carpet at the door of his study so that visitors had to pass them as they entered. A story, perhaps apocryphal, was current in Addis Ababa that one day when Sir Sidney Barton confronted two lions at the door he took out a pistol and shot them dead, then warned the Emperor he would do likewise the next time he was met by such dangerous beasts. True or not, the Emperor no longer allowed lions the freedom of his study. When he entered the room for his interview with Farago, he had exchanged the two lion cubs for three cocker spaniels which he said were the gift of the Duke of Abruzzi, the King of Italy's uncle.

The most striking immediate impression of Haile Selassie, for most people who met him, was not his small stature but the large brow and the full bush of hair above the quick eyes and slender, handsome features of his face. Though his skin was brown, these features were Caucasian. Amharic people made careful distinction between themselves and Negroid people.

The Emperor's composed expression appeared to reflect not calmness but a determination to conceal sadness and anxiety. Even if he could prevent his melancholy from showing in the rest of his face, he could not banish it from his eyes. He wore a black silk cape with white jodhpurs. His movements were quick. When he spoke, he gesticulated with his hands. He looked much younger than his age, which was either forty-three or forty-four or forty-five years—no one could say with certainty; the keeping of records was so casual in Ethiopia that the precise age even of the nation's most important man could not be certified. He went to his large desk in the center of the room and invited his visitor to sit down in a nearby chair. An interpreter stood by waiting to translate.

"Would Abyssinia resist a foreign invasion?" Farago asked.

The Emperor answered in Amharic, which was duly translated: "Ethiopia is a member of the League of Nations and has signed the Kellogg Pact [the Kellogg-Briand Pact of 1928, an international agreement to outlaw war, cosponsored by the United States and France, and signed by fifteen nations, including Ethiopia], so she feels in duty bound to make every effort to reach conciliation before resorting to weapons. Should a foreign power attack the country while these negotiations are in progress, then we should naturally oppose it."

When the Emperor paused, the interpreter began translating his first sentence, but soon the Emperor became noticeably restive and waved the interpreter aside to begin speaking for himself in French.

"The Italians have no reason for mobilizing," he insisted. "The incidents of December fifth, 1934, and January twenty-ninth, 1935, were attacks made by Italian troops." He broke into a complicated explanation of the January 29 clash, after which he said, "I have always tried to create an atmosphere favorable to friendly conciliation, but I am not prepared to turn a blind eye while these discussions drag on and more Italian forces are sent out to the neighboring colonies. I feel compelled to make preparations for defending my own country."

Farago turned to a question which the Emperor had often faced in recent weeks. "Does Abyssinia wish to expand her frontiers?"

The Emperor became vehement. "What we want at the moment," he said, "is the liberation of those districts that the Italians are now occupying unlawfully. We would also like an outlet to the sea, but we intend to get that by peaceful negotiation with our neighbors, and in that connection I look upon Italy's territorial expansion in Africa as a real menace to Ethiopia. At the time of the Treaty of 1906 [in which England, France, and Italy had defined for each other, without consulting Ethiopia, their spheres and aspirations in East Africa], Italy had already expressed a wish to unite its two colonies of Eritrea and Somaliland [between which lay Ethiopia as well as French and British Somaliland], which would automatically damage Ethiopia's integrity."

The Emperor was now so animated he continued talking without bothering to wait for questions. "We welcome everyone's assistance," he said, "but we shall never surrender our political or economic freedom. We have no grounds for conflicts apart from a section of frontier that has not been delimited; that ought to be done soon because the people in those districts do not know where they belong, and as a result, the incidents that occasionally happen are, unfortunately, unavoidable. This frontier could be decided quite peacefully. There were no disturbances while the frontiers were being adjusted between British Somaliland and Ethiopia; the English and Ethiopian commissions worked together very quietly for three years."

The Emperor went on talking at length, and when he finished Farago sensed the interview was nearing its end. He concluded it by changing the subject to probe the Emperor's views on a more general topic—the future of the African continent. He was surprised to hear this ruler of a nation only now emerging from feudalism express ideas so radically advanced they would be unacceptable to all but a few Europeans of that day.

"If the European powers were to renounce their political and economic interests in Africa," Haile Selassie said, "the half-independent native peoples would enact modern laws that would eventually make them independent and responsible members of the League of Nations. Then peaceful cooperation would be possible in Africa."

It was perhaps indiscreet of him to climax an interview at a time when he was seeking the help of France, England, and other colonial powers within the League by expressing such a revolutionary dream as African independence, but in fact it was safe enough for him to say what he pleased because the world had not yet paid him heed. To fellow Members of the League of Nations, Ethiopia's complaint was still more a nuisance than an issue. With every passing day since the January Council, the Emperor's frustration had grown. It was driving him toward a move which he hoped would force the nations of the League to hear him and save his country from despoliation by Italy.

On March 17, Ethiopian League delegate Tecle Hawariate (who was also Minister to France) submitted to Secretary-General Avenol a new appeal for help, this time invoking Articles 10 and 15 of the Covenant. Article 10 declared:

> The Members of the League undertake to respect and preserve as against external aggression the territorial integrity and existing political independence of all members of the League.

Article 15 declared:

> If there should arise between Members of the League any dispute likely to lead to a rupture, which is not submitted to arbitration or judicial settlement in accordance with Article 13, the Members of the League agree that they will submit the matter to the Council. Any party of the dispute may effect such submission by giving notice of the existence of the dispute to the Secretary-General, who will make all necessary arrangements for a full investigation and consideration thereof.

The Ethiopian letter of submission, on which the Emperor and his advisers had been working for several days, began by stating that "in consequence of the mobilization ordered by the Royal Italian Government and of the continual dispatch of troops and war material to the Italo-Ethiopian frontier, there now exists between Ethiopia and the Royal Italian Government a dispute likely to lead to a rupture." After accusing the Italians of refusing to conduct "real negotiations" in the spirit of the agreement to negotiate, signed by the two countries at Geneva on January 19, and after repeating Ethiopia's willingness to accept any arbitral decision by a third party, the letter, addressed to Avenol, concluded with a virtual demand for League action: ". . . the Ethiopian Government, availing itself of the right conferred upon it by Article 15 of the Covenant, requests you, Sir, to lay the Italo-Ethiopian dispute before the Council of the League of Nations with a view to full investigation and consideration."

This was the strongest Ethiopian appeal for help since the Wal Wal incident had taken place. By pointing out the continuing Italian arms build-up on the Ethiopian borders, it made clear that the dispute between the two countries was now much larger than the Wal Wal issue. It had become a question of Ethiopia's national integrity and survival. The issue was so precisely defined that when Emperor Haile Selassie dispatched his letter to the League, he had reason to feel it would be difficult to ignore. He did not yet know that he was about to be victimized by another event which would make his appeal appear unimportant. His letter reached Geneva at a moment when nobody there had even the slightest inclination to worry about Ethiopia. On the previous day, March 16, 1935, in Berlin, Adolf Hitler had heightened his defiance of the Versailles Treaty by announcing the reinstitution of conscription in the German armed forces.

CHAPTER FOUR

BECAUSE of the concern that Adolf Hitler's announced military build-up had caused among the governments of Europe, Italian dictator Benito Mussolini, on April 11, 1935, played host to the prime ministers and foreign ministers of France and Great Britain on a lovely little island off the western shore of Lake Maggiore, near the resort town of Stresa. The meeting, in the medieval castle of Prince Borromeo, had been assembled primarily to establish a three-nation pact against resurgent Germany. The agreement that was to result, called the "Stresa Front," had little chance to become more than a mere "front" for several reasons, not the least of which was the fact that the British government had simultaneously reacted to Hitler's March 16 conscription announcement in two astonishingly opposite ways. While hastening to arrange the Stresa conference, it had also sent Foreign Secretary Sir John Simon and League of Nations representative Anthony Eden to Berlin in an ill-fated effort to learn Hitler's intentions and perhaps to placate him. Neither the French nor the Italians were in a mood to appreciate Simon's already consummated Berlin trip when they greeted him at Stresa. For this meeting Simon had brought along, instead of Eden (who had suffered something approaching a heart attack after talking to Hitler), the old and doddering British Prime Minister, Ramsay MacDonald. Also included in the top level of the British contingent was Sir Robert Vansittart, the debonair and extremely influential Permanent Undersecretary at the Foreign Office. As a civil servant who remained at the Foreign Office even when governments changed, the Permanent Undersecretary had the responsibility, more than any other man, of maintaining consistency and continuity in Great Britain's relations with other nations. Vansittart's healthy concern about what was happening in Germany sometimes kept him from seeing what was happening elsewhere.

On the day the Stresa conference began, these three members of the British party devoted their thoughts almost exclusively to Germany, as did their French counterparts, Prime Minister Pierre-Etienne Flandin,

Foreign Minister Pierre Laval, and Secretary-General of the Foreign Office Alexis Léger. The principal Italians—Mussolini as Premier and Foreign Secretary, and Fulvio Suvich, his Undersecretary—were perhaps more concerned at the moment with Ethiopia than with Germany. While Mussolini in 1935 still looked upon Hitler with fear and suspicion (especially his lust for *Anschluss* with Austria), he also saw the new German military move as an opportunity to facilitate his own aspirations in Africa. The Stresa conference represented to him such an excellent opportunity to wrest African concessions from Britain and France in exchange for promises to support them in Europe that he had urged the British, through his London ambassador, Dino Grandi, to bring to Stresa their principal African expert, Geoffrey Thompson.[1] Foreign Secretary Simon, who had intended to leave Thompson at home, finally agreed to take him along (at the insistence of the ailing Anthony Eden), with the instruction that he limit his talks with his Italian counterpart, Giovanni Guarnaschelli, to discussions of Ethiopian pasturage problems and avoid any mention of the Italo-Ethiopian dispute. But Thompson was so disturbed by Mussolini's apparent intention toward Ethiopia that he couldn't keep his feelings to himself.

On the morning of the eleventh, while the top-level conferees were launching their discussion of the German problem in the island castle, Thompson and Guarnaschelli met in a Stresa hotel room.[2] Thompson broached the subject at the front of his mind by mentioning his disturbance at the "widespread rumors of a possible forward move by Italy against Abyssinia in September," when the rains would have ended. "I hope these rumors are baseless," he said.

"The possibility of an offensive cannot be entirely dismissed," Guarnaschelli admitted. He was not, of course, aware of what was in Mussolini's mind; but he did know that the Duce was seriously disturbed over the whole situation. The Ethiopian question would not be settled by conciliation commissions; at the same time the necessity for a settlement (of some kind) was daily becoming more urgent. He went on to say it was impossible to believe that the Ethiopian empire, with its fourteenth-century policy and outlook, could effectively continue to resist the march of progress. One had only to contrast the state of affairs in Abyssinia, with its slavery, cruelty, xenophobia, lack of resource development, and all the rest, against the work being carried out by the British in their colonies and mandated territories. Italy was largely denied such opportunities for constructive labor. Her possessions in Africa were mainly desert areas. "Something will have to be done to remedy this situation," he insisted, "and I can see only one way of doing it, either sooner or later. It will be a big task but its magnitude has been appreciated and taken into account."

Thompson told Guarnaschelli he was very perturbed by these remarks.

"Italy can expect no cooperation from the United Kingdom in any attack on Ethiopia," he said. A forward policy against that country would be extremely dangerous, from the Italian point of view, because it might be inordinately expensive in blood and money, and also because it might react adversely upon Anglo-Italian relations. There was a very vocal and humanitarian element in the British public which would not conceal its feelings.

Thompson was, of course, speaking for himself when he pursued these points. Guarnaschelli was not impressed. "British public opinion did not take kindly to Japan's policy in Manchuria," he pointed out, "but that will doubtless not prevent the eventual recognition by His Majesty's Government of the existence of the new state of Manchukuo."

The two men closed their discussion amicably with the remark by Signor Guarnaschelli that he thought the Ethiopian question might be mentioned during the present conference.

This apparent hint that the Italians wanted to put Ethiopia on the Stresa agenda was not lost on Thompson, who went to Vansittart that afternoon and reported Guarnaschelli's remarks. Vansittart's response was that he would speak to Suvich and that, in the meantime, Thompson should raise the subject again the next day to suggest that the Italians carefully weigh their intentions because a forward military move might lead to "grave complications." Vansittart's conception of these "grave complications" did not coincide, however, with Thompson's own conceptions.

On the afternoon of the twelfth, in compliance with Vansittart's instructions, Thompson pointed out to Guarnaschelli and to Leonardo Vitetti, counselor at the Italian Embassy in London, that if Italy became seriously involved in Ethiopia it would "react upon her influence in Europe" and "might easily have repercussions in Italy itself." Thompson did not repeat on this second day his first day's warnings that it might have repercussions in Great Britain. He concluded by saying merely that Vansittart intended to "have a word" with Suvich on the matter.

Thompson found that both Guarnaschelli and Vitetti took what he had said "in good part," as well they might since his remarks after he had absorbed Vansittart's instructions represented a significant retreat from the sentiments he had expressed the previous day. Vitetti proceeded to give Thompson a good-natured lecture on the realities of the European colonial situation.

"Thanks to Britain and France," he pointed out, "Italy has been denied any of the colonial fruits of the victory [in the 1914–1918 war] over Germany." Now Germany was once more becoming a threat, and her demand for equal rights was understood to include the right to overseas possessions. How was this claim to be satisfied? Were the British likely to give up to Germany any of the territories that the Versailles Treaty had given them. Was France, or even Portugal, disposed to satisfy Germany's ambitions? Or was it intended that Italy should once more have the cup—in this case Ethiopia—dashed from her lips?

Thompson, handicapped by the difficulty of explaining Great Britain's colonial policies, decided to offer no answer.

Whether Vansittart actually intended to discuss Ethiopia with Suvich is questionable in light of the fact that he did not avail himself of the easy opportunity to do so. Sir Eric Drummond, the British ambassador to Italy, had asked Vansittart to warn Mussolini personally against an attack on Ethiopia, but there is no record that Vansittart followed this advice. Thompson, after his April 12 discussion with Guarnaschelli and Vitetti, reported once more to Vansittart, who indicated he would like to see the matter presented in a memorandum.

Thompson's talk with Vansittart on the twelfth was hardly encouraging. But his hopes were renewed unexpectedly late that night when he received an invitation to breakfast the following morning (April 13) with the Foreign Secretary himself. Thompson optimistically took this as a sign of Sir John Simon's eagerness to be briefed about Ethiopia in anticipation that he would be discussing it with Mussolini. If Thompson was as familiar as he should have been with Simon's recent correspondence on the subject, it is difficult to understand his optimism.

On March 22, in a telegram to Sir Sidney Barton at Addis Ababa, Simon had outlined a proposal which Vitetti told him the Italians had made to Emperor Haile Selassie on the eleventh, and which the latter had rejected. This proposal was that the Emperor write a letter to Italy deploring the occurrence at Wal Wal; that he pay two hundred thousand Ethiopian dollars on deposit; and that the two countries then appoint a commission, not to find out what had happened at Wal Wal and fix responsibility, but to settle the boundary lines and also settle "the compensation to be paid to Italy."

This offer, which assumed Ethiopia's complete guilt in the Wal Wal incident, sounded very attractive and reasonable to Simon. "Though I realize the difficult position of the Emperor," he wrote, "and naturally sympathize with his legitimate desire to settle matters in dispute by methods of arbitration in the last resort, I think he was unwise if he indeed flatly rejected these proposals."

Barton, who had previously swallowed some fairly indelicate suggestions from his chief, decided that this one was more than he could digest. In a telegram March 25, he answered:

> The version given by the Italian counsellor [Vitetti] is misleading in that it ignores completely the fact that the proposals made by the Italian minister were made with the object of avoiding arbitration, and were

persisted in long after the Abyssinian Government had, by their note of 20th Feb., definitely asked for arbitration under the Geneva arrangement of 19th Jan. .... Mistrustful as the Abyssinian Government have always been of the Italian good faith, this mistrust was increased beyond measure when every Italian effort here was devoted to evading Geneva arrangement while pouring in troops.

At exactly eight o'clock in the morning of the thirteenth, Simon welcomed Geoffrey Thompson into his Stresa hotel suite for breakfast.[3] Thompson, whose head was full of Ethiopia, later recalled his satisfaction at finding the table set for only two. The prospects seemed good for an uninterrupted discussion of what he had learned from Guarnaschelli during the previous days. As the two men sat down and the waiter began bringing food, Sir John made some opening remarks about Thompson's memorandum, which he had apparently read. Thompson was about to report more fully on the attitudes of the Italians when, after five minutes, Sir John's chief private secretary entered and said to him, in a confidential manner, something Thompson could not quite hear. This began a conversation between Simon and his secretary which lasted twenty-five minutes.

At eight-thirty, Sir John turned to Thompson and indicated it was time to leave for the day's sessions in Mussolini's Lake Maggiore island retreat. This breakfast meeting with the Foreign Secretary completed Thompson's work at Stresa.

The conference at the top level was proceeding so smoothly, despite Britain's recent duplicity in its overtures to Germany, that Sir John was not disposed to spoil it by introducing unpleasant subjects. Mussolini had proved friendly. His aides were amiable. Mutual compliments flowed as freely as the wine at the lunches and dinners the Italians provided for their visitors. Even the setting conspired to produce agreeable results. Stresa was a town full of gardens and magnolia groves. The statesmen were quartered in hotels with broad lawns stretching down to the shore of the lake. Their windows overlooked the blue-green lake in the foreground, and beyond it, a panorama of snowy mountains. The island on which they held their meetings, Isola Bella, was a flowery paradise. Platoons of Fascist guards were the only disquieting element in this peaceful scene. The one afternoon when Mussolini decided to leave the island and go ashore, Fascist guards made certain all visitors were cleared from the hotel balconies. In 1926, he had been shot and wounded by a deranged woman and he retained, even in this protected location, some of his morbid fear of assassination.

By the afternoon of the fourteenth, which was the last day of the Stresa conference, the draft of the three-power agreement had been completed and Mussolini, seated at the head of the conference table in the Borromeo castle's "Hall of Medals," was rereading it, phrase by phrase, to his British and French guests.[4] He read loudly and carefully, pausing for effect when he came to the following sentence: "The three Powers, the object of whose policy is the collective maintenance of peace within the framework of the League of Nations, find themselves in complete agreement in opposing, by all practicable means, any unilateral repudiation of treaties which may endanger the peace and will act in close and cordial collaboration for this purpose."

He stopped and looked down both sides of the table. Was it not necessary, he asked, to add the words "in Europe" to the text?

No one said anything.

Mussolini repeated himself. Shouldn't the agreement say, "opposing, by all practicable means, any unilateral repudiation of treaties which may endanger the peace in Europe"?

After Mussolini had pronounced the additional phrase the second time, Vansittart leaned over to Prime Minister MacDonald and pointed out to him, quite needlessly since MacDonald wasn't that feeble, exactly what its addition to the text would mean—that the agreement would exclude anything Mussolini might be planning to do in Africa.[5]

MacDonald said to him, "Don't be tiresome, Van, we don't want any trouble. What we want is an agreement that we can put before the House of Commons."

French Premier Flandin, noticing no negative reaction from either MacDonald or Simon, received the impression, as he later said, of "a tacit acquiescence given by the British Government to the Italian ambitions in Ethiopia."[6] Since Flandin was France's head of state, he must also have regarded his own silence as a tacit acquiescence by the French government. Italian Undersecretary of State Suvich, speaking of the incident many years later at his own war-crimes trial, said "the Ethiopian war was made by a gentlemen's agreement with England."

Mussolini, in an interview with a British journalist five months after the Stresa meetings, said he had been "especially disposed" to talk about Ethiopia at the time, and he had been annoyed at the British for avoiding the subject. He had hoped for an opening which would allow him to bargain with Great Britain over Ethiopia. What he got must have looked even better to him when he stopped to think about it. The British had apparently decided to let him have his way in Ethiopia without raising a word of objection.

As soon as the Stresa conference ended April 14, the diplomats of the three powers hurried to Geneva, where the Ethiopians were tediously insisting that their dispute with Italy, which they had been prevented from discussing at the League Council session in January, be placed on the agenda of the extraordinary session of the Council scheduled for the following day. After Haile Selassie's March 17 note asking investigation and protection by the League under Articles 10 and 15 of the Covenant, he had sent two more notes to Geneva, on March 29 and April 3, renewing his request that the League investigate a situation which, in the words of the March 29 note, had "entered upon a new phase, as a result of the military mobilization ordered by the Royal Italian Government, the dispatch to Africa of a large number of troops and a considerable amount of war material, and the appointment of a military chief of high rank [De Bono] to command all those troops."

This same March 29 note, implying that Italy showed no intention of pursuing the arbitration promised to the League January 19, proposed "that a time limit of thirty days should be agreed upon with the Italian Government, during which the two Governments should negotiate, either at Geneva, Paris, or London, as the Italian Government may prefer, on the absolutely free appointment of arbitrators of their choice, on the drafting of the arbitration agreement, and on the fixing of all the details of the procedure of arbitration."

In this note, Haile Selassie had, in effect, let the League know he, too, could see what was plain to most of the world—that the Italians were stalling all diplomatic moves until the end of the torrential Ethiopian rainy season, at which time they would be ready to attack. Only Sir John Simon seemed unable to see this. In a telegram to Sir Eric Barton in Addis Ababa April 3, he had written:

> ... the latest Abyssinian proposal to negotiate in a 30-day time limit ... is a legal rather than a practical step. It is felt in this quarter that the step seems to indicate that the Abyssinian Government no longer favor giving effect to conciliation procedure of Article 5 of the Italo-Abyssinian Treaty of 1928, and this when the Italians appear ready to carry out [their] obligations under that treaty. ...

When Sir John wrote those deceptive words April 3, he had seen no such signs that the Italians were ready to carry out their obligations, but he had one such indication at hand when he arrived in Geneva April 14. In the intervening time, on April 10, the Italians had provided an instrument with which France and England, if they were as cooperative as they seemed at Stresa, could once more stall Ethiopia. This instrument was a note to the League from Undersecretary of State Suvich which declared that

> the Italian Government ... is taking steps to notify the Ethiopian Government direct that it is prepared to make the necessary arrangements with

63

that Government regarding the details of the conduct of the procedure provided for in Article 5 of the Treaty of 1928. The Italian Government, thus conforming for its own part to the undertakings into which it has entered, considers that the procedure of conciliation and arbitration to which the dispute is submitted, in accordance with the agreement of January 19th, 1935, . . . should be applied as fixed by the Conventions in force between the two countries.

To Simon and Laval, flushed with the friendly mood of Stresa, this Italian promise was an opportune diplomatic tool. They went to work immediately on the aging Ethiopian League representative, Tecle Hawariate, pointing out to him with all their powers of persuasion that, since the Italians were now ready to negotiate, there was no reason for League intervention. Tecle Hawariate, awed and perhaps even somewhat confused by their pressing attentions, was nevertheless constrained by his instructions from the Emperor. Simon and Laval decided finally that the whole matter could be dispatched most discreetly at a private session of the League Council on the afternoon of the fifteenth, just before the first public session.

The private session began at three-thirty p.m., and since its purpose was to discuss a request initiated by Ethiopia, Tecle Hawariate began it by presenting himself at the Council table. But the Italian representative, Baron Pompeo Aloisi, spoke first. After his introductory remarks, in which he reminded the members of the January 19 agreement between the two countries to pursue "direct negotiations by ordinary diplomatic methods," he insisted that "the Italian Government has pursued the direct negotiations in the broadest spirit of conciliation and, for its part, thinks it advisable to continue them."

Alluding to the Italian note of April 10, of which all the members were aware, he assured them that his government had informed the Ethiopian government that it was "prepared to embark on the procedure of conciliation and arbitration provided for in Article 5 of the Treaty of 1928." (Though Aloisi did not remark upon it, this article provided for conciliation and arbitration of any and all disputes between the two countries.)

"In these circumstances," he concluded, "I do not think that any member of the Council would feel called upon to propose that the Ethiopian request be placed on the agenda of the present extraordinary session, which has been specifically convened to examine a question of the highest international importance."

When Tecle Hawariate arose to answer Aloisi, he would have served his country well by insisting that the Italian-Ethiopian dispute was now itself a matter of the highest international importance because it threatened war, that the whole issue had become larger than the Wal Wal incident and the demarcation of boundaries, and that Ethiopia's very existence was now at stake. Such arguments, already stated in notes to the League from Addis Ababa, would have been difficult to counter. But Tecle Hawariate simply touched in passing upon the danger of Italian military preparations, basing his principal complaint on the failure of the Italians to observe the "solemn undertakings" to which they had agreed in January.

"The Ethiopian Government," he said, "has made many proposals for prompt arbitration, without avail. It has done so both in notes addressed directly to the Italian Government and by successive representations made on two separate occasions to two friendly Powers [England and France] which have seats on the Council."

Taking cognizance of the April 10 Italian note signifying readiness to arbitrate, he informed the Council members that the Ethiopian government had subsequently proposed immediate designation of the arbitrator and that the Italian government had "avoided giving a precise reply in the affirmative."

The Ethiopian government, he said, had already chosen its arbitrators and would be glad if the Italian government would do the same by April 20 "or some other very early date."

It should also be understood that during the period of arbitration, each government would refrain from making any military preparations under any pretext. "The Imperial Ethiopian Government," he concluded, "expresses its profound confidence in the wisdom of the Council in seeing that the Covenant is applied to the present dispute and that relations of confidence and friendship between the two Governments . . . be restored as promptly as possible by the arbitration provided for in the Treaty of 1928."

The diminutive old man stopped talking. He had come to the end of his remarks without once mentioning the purpose for which his country had demanded this meeting—to request that the differences with Italy be placed on the agenda of the current Council session. The awesome British and French pressure of the last twenty-four hours had gotten to him so effectively he was accepting the apparent good faith of Italy's April 10 note and was surrendering to it without a struggle.

The President of the Council, Rustu Aras of Turkey, seizing the opportunity, declared that, inasmuch as the dispute was already on the agenda for the May session, the Council might take note of the declarations of the two parties, but that there was no need to place this item on the agenda of the current extraordinary session.

Tecle Hawariate, as if suddenly awakened to the fact that he had lost the day, stood up to remind the members that the Treaty of 1928 also forbade the two governments to use force against each other. "It is a fact, however, that [Italian] troops are being dispatched daily," he said. "That situation cannot last indefinitely and the Ethiopian Government cannot wait unless it receives a definite assurance."

His afterthought had come too late. Aras calmly overrode him. "While taking into consideration the Ethiopian representative's remark," he said, "I will repeat my previous suggestion, unless the members of the Council have any objection. The two parties have both made perfectly clear declarations as to their pacific intentions and their desire to settle the question. . . . Consequently, if there are no further objections, I shall consider that . . . there is no reason to place this item on the agenda of the present extraordinary session."

Only the formalities were needed now to make it official. Simon and Laval had managed to get the Italians what they wanted once more—another month's delay. But when Simon stood up to ratify the proceedings, his words first puzzled then troubled the Italian delegation. It began to sound as if he had forgotten for whom he was working.

After sharing the President's "satisfaction at the spirit of conciliation shown by both parties," Sir John went on to say, "there is only one consideration which occurs to me, and I think it is my duty as a member of the Council to mention it. It would manifestly be very unfortunate if, when the Council meets for its ordinary session in May, the situation is exactly the same as it is today; that is to say, if no conciliators have been appointed and no terms of reference settled."

He did not think the Council should step in and fix dates, or anything of that kind. "But would it not be possible," he asked, "to ascertain from both parties whether they could inform the Council that, if it now accepts the President's suggestion, it might safely do so on the assumption that the conciliators on both sides will be appointed before the May session and that the terms of reference will be fixed?"

Though it is conceivable that Simon himself didn't realize what he was saying, everyone else did. Tecle Hawariate leaped to his feet and accepted the proposal. The Italians sat in stunned silence at this suggestion that they might actually be held to their promise of prompt arbitration. Simon, after Tecle Hawariate's enthusiastic interruption, continued in the same vein, offering his opinion that the assurances he had just suggested would not be difficult to receive from the two parties.

"The Council will then be in a position to know," he said, "that when it meets in May, something practical can be undertaken."

Baron Aloisi, in obvious alarm, jumped up to remind Simon and the Council of a statement he himself had just made to the effect that the Italian government would "do its utmost" to see that the conciliation and arbitration would open "as rapidly as possible." He spoke as if the words "as rapidly as possible" were a much greater assurance of promptness

66

than a definite time limit. He knew that if the British intended now to press for an actual time limit, he was in trouble.

Fortunately for Italy, Pierre Laval, who understood the entire situation better than anyone in the room, stepped in quickly. The Italian representative, he pointed out, had just agreed that Article 5 of the Treaty of 1928 should be applied both in the letter and in the spirit. "I therefore support the observation made by the President of the Council," he concluded, "and I hope that the Council, in once more inviting the parties, as it did at the last session, to reach agreement as rapidly as possible, will never have to deal with the dispute."

Even the Spanish delegate, Salvador de Madariaga, felt compelled to leap in and help the Italians. "I very well understand Ethiopia's nervousness," he said, "notwithstanding the clear statements which have just been made to the Council—and which indeed were hardly necessary in view of the country concerned—to the effect that Italy has only pacific ends in view." In an effort to allay Ethiopia's nervousness, he then went on to point out that Italy was, at that precise moment, taking part in "a clear demonstration of good will which gave evidence of a constructive spirit of international peace." Señor de Madariaga was apparently speaking of the Stresa agreements. In less than two years, he and his government were destined to become better informed about Italy's "pacific ends" and "constructive spirit of international peace."

By this time, Simon himself was aware that the Italians were angry at him for some reason, but it is quite possible that he didn't yet know why. As he had once said to Anthony Eden, he never knew what people were thinking.

The Italians soon made it clear that Simon's suggestion to the Council was, to them, another instance of British perfidy. Aloisi later called it "underhanded,"[7] and Mussolini described it as one more attempt to block off every Italian "just demand."[8] Perfidy was a subject on which Italian opinion could not be taken lightly. Also on April 18, the same day as the private meeting of the League Council at which Italy gained another month's delay on the promise of prompt negotiation in good faith, the Italian Minister in Addis Ababa, Count Luigi Vinci-Gigliucci, delivered to the Ethiopian foreign minister a note, dated April 14, which stated:

> ... The Ethiopian Government, laying stress in Your Excellency's note No. 23 on the alleged illegality of the establishment of Italian posts at Wal Wal and Wardair, is endeavouring to evade the fundamental question—that of the responsibility for the fight at Wal Wal on December 5th and the subsequent incidents. This is the precise point at issue that has to be settled, while the determination of the Italo-Ethiopian frontier must be effected in accordance with the provisions of Article 5 of the Italo-Ethiopian Treaty of 1908, which the Royal Government has always been ready

67

to carry out, as it still is—that is to say, after the present dispute has been settled.

In other words, the Italians were already vitiating, with a note predated to make it look as if the Ethiopians had received sufficient notice of it, the promise they were making that same afternoon to negotiate on the basis of the 1928 Treaty, which encompassed all aspects of the dispute. And they were contending that the question of whether Wal Wal was on Ethiopian soil had no pertinence to the question of responsibility for the incident there. As Emperor Haile Selassie indicated to British Minister Barton, he felt he had been tricked again. When he received the note from Count Vinci, it was already too late to send fresh instructions to Tecle Hawariate, who was therefore led in ignorance to accept what was destined to be an insignificant gesture of arbitration.

Though this Italian breach of good faith offended the Emperor, it did not offend British Foreign Secretary Simon, who set down his reaction to it in a confidential telegram to Barton on April 20. After noting Italy's refusal to acknowledge the connection between the frontier issue and the Wal Wal incident, Sir John wrote:

> In support of this contention the Italians argue that the uncertainty over the ownership of the territory, which has been in Italian occupation for some years, in no way affects the question of responsibility for the encounter on the above date [December 5] and that the delimitation of the frontier, to which both sides have agreed, must be carried out by a special Italo-Ethiopian Boundary Commission.
> Whether this attitude is right or wrong is, in the face of realities, beside the point; and you may consider that in these circumstances, and in the light of the fact that the Italians give no indication of any desire to hurry matters, the Emperor would be well advised to refrain from seeking to impose conditions likely to result in further delays, and to exploit to the fullest possible extent the undertakings the Italians have given publicly, that is: (1) to follow out Article 5 of the 1928 Treaty (so far as the main issue is concerned) and (2) to set up (in due course) a joint boundary commission.

Sir John knew, of course, that the "uncertainty" over the ownership of the Wal Wal area had long since been settled by official maps which the Italians themselves had published. He knew that any "further delays" would be caused not by Emperor Haile Selassie but by Mussolini. And he knew also that the "main issue" was no longer, as he indicated, the Wal Wal incident; it was the very survival of Ethiopia. After all, it was he who had said to Geoffrey Thompson in January, "the Italians intend to take Abyssinia."

CHAPTER FIVE

ANTHONY EDEN, on his feet again after the illness he had suffered during his March trip to Germany, arrived in Geneva May 19 with an assignment which would fairly well test his recovery. As Britain's delegate to the League of Nations, he would have the primary responsibility of restraining Italy and putting the Italian-Ethiopian situation into some kind of order during the May session of the Council, due to begin the twentieth.

Despite Italy's April 15 promise to negotiate promptly, nothing had happened except Mussolini's appointment May 15 of his own two arbitrators (Count Luigi Aldrovandi-Marescotti and Raffaele Montagna, both Italian diplomats) and his refusal to accept the Ethiopian arbitrators who were named the next day. He objected to them because they were not Ethiopian, one being a distinguished French law professor named Albert de La Pradelle, and the other, Pitman B. Potter, an American professor at the Graduate Institute of International Studies in Geneva. Since the extraordinary session of the Council in April, the Italians had shown no indications of peaceful intentions in Ethiopia. On April 18, the first battalion of the Gavinana Division had reached Eritrea. In early May, three more divisions were mobilized, then another three. And on the fourteenth, in a brief but pugnacious and loudly cheered speech to the Italian Senate, Mussolini had declared, "It is worthwhile to point out that up to this time the number of workmen sent out [to Africa] surpasses the number of soldiers. But I wish to add immediately in the most explicit and solemn manner that we will send out all the soldiers we believe necessary. And no one can take upon himself the intolerable presumption to dictate to us concerning the character and volume of our precautionary measures."

After a burst of applause, he had gone on to say,

> No one can judge this most delicate matter except Italy, who has in her history a dramatic, sanguinary and not forgotten experience in this regard. I prefer to be removed tomorrow for doing too much rather than

for doing too little when it is a question of the safety of our colonies and the life of even a single one of our native or metropolitan soldiers. . . . One might reply to these zealous, disinterested counselors who consider our presence in Europe indispensable that we are also of the same opinion. But it is precisely because we wish to be tranquilly secure in Europe that we intend to be well guarded in Africa.

This was the mood of the Mussolini with whom Eden would have to cope in the upcoming Council session. The handsome, tall, but frail British diplomat realized many of his disadvantages, but he didn't realize all of them. He was not privy, for instance, to a letter the Duce had sent his African commander, General Emilio De Bono, on May 18, the day before Eden arrived in Geneva.

Mussolini wrote:

> I have made it understood that we shall not turn back at any price. In the meantime, with the nomination of the two arbitrators on the Italian side, we shall get the better of the next Council of the League of Nations [just two days away], but in September we shall have to begin all over again. It may be that we shall then find it necessary to withdraw from Geneva.
>
> It is precisely in view of this eventuality that it is absolutely indispensable not to alter the date—October—which we have fixed for the beginning of the eventual operations.
>
> Preliminary to this date you must have on the spot the whole ten Italian divisions. . . .
>
> You must make sure beforehand of victuals and munitions for at least three years, and also, however absurd it seems, because there are formal conventions in existence relating to the passage of the Suez Canal in peace and war, one must expect difficulties in respect of its passage. In the House of Commons there has even been talk of closing the Canal.

Such talk, mostly from members of the British Labour Party, distressed Mussolini because, while he might tell De Bono to stock up three years' worth of supplies, he knew it could not be done. In order to conquer Ethiopia, he had to have unrestricted use of the Suez Canal.

In this respect, Anthony Eden's key limitation was not the attitude of Mussolini, who was neither strong enough nor foolish enough to go to war with Great Britain, but the private attitude of Eden's own associates and superiors in the British National Coalition Government. The Italian dictator knew that if the British were to close the canal and send their fleet to enforce the closure, his entire expeditionary force in Africa would be stranded. He also knew enough about the men in the British Cabinet to feel confident that they would never close the canal just to save an African nation in which they had only a minimal interest. The Ramsay MacDonald government had made exceedingly plain to him its eager desire to retain him as an ally in Europe, even at the expense of a certain amount of international embarrassment and handicap to the League of Nations. Eden himself, having become only recently a champion of the League, wanted to save Ethiopia because he realized that if Ethiopia were to be lost, the League itself might be lost. If he was to receive any support from home, it would have to come, ironically, not from his own party and Cabinet, but from a very vocal segment of the opposition Labour Party, and from an increasingly vocal British public.

Feelings on the Ethiopian question were changing rapidly in England. There were growing signs in the press that the British people were deeply offended by Mussolini's apparent intentions toward Ethiopia, and apprehensive about the actions of their own government and the League in the matter. The MacDonald Cabinet, aware of the shifting public opinion, felt the political desirability of restraining Mussolini, but was willing to undertake the job only if it could be done without exercising any power. In a conversation at the end of April between Mussolini's London ambassador Dino Grandi and Permanent Undersecretary Sir Robert Vansittart, the latter acknowledged that he was quite aware of Italy's determination to conquer Ethiopia, and he even acknowledged that in his opinion there was some justification for the plan.[1] As Vansittart saw the situation, Britain and Italy had no irreconcilable differences in Africa. But he warned Grandi that the British people would be so strongly opposed to the Italian forward movement that the British government would have to do as much as possible to convince its own constituency that it stood behind the League.

Having thus learned from Vansittart that the British Cabinet would cause no more trouble than the British people demanded, and perhaps not even that much, Grandi went next to Foreign Secretary Simon, who was even more reassuring.[2] He wanted Grandi to know first of all how much he admired Mussolini. In this respect, he did not differ from many other influential British statesmen at the time, including former Foreign Secretary Sir Austen Chamberlain, who had said of Mussolini, after meeting him twice in the mid-twenties, that he was

> the simplest and sincerest of men when he was not posing as the dictator. . . . It is not part of my business . . . to appreciate his action in the domestic policies of Italy, but if I ever had to choose in my own country between anarchy and dictatorship, I expect I should be on the side of the dictator. . . . I am confident that he is a patriot and a sincere man; I trust his word when given and I think we might easily go far before finding an Italian with whom it would be as easy for the British Government to work.

Chamberlain, who was still one of England's most powerful men in 1935, had never repudiated that assessment. Simon, in his conversation with Grandi, did have one mild criticism of the Italian dictator. He thought it a shame that Mussolini hadn't mentioned Ethiopia during the Stresa conference.

Grandi, taking encouragement, had told Simon almost exactly what Italy intended to do in Ethiopia. Sir John was sorry to hear all this. It would put the British government in a most embarrassing position. If England did not support the principles of the League, how would he, Simon, as Foreign Secretary, answer questions on the subject in the House of Commons?

Eden, receiving from Simon a report of this conversation with Grandi, found it depressing. What Grandi had demanded for Italy was a free hand in Ethiopia. Eden in his memoirs charitably characterized Simon's answer to him as "nothing like stiff enough." On May 15, four days before traveling to Geneva, Eden met with Simon and the rest of the Cabinet for further guidance, which turned out to be no stiffer. That was the day Mussolini had announced his selection of arbitrators in the Ethiopian dispute, making it plain, even to Simon, that he intended at Geneva to use this action as proof that conciliation was in progress and another delay was therefore in order. Some members of the Cabinet thought his appointment of arbitrators should be accepted as a sign of good faith and that he should be granted the delay, but even in this Cabinet there were men for whom such a complete evasion would be intolerable. The majority favored something which would look better. They agreed that the British government should refuse, in Eden's words, "to agree to a procedure which would result in no action being taken to prevent hostilities before the Council held its next meeting in September." Such were the instructions, if he could understand them, that Anthony Eden carried with him to Geneva May 19.

One of his first moves was to talk to Ethiopia's League delegate, Tecle Hawariate, which was not easy because he had with him a new French adviser, Gaston Jeze, who was inclined to do all the talking. The Ethiopians were now deeply worried about the Italian military build-up and Mussolini's delays in arbitration, and were determined to have Council action. Eden was able eventually to learn their minimum demands. They would accept the arbitration delays, Tecle Hawariate said, if Italy would join them before the Council in an agreement that there would be no military aggression on either side until a final settlement was reached. But because they did not trust Mussolini's government, such an agreement would have to be enforced by League authority.

Informed of this demand, which he knew was impossible to attain, Eden sat down that evening to a dismal dinner with Italy's League delegate, Baron Aloisi, for whom he entertained surprising respect, considering the methods Aloisi employed at Geneva. Aloisi began by telling him it would be difficult to accommodate the Ethiopians and ended by telling him it would be impossible. The prestige of the entire Fascist regime was at stake, he said in a burst of honesty. A man like Signor Mussolini could not be expected to spend six hundred million lire (the estimated outlay to date) in order to change his mind at the request of the League of Nations. There was the earlier defeat at Adowa which would have to be "washed out in blood." And there was the "pin-pricking" Abyssinian conduct toward Italy which had been a constant source of aggravation. Italy could not be expected to forgo an opportunity to settle all this. As for the League, Italy had always been too realistic to base her entire policy upon it. The matter of Ethiopia should have been discussed at Stresa. He understood the importance of saving the League's face and he felt sure Signor Mussolini was prepared to do all he could to cooperate, but only with the understanding that it must not affect the final outcome.

It is unclear what Eden hoped to gain by continuing the conversation beyond this point. Though the Italians had not been honest with the world in the Ethiopian matter, they had, at least during recent weeks, been honest with the English. Aloisi was simply repeating to Eden, quite candidly, what Guarnaschelli, Vitetti, and Grandi had already said to Thompson, Vansittart, and Simon. As far as Italy was concerned, the matter was settled. *Delenda est* Ethiopia. Further discussion would not dissuade Mussolini. Only a firm threat of action would stop him now. But Eden, deprived by his government of the power to threaten, nevertheless pursued the conversation on the assumption that talk was better than nothing at all.

"If the Italian Government is really engaged in a policy of military aggression in Abyssinia," he said, "I view the future with the utmost concern. In our judgment, Italy is indispensable to peace in Europe at the present time. It is hard for us to believe that Signor Mussolini does not understand this all-important fact as clearly as we and the French Government understand it. There is nothing I deplore more than that you and I should, as the outcome of this dispute, witness a steady deterioration in Anglo-Italian relations."

If Eden intended this to be a statement of the British position, he must have realized that it was, as he himself had said of Simon's statement to Grandi, "nothing like stiff enough." Aloisi simply reiterated, no doubt with full confidence, the Italian insistence that any conciliation must be confined to the Wal Wal incident, thus ignoring what he himself had just defined as the true issue—the question of whether Italy should be allowed to conquer Ethiopia. This was almost like a bank robber, having been caught in the act, insisting he didn't have to stand trial because he was willing to discuss only his conveyance to the scene of the crime and not the crime itself. Eden, however, registered no outrage at Aloisi's declaration. He asked merely how the Italians thought the Council, once adjourned, could keep in touch with the progress of the conciliation under such circumstances. It was a question which must have amused Aloisi, who was less than eager to have the Council keep in touch. Eden suggested that the Council might appoint a committee or a *rapporteur* to observe the conciliation efforts. Aloisi, while showing his distaste for the idea, eventually took a more sporting view and agreed to think about it.

In Rome on the twentieth, British Ambassador Sir Eric Drummond had another audience with Mussolini, who, as on a previous occasion, kept him waiting several days before receiving him. Drummond deferentially began by rephrasing Eden's suggestion of the previous day to Aloisi. What did Signor Mussolini think about having a League Council member sit in on the Italian-Ethiopian negotiations?[3]

Mussolini brusquely let him know that he didn't think much of the idea. He failed to see the usefulness of such a measure while the conciliation procedure provided by the Treaty of 1928 was still in progress. Now that Italy had nominated her two members of the Conciliation Commission, he expected that the Council would simply take note of the fact that the commission had been formed and wish it all success.

Drummond remarked that the Italian-Ethiopian dispute concerned England greatly because majority public opinion at home upheld the League of Nations and its concept of collective security. What the British government sought from Italy was a solution which would preserve the prestige and the principles of Geneva. "If you force Britain to choose between her old friendship for Italy and her support for the League," he warned, "she might well choose the latter."

Mussolini was unperturbed. "Italy has chosen its road in the Ethiopian question. Nothing can make us turn back, because we have decided to go to any limit to regulate our colonial situation. I don't believe that the English Government and people will compromise their relations with Italy for Abyssinia." Just in case Drummond might have failed to understand him, he then went on to describe more explicitly Italy's intentions in Ethiopia. "We cannot be satisfied with the wells at Wal Wal," he said, "nor with mining and public works concessions. We must resolve the question of the security of our colonies. Every time we've been occupied in Libya or in Europe, Ethiopia has tried to throw us into the sea. And today its army, since it is being trained by the Swedes and the Swiss, represents a considerable force."

Drummond at this point interjected the idea that the strength of the Abyssinian army could be reduced by imposing upon it an officer cadre from several European nations, including Italy.

At this suggestion Mussolini lost his patience. "I have not carried through all these preparations," he said, "and spent all this money simply to obtain a settlement of the Wal Wal incident. If in order to clarify the

74

situation and to obtain security it is necessary to resort to arms, even to go to war, I shall do so, and I shall send sufficient men to gain my objective." As an afterthought, he pointed out that France and England had done the same thing—in Egypt, for example.

Drummond, alarmed at Mussolini's open avowal of warlike intentions, pointed out the seriousness of his statement not only in regard to Great Britain but also in regard to the League of Nations. "To destroy the League," he said, "would be to destroy the whole existing political system."

To this Mussolini replied, "Collective security should be confined to Europe, as was emphasized at Stresa. If the League seems to support Abyssinia against Italy, I shall have no choice but to leave it, never to return."

On the same day, May 20, Emperor Haile Selassie sent a personal note to the League, reviewing the situation and pleading

> that the Council should take steps to ensure the execution of the Covenant and that it should stop Italy's military preparations, the character of which is falsely described as defensive. We ask that it [the Council] should decide that unless Italy agrees that the arbitrators should interpret the Treaty of May 16th, 1908, and pronounce on all the incidents which have occurred since November 23rd last in the vicinity of the Somali-Ethiopian frontier, it [the Council] will take up the dispute itself and make full enquiry and examination on the basis of Article 15 of the Covenant.

In this letter the Emperor made a significant retreat from his previous demands. Hitherto he had pleaded that arbitration be conducted in accordance with the Treaty of 1928, which covered any and all differences between Italy and Ethiopia. Now he was asking only that the arbitrators interpret the Treaty of 1908, which covered no more than the definition of boundaries.

Anthony Eden pronounced himself deeply worried when he was informed, the morning of the twenty-first, of Mussolini's remarks to Drummond. French Foreign Minister Pierre Laval, who had arrived in Geneva during the night, assured Eden that he, too, was perturbed. "Mussolini must be mad," he said.

Eden, remembering that Mussolini's first assurances concerning the Ethiopian operation had come from Laval in early January, now asked the untrustworthy French diplomat pointedly if he had, during his visit to Rome, offered the Italians a "free hand" in East Africa.

Laval insisted that at no time during the Rome conversations did France give Italy any encouragement to military action in Abyssinia. On the contrary, Laval recalled that he had warned Mussolini to make certain his efforts in Abyssinia were confined to economic objectives. Eden has not recorded whether he believed Laval's assertions to him. The two men did agree, however, that the French and English delegations should work together in applying pressure upon Mussolini.

Eden then sent an urgent wire to the Foreign Secretary in London, making special note of Mussolini's remarks to Drummond that he was ready to resort to war. "It seems to me impossible for us to allow this statement to go unchallenged," Eden's telegram said,

> and I suggest that as a first step Mussolini should be reminded of these treaties [Kellogg Pact, League Covenant, and tripartite Treaty of 1906] and of obligations we share under them. It should be made clear to him that if he should decide to engage upon a policy which from his own showing would run counter to obligations he has assumed under these treaties, then he cannot expect us to condone much less to support him in doing so either at Geneva or elsewhere.

Eden received no answer from Simon, perhaps because Simon had little time that day to think about Ethiopia and Mussolini. Some weeks earlier, the British Cabinet, despite the Stresa pact and a February agreement with France to make no separate alliances, had decided to develop friendly unilateral relations with Germany. Simon had therefore, without informing his Stresa allies, invited Adolf Hitler's representative, Joachim von Ribbentrop, to London for cordial conversations. As it happened, Eden's May 21 telegram arrived just at the time when the von Ribbentrop conversations were bearing first fruit in the form of a Reichstag speech by Hitler which excited the imagination of Simon and his Cabinet colleagues. In this speech Hitler said he recognized the vital importance of "a dominating protection for the British Empire on the sea." It was his straightforward intention to "prevent for all time a repetition of the only struggle there has been between the two nations." And, in that regard, "an Anglo-German alliance would hallow the ancient ties of friendship and kinship."

These were seductive words to poor old Ramsay MacDonald, to his stand-in and successor-elect, Stanley Baldwin, and to his foreign minister, Simon. Perhaps Hitler was a decent chap after all. They prepared immediately to seek a pact which would "hallow the ancient ties of friendship and kinship" with Germany and insure Hitler's blessing for the British Empire on the sea. Vansittart, the great exponent of restraints upon Germany, professes to have washed his hands of the whole matter, but admits he "did not object to it."

If these British statesmen had been less enchanted by Hitler's nice words about their country, they might also have noticed that in the same speech, Hitler, while courting them, had also courted Mussolini, with whom they had so recently exchanged a solemn pledge against Germany at Stresa. Referring to a subject which made Mussolini acutely nervous, Hitler told the Reichstag,

> Germany neither intends nor wishes to interfere in the internal affairs of Austria, to annex Austria, or to conclude an *Anschluss*. . . . The German government regrets the tension which has arisen from the conflict with Austria all the more because it has resulted in disturbing our former good relations with Italy, a State with whom we otherwise have no conflict of interest.

These words affected Mussolini as profoundly as did his growing distrust of British intentions in Africa. At Stresa he thought he had the British, but with young Anthony Eden running Ethiopia's errands in Geneva, he was no longer so confident. Though he might fear Hitler, he could now see Germany as a possible new friend if England betrayed him, just as the British could see Germany as a possible new friend if Mussolini betrayed them. Mussolini was moved to suggest this new friendship four days later to the German military attaché in Rome. He told the attaché he hoped a gradual *rapprochement* would draw their two countries together within the framework of a "basic reorientation" of Italian policy.[4] So much for the Stresa Front. With a friend like Hitler, perhaps neither the British nor the Italians would need each other.

In Geneva, meanwhile, Eden had little time to think about Hitler's Reichstag speech. He was left to flounder through the Ethiopian matter with only a querulous note from Sir Eric Drummond in Rome to guide him. The words Eden proposed to use on the Italians, Drummond warned him, would lead to a serious explosion on Mussolini's part and to anger directed against His Majesty's Government. He greatly feared that a communication in such terms would cause the Duce to refuse any concessions at Geneva and prejudice altogether the remaining chances, however small, of an agreed solution at the Council meeting.

Even more remarkable than Mussolini's ability to make Italian trains run on time was his ability to make the statesmen of strong nations fear the ineffectual country over which he held sway, and which was propelled by little more than the power of his voice. The British statesmen of this era, at the helm of the largest empire ever assembled in the history of the world, have never explained why they feared Mussolini. Perhaps it was the volume of his voice. The British, unaccustomed to hearing the rulers of lesser nations shout at them, seem to have retreated in astonishment at the very sound of loud, harsh words.

Eden, ignoring Drummond's advice, and receiving no guidance from

Simon, decided to act on his own authority. Early that evening, he and Laval agreed to put forward a Council resolution, which the French delegation would draft, based on Emperor Haile Selassie's plea that all the border disputes between Italy and Ethiopia be subjected to arbitration, and making it a condition that there be no hostilities during arbitration. It was a resolution which sounded good, but which included another provision that rendered it virtually meaningless. If no settlement was reached within a time limit to be decided, the Council would then meet again to "examine the situation." Such a provision would, of course, allow Mussolini to use the allotted time for another stall so that when the Council met again it would have to start exactly where it was now.

Before the French had finished drafting the resolution, Eden again talked to Aloisi and used upon him the firm language he had asked permission to use in the unanswered telegram to Simon. Aloisi said he very clearly understood the British position and that it caused him "grave anxiety." Eden, assuming this statement to be sincere, felt quite pleased with himself.

Eden was also quite pleased, for some unexplained reason, with the proposed resolution which the French finished drafting that night. The morning of the twenty-second, he and Laval presented it to Aloisi, who must also have been secretly pleased with it, since it was designed to grant Mussolini the delay which everyone now knew he wanted. But if the first proposal offered the Italians this much, perhaps they could get even more. Aloisi professed himself horrified at such rigid terms and warned that, though he would reluctantly show them to Mussolini, the odds were at least ten-to-one against his Duce accepting them.

The next day, Aloisi was back with what Eden called a "counteroffer," but which was simply a restatement of the conditions Mussolini had already demanded, limiting the scope of the arbitration to Wal Wal, and excluding any assurance against the use of force before settlement was reached.

Eden found this so unacceptable that instead of sending a telegram to Simon, he picked up the telephone and called the Foreign Office in London, explaining his position to whoever answered the phone (it was not Simon) and asking that Simon please not undercut him—in other words that he not give Italian Ambassador Grandi any "encouragement to suppose" that the British stance would weaken.

On this occasion, Simon did give Eden enough support so that Mussolini, deciding he had got as much as he could get, finally agreed to the resolution in a modified form.

At a Council meeting half an hour after midnight the morning of May 25, the revised resolution was passed. It stated that the Italians would accept the arbitrators already named by Ethiopia, that if the four arbitrators now named could not agree upon a fifth one by July 25 the Council would meet to examine the situation, and that if the process of arbitration was not completed by August 25, the Council would meet again to examine the situation.

The resolution thus gave Mussolini a new three-month delay, which would bring him to within one month and one week of his October schedule for the opening of hostilities. In one of its other provisions it gave him something else equally important. While it stipulated that the arbitration would encompass other border incidents as well as the one at Wal Wal, it did not provide for the actual demarcation of the borders, nor did it mention what was now the true issue between the two countries: the apparent Italian intention to conquer Ethiopia. When Jeze, speaking for Ethiopia, told the Council that he and Baron Aloisi were in "complete agreement" as to the interpretation of the resolution, he was allowing the Council members to comfort their consciences by dealing with only what were now the secondary aspects of the dispute. The Council's acquiescence, stemming largely from the Emperor's most recent letter to the League, represented an irretrievable mistake on the part of the Ethiopians. Eden, however, was much congratulated for bringing the measure to fruition. Those who read it less than carefully seemed to think it represented Italian rather than Ethiopian concessions. Eden also earned for his troubles increasing enmity in Rome, where he was now the symbol of whatever resistance the British might provide against Mussolini's ambitions in Africa.

To make certain the entire world would understand how little the Geneva resolution meant to him, Mussolini spoke that same day before his Chamber of Deputies. "No one must hope to make of Ethiopia a new pistol that would be pointed perennially against us," he said, "in which case European trouble would render untenable our position in East Africa. Let everyone keep well in mind that when there is a question of security of our territories and the lives of our soldiers, we are ready to assume all, even the supreme responsibilities."

When Anthony Eden returned to London May 26, he found himself involved in Cabinet changes which had been long expected. The three-party coalition National government, headed by the almost senile, disavowed Labour Party leader Ramsay MacDonald and by the indolent, stodgy Conservative Stanley Baldwin, was so unsatisfactory that even its own members realized it had to be altered. Baldwin, who, since 1931, had been exercising whatever power there was behind Prime Minister MacDonald, prepared now to replace him officially. Eden, despite his youth, had gained fame so rapidly as a champion of the League of Nations that everyone, including himself and perhaps even Baldwin, expected him to replace Sir John Simon as foreign minister.

On June 5 at noon, the Secretary of the Cabinet, Sir Maurice Hankey, called Eden at the Foreign Office and told him it was settled. He had only to await the official announcement before moving his things into the huge, chilly, high-windowed chamber that was the Foreign Secretary's office. When Prime-Minister-to-be Baldwin tapped him on the shoulder after the House of Commons session that afternoon and said, "Come to my room, please, after this," Eden expected he was about to get the good news from the man himself, whose political protégé he had been since entering the government.

As soon as they reached Baldwin's office, which was the Lord President's room, Baldwin quickly turned to Eden and without ceremony announced, "Sam is to go to the Foreign Office and I want you to stay on and help him there."

The "Sam" of whom Baldwin spoke was Sir Samuel Hoare, a member of a prominent British banking family who had made a career in government. As the Secretary of State for India, he had just spent four years steering a new Government of India bill through Parliament despite a vigorous opposition led by the maverick Conservative, Winston Churchill. Baldwin, after almost deciding to name Eden Foreign Secretary, had changed his mind and settled upon Hoare at the urging of Geoffrey Dawson, the editor of the London *Times*, and Neville Chamberlain, then Chancellor of the Exchequer and a close friend of Hoare.[5] Dawson and Chamberlain thought Eden too young for the job and less solid than Hoare, who was in their view altogether better qualified.

There is some doubt that even Hoare himself shared their view. As he later explained, he was then so tired from the strain of his India assignment that he had fainted on several occasions and had once collapsed for several days. As for his knowledge of foreign affairs outside the Indian sphere, he recalled in a book published in 1954 that, in 1935, "I had not before realized the imminence of the German danger, and the slowness of our rearmament programme. Hitler had appeared on the scene when I was thinking of Gandhi." In that same 1954 volume of memoirs, writing about the Ethiopian crisis of 1935, he referred to the wells at Wal Wal as being "situated in what had been recognized in fact as a part of the Italian colony" of Somaliland.

Hoare's 1954 version of what happened at Wal Wal in 1934 is so extraordinary, especially in light of his subsequent record as Foreign Secretary, that it deserves quotation. After describing the arrival of the Anglo-Ethiopian Boundary Commission, he wrote:

A crowd of Abyssinian tribesmen gathered around Colonel Clifford's survey party. Their appearance made the local Italian commander believe that he was threatened with a hostile attack. Having only a handful of native troops, he telegraphed for reinforcements. In due course the reinforcements, amounting to 350 askaris [native East African soldiers], arrived, together with two aeroplanes that appeared from the ground to be pointing machine-guns at Colonel Clifford's party. It afterwards transpired that the supposed machine-guns were cameras for photographing the position. Colonel Clifford, having made a vigorous protest and carried on a heated correspondence with the Italian commander, eventually withdrew from the area in order to avoid a serious international clash. His departure was the signal for the Abyssinian camp followers, who had tacked themselves on to the British party, to attack the Italian fort.[6]

If in 1935 Sir Samuel was as ignorant as he acknowledged himself to be on the subject of Hitler and Europe, it is conceivable that at the same time he was capable of equal ignorance on the subject of Mussolini and Africa, though he could not have remained long in such ignorance except by refusing to read either the Ethiopian or the Italian description of what happened at Wal Wal. It would be insupportable to suggest that Hoare, writing twenty years later, after the facts of Wal Wal were known to the entire world, could still believe his own version, inaccurate as it was regarding even the particulars on which the Italians and Ethiopians agreed.

This was the man Stanley Baldwin chose, at the urging of the London *Times* editor and Neville Chamberlain, as Foreign Secretary in the new Cabinet he formed June 7, 1935. Eden was to fill a newly created Cabinet post with the title of Minister for League of Nations Affairs.

On hearing the bad news from Baldwin, Eden had the good sense to say he did not like the idea of dividing responsibility for foreign affairs between two Cabinet ministers. Baldwin explained that Hoare would handle foreign affairs in general, while Eden would handle League affairs. To this, Eden said, "League affairs are foreign affairs and it is not possible to separate them." Baldwin, unmoved, told the young man to go see "Sam," who, he said, was "most anxious to have your help."

Ultimately, Eden did as he was told. On June 7, he tried to answer in the House of Commons both the growing attacks Italy was making against England and the opposition attacks against the government. Of the Italians he said,

It is alleged we have encouraged the Ethiopian Government for our own end to adopt a hostile attitude toward Italy. This story is as mischievously absurd as the suggestion that our colonial football fields are aerodromes in disguise.

81

Equally fantastic is the assertion that for years we ourselves have had in mind the possibility of some sort of protectorate over Ethiopia. What have we to gain by adding fuel to a fire yet only smouldering? Our interest, of course, is precisely the reverse. It has been our constant endeavor to help bring about a permanent settlement, mutually satisfactory to Italy and Ethiopia. . . .

In his attempt to answer the opposition, Eden encountered more difficulty. Deputy Labour Party leader Clement Attlee attacked both Italian and British policy. What Attlee said was especially significant because only three months earlier he had denounced a government rearmament program on the grounds that aggressors should be handled by the League and the whole world, and that rearmament, instead of insuring national security, "will lead to international competition and the insecurity thereby engendered and will ultimately lead to war." In three months, if Attlee's new pronouncement was an accurate measure, he had changed his mind in favor of a more aggressive stance.

"If you have a failure to renounce force," he said, "and if that is acquiesced in by the League, you have practically brought the whole system of the League and the Covenant into disrepute. There is today a great opportunity in this incident for re-establishing the authority of the League and the rule of law in Europe. We require a clear statement by our Government. We want to tell Signor Mussolini that this Government, like other Governments, upholds the Covenant against an aggressor State, that it believes it a matter that affects our honor and our vital interests, that the refusal to accept the League's authority constitutes a refusal by an aggressor, and that we shall in that event be bound under Articles 10 and 16 of the Covenant to see that we give no assistance whatever to an aggressor, but, on the contrary, that we are bound to act against an aggressor. . . . The League will be destroyed altogether if, within the circle of the League, powers are enabled to carry out imperialist, filibustering enterprise."

He then went on to suggest what Eden and his colleagues least wanted to hear. If Italy intended to use force against Ethiopia, Attlee said, "she ought to be told quite plainly that in that event she would not have the use of the Suez Canal."

Eden was at a disadvantage trying to answer this Attlee plea because the new Cabinet was no more willing than the old one to bar Italy from using the Suez Canal. The Italians were now the principal source of profit for the British-controlled corporation which owned the canal. On May 16, the old Cabinet, in conjunction with France, had tried to still the growing clamor for canal closure by banning unofficially all exports of arms to Italy and closing all of Ethiopia's avenues of access to arms. This latter was a simple procedure, since Ethiopia was completely surrounded by the colonies of England, France, and Italy. The joint British-French measure was supported with enthusiasm by Italy (Mussolini reported it gleefully in a May 18 letter to De Bono) because the Italians, able to manufacture all the arms they needed, welcomed any move that would deprive Ethiopia of arms.

Eden, in a reply which must be labeled less than candid, coming as it did from a man with real knowledge of Italy's intentions, told Attlee that Mussolini, by accepting Article 5 of the Treaty of 1928, had agreed not to resort to force.

"It is a cardinal principle of British law," Eden said, "that a man is innocent until proven guilty." He did not mention the Suez Canal.

Anthony Eden's problems with Clement Attlee June 7 were only a soft prelude to the troubles he was destined to encounter June 23 when he arrived in Rome to spring a new proposal upon an astonishingly bitter Mussolini, who seemed not to recognize that the British were eager to please him. What exasperated him, of course, was that on some days they were as subservient as the French, while on other days they raised objections, however timid, which threatened his whole colonial project. The proposal Eden brought to Rome had grown out of England's overweening desire to regain Mussolini's friendship and to maintain the balance-of-power arrangements which, though they might be destructive to the League of Nations, were considered by most British statesmen to be essential to the containment of Hitler and the maintenance of peace. Ironically, these same British statesmen, while they were trying to contain Hitler, were also seeking his friendship. When Sir Samuel Hoare moved into the Foreign Secretary's office, his major concern was to help the Admiralty work out a naval treaty now developing with Germany as a result of England's friendly overtures to Hitler. But at the behest of Eden and Sir Robert Vansittart, Hoare also devoted some attention to the Italo-Ethiopian crisis.

Hoare saw the troubles with Italy as an opportunity for personal diplomacy.[7] He had done business with Mussolini during the 1914–1918 war when, as a British agent, he had paid the obscure leader of the Fascist rabble a certain sum to turn his goon squads loose on pacifists in Milan who wanted Italy to retire from the battlefields and make a separate peace with Germany. As soon as Mussolini got the money, he had said in a message to Hoare, "Leave it to me. I will mobilize the *mutilati* in Milan and they will break the heads of any pacifists who try to hold antiwar meetings in the streets."

Mussolini was, as Hoare recalled, "true to his word," and on occasions when the two men had met in later years, after Mussolini's rise to power, they had reminisced happily about the distasteful incident. It was a comradely link between them which Hoare felt he could use to advantage now that he had to deal with a less-than-friendly Mussolini.

"I somewhat lightly flattered myself," he observed,

> with the feeling that my past associations with the Duce might still have some effect upon him. . . . No doubt I was foolish to imagine that an almost forgotten incident of many years before would influence the dictator. Yet as almost anything was worth trying, I did my best in the personal letters that I sent him to remind him of my work for Italy.

Since something more substantial than this shared memory was obviously needed, Hoare also devised with Vansittart, and with a skeptical Anthony Eden, a unilateral British offer which he thought might induce Mussolini to forgo his military plans. Ethiopia had always wanted access to the sea and had already broached the possibility of acquiring the little British Somaliland port of Zeila in exchange for a piece of the Ogaden desert. Hoare and Vansittart decided they might be able to settle the Italian-Ethiopian crisis by giving Ethiopia the port, plus a corridor to it, if Ethiopia would then give Italy a sizable chunk of the Ogaden plus certain other concessions to be defined during negotiations.

Though this was a patently fatuous offer in light of Mussolini's stated aspirations, and one which Vansittart must have known would be rejected (he had already heard Mussolini's daughter, Edda, at London dinner parties that summer assert, "Father means to have it all"),[8] he and Hoare asked their ambassador in Rome, Sir Eric Drummond, what he thought of it, and Drummond replied that he thought it had a fifty-fifty chance of success. They decided, therefore, to send Eden to Rome to present it, but when Drummond proposed the Eden visit to Italian Undersecretary of State Fulvio Suvich, the latter labeled the idea "undoubtedly interesting," then quickly put a lid over it by observing the improbability that Eden could "bring proposals that would please the Italian Government."[9]

Drummond, who was not always as cool as he might be in the presence of Italian officials, reacted with some desperation to this sign that his fifty-fifty odds were dropping. He hastened to assure Suvich that the suggested Eden visit was an outgrowth of the fact that officials in London were changing their minds about the Ethiopian crisis. The matter was now being presented on a different plane, he said, from that on which the British government had originally placed itself.

Suvich countered by reminding Drummond of something he already knew—that the issue between Italy and Ethiopia was no longer the Wal Wal incident, or economic concessions. The dispute had now reached a point at which the only solution would be "the definitive liquidation of the Ethiopian question." There would be no point in Eden's coming unless he intended to agree to such a solution.

Drummond, unwilling to accept failure, kept talking beyond the limits of his instruction. Eden, he said, would be bringing a new offer, and though he couldn't divulge its exact provisions, he could say that in his opinion it would satisfy at least half of Italy's demands, and would make it possible for Italy to realize at least a good portion of the other half.

Suddenly Suvich was interested. If the British were actually offering the Italians that much, the necessity to resort to arms and the danger of diplomatic ruptures in Europe might be averted. And once Italy had achieved at least half of its demands against Ethiopia, it could quietly and easily usurp the other half. With this prospect in view, the Italians decided to invite Eden.

Sir Samuel Hoare and the British Admiralty had, in the meantime, managed to consummate their naval pact with Germany. It provided that the German Fleet (which Hitler had already begun to rebuild in defiance of the Versailles Treaty) would not exceed thirty-five per cent of the British Fleet, except in submarines. Hitler would be entitled to sixty per cent of British U-boat strength, and eventually he would be entitled to full parity. British satisfaction with this pact is difficult to explain in light of the fact that it (1) gave Germany official approval of its violation of the Versailles disarmament provisions; (2) licensed equality and actual superiority for the German submarine fleet, which had been, and might one day be again, the major German sea threat to Great Britain; (3) allowed Germany to build cruisers and battleships which, being new and modern, would make most of the existing British capital ships obsolete; (4) abrogated the February agreement with France against unilateral pacts with any third nation; (5) destroyed whatever was left of the Stresa Front against German encroachment; and (6) bypassed the League of Nations from which Germany, under Hitler, had scornfully withdrawn.

During later years, most British statesmen of the time were rather sheepish in their explanations of this first pact with Hitler. In 1935, however, they were quite proud of it, with the possible exception of Anthony Eden, who, on the way to Rome June 21, had the odious assignment of stopping in Paris in the hope that he could explain it all to the French. Laval, who had become Prime Minister as well as Foreign Minister June 7, after Pierre-Etienne Flandin's government succumbed to France's latest economic crisis, greeted Eden coldly and made clear his displeasure at Great Britain's astonishing new diplomatic maneuver. He observed with impeccable logic, after listening to Eden's explanation of the British-German pact, that it was in violation both of the Versailles Treaty and the February British-French agreement, and that, in addition, it would destroy whatever remained of the Stresa Front. Why, he asked, should not other powers now deal separately with Germany? France might have done so, but she had not, and would not do so. It was German policy to deal separately with each party. He wished to make peace with Germany, but on the condition that Germany would make peace with everybody else.

Eden had no satisfactory answers. It soon became apparent that the architects of the British-German Naval Treaty had achieved at least one remarkable accomplishment. They had made Pierre Laval look, by comparison, like a statesman.

Eden, while chagrined by Laval's lecture, was not sufficiently chastened to mend the British ways. Though he was now en route to Rome with another unilateral British proposal, he didn't say a word about it to his French allies. Laval was wise enough, however, to realize that the British would not send Eden to Rome for the single purpose of soothing Mussolini's anger at their pact with Germany. For such a mission Eden would be the worst possible man to send, considering the attacks Mussolini had been leveling against him in the Italian press. Convinced that the British must be launching a new Ethiopian initiative behind his back, Laval sent Mussolini a message through Comte Charles de Chambrun, the French ambassador in Rome.

Chambrun, delivering the message to Suvich on June 22, said Laval had expressly charged him to tell Mussolini that he would "adhere faithfully" to the policy on which they had agreed in January, and that Italo-French friendship could not be disturbed by England or any other country.[10]

But what about the League of Nations, Suvich asked Chambrun. Could it not disturb Italo-French friendship?

"Laval trusts that the Ethiopian question will be settled without causing any trouble at Geneva," Chambrun replied. "Laval hopes too that the Italian demands will be accepted [by the Ethiopians] without any recourse to arms. He will do everything in his power to help Italy obtain what she wants peacefully."

Suvich said, "I think it is not improbable that the Negus will accept our demands peacefully."

Chambrun concluded reassuringly. "On the Ethiopian question," he said, "France is for you."

Eden's position when he arrived in Rome on the evening of the twenty-third was not enviable. There was an expression current in England at the time: "We shall have to send the boy scouts to deal with the Dagos." In the opinion of Mussolini and some others, this was what the British were doing when they sent Eden. Unlike Laval in January, he was not greeted by Mussolini with a red carpet underfoot and a cheering mob in the background. He was not greeted by Mussolini at all. The only Italians to greet him were Fulvio Suvich and Baron Aloisi, both dressed in lounge suits and soft hats instead of the morning suits and top hats which a Cabinet minister had the right to expect. Also on hand was Drummond, with one of his aides.

Eden shook hands with everyone and, after a few minutes of polite talk, emerged from the station to find a modest crowd which had probably gathered not so much to see the archvillain about whom Romans had been reading in their newspapers as to see why there were so many policemen surrounding the area. The people neither cheered nor booed when Eden appeared. Many may not even have known who he was. There had been no announcement of his pending arrival. He smiled perfunctorily, got into a closed car with Drummond, and headed for the British Embassy, where he would be staying. His aide, William Strang, and Foreign Office Africa expert Geoffrey Thompson, who had accompanied him, went to the Royal Hotel near the Embassy.

That evening, Drummond held a dinner for Eden at the Embassy, but neither man was in a mood to enjoy it. They had now learned one of the reasons for the cold Italian reception. A member of the British Cabinet had leaked all the details of Eden's intended proposal to one of the London papers, which had published it immediately, thus giving the Italians full knowledge of its limitations and arming them against it before he had a chance to present it in its best light.

Another breach of British security, about which Eden didn't yet know, might also have been working against him. In early March, the British Cabinet had assigned a commission under Sir John Maffey, Permanent Undersecretary for the Colonies, to review the entire field of relations with Ethiopia, and to make a study of Great Britain's interests in that country. On June 18, the Foreign Office received the report, the major conclusion of which was that the area of Lake Tana, the waters of which fed the British-held Nile, was Great Britain's only vital interest in Ethiopia, and that there were "no vital British interests . . . in Ethiopia or adjoining countries sufficient to oblige His Majesty's Government to resist a conquest of Ethiopia by Italy. . . . It is a matter of indifference whether Ethiopia remains independent or is absorbed by Italy." The report even suggested that in frontier regulation, Italian control of Ethiopia might be beneficial.

The Maffey report was sent by the Foreign Office to the British Embassy in Rome. Eight months later, in February, 1936, it was destined to be summarized in one of Mussolini's favorite Roman newspapers, *Il Giornale d'Italia*. When this happened, the British, assuming there was a leak in the Foreign Office, tightened security there, but apparently gave the matter very little more thought. At the time of King George VI's coronation in 1937, the Italian citizen who was chief messenger at the

British Embassy in Rome was invited to London "as a reward for long and devoted service." When British and American forces occupied Rome during World War II, documents were discovered which proved that this "devoted servant" had, for many years, fed copies to Mussolini of the Embassy's secret communications. *Il Giornale d'Italia*'s source of the Maffey report then became clear. Though the date this report was transmitted from London to Rome is untraceable, it is likely that it was sent shortly after June 18, in time to help guide Eden in his negotiations. It is also likely that when Eden and Mussolini met, the Italian dictator had his own copy of the Maffey report to help guide him in his negotiations.

The first meeting between the two men took place in Mussolini's Palazzo Venezia office the morning of the twenty-fourth.[11] The Duce appeared wearing sneakers without socks, white linen trousers, an open-necked shirt, and a sport jacket. Suvich and Aloisi were with him. Eden, dressed in diplomatic black, was accompanied by Drummond and Strang, but after the preliminary talks, Aloisi, Drummond and Strang withdrew. The conversation was in French, which both Eden and Mussolini spoke fluently. It was rumored later that their words were often bitter, sarcastic, contemptuous, sometimes even loud. Eden insists the atmosphere was much less explosive than advertised. But there are, of course, other ways than words to indicate contempt, as Mussolini had demonstrated when he chose his costume. Italians have a whole unspoken language of gestures at their disposal, which they use very effectively—the rolling eyes, the turned-down mouth, the incredulous stare, the pointing fingers at various angles and in varying combinations. Eden, while insisting later that Mussolini's mood had been "calm, relaxed, and reasonable," observed, nevertheless, "a gloomy fatality about his temper."

They spoke first of the British-German Naval Treaty, which seemed to upset Mussolini less than it did Laval, perhaps because, as noted earlier, he was now beginning to have second thoughts about Germany as an ally instead of an enemy. His own duplicity did not, however, decrease his annoyance at England's duplicity. He had, in fact, directed that a note be prepared for transmission to England in protest against the treaty with Germany. The gist of the note was: In responsible Italian circles, the communications coming from London with regard to the Anglo-German naval agreements are being followed attentively and also with some surprise. It is curious that Great Britain, who has recently turned herself into a paladin of the so-called collective systems, wanted to discuss an agreement with Germany separately in such a delicate subject as naval affairs, which imply very important interests of other states and which up to now have been the subject of international conversations and agreements.[12]

It was a remarkably apt and well-constructed communication, which the British, however, were not destined to receive. After agreeing to the Eden mission, Mussolini had decided not to send the note. This was the only gesture he had made in honor of Eden's arrival. He conveyed to Eden in person his feelings about the Anglo-German pact, after which there was some inconclusive talk about an air pact with Italy (which was one of the publicized reasons for their conference) and about the situation in eastern Europe. As soon as possible, Eden addressed himself to the true purpose of the conference. During this discussion, Suvich was the only other person in the room.

Eden began by saying, even in the face of the facts about the German naval pact, that British foreign policy was founded on the League of Nations and that therefore his government could not assume indifference to events which might profoundly affect the League's future and concerning which public opinion in Britain was very strong. Even men of the Right, like Churchill and Austen Chamberlain, as well as the Labourites, were committed to the League. It was only in collective security, he declared, that peace could be preserved, and only through the League could Britain play her full part in Europe. For these reasons, he said, his government wanted to make a constructive contribution to the solution of the Italian-Abyssinian dispute.

Eden then outlined the Zeila proposal while Mussolini listened with a straight face, as if he were hearing it for the first time. As soon as Eden stopped talking, Mussolini began enumerating all the objections the British should have known he would recite to them. The plan would give Abyssinia an outlet to the sea, which would make her stronger, and also give her a corridor through which she could import arms.

If this was the only difficulty, Eden interposed, some means might be found of meeting it in any final settlement.

The scheme, Mussolini continued, had still more serious disadvantages. It would prevent Italy's two colonies (Eritrea and Somaliland) from being connected, and it would result in Abyssinia's claiming a victory by pointing out that concessions had been made, not to Italy, whom she detested, but out of friendship for England. The British government would then appear to the world as Abyssinia's protector and benefactor, in exchange for whose gift Abyssinia had consented to make some territorial adjustments with Italy.

But Italy could surely trust England, Eden said, to put the matter in a fairer perspective.

Mussolini assured him he did not doubt England's good intentions, but, at the same time, neither did he doubt the outcome of this proposal if any attempt were made to put it into force. It was not only unsatisfactory, but positively dangerous. "I cannot accept it," he said flatly.

Eden, seeing his whole mission collapse in less than an hour, resorted to a rather lame plea. Since the British government had been at pains, he said, to think out this scheme, which involved a land concession on England's part, simply in an attempt to secure a final settlement and to avoid conflict, "I ask you not to reply to me now."

Unfortunately, Eden has not reported Mussolini's gesture at this moment. The Duce said, "In any case, my point of view will not be modified." He realized Abyssinia wanted an outlet to the sea and Italy might have offered one if the Abyssinians had been more agreeable. As for Eden's mission, since he had come all the way to Rome, and since Mussolini appreciated the sincerity of the British government, he would "reciprocate" this good will by telling Eden exactly what he demanded in Africa. This was a *quid pro quo* which Eden didn't need, but which he accepted anyway.

"If Abyssinia comes to terms without war," Mussolini said, "I shall be content with the surrender of those parts of the country which have been conquered by the Abyssinians in the last fifty years and which are not inhabited by Abyssinians." He was referring to the regions Menelik II had consolidated into his empire. To indicate them, he made a circular gesture which seemed to encompass the country's entire perimeter. "The central plateau," he continued, "can remain under Abyssinian sovereignty, but only if it is under Italian control. If, however, Abyssinia does not come to terms on these lines, if Italy has to fight, our demands will be proportionately greater."

To dramatize this last statement, Mussolini made a sweep of his hand, indicating he would demand the whole country. Inasmuch as his alternative without war would also have given Italy the whole country, the difference between his two demands was negligible, amounting only to the preservation of the Emperor, whom, however, he could banish at leisure, once he controlled the country.

Eden, having failed in his attempt to be friendly, tried now to be forceful. "Our offer has not been lightly made," he said. "I shall not conceal from you how gravely I view the future of relations between our two countries if this offer is rejected and no final settlement reached. If Italy takes the law into her own hands in Abyssinia, and if the consequences are fatal to the League, the British people will inevitably and deeply resent it."

It was a statement which sounded strong until analyzed. If Italy took the law into her own hands, why should the consequences be fatal to the League? Why shouldn't they be fatal to Italy? Eden was in fact admitting, perhaps inadvertently, that the League would do nothing to stop the Italian aggression. If so, then Mussolini was not the only one whose policies threatened the League. The British, acting in accord with the League (or even acting independently), were in a position easily to forbid Mussolini his adventure, as Mussolini's own military advisers were quick to inform him. Had the British been resolved to do so, had they been prepared to drop the obvious double fiction that Mussolini was a dependable ally and that he was strong enough to threaten war against them, they would not have found it necessary to send Eden to Rome. They could have sent an office boy to tell Mussolini the game was over and he had lost. The very act of sending Eden with his obsequious little offer and empty threats indicated to Mussolini that the game was over and he had won.

Mussolini responded by threatening to leave the League, though he had no desire to do so. He observed that Germany and Japan had already done so "without loss to themselves."

Eden then referred to the fact that Ethiopia's membership in the League was at the heart of the problem. Great Britain must support the conditions of the Covenant, to which Ethiopia was now appealing. There was in this Eden remark a reminder to Mussolini that he had supported Ethiopia's application for League membership, while England had opposed it.

Suvich broke in at this point to observe that France was also a member of the League. His implication was that Italy's intentions did not worry France; therefore they need not worry England.

"But Monsieur Laval is also very anxious," Eden replied. "He himself told me so and asked me to inform Signor Mussolini."

The Duce took immediate exception to this analysis of Laval's feelings. In January, when Laval was in Rome, Mussolini said, it had been clearly understood by both of them that Italy was to have "a free hand" in Abyssinia.

Only in economic matters, Eden insisted.

"That might be so as far as a written document is concerned," Mussolini said, "but since I had yielded to France the future of a hundred thousand Italians in Tunis, and received in return a half-dozen palm trees in one place and a strip of desert which does not even contain a sheep in another, it must be clear that I understood that France had disinterested herself in Abyssinia."

Eden did not yield the point. He recalled that, in Geneva, Laval had described to him the January talks in Rome. At that time, Laval had emphasized that France had given Italy a free hand only in economic measures, and that he had remarked to Mussolini at that time, "*Vous avez les mains fortes. Faites attention.*" Laval was thereby making it clear, Eden said, that French good will toward Italy in its Abyssinian venture did not apply to anything other than economic enterprises.

Mussolini, upon hearing this, flung himself back in his chair with a gesture of incredulous astonishment.

Though their talk continued a few more minutes, Mussolini remained firm in his rejection of the Zeila plan. When Eden left the Palazzo Venezia, he returned to the British Embassy to prepare himself for the luncheon Mussolini had scheduled in his honor at the Hotel Excelsior.

Mussolini, in the meantime, was not bothering to prepare himself. When a Foreign Ministry official named Mario Panza, who was to escort the Duce to the Excelsior, arrived at the Palazzo Venezia at one p.m., just fifteen minutes before the luncheon was to begin, the Duce was still wearing his stockingless sneakers and open shirt.

Panza said to him, "But we shall be late for the lunch, Your Excellency. You can't possibly change in five minutes."

"Do you think I'd change for that fellow?" Mussolini said. "The idea never occurred to me. Let's go." He had reportedly said to an aide after Eden's departure, "I never saw a better dressed fool."[13]

At the luncheon he was less than polite. Eden, who was already present in the Excelsior's large, plush, and crowded reception room when the Italian dictator arrived, almost felt he was looking at a different man from the one with whom he had conferred that morning. In his office, the Duce had shown no "attitudes or airs." But now, with an elite crowd of ladies and gentlemen watching him, "the man was transformed, jaw thrust out, eyes rolling and popping, figure strutting and attitudinizing." As soon as the luncheon was announced, Mussolini made what Eden interpreted as "an imperious gesture" toward him, then, without looking back, marched on alone into the banquet room. Eden "hung back, English style, waiting for the ladies."

Mussolini was just barely willing even to talk to Eden at this luncheon, but when Eden forced the issue, to ask that they have another meeting the following day, he did consent, at the same time showing his intractability by asserting the Italian army's great need to avenge its 1896 defeat. Eden protested that no country could refight past campaigns and turn them into victories, and that included the British, who would have to start at Bunker Hill. Mussolini did not appreciate the humor in Eden's remark.

The next day, after a luncheon given by the Foreign Ministry at Castel Fusano, Eden indicated his eagerness to salvage something from his collapsing mission. When the guests arose from the table, Baron Aloisi, noticing the apparent depression of the British visitor, approached him with a new idea.[14] Since Eden's talks with Mussolini the previous day had left the impression that it was the prestige of the League which most concerned England, the major problem seemed to be not to stop Italy but simply to relieve the League of the blame for not stopping Italy. Aloisi had already worked out a plan. He would make a speech at Geneva stating what he called the facts about Abyssinian barbarity, cruelty, and irresponsibility, especially toward Italy, during the years since 1928, when the two countries signed their last treaty. He would then refer to England and France the question of whether a nation as uncivilized as Abyssinia should

92

be allowed to remain a member of the League. The English and French would examine and publicize the facts as Aloisi presented them, after which the people of both countries would be quite satisfied to see Abyssinia read out of the League.

Aloisi later recalled that Eden did not immediately turn his back on this suggestion. The following morning, June 26, he even sent William Strang to Aloisi's office to learn more precise details of the plan. This may, however, have been a gesture of desperation on Eden's part after his last interview with Mussolini the previous evening at the Palazzo Venezia.

The second meeting between the two men had served no other function than to fill out time and perhaps avert the public impression that Eden had been sent away after only one day in Rome. Mussolini proposed on this occasion an Italian protectorate over Ethiopia similar to England's protectorate over Egypt. He said he would not take the initiative in leaving the League, but that he should not be put in a position of *having* to leave the League. There was no point in further discussion of the Zeila proposal. Eden must surely know that "the decision to follow our own path is clear and irrevocable."

Eden meekly packed and departed on the twenty-sixth, but not directly for home. He had promised Laval he would stop again in Paris en route to London and brief the French on his conversations with Mussolini. Of course, by the time he reached Paris, the Italians had already briefed the French with enough information, interpretation, and innuendo to prevent the outbreak of any good will between Eden and Laval.[15] Mussolini, while rejecting the Zeila proposal, still found a use for it. Through Suvich and the Italian ambassador in Paris he sent Laval not only the details of the British suggestion but also a ready-made analysis of its implications. The British were again trying to promote their own interests behind the backs of their allies. They were trying to mask their own intention of seizing territory or advantages in Ethiopia. They were abrogating the British-French-Italian Treaty of 1906, which defined the interests of the three countries in East Africa. And in offering the port of Zeila to the Ethiopians, they were threatening to put out of business the French Somaliland port of Djibuti. When Eden arrived at the Quai d'Orsay, Laval was ready for him.[16]

The British had very nearly played a trick on their French ally, he said. If the Italians had accepted the proposal, and if Zeila were ceded to Abyssinia, the French might have been forced to declare Djibuti a free port. Moreover, if the Abyssinians had a port of their own, they would no longer use the Addis Ababa–Djibuti railway, which was perhaps one of the few in the world operating at a profit at the time, and which provided for nine-tenths of the French expenditures in their Somaliland colony.

To these remarks, Alexis Léger, who was with Laval, added the contention, also inspired by the Italians, that Britain's action had violated the Treaty of 1906. Cynical though these observations may have been, they were nevertheless germane to the British Zeila proposal, within the context of Britain's alliances with France. Once again Eden's friends in Whitehall had hung him out to dry. His only answer was one which could hardly appeal to a thrifty, money-conscious Frenchman like Laval who had, during his political career, progressed by sometimes mysterious means from penury to significant wealth.

"If we had been able to obtain agreement between Italy and Abyssinia at this price," Eden insisted, "thereby saving the League and ourselves from a grave crisis, it would certainly have been worthwhile."

Such a solution to the Abyssinian crisis did not recommend itself to Laval. He wondered if Mussolini had thought of the possibility of a protectorate over all of Abyssinia. The Emperor would thereby gain the "advantage" of maintaining the integrity of his country, merely by accepting "some relaxation of control." He might also in this way obtain a guarantee of his throne against rebellious rases. As for a guarantee of his throne against a victorious Mussolini, Laval said nothing. It seemed to him if Emperor Haile Selassie were informed that Britain and France looked favorably upon such a protectorate, he might acquiesce.

"The Emperor would prefer to fight," Eden said. "And if he did not fight, he would probably be deposed by the rases."

The conversation between Eden and Laval was a lengthy one, and as Eden listened he became convinced gradually of something he should have known several months earlier—that he could expect no more than token support from France in any attempt to stop Mussolini. Finally, in desperation, he said he thought the British had done "all they could for the present," and asked whether France would be "willing to take the British Government's place in the mediating action."

If by this time Eden still retained any hope of French assistance, Laval quickly disabused him of it with a firm reply in the negative. Eden left Paris feeling more depressed and frustrated than he had felt leaving Rome.

He might have been additionally depressed if he had known what his French allies were to do as soon as they said good-by to him. Léger quickly communicated to Italian Ambassador Moreno Pignatti a full report of the Eden-Laval confrontation.[17] He also confidentially informed the Italians that the British government's attitude was "chiefly determined by considerations of a domestic nature." He believed that, in the end, the British would "safeguard their interests by occupying, at the right moment, those parts of the Abyssinian territory to which they aspire." As for now, however, their greatest concern was about internal politics. The Conservative Party (which effectively controlled the National

Coalition Government) was afraid that it might be charged with "a lack of skill in not knowing how to manœuver the League of Nations with sufficient ability in order to have it block Italian ambitions. The matter might be exploited successfully in the [upcoming] electoral campaign by arousing the public against the Conservative Party, as was done in the case of Manchuria. To prevent the Abyssinian war preceding the elections, there was even some thought of having the latter held earlier. But, according to Eden, this solution was discarded in the end."

Either Eden had said much more than he later admitted saying, or Léger had a remarkable talent for interpolation. In any case, Mussolini could not fail to be delighted when he heard the report. Though he controlled only a weak, impoverished, and militarily inept country, he had obviously hit upon a powerful technique for handling the two strongest nations in Europe. To make the British and French think of him either as an indispensable friend or a formidable enemy, he had only to expand his chest, stick out his jaw, raise his voice, treat them rudely, and divide them against each other.

On the day the unfortunate Anthony Eden returned to London, June 27, another development arose to complicate the British Cabinet's policy in the Ethiopian crisis: publication of the results of a vast private poll throughout England by the League of Nations Union on questions relating to the League, and to national armaments. A total of 11,599,165 people (27.9 per cent of the eligible voters in Great Britain and Northern Ireland) took part in this poll (which came to be known as the "Peace Ballot"), each answering five questions with the following results:

1. Should Great Britain remain a member of the League of Nations?

Yes	No	Doubtful	Abstentions
11,090,387	355,888	10,470	102,425

2. Are you in favor of an all-around reduction of armaments by international agreement?

10,470,489	862,775	12,062	213,839

3. Are you in favor of an all-around abolition of national military and naval aircraft by international agreement?

9,533,558	1,689,786	16,976	318,845

4. Should the manufacture and sale of armaments for private profit be prohibited by international agreement?

10,417,329	775,415	15,076	351,345

5. Do you consider that, if a nation insists on attacking another, the other nations should combine to compel it to stop by
(a) economic and non-military measures?

10,027,608	635,074	27,255	855,107

(b) if necessary, military measures?

6,784,368	2,351,981	40,893	2,634,441

The polling was not as scientific as it might have been. It was hardly surprising that such a vast majority would vote against arms profiteering and favor the reduction of armaments by all nations. No one would have guessed, however, that such an overwhelming proportion of the British people supported not only membership in the League but also economic and even military measures against an aggressor nation. Though few people questioned the honesty of the "Peace Ballot," it became a subject of sharp discussion and argument throughout England, and there were many interpretations of it. The one interpretation most difficult to avoid was that a large majority of the British people believed the League of Nations should step in forcefully and stop Italy from swallowing and digesting Ethiopia.

The most astonishing reactions to the "Peace Ballot" came from the men in power, the members of the government, and the Establishment. Prime Minister Stanley Baldwin said it was "misleading." Foreign Secretary Sir Samuel Hoare, writing about it nineteen years later, still referred to it as a "so-called ballot," and blamed it for England's lack of war preparation. (He also placed it, inaccurately, in 1934, a year ahead of its time and its pertinence.) Chancellor of the Exchequer Neville Chamberlain said the poll was "terribly mischievous." Sir Robert Vansittart called it a "free excursion into the inane." *The Times*, whose editor, Geoffrey Dawson, was in the front ranks of those courting friendship with Hitler, said it was "a deplorable waste of time and effort." Sir John Simon, the recently deposed Foreign Secretary who was now Home Secretary, made perhaps the most candid and unguarded statement about it. He said, "The question of war and peace is not one on which the opinion of the uninstructed should be invited." The "Peace Ballot" was a dreadful nuisance to Stanley Baldwin and his new Cabinet. But while they could belittle it, they could not ignore it. If the British people were actually as firm as they seemed to be in support of strong League action against Italy, they were going to need some subtle guidance in the weeks and months ahead.

CHAPTER SIX

THE American Chargé d'Affaires in Addis Ababa, W. Perry George, having been summoned to the Imperial Palace, was ushered into a room where Emperor Haile Selassie greeted him with friendly respect.[1] The Emperor sat at a heavy gilt table with a high window behind him. Having put aside other matters of business, he took in hand a five-page letter which he intended to submit to George for transmission to Washington. For some time the Emperor had been acutely aware that two of the world's most powerful voices, those of the United States of America and the Roman Catholic Church, had not yet been raised regarding Italy's aggressive intentions toward Ethiopia. He was now hoping to smoke out one of them on the subject. Though he could scarcely count on any help from the Italian-dominated Catholic Church, he still had some faith that the United States, a country which often advertised its fair-mindedness, would at least register disapproval of Mussolini's preparations to devour his country. The Emperor had pointedly chosen this day, July 3, the eve of America's Independence Day, as a most appropriate occasion to seek United States President Franklin D. Roosevelt's help in maintaining Ethiopia's independence.

After George was seated comfortably, the Emperor, speaking in French, gave the first indication of his purpose by outlining briefly the development of the dispute with Italy since Wal Wal, and by reminding the American diplomat of an audience here at the Palace December 18, during which he had asked the United States to make some kind of gesture, undefined, that might encourage a peaceful settlement of the Wal Wal controversy.[2] At that time the United States had declined to intervene because, in the words of Secretary of State Cordell Hull, "it was the League's function to act, if it wished, and any individual move [on the part of the United States] would only confuse the issue."[3]

In the almost seven months since that time, the situation had deteriorated steadily, as witnessed by Italy's continuing military build-up on the Ethiopian borders, and by the total failure of Anthony Eden's recent visit to Rome. It was no longer possible to doubt, the Emperor insisted, that Italy intended to conquer his country. Ethiopia was unswervingly determined to resist an Italian invasion. In the meantime, Ethiopia would, of course, continue its cooperation with the League of Nations, but at the same time, in the hope of adding strength to the League's efforts, the Emperor was hereby formally requesting by letter that the United States "examine means of securing Italy's observance of engagements as signatory of the Kellogg Pact."

George accepted the letter from the Emperor graciously. He could not say, however, that his superiors in Washington would welcome it.

When Cordell Hull received the five-page communication from Haile Selassie by wire the following day, he was faced with a problem he had anticipated and dreaded since December, at which time he had instructed George "to refrain scrupulously from encouraging any request by the Emperor for mediation by the United States."

The actions of Roosevelt and Hull in the Italian-Ethiopian dispute, as in many other foreign-policy matters, were limited by an intense mood of isolationism which at that time pervaded the United States. In this respect the contrast between America and England was striking. The British Cabinet wanted to take no significant action against Mussolini while the majority of the British people favored a firm stand against him. Roosevelt's Cabinet, on the other hand, would have been tempted to take some kind of action against Italy were it not for the strong disinclination of the American people to get involved. The majority of Americans agreed that Mussolini was a dreadful fellow and they would be glad if someone were to stop him, but it should be someone else.

When Haile Selassie asked for American help against Italy, he was acknowledging a fact most Americans still refused to acknowledge—that the 1914–1918 war had shown the United States to be the wealthiest nation in the world, and had thrust it into an inescapable position of world leadership. The United States Senate, by rejecting Woodrow Wilson's plea to join the League of Nations in 1921, had refused to assume responsibility for whatever might happen in the rest of the world. Even fourteen years later, the majority of American Senators, as well as the American people, still believed that international disputes were of no consequence to the United States. Because of this tragically nearsighted American attitude, because the United States refused to assume international responsibility between 1919 and 1939, it could not escape its share of responsibility for the war that started that year, the most horrible war in the history of mankind.

The Ethiopian crisis of 1935–1936 was such a crucial and irretrievable step toward World War II that America's reaction to Haile Selassie's plea for help becomes, in hindsight, too important a factor to be ignored. To shake the American people from their isolationism in 1935 would have taken strong leadership. President Roosevelt was not yet ready to exert such leadership. Though he and Cordell Hull were both Wilsonian Democrats and confirmed internationalists, they were so apprehensive of losing the 1936 Presidential election that they feared even to speak out in support of their own beliefs. In the event, they need not have been so timid. Roosevelt, thanks to his domestic economic and social policies, was destined to win the 1936 election so overwhelmingly (capturing every state except Maine and Vermont) that it is scarcely possible to conceive of his losing even if he had arbitrarily sent the United States Navy to blockade Italy. On the fourth of July, 1935, however, he was not convinced of this, and while his sympathies for Ethiopia were already as pronounced as his loathing for Mussolini, he was not courageous enough to act upon them.

His courage had been tested in January 1935 by the reaction which buffeted him when he proposed, not very forcefully, that the United States adhere to the World Court and make a small yearly contribution to it. The Hearst newspapers, and such intemperate agitators as Father Charles E. Coughlin, the anti-Semitic radio priest, leaped so hard upon the suggestion that it was defeated in the Senate. But innocuous as the measure would have been, it filled Congressional isolationists with so much distrust of Roosevelt's international proclivities that they decided to saddle him with a Neutrality Act which would virtually prevent him from taking any stand in disputes between other nations. Roosevelt's resistance to them did not go so far as to be called opposition. He had, indeed, announced himself in favor of a Neutrality Act, hoping only that he might get one flexible enough to leave him some options. The provisions of the act were now being cemented together in the Senate under the insistent guidance of such rigid isolationists as Gerald P. Nye of North Dakota, Arthur Vandenberg of Michigan, William E. Borah of Idaho, and George Norris of Nebraska. The act would almost certainly include an embargo of war goods to belligerents. Roosevelt was hoping the embargo would be at the President's discretion. He hoped also that the act would allow some cooperation with the League of Nations in settling international disputes, and that it would not cancel completely the provisions of the Kellogg Pact.

Hull, who was so convinced of Mussolini's intentions that he had issued an evacuation warning to the approximately 123 United States citizens in Ethiopia only two days earlier, reacted nervously to the Emperor's message, undertaking to answer it even before the full text had reached

Washington. The Secretary of State had already evolved a rationale to satisfy his own self-respect. "There was still no point," he later explained, "in taking any step that might impede the action of the League."[4] To accept this argument, one would have to believe that in July 1935 the American State Department was still expecting the League to take action.

After working out a carefully worded draft of a reply, Hull took it to the White House, where President Roosevelt made some small, penciled additions. On the fifth, it was ready for transmission to Addis Ababa. Beginning with some pious remarks about America's desire for world peace, the communication expressed gratification that the League of Nations had taken an interest in the Ethiopian crisis and had arranged an arbitration process. After this preamble, the message went directly to its point: "Furthermore, and of great importance, in view of the provisions of the Pact of Paris [the Kellogg Pact], to which both Italy and Ethiopia are parties, in common with sixty-one other countries, my government would be loath to believe that either of them would resort to other than pacific means as a method of dealing with this controversy or would permit any situation to arise which would be inconsistent with the commitments of the Pact."

Coming, as it did, so soon after the State Department had advised United States nationals to get out of Ethiopia before the war began, this statement was almost cynical enough to qualify Roosevelt and Hull for the big league of European diplomacy. It neither affirmed nor denied, but completely ignored the heart of the Emperor's message, which stated flatly that one of the countries in the controversy, Italy, was about to "resort to other than pacific means." Though the Kellogg Pact was only a moral deterrent to war, calling for no economic or military measures to enforce it, though nothing more than straightforward words would have been needed to invoke it, Roosevelt and Hull withheld the essential words.

It was noon, July 6, in Addis Ababa when W. Perry George received the message. After having it decoded, but without having it translated into French, he took it, at seven p.m., to the Palace, where the Emperor was anticipating it with unconcealed anxiety and agitation.[5] The failure of Anthony Eden in Rome was only one of the immediate problems on his mind. Most distressing was the information he had recently received that Belgium was canceling an Ethiopian order for ten million cartridges after having delivered only two and a half million; that Czechoslovakia's Skoda arms factory, after accepting an order for artillery weapons, had decided not to deliver them; and that Denmark had also canceled an armament order after having welcomed it. France and England had, of course, agreed in May to embargo arms shipments both to Italy and Ethiopia, and to prevent passage through their colonies of any arms destined for Ethiopia, although they had not barred passage of arms through the Suez Canal to the Italian colonies. For Haile Selassie, it was hardly profitable even to speculate on the reasons why Belgium, Czechoslovakia, and Denmark had canceled their commitments. His mind was occupied with the problem of replacing the armaments these countries were withholding. If the message from Washington contained a forthright invocation of the Kellogg Pact and a warning to Italy to leave Ethiopia alone, it was at least conceivable that America might agree to sell him arms, in which case the British and French would be hard put to prevent the shipments.

When George entered his study, the Emperor quickly dispensed with the formalities. Because the note was in English, George translated it aloud into French as he read it. The Emperor listened in silence, which continued for some minutes after George had finished. Eventually, the Emperor, arousing himself from deep thought, asked George to translate the last paragraph for him again, slowly. It was this paragraph which said the United States government would be "loath to believe" that either Italy or Ethiopia would resort to war as a method of dealing with their controversy.

The Emperor now abandoned hope of help from America. Instead of invoking the Kellogg Pact, President Roosevelt had merely referred to it. The Emperor, to be polite, thanked George for the message and asked him a few questions about details of the Kellogg Pact before dismissing him.

Roosevelt and Hull, who seemed to consider their message quite carefully clever when they sent it, were astonished in the next few days to find that in all quarters it had been recognized for what it was.[6] Emperor Haile Selassie, on the very evening it was delivered, had let it be known to correspondents in Addis Ababa that the United States note was so disappointing he would have to turn again to England for whatever help he could get.

In London, according to a dispatch published in the *Boston Transcript*, the British public now considered the Kellogg Pact dead as a result of the "brusque refusal of the American government" to invoke it.[7]

In Rome, as Hull quickly learned from an Associated Press dispatch, Italians were interpreting the note as "evidence of the United States' friendliness toward Italy," and as an acknowledgment that Italy was "justified in its stand." American Chargé d'Affaires Alexander Kirk, in a telegraph which arrived from Rome July 12, informed Hull that Italian officials had contrasted the United States viewpoint favorably against that of Great Britain and "have voiced the opinion that the American attitude has served to moderate British policy." One Italian newspaper, in a dispatch from its Washington correspondent, quoted a "State Department spokesman" as saying, "In no case will America agree to join in any economic or other sanctions against Italy. Still less does America intend to follow the British suggestion of making representations at Rome calling the attention of the Fascist Government to its obligations under the Kellogg Pact. The affair does not concern us in any way." Whether a State Department official actually made such a statement might be doubted. Italian newspapers under Mussolini were capable of complete fabrication. But while no State Department spokesman came forward to claim the words, neither did the Department deny them, perhaps because it would have been difficult to do so in light of intended policy. The Italian public, at any rate, was much heartened by such reports.

Cordell Hull, on the other hand, professed himself bewildered at being so grossly misunderstood. In what he regarded as an attempt to clarify the American position and eliminate Italian misconceptions, he summoned to his office Italian Ambassador Augusto Rosso and told him that, while he was not familiar with all the matters at issue between Italy and Ethiopia, the United States government was "deeply interested in the preservation of peace in all parts of the world,"[8] and particularly interested in "those international arrangements designed to effect the solution of controversies by peaceable means." He told Rosso also that he wanted to impress upon him "my increasing concern" and "my earnest hope that a means may be found to arrive at a peaceful and mutually satisfactory solution of the problem." He concluded by saying, "A war started anywhere would be awfully dangerous to everybody." This weak and self-evident little observation was as close as Hull came to suggesting that the Italians behave themselves. He did not utter to Rosso the words "Kellogg Pact," nor did he criticize what he later called "Mussolini's propaganda machine" for distorting the significance of his letter to Ethiopia. Rosso, who had come to Hull's office not knowing what to expect, left it with a fairly clear assurance from the Secretary of State himself that the United States intended no serious action to block Italy's progress in Ethiopia.

The meeting between Hull and Rosso left America's position more equivocal than ever. He hadn't warned the Italian ambassador about anything. He had simply consulted with him and expressed concern. Hull was now exasperated because nobody seemed to feel any purpose or menace in his vague and tepid words. Why should everyone persist in missing his meaning simply because he had refused to express it? On the eleventh, he called in both the British and French ambassadors and insisted to them that the Kellogg Pact was not dead, that this impression was "entirely contrary to the sense of our note to the Emperor of Ethiopia, which emphasized the principles of the pact." Since he did not say to them, however, that his country planned to invoke the pact, they would have had to be quite naïve to come away with the impression that the pact was still alive.

Finally, to his annoyance, Hull was forced on July 12 to issue a press statement which said that the Kellogg Pact was "no less binding now than when it was entered into by the sixty-three nations that are parties to it," and that it constituted "a treaty by and among those nations." In his statement he went on at some length to explain the details and peace-promoting purposes of the pact. He did not go so far as to say what he later admitted knowing—that Italy was at this very moment threatening to violate the pact. He did not warn Italy against doing so.

Mussolini, under these circumstances, was able to continue his preparations with only a momentary uncertainty about possible interference from across the Atlantic. On July 6, at Eboli, he had allowed himself to venture beyond prudence in an address to four Black Shirt divisions which were about to embark for Africa.[9] Speaking from the back of a truck, he had completely exonerated Italy's soldiers of 1896 for their defeat at Adowa, blaming instead the "abject" government in Rome at that time. With his Fascist government in power, he assured the Black Shirt troops, their efforts in the field would get full support at home. "Abyssinia, which you are about to conquer, we shall have totally," he shouted. "We shall not be content with partial concessions, and if she dares resist our formidable strength we shall put her to pillage and to fire. You will have powerful armaments that nobody in the world suspects. You will be strong and invincible, and soon you will see the five continents of the world bow down and tremble before Fascist power. . . . To those who may hope to stop us with documents or words, we shall answer with the heroic motto of our first storm troops: '*Me ne frego*' ['I don't give a damn']. We shall snap our fingers in the face of the blond defenders of the black race. We shall advance against anyone—regardless of color—who might try to bar the road. We are engaged in a fight of decisive importance and we have irrevocably decided to go through with it."

Never before had Mussolini stated publicly his naked plans for Ethiopia. It was not an impromptu outburst. Mimeographed copies of his speech had been sent to Fascist organizations throughout Italy, and had reached some foreign correspondents. After he made the speech, however,

Mussolini had second thoughts about it, perhaps because he did not yet know at the time the contents of the United States response to Ethiopia's call for help under the Kellogg Pact. July 6, the day of the Eboli speech, was also the day on which the Roosevelt-Hull response reached Addis Ababa. This may have explained the fact that the account of the speech published in Italian newspapers July 7 was quite different from the speech itself. The controlled news stories said simply that Mussolini "had pronounced words of greeting and incitement to the Black Shirts."

The self-censorship of his remarks did not, however, lead to any retreat from their intent. On the morning of July 7, the weakness of America's message to Ethiopia became public knowledge. Thereafter, the four Black Shirt divisions left for Africa on schedule. On July 9, Italy's two members of the Wal Wal Conciliation Commission, meeting at Scheveningen in the Netherlands, walked out in righteous pique because one of the Ethiopian members kept insisting that Wal Wal was in Ethiopia. And on July 16, Mussolini wrote, in answer to a report from General De Bono about progress of military preparations in Eritrea,

> It appears ... that the work of the High Commissioner has expanded into every field with an intense alacrity and without intermission in order to put Eritrea into a position to face present and future tasks. All that is necessary for the life of a population increased tenfold and a great Italian and native army, that is roads, water, victuals, barracks, stores, hospitals and an infinite number of other necessities, has been successfully provided in spite of difficulties which for various reasons were at first enormous. The congestion of the port of Massawa which gave us such anxiety at one moment is nearly ended. Fascist loyalty and determination have bent things to their will. In the logistic sector much still remains to be done, but on the basis of the data of the outline report I consider that your second half-yearly document will be even more satisfying than the first. . . .[10]

One of the "other necessities" for which De Bono had provided, under Mussolini's orders, was the organization, during July, of a Chemical Warfare Service, to be called the "K" Service. General Fidenzio Dall'Ora who, as Quartermaster General for all Italian forces in East Africa, took charge of the formation of the "K" Service, wrote in 1937 about how it came into being despite the fact that both Italy and Ethiopia had signed the 1925 International Protocol against the use of poison gases.

"We limited ourselves," Dall'Ora wrote, "to the preparation of a means of defense against chemical-bacteriological warfare, and only very partially [prepared] offensive means to be able to respond with arms equal to the enemy if he ever made use of such arms."[11]

The Italian general staff was, no doubt, filled with uncontrollable anxiety at the possibility that Ethiopia's barefooted army, still using spears to compensate for a shortage of rifles, might suddenly provide itself with such a sophisticated and difficult weapon as poison gas. Before the "K" Service was formed, the Italians conducted an exhaustive study of the possible uses of gas. One of the conclusions of this study, as Dall'Ora later explained it, was that "the high temperatures and the vast sinuosity of the terrain produce concomitant causes of ascending air currents which make the formation of strong concentrations of gas difficult. Consequently, the offensive weapons would have had to be used with a greater density than that predicted for a European war; particularly for the blistering gases [which include mustard gas], aggressive action would have been predictably limited to that action coming from direct contact with the liquid. . . ."

Dall'Ora used the past conditional to indicate that such gases had not been employed in battle. According to Dall'Ora, 617,000 kilograms (680 tons) of chemical material was shipped from Italy to Ethiopia for the "K" Service, and was stored in three warehouses, two near Asmara and one on the plain of Ala near Nefasit, where it would be ready, if needed, to carry out the missions for which it was intended.

While General Dall'Ora was building up his Chemical Warfare Service in Eritrea, British Foreign Minister Sir Samuel Hoare, in the House of Commons July 11, was thinking out loud about the dilemma into which the Ethiopian crisis had thrown England. "We have always understood Italy's desire for overseas expansion," he told the House. "In 1925 [it was actually 1924] we ceded Jubaland [a bleak piece of East Kenya bordering Italian Somaliland] to Italy. Let no one in Italy suggest that we are unsympathetic to Italian aspirations. We admit the need for Italian expansion." He also admitted that "some of the criticisms that have been made against the Abyssinian Government" were justified. However, these were not sufficient reasons, he said, for going to war.

He spoke also of the League of Nations, which he freely characterized as being not strong enough to handle the problems of the Italian-Ethiopian conflict. This extraordinary observation by the representative of one of the League's two most powerful members was as unanswerable as it was disturbing. Since the League was virtually controlled by Britain and France, it could not be any stronger than these two countries wanted it to be. If Hoare and his government said the League was weak, that meant it had to be weak because they didn't intend to give it strength. He was therefore unquestionably correct when he said it was weak. This being the case, he felt it had to be shielded from such difficult issues as the present one, and the best way to shield it was to bypass it in favor of traditional power diplomacy.

Having thus disposed of the League, Hoare addressed himself with much greater respect to Italy. Mussolini, he said, should take into account that England was a member of the League and that the Covenant pledged the British government to prevent the pending Italian-Ethiopian War. But to make sure Mussolini would not misunderstand this statement and feel threatened by it, he hastened to continue reassuringly. "Let the honourable Members dismiss from their minds," he said, "the rumours, altogether without foundation, that we have asked the French Government to join in a blockade of Italy and that we ourselves are preparing some isolated form of coercion."

He was approaching now a theme which might prove useful in the months ahead. It was a train of thought designed to disguise the timidity of England by calling attention instead to the timidity of France. "As things are," he concluded in his address to the House of Commons, "and as long as there is an effective League, we are ready to take our full share of collective responsibility. But when I say collective responsibility I mean collective responsibility."

He seemed at the moment to have forgotten that he had just rendered the League less than effective by certifying its weakness. But perhaps he hadn't forgotten. Perhaps Sir Samuel was more subtle than he sometimes appeared to be. If Mussolini were to trace the logic of this July 11 speech, he would see that Hoare, in addition to discounting the League, was, at the same time, tying British policy tightly to French policy. He was informing Mussolini and the world that the British would do no more than the French to stop Italy. Since Mussolini already had a French promise to do nothing, he could read with profound pleasure everything Sir Samuel said to the House of Commons that day.

This new line of thought was not something Sir Samuel had devised on the spur of the moment. In his efforts to prevent the Italian-Ethiopian crisis from embarrassing Great Britain, he had already talked privately to several of his colleagues and other national leaders, one of whom, Winston Churchill, also stood up in Parliament July 11 to support Hoare's reasoning.

"We must do our duty," Churchill said, "but we must do it with other nations only in accordance with the obligations which others recognize as well. We are not strong enough to be the lawgiver and spokesman of the world. We will do our part, but we cannot be asked to do more than our part in these matters."[12]

In private conversation with Hoare, Churchill enlarged upon this view. "Go as far as the French will go," he said. "Take them along with you, but remember their weakness and don't make impossible requests to Laval. It is doubtful whether the French will go as far as economic sanctions, but that is no reason for not pressing them. The real danger is

Germany, and nothing must be done to weaken the anti-German front. The collapse of the League will mean the destruction of the instrument that may be chiefly effective as a deterrent against German aggression." Even Churchill seems not to have realized at this time that if the League failed to stop the Italian army now, it could hardly be expected to stop the German army later.

Former Prime Minister David Lloyd George, in conversation with Hoare, echoed Churchill's sentiments. As Hoare recalled in 1954, he pronounced himself "strongly against any unilateral action on our part." What was needed, Lloyd George said, was collective action, and by "collective action" he particularly meant Anglo-French cooperation. Hoare also recalled that such other Parliamentary leaders as Clement Attlee, George Lansbury, Herbert Samuel, Robert Cecil, and Austen Chamberlain were of like minds in their insistence on collective action. He apparently did not explore their thoughts on the question of what should be done to insure such collective action. What to do was not Sir Samuel's concern at the moment. He was much more interested in what not to do. By pressing the point that there must be collective action or no action at all, he might now be able to develop a policy of opportune in-activity which, if pursued in Paris and Geneva, could save the British government from an ever-deepening embarrassment without depriving the Italians of that "overseas expansion" which he had told his colleagues in Parliament England understood and admitted.

On the warm, sunny morning of July 18, the Ethiopian Imperial Guard, four thousand strong, formed precise ranks in their khaki uniforms and lion-hair caps on three sides of the square in front of the new Imperial Palace.[13] These troops, trained by European officers, were the nation's finest. Some carried rifles, others lances. Some wore heavy military shoes; others were barefooted. Their precision was a new-found military virtue, gained after countless hours of close-order drill on the Palace grounds under Swedish and Belgian supervision.

In the center of the square was a silk-embroidered, gilt-painted chair beneath an orange umbrella. Waiting behind the chair were the European military advisers who had remade the Imperial Guard, plus a crowd of Ethiopian dignitaries, many of whom would be viewing for the first time a European-style military review.

At ten a.m., Haile Selassie arrived with his fourteen-year-old son, Prince Makonnen, and his more-than-seventy-year-old War Minister, Ras Mulugeta. After the Imperial Rolls-Royce had circled the square, it stopped in the center, where the Emperor took his place in the chair awaiting him. His uniform included, on the cap and epaulets, the lion-hair symbol of the Imperial Guards. Thirty-two new Guards officers, some trained in Europe, began the ceremony by stepping forward to be sworn in with their hands upon the Ethiopian flag. Thereafter, the drill and parade of the Guards commenced with Haile Selassie watching impassively as four thousand men marched smartly past him. They did not represent the full strength of the Imperial Guard, which was now in the process of expansion. Three more battalions were stationed in the province of Harar and several more new battalions were being trained.

Whatever his composure, the Emperor must have been worried. The procrastination of the League, the failure of the Eden proposal in Rome, the American refusal even to speak out against Mussolini, the cancellation of Ethiopian munitions orders by so many European countries, the problems of military finance, the inability to procure even basic military training for more than this small handful of men marching past his chair left him in the helpless position of having to face a war he could neither avoid nor win. He could not avoid it because the chiefs who supported him would not tolerate surrender without a full fight. Many of them, indeed, still believed that because their fathers had defeated the Italians forty years earlier, they could do so again now. The Emperor, a man of remarkable knowledge and sophistication, knew himself doomed to lead these chiefs and their unsuspecting followers into the range of modern weapons whose ferocity they could not conceive. One of the few hopes he had left was that England might yet take some action, either unilaterally or in conjunction with the League; but since he, too, could read and understand the speeches of Sir Samuel Hoare, he realized that if any help was to be forthcoming from England, it would have to arise from the demands of the British people, a great number of whom were now raising their voices in his support.

Throughout the world, in fact, wherever people were free to speak, they were speaking up in anger at Mussolini's apparent intentions. The growth of moral indignation against Italy and against the men in the League of Nations who were fostering Italy's designs had now become Haile Selassie's principal asset in his struggle to save his people. Ethiopia's shortcomings might be great and her cultural needs enormous, but did the country's hope for civilization lie with men like Benito Mussolini, Pierre Laval, or Sir Samuel Hoare? Against these powerful personages, Haile Selassie had only one advantage, a rather tenuous one in power diplomacy—he was right and his opponents were wrong. If he could make enough people acknowledge this fact and act upon it, he might still have a chance of salvation. If not, he was doomed to total defeat.

At the end of the military review in front of the new Palace, the Emperor again got into his car, with one of his little cocker spaniels, for a ride down the hill to the Ethiopian Parliament, which he had summoned only that morning, at six a.m., for an extraordinary session at noon. The Parliament was a fairly new institution which he had created because most other countries had them and therefore Ethiopia needed one. Ethiopia's Parliament was not, however, a deliberative and legislative body like England's. It was more like Italy's, an assembly whose members were privileged to hear, though not to debate, the policies and decisions of the man who ruled the country.

From the moment the news of the special session had begun circulating by word of mouth that morning, the streets of Addis Ababa had filled with hordes of people, clad in white or dun-colored shammas, surging up the hill toward the impressive, one-year-old Parliament building near the Palace of Menelik. Great and lesser chiefs, their heads swathed for protection from strong sun and vulgar eyes, moved majestically on jeweled donkeys, surrounded by swarms of retainers. By the time Haile Selassie's car had arrived from the new Palace, even farther up the hill, the area around the Parliament building was white with shammas almost as far as the eye could see.

Ahead of the approaching car, court officers cleared a path for it through the crowds with wands and scabbarded swords. The multitude, standing ankle-deep in mud from the seasonal rains, broke into a chorus of "Li-li-li-li," the Ethiopian welcome call. The Emperor quickly passed on into the building where members of Parliament, national dignitaries, and representatives of the foreign press were awaiting him. Actually, there were more dignitaries and correspondents than members of Parliament because those members living at any distance from Addis Ababa had not had time to arrive. The notice had been so short many hadn't even received it, since it could be sent to some regions only by foot messenger. The Cabinet ministers were all present, wearing mantles of various colors and sitting together on high seats within a paneled box at a level just above the members' benches. The Emperor's box, flanked by two others, was in an enclosed balcony about fifteen feet above the floor of the assembly chamber. In the box on the left, War Minister Mulugeta took his place with Abuna Kyrillos, Chief Bishop of the Ethiopian Orthodox Church, and other prelates. In the box on the right were several court officials.

At precisely eleven-fifty-five a.m., a pink silk veil dropped from the draped front of the Emperor's box to reveal him standing before his throne, wearing his military uniform, his written speech in hand.[14] The Court Chamberlain, with silver-topped staff, took his place in the center of the chamber and the Emperor began reading without ceremony.

Addressing his people in Amharic, the nation's official language, he first outlined the background and development of the dispute with Italy, then, in reference to the Wal Wal incident, declared, "We were resolved to defend our honor but we have always believed that a government ennobles, not debases itself, when it voluntarily submits a quarrel to the judgment, perhaps the condemnation, of a qualified, impartial international body."

He explained the efforts through the League of Nations to settle the Wal Wal dispute, the enlargement of the dispute by Italy, the refusal by Italy to engage in meaningful arbitration, and the offer by Great Britain to settle the matter by ceding the port of Zeila in exchange for the relinquishment of some Ogaden territory to Italy. This offer, he said, he was willing to discuss.

"Ethiopia desires only [to procure] safeguards of her integrity and independence for all time," he said. "The Italians, trying [in their words] 'to civilize' the Ethiopian people by aggression, will find us a united people."

He then launched a vigorous exhortation to personal courage. "Soldiers, when, in the course of battle, you hear that your loved and respected chieftain has fallen, do not weep or despair. The man who dies for his country is happy. Blind death destroys in peace as well as in war. Better die free than live as slaves."

And, in conclusion, he promised them, "Your Emperor, who addresses you, will be in your midst, not hesitating to pour out his life blood for the independence of Ethiopia."

A deep murmur arose in the crowded room as Haile Selassie finished speaking and put away the papers in his hand. The silk veil, which had dropped before he began, now rose to cover him. A few minutes later he appeared at the door of the building and entered his Rolls-Royce for the drive back up the hill to the new Palace. Once again the chorus of "Li-li-li-li" arose from the crowd as officers pushed people back to clear a path for the automobile. The Emperor had little time to waste. He had arranged also to speak on the Ethiopian radio station that day, promising his people, and warning the world, that Ethiopia would never become an Italian protectorate. He had now launched a well-planned campaign to arouse world support by making certain the whole world was aware of what was happening to his country.

In the House of Commons July 25, Labour Party leader George Lansbury addressed a polite question to Foreign Secretary Sir Samuel Hoare. "Is His Majesty's Government in a position to make a statement," Lansbury asked, "with regard to the export of arms?"

Lansbury, a confirmed pacifist, was such a vocal spokesman for the pacifist faction within the Labour Party that his position as party leader had become endangered by the issue. Despite this, however, he found the possibility of another war so abhorrent he could countenance no measure which might in any way foster it. He apparently anticipated today a reply from Sir Samuel that would please him.

When the Foreign Secretary stood up he said, "The transit of arms destined for the Government of Ethiopia across British territory or British protected territories adjacent to Ethiopia will be permitted in accordance with Article Nine of the Treaty of August 21, 1930. The French Government, I understand, interpret their obligations under the treaty in the same manner. As to the issue of export licenses, His Majesty's Government are doing their best to make possible a peaceful outcome of the present unhappy dispute, and would not wish to do anything which might prejudice the situation. They will, therefore, for the present, not issue licenses for the export of arms either to Italy or Abyssinia."

There was a scattering of cheers from the House. No one arose to attack the statement, which had been carefully and cleverly worded to preclude criticism for allowing the passage of Italian arms through the Suez Canal. If arms for Ethiopia were allowed to pass through British territory, it would be unfair to prevent Italian arms from passing through the canal. The practical question of how much armament for Ethiopia would actually travel through British territory—a question which depended on the ability of Ethiopia to find sources of arms and the discretion of British customs officials in either facilitating or delaying their flow—was not discussed by the Members of Commons. No one raised the question of whether this apparent neutrality policy of Britain and France was consistent with the Treaty of August 21, 1930, to which Sir Samuel had referred in his statement, and which promised help for the Emperor in obtaining "all the arms and munitions necessary for the defense of his territories from external aggression." The House passed over this opportunity to debate the practical equity of the British-French arms-embargo policy.

Emperor Haile Selassie, painfully aware of the embargo since May 16, when it was instituted unofficially without public announcement, had raised these questions forcefully on several occasions, but without much reaction. Just two weeks earlier, on July 10, he had called in the British, French, and Belgian ministers to protest the inequities of their countries' armament policies. Their restrictions against his procurement of arms, he told them, had placed Ethiopia "in a difficult position, inasmuch as, unlike Italy, she possesses no local manufactures." In conclusion, he reminded them obliquely of their obligations under the 1930 treaty. "At the present time, war does not exist," he pointed out, "hence, the refusal to supply arms cannot be explained by a simple desire to observe an attitude of neutrality and impartiality."

Since this protest was reported in the London *Times* of July 11, it can hardly be said that the Members of Parliament were unaware of the practical effects of Britain's armament policies. There was, however, an issue involved which no British statesman wanted to discuss in public. Englishmen were uncomfortably aware that what Italy was planning to do was nothing more than what England had already done all over the world in the process of amassing her Empire. Among some Englishmen there was also a feeling that if Italy failed, if the nonwhite people of Ethiopia succeeded in repulsing again a European attempt to subjugate them, their success might stimulate unrest among nonwhite peoples elsewhere who had already been subjugated.

One of the Englishmen to whom this thought occurred was the redoubtable Sir Samuel Hoare. In a conversation with United States Ambassador Robert Bingham that summer, he said, "Mussolini has now put the issue in the shape of a contest between the black and white races which has had already unfavorable effects in Egypt, in Great Britain's African colonies, and in British Dominions where there is a population of blacks."[15]

Hoare's viewpoint was not an isolated one. A "distinguished British officer [unnamed] who had participated in the Somaliland campaign" enlarged upon the same attitude during a conversation with the American Military Attaché in London, Lieutenant Colonel Raymond E. Lee. After a general discussion of the situation, Colonel Lee asked this distinguished officer about the possible effects of a war between white and black races.[16]

This was one of the chief factors perturbing the British government, the officer replied. An Abyssinian victory might result in serious disaffections within British possessions. The Abyssinian victory over the Italians at Adowa in 1896, he said, was one of the governing factors which led to the Anglo-Egyptian campaign in 1898, because British authorities then felt strongly that the blow to white prestige in that area required a victorious campaign of whites against blacks.

These were private and discreet conversations. The subject of race was an implied but not an open issue in England. There were some men, however, who implied their racism so strongly as to profess it almost openly. One of them was Lord Rothermere, the powerful and influential publisher of the London *Daily Mail*. In a signed editorial on July 24, he wrote:

> Armchair critics of Italy's action in Abyssinia are trying to make fools of the British public. There is no basis for the moral indignation they profess. The claim that Abyssinian independence concerns the League of Nations is fallacious. The League is an association of civilized states. Abyssinia is a semi-barbaric country, characterized by cruelty, slavery and feudal anarchy.
>
> Her application to join the League was an adroit move to secure a

protection to which she is not entitled. ... As soon as Italian rule is established in that country, the futility of present objections to it will appear, for everyone concerned will be better off. The Abyssinians will benefit by the opening up of their territory just as the Moors and Berbers have benefited from the French occupation of Morocco, or the Sudanese by the British conquest of Sudan. ...

With one of England's most powerful publishers expressing such sentiments, and with the British Foreign Secretary making almost overt assurances that Great Britain intended no action against Italy, Mussolini should now have been feeling quite friendly toward England. But it was not so. More disturbed by the peculiar behavior of the British government than he was reassured by its ineptitude, he now began lashing out at England as if he were getting ready to fight the British rather than the Ethiopians. The Italian press intensified daily its attacks against "Perfidious Albion," and the Duce himself found occasion, during an interview with a Le Matin correspondent, to issue a flat warning of war if the English continued to meddle in Italy's business.

"We have had a sincere and faithful relationship with the British people for many years," he declared, "but today we find it monstrous that a nation which dominates the world refuses us a wretched plot of ground in the African sun. Many times and in every way I have given the assurance to Great Britain that her interests in Abyssinia would be scrupulously safeguarded. But the interests for which she so strongly opposes us are other interests. . . . Never from our side will come any hostile act against a European nation. But if one is committed against us, well, it means war. . . ."

When Mussolini referred to "other interests" which might be causing Britain to oppose Italy, he was expressing a belief now dominant in his mind that Britain also entertained territorial ambitions in Ethiopia, especially around the Lake Tana region. He had in his possession a copy of the secret Maffey report which, while disavowing any territorial interest in Ethiopia, nevertheless made certain reservations about the waters of Lake Tana, so vital to the British-held Nile. Mussolini shared with millions of other continental Europeans that deep distrust of England which was one of the prices the English had to pay for their unparalleled success in acquiring the world's greatest empire. The long-time success of the British had created a mystique about their cleverness, their deviousness, their knack of doing the brilliant, successful thing even when they appeared to do the stupid, disastrous thing. The British might appear weak at the moment, but Mussolini knew how unpredictable they were. At any time they might become strong simply by deciding to be so. It took only a firm decision on their part to put an end to his African venture. Fortunately for him, the men now ruling Great Britain had so far been mesmerized by his bluff and bluster. He had them down, and his purpose in intensifying his threats against them was obvious. He had better keep pounding at them while they were down to forestall the possibility that they might get up and fight.

Mussolini at the same time was using a quite different method of dealing with another possible threat to his enterprise—the Vatican. All he needed from Pope Pius XI was silence. It might prove intensely embarrassing if the "Vicar of Christ on Earth" were to take Christ's precepts so seriously as to apply them to Italy's intentions in Africa. Though the Pope had been quite cooperative in ignoring the gangster methods of Fascism within Italy, he might feel obliged to speak out against using the same methods in other parts of the world. Africa was an especially sensitive area for the Church because it did extensive missionary work there. To insure Vatican silence about his Ethiopian venture, Mussolini depended upon the Italianism of the Pope himself, the cooperation of certain high Church officials, like Eugenio Cardinal Pacelli, the Papal Secretary of State (later Pope Pius XII), and the unspoken threat that the Fascist government, guardedly friendly with the Church since the Lateran Pact of 1929, might at any time revert to the open hostility of previous Italian governments since 1870.

Between 1870, when the newly created Italian central government nullified the temporal power of the Popes, and 1929, when Pope Pius XI arrived at a comprehensive working relationship with Mussolini's Fascist government, successive Popes had protested Italian restrictions by living as voluntary prisoners within the Vatican. They had refused even to accept a very sizable yearly stipend which the Italian government, despite its anticlericalism, continued to offer for the support of the Church. Though an ever-increasing flow of money from American Catholics replaced this stipend, several Popes, including Pius XI, accepted it with reservations because they felt that American money brought with it demands for greater influence by American prelates in the affairs of the Vatican, which had been, for most of the previous fifteen hundred years, an Italian preserve.

The Lateran Pact, negotiated largely by Cardinal Pacelli, made the Pope once again not only a spiritual but a temporal ruler, with absolute dominion over the small area in central Rome defined as Vatican City. It reconstituted the Roman Church as the official national religion and incorporated canon law into the code of Italian law. It acknowledged the right of the Church to educate Italian children. And it provided a staggering financial settlement of the yearly stipends uncollected since 1870 by presenting to the Vatican seven hundred fifty million lire in cash plus one billion lire in Italian government securities, with the single restriction that these securities not be put on the market for a period of several years.

This financial settlement was especially gratifying to the Pope because it appeared to make the Vatican self-supporting, and therefore independent of American money. He seemed to have overlooked the fact that he had exchanged the diffuse and almost ignorable influence of the distant American Church for the assertive and concentrated influence of the Italian Fascist State which totally surrounded and threatened to smother him. He seemed also to have overlooked the fact that with one billion lire worth of Italian securities in his possession, he would have a very strong vested interest in the welfare and continuation of the Italian Fascist State. On the other hand, he may not have overlooked any of these factors. He may simply have accepted them with equanimity. In his first encyclical, Pius XI called his native Italy "Our beloved country, chosen by God himself as the place wherein to establish the seal of His Vicar on earth. ..." And in an audience he granted to French Ambassador François Charles-Roux during July 1935 he said, "I am very worried, very preoccupied by this Italian-Abyssinian conflict. Already I've been informed of the repercussions it is having on Catholic interests in Ethiopia, and even in all of black Africa. The Catholic missionaries in Abyssinia are denounced as so many spies. Elsewhere, also, the situation is exploited among the blacks to stir them up against the whites."[17]

What did the Pope conclude from these observations? Did they lead him to oppose or denounce Mussolini's colonial venture? On the contrary, he was concerned most about its possible failure. "The defeat of the Italian enterprise," he told Charles-Roux, "would work to the detriment of the European colonizers in Africa." Without these European colonizers, there could be no Catholic missions in Africa. While the Pope might abstractly deplore violence, his mind was clear as to the interests of the Church in the war Mussolini planned to wage against the blacks in Ethiopia.

There were already some Catholic missions in Ethiopia, thanks to the zeal of a nineteenth-century Italian missionary named Giustino De Jacobis and thanks also to the fact that, under Haile Selassie, there was more religious freedom in Ethiopia than in Italy. Pope Pius, with these missions in mind, took occasion on July 28, 1935, to deliver an address in support of De Jacobis's eventual beatification. Referring to De Jacobis as an "Abyssinian by adoption," he expressed concern that the deliberation over the man's possible sainthood should coincide with the Italian-Ethiopian crisis. He referred to the crisis as "a cloudy sky, of which no one is able to evade the presence, the significance, indeed the mystery, because there is yet more cloudiness to come. ... We trust, we shall always continue to trust, in the peace of Christ within the reign of Christ, and we cherish full faith that nothing will happen except according to truth, according to justice, according to mercy."

Pope Pius had, apparently, more faith and trust in the "peace of Christ" than did his Secretary of State, Cardinal Pacelli, who had said to French Ambassador Charles-Roux in February, "The Italians have let us know that they are going to march." Charles-Roux talked the same day in February to another Vatican official who confided that, not surprisingly, the Pope was equally aware of Italian intentions. Had the Pope forgotten this by July, when he informed the world of his faith that "nothing will happen except according to truth, according to justice, according to mercy"?

On July 30, 1935, Anthony Eden left England for Switzerland by way of Paris because the time had come to play another session of Geneva poker, with Ethiopia again supplying the stakes. The last session, played in late May, had ended with the understanding that the winner, Italy, could have until July 25 to settle its dispute with Ethiopia, but if during that time the Italians didn't get around to settling the dispute, they were to be given another month to do so, under the eye of a neutral arbiter to be appointed by the League Council. July 25 having now come and gone without any movement toward a settlement, the League Council members, embarrassed and uneasy, were preparing to meet again for a new session which appeared destined, even before it started, to end the same way as the last one.

Again, as in May, Eden began preparation for the Council session by stopping at Quai d'Orsay to spend a day with Pierre Laval. Despite everything that had passed, Eden still entertained a wondrous and persistent hope that something might yet be done to save Ethiopia.[18] His hope arose, perhaps, from the knowledge that something could very easily be done, if Britain and France chose to do it. His Cabinet colleagues in London had humored him in this hope to the extent of having the Foreign Office draw up an Italy-Ethiopia policy paper, which Sir George Clerk, the British ambassador in Paris, handed to Laval the morning of Eden's arrival. It is not clear why Eden himself did not bring the document to Paris; perhaps it was because he didn't feel very comfortable with it. Actually, the document was rather impressive, containing a fairly good summary of the situation and taking cold cognizance of the fact that, despite Mussolini's bombast, his country was still almost as weak and manipulable as pre-Fascist Italy. The Foreign Office paper's only flaw was that it ended where it should have begun—when it came to the question of what should be done. The purpose of an Italian-Abyssinian war, it said, would not be in doubt outside Italy. All ordinary persons would consider it a war of aggression by a strong League Member against a weak one, with the aim of annexation. If the League acquiesced it would fall into universal and everlasting contempt. If it thus became divided against itself, it would be no longer an organ of peace but an arena for power diplomacy.

Here was a document which seemed to promise a rousing conclusion. Since it would be disastrous not to take strong action within the League, we must do so. Unfortunately, the document contained no conclusion at all, as Laval quickly pointed out to Eden when they met. "I agree with its principles," he said, "but I have sought in vain for any practical suggestion toward solving the difficulty."

Perhaps Laval expected that Eden, having sent the document on ahead so it could be digested, had brought the "practical suggestion" in person. Eden, taken aback by Laval's immediate perception of the document's weakness, fervently wished he had with him something to give it strength. He had pleaded with the Cabinet before leaving London for permission to say that Great Britain was ready "to fulfill our obligation under the [League] Covenant," but as he later recalled, "my request to be authorized to do so . . . had not been approved by my colleagues."

The Cabinet had approved instead, in another astonishing move, a plan which would work diametrically against the sense of the document the Foreign Office was sending to Paris, a plan that would in effect, without technically bypassing the League, actually take the crisis out of its jurisdiction in the hope that Britain, France, and Italy might solve it under the terms of the Tripartite Treaty they had concocted among themselves in 1906, acknowledging each other's interests in East Africa. The British Cabinet showed no concern over the dubious legitimacy of this 1906 treaty, even though it was an agreement among three nations to parcel out rights, territories, and spheres of influence within a fourth nation, Ethiopia, which had not been even casually consulted in the matter. This new policy grew out of a simple notion that the prestige of the League could be preserved by stripping it of responsibility for what was about to happen.

Laval, after laying the British document aside, told Eden that in his opinion there was little hope of stopping a war between Italy and Ethiopia.

Alexis Léger, who was also present, interposed a different view, perhaps because, knowing France's intention to let Mussolini have his way, he wanted to discourage England from taking any embarrassing action. Mussolini had, a month earlier, regarded war as "inevitable," Léger said, but now regarded it only as "possible," and in another month would think it "out of the question."

Eden was not deceived by this transparent attempt to lull the British.

Disregarding Léger, he urged Laval to work out with him a *modus operandi* for the coming League Council session. But Laval already had his *modus operandi*, which was to sit still and do no more than the British pressed him to do. Laval and Léger were keenly aware of one serious vulnerability in their policy of accommodation to Mussolini. Eager as they were to retain Italy's friendship, they knew that the French-English partnership, with all its exasperations, was still the bedrock foundation of their country's foreign policy. If the British were to force the issue against Italy, France would ultimately have to go along with them. Laval, in apparent sympathy with Eden's aims, said he did not understand the "shock tactics" Mussolini was using.

Eden asked ingenuously if Mussolini knew how gravely the situation troubled the French government. What he was trying to find out was whether the situation troubled the French government at all. He had heard reports that the French ambassador to Italy, Comte Charles de Chambrun (who was to become Laval's son-in-law), had shouted, "*Evviva Italia!*" to a crowd of Italians demonstrating outside his embassy. It did not seem suitable conduct for the representative of a nation which was concerned about Italian policy.

Laval assured Eden it meant nothing. "Mussolini clearly understands the French attitude," he said.

This was undoubtedly an accurate statement. Mussolini not only understood the French attitude but was quite comforted by it. The same could not be said for Anthony Eden. The most he could get out of Laval July 30 was an agreement that they would meet again in Geneva, and then perhaps decide upon some joint action.

In Geneva, on the morning of the thirty-first, Eden sought out the Italian delegate, Baron Pompeo Aloisi, who reacted with some astonishment to Eden's concern about the Council session scheduled for that afternoon. "All the Council needs to do," Aloisi said, "is to interpret its decision of last May and set the four conciliators to work again. There is no necessity even to appoint an arbitrator."[19]

Eden quickly pronounced that position untenable. "The Council cannot be expected to adjourn discussion of the dispute," he said, "unless it can be assured of progress with negotiations for a peaceful settlement."

Aloisi tried to be understanding about Eden's apparent petulance. "Your chief object," he said, "is to satisfy Labour [Party] opinion at home."

In an effort to correct this impression, and to create a picture of British solidarity behind the League, Eden referred to some remarks by Sir Austen Chamberlain, who had long since certified his deep admiration for Mussolini. During a recent speech, Chamberlain had said, "It is not to be supposed that the League can be flouted under the eyes of Europe, that League methods can be repudiated, a policy of force and conflict engaged in, and that the League can pass all that by, because it happens to occur in Africa and not in Europe, without thereby destroying the value of collective security not for Africa only but for Europe." Eden warned Aloisi that if Italy went to war in defiance of her engagements under the Covenant, her friends in England would be both few and unimportant.

It was a hopeful statement by Eden, but not a very frightening one. Aloisi was quite able to read, and had no doubt read the rest of Sir Austen Chamberlain's latest speech, which concluded: "We have to take the risk of saying, 'We are prepared to fulfill our obligations under the Covenant if others will do the same.'" This was simply a new phrasing of the line Sir Samuel Hoare had laid down July 11 and Winston Churchill, for one, had done him the favor of repeating. The code words were, "if others will do the same." What it meant, as Aloisi knew, was that England would not insist unless France insisted.

Aloisi was ready, however, to humor the British. When Eden, with some support from Laval, suggested a three-power meeting to solve the crisis under the 1906 treaty, but with League authorization, Aloisi at least agreed to telephone Mussolini and get his reaction to the idea. It took a series of calls to Rome, during which time Eden received an alarming telegram from Hoare in London. The Foreign Secretary had become so worried about the possible failure of this latest scheme that he told Eden to push the three-power meeting even without League auspices if necessary. Italy would surely have agreed to this, since it would have constituted a formal acknowledgment by Britain and France that Italy could henceforth ignore the League. But Mussolini, not knowing that Hoare was prepared to make such a generous offer, indicated his willingness to bargain on the basis of a three-power meeting under League sponsorship.

From the Italians' point of view, this was also a good offer. They now needed only a two-month delay until the rains ended in Ethiopia and military operations could begin. A three-power discussion would use up at least one of these two months. Mussolini was feeling so expansive at the moment he even agreed to the appointment of a neutral arbitrator of the Wal Wal dispute, if the League Council wanted to name one, and a review of the whole dispute at the September Council meeting. All he demanded in return was a stipulation by the Ethiopians that they would drop one tiresome claim which they had endlessly repeated. If the Ethiopians wanted their efforts toward a peaceful settlement to continue, they would have to stop insisting that the location of Wal Wal, the question of whether it lay in Ethiopia or in Italian Somaliland, was pertinent to the question of which side was responsible for the Wal Wal incident. One can easily understand the annoyance of the Italians on this point. It was as if the United States Army were to attack Toronto, for instance, and the Canadian government were to make the pusilanimous observation that the attack had taken place in Canada, ignoring the vital fact that, before the attack took place, the United States had unofficially and unilaterally annexed Toronto.

Since Wal Wal lay at least sixty miles inside Ethiopia, and since the Italians had absolutely no right to be there, the location of the place was, of course, the most pertinent question in the entire dispute about the battle which occurred there. Incredibly, Eden and Laval suggested to the Ethiopians that they concede the point, and when they registered their disinclination Laval suggested, at the first Council session on the afternoon of the thirty-first, that the meeting be adjourned to give the interested parties more time for private conversations and persuasions.

During the private conversations, which filled the first two and a half days of August, it was strongly suggested to Ethiopian delegate Tecle Hawariate and his French adviser, Gaston Jeze, that their refusal to acquiesce would lead to the end of all arbitration, to Italy's withdrawal from the League, and to an early launching of outright war.[20] It was difficult to alarm the Ethiopians with these arguments in light of Mussolini's recent public statements, which indicated his intention to wage war, whatever might happen in Geneva.

Mussolini's most explicit remarks to date were included in an *Il Popolo d'Italia* article which was published July 31, the day this League Council session began. He had said in the article:

> The essential arguments [in favor of military action against Ethiopia], absolutely unanswerable and such as to end all further discussion, are two: the vital needs of the Italian people and their military security in East Africa. The first of these arguments has been specifically admitted by the British foreign minister. The second is the decisive one. It is clear that the strategic situation of our colonies, precarious in normal times, would become untenable in exceptional times, if Italy found itself engaged in Europe, for instance. ... Put in military terms, the Italian-Abyssinian problem is immediately simple, with the force of a logical absolute. Put in military terms, the problem admits of only one solution—with Geneva, without Geneva, against Geneva.

If Mussolini actually meant what he was saying, how could anyone convince the Ethiopians that any concession on their part would be efficacious? Instead of conciliating him, why shouldn't they use his own latest words against him in a renewal of their demand for immediate League action? By quoting his *Il Popolo d'Italia* remarks of July 31 they could prove that Italy's aggression was now directed not only against themselves but against the League as well. By confronting the Council with Italy's open defiance of it, they could force it either to take action or to admit officially its abdication of responsibility.

Such an argument would, however, confound Ethiopia's "friends," England and France, more than her enemy, Italy, because it would make British and French intentions open and official. As long as Ethiopia refrained from forcing the British and French to acknowledge their actual hands-off policy, a slight possibility remained that, before the shooting began, that policy might yet change.

Because it took the Ethiopians three days to ponder and resolve all these bewildering and intimidating considerations, the second meeting of the Council was not called until seven p.m., August 3. By this time Ethiopia was ready to accept two resolutions which Russian delegate Maxim Litvinov, in the President's chair, read to the Council members as soon as the meeting began. The first resolution excluded the location of Wal Wal as a consideration in placing responsibility for the December clash there; and it took note that the two parties to the dispute had agreed to continue their arbitration procedure, with the addition of a fifth arbitrator. The second resolution stipulated that the Council would meet again September 4 "to undertake a general examination, in its various aspects, of the relations between Italy and Ethiopia." The British-French-Italian agreement to try to settle Ethiopia's future among themselves in the meantime, under the 1906 treaty, was not mentioned.

The Ethiopians, who hadn't even been invited to sit in on the planned three-power talks, were once again bowing reluctantly, not so much to the threats of their enemy as to the pressures of their "friends." But it was not a lack either of courage or intelligence which led them to accept this latest setback. Gaston Jeze, their French representative, said to the Council after the resolutions were read:

> For political reasons of expediency the Imperial Ethiopian Government is called upon to make a considerable sacrifice in the interests of world peace. . . . It realizes the value of what it is giving up for the sake of world peace. . . . The Ethiopian Government is firmly convinced that, even after this sacrifice, which weakens its position before the arbitrators by the abandonment of a very important part of its case, impartial arbitrators, under the chairmanship of a fifth arbitrator enjoying world-wide prestige, will recognize the justice of the Ethiopian cause.

Though the Ethiopians did not say so, they may also have felt that even if this weakening of their case led the arbitration commission to rule against them and penalize them, the penalty could not approach the severity of an invasion by the Italian army, and their willingness to pay such a penalty, even if undeserved, would leave the Italians with scant excuse for an invasion.

Before the votes on the two measures (both approved unanimously, except that Italy abstained from the second), Eden and Laval each said a few words. Eden reminded the members that at the September 4 meeting, "it will be the duty of the Council to deal with the whole question as it then exists."

Laval, on the other hand, was so lacking in grace as to remark that with passage of these resolutions "the Council will thus have fulfilled once more its great and noble mission. All those throughout the world who remain attached to the Geneva institution will rejoice." Because of men like Laval, those who remained attached were, unfortunately, a fading multitude. *Paris-Soir*, commenting that same day on the outcome of the Council meeting (which was known to the press several hours before it met), said, "It is certain these decisions will not raise the prestige of the League, but could anyone have done better or more cleverly than M. Laval to conciliate painlessly what was irreconcilable?"[21]

Paris-Soir did not ask whether Italy's irreconcilable demands should have been conciliated. During the session, League Secretary-General Joseph Avenol told Anthony Eden that "almost every delegate has instructions to follow the British lead." And Russian representative Litvinov, who was presiding, suggested privately to Eden that "the Council as a body should declare that it was prepared to carry out its obligation under the Covenant."

Eden telegraphed this to London, but received no permission from Prime Minister Stanley Baldwin, Foreign Secretary Sir Samuel Hoare, or the Cabinet to take such an initiative. Sir Samuel was now unmindful of his July 11 speech to the House of Commons in which he had said, ". . . we are ready to take our full share of collective responsibility. But when I say collective responsibility, I mean collective responsibility." It must have been at least slightly embarrassing to him (and to influential men like Winston Churchill, Sir Austen Chamberlain, and Neville Chamberlain who had supported this view) when Eden reported that all these other nations were ready to share with England this collective responsibility. There was not enough embarrassment in London, however, to provoke any action.

Mussolini was still unable to convince himself that the apparent British paralysis was real. Having now received from England's French "ally," Pierre Laval, an exact copy of the British Foreign Office paper derogatory to Italy, he sensed that the British were finally grasping the actual weakness of his situation.[22] When they realized they were being deceived and thrown off balance by nothing but the force of his bombast, they might yet descend upon him in full wrath. Baron Aloisi, who received the British memorandum from Laval in Geneva, July 31, included a fearful notation about it in his diary that night:

This is terrible for us. It clears up completely the intention of the British Cabinet in our regard. London, which treats us a little like fools, is uneasy for the League, for its colonial empire, and will prevent at all cost our making war.

When Aloisi sent the offensive document to Rome, it so upset Mussolini that on August 9, he directed the chief of staff of his armed forces, Marshal Pietro Badoglio, to study the question of how well Italy might do in a war against England.[23]

Badoglio's report, put together after consultations between the army and navy, and delivered August 14, confirmed what Mussolini already knew. Badoglio's assessment was uncompromisingly professional and therefore dismally pessimistic. Referring to the strength of the British navy, he wrote,

> It is not possible to nurture any hope at all of having positive results in a fight against such forces, given that our navy is only an advance guard without real substance. Nor should we delude ourselves about a daring campaign which might be possible in a sea as narrow as the Adriatic, but not possible in a sea like the Mediterranean.
>
> In fact, at least 12 or 15 of our submarines could not operate in a sea which is more than 2,000 miles long. Each would have to assume such a large zone of responsibility that the probability of their finding something worth hitting would be almost zero.
>
> On the other hand, the English battleships, escorted by an imposing mass of destroyers, could cruise around the Mediterranean inflicting all the damage they pleased to our coasts, which are sparsely defended.
>
> Nor can we be happy about the aviation which . . . is in a state of crisis; all the older equipment, constituting most of what we have, would be out of use after a few days of intense work. It is true that new squadrons are being formed but the crews must be prepared for the new planes, and we cannot pretend that they will produce any results until they have had a long enough period of training.
>
> In conclusion, and to use precise terms which the gravity of the situation requires, such a war [with England] would bring us to certain catastrophe. . . .[24]

There is no record of Mussolini trying to refute this report. Though he may have been a bully, he was not a fool. If England was, indeed, developing warlike plans against him, the only weapon he had to stop them was the one he had already used so effectively—his mouth. To German Ambassador Ulrich von Hassell he said, on August 3, that some people obviously hadn't yet grasped the fact that Italy was now a different country. He had laid two mines, one in Africa, one in Europe, and he was ready to explode them under anybody who refused to understand this. To French Ambassador Charles de Chambrun, on August 13, he said, "My victory in Abyssinia is certain. I have 170,000 infantry soldiers there and I'm sending more. Whatever the price, I shall avenge Adowa, and if England . . . closes the Suez Canal . . . I shall reopen it myself. Out of desperation I would not hesitate, if it were necessary, to make war [against England]."[25]

At least the French ambassador, if not the German, could be counted upon to pass along in the direction of London these brave words of determination. Everything conceivable had to be said and done to convince the British that Italy was not afraid. With this end in view, Mussolini even set about shoring up the courage of Baron Aloisi, who had been thrown into a near panic when he first read the British memorandum. It was absolutely essential that Aloisi put on an aggressive front because it was he who would be dealing with the British and the French at the three-power talks now scheduled to take place in Paris beginning August 15. When the Duce gave Aloisi his instructions for these talks, he said, "I want no agreement unless I am conceded everything, and that includes the decapitation of the Emperor."[26] He also told Aloisi, "You must act henceforth as a soldier rather than as a diplomat, as a Fascist rather than as a negotiator. Even if I am accorded everything I prefer to avenge Adowa." He would settle, he said, for nothing less than one hundred per cent control of Ethiopia. Aloisi was so impressed by his chief's ferocity that he went to Paris completely convinced the tripartite conference would be a waste of time.

The Duce had also succeeded in scaring the British. They were now so concerned about the possibility of a "mad dog attack" by the Italians, perhaps against their naval base at Malta, that the chiefs of staff in London, on August 6, undertook an analysis of their strength in the Mediterranean. First Lord of the Admiralty Ernle Chatfield, summing up the findings of the naval staff, reported that, while they were reluctant to fight a war against the Italians, because it might be costly in terms of their limited peacetime strength and because they lacked sympathy for its purpose, they had "no hesitation tactically" about engaging the Italians in the Mediterranean as soon as necessary reinforcements were sent there from other waters. The Admiralty was certain the British fleet could defeat Italy on the sea, and therefore equally certain it could stop Italian shipping to Ethiopia, thus ending Mussolini's African adventure.

Sir Samuel Hoare's interpretation of this report from the naval staff was that they "could not have been more insistent with their warnings against diminishing or dissipating our limited strength." So great was his desire to placate the Italians and preserve peace that he saw in the report only what he wanted to see. He missed completely its primary message, which was that the Italians had much greater reason than the British to avoid war. Stanley Baldwin, who was now hurrying off on vacation, had "repeatedly" told him, "Keep us out of war. We are not ready for it." Such remarks, fairly well exemplifying the limits of the Prime Minister's interest in foreign policy, impressed Hoare so deeply he was afraid even to take advantage of the navy's great usefulness as a deterrent to war. Ironically, the British foreign minister had less respect for the power of the British navy than did the Italian dictator and his military staff.

Sir Robert Vansittart, who accompanied Anthony Eden to Paris for the tripartite talks, agreed with Hoare.[27] It was not to be expected, therefore, that he would speak up very firmly to the Italians. Baron Aloisi was assured of this on August 15, the first day of the meeting, by Pierre Laval, who told him that the British front was softer than it appeared, and that the primary interest of both the French and the British was to safeguard the League and avoid war. Thus comforted, Aloisi was able to employ during the four-day meeting an extension of Mussolini's successful methods in bullying the British. When they presented their plan for a settlement of the crisis, similar in design to their earlier Zeila proposal, he took it no more seriously than Mussolini had done when Eden first presented it in Rome. The French then proposed, on August 16, a settlement that would make Ethiopia technically a protectorate of Britain, France, and Italy, but with Italy in real control of the country. Aloisi went through the pretense of entertaining this notion for two days, before announcing to the British and French on the morning of the eighteenth that Mussolini had rejected it completely. As if Mussolini's cavalier treatment of the British were not sufficient insult, Vansittart sought more of the same by asking the Italian dictator, through the Italian Ambassador in Paris, Vittorio Cerruti, if it would be "useful or pleasing for him to visit Rome." Mussolini rebuffed the timid bid, informing Vansittart that he considered war with Abyssinia inevitable.

Vansittart showed signs now that he was beginning to understand the gravity of the situation, though he could not acknowledge his own role in creating it. On the eighteenth, before he left Paris, he said to Eden, "You are faced with a first-class international crisis. We've got to reinforce the Mediterranean fleet."

Eden agreed. He even sent a secret message to Hoare that night asking him to hasten British defenses "against possible action by Mussolini."[28] At the same time, he was burdened by an additional worry which did not concern any of his British colleagues. He was now so intimately involved in the situation and had gotten to know the Ethiopians so well that he actually cared about their fate. Before leaving Paris, he received Tecle Hawariate (the Ethiopian Minister to France as well as the delegate to the League of Nations), who had come to Paris to make an appeal on the

Emperor's behalf for the relaxation of England's arms embargo against Ethiopia.

"It is surely evident to everyone now," he said, "that Italy intends to attack Ethiopia, and to attack soon. All we ask of the world is the right of self-defense. Even that is being denied us by withholding arms." He implored Eden to intercede with the British government for a partial relaxation of the embargo so that Ethiopia could supply herself with "at least a few arms" for her national defense.

Though Eden was personally sympathetic to this appeal, he could offer no promises. He himself had already made the same appeal to his colleagues in London, pointing out that an embargo of arms to Italy and Ethiopia was actually a boon to Italy, since Mussolini had all the arms he needed, while the Ethiopians were virtually defenseless. So far, this argument had not prevailed against the Cabinet's determination to avoid trouble with Italy. Eden could only assure Tecle Hawariate that he would try again.

On August 27, 1935, Pope Pius XI spoke to about a thousand members, from twenty-seven nations, of the International Congress of Catholic Nurses, who had gathered at his Castel Gandolfo summer palace.[29] He treated these Catholic daughters to an unexpected address, carefully obtuse, parts of which made him sound quite uneasy about the approaching war, though he did not even suggest any condemnation of it. After protesting his desire for peace and his terror of war, he said:

> ... we see that abroad there is talk of a war of conquest, of a war of aggression. That is a hypothesis which we even fear to think of; it is a hypothesis which is truly disconcerting. A war which is only a war of conquest would be clearly an unjust war; it is something which exceeds imagination; it is something indescribably sad and horrible. We cannot think about an unjust war nor admit its possibility. . . . On the other hand, in Italy it is said that this is a question of a just war because it is a war of defense, to ensure the nation's frontiers against continuing and ceaseless assaults; a war made necessary by the daily expansion of population; a war undertaken to defend and assure the material security of the nation— that such a war is justified.
>
> It is true, however, dear daughters, and we cannot prevent ourselves from meditating upon it, that if this need of expansion does exist, if there exists also a necessity for assuring the defense of frontiers, we can only hope all these difficulties may be resolved by some means other than war.
>
> One thing seems to us beyond question—that is, if the need for expansion is a fact to which consideration must be given, the right of defense

has its limits and restrictions, and if it is to be blameless, it must be held to a certain moderation.

The Pope's analysis of the matter was hardly what one might have expected to hear from the "Vicar of Christ on Earth." Was he asking people to believe that the Vatican, situated in Rome and with its vast world-wide sources of information, did not know whether Mussolini's intended venture would be a "just" or "unjust" war? Was he asking people to take seriously the Italians' claim that they were preparing only a "defensive" action against Ethiopia? When he mentioned Italy's "need of expansion," could he properly ignore the fact that, if there was such a need, it had been created by Mussolini's blatant campaign for bigger Italian families—a campaign which the Church had abetted? Coming from a man whose exalted ecclesiastical position proclaimed him the world's foremost symbol of spirituality and the highest authority in matters of orthodox morality, the Pope's remarks on August 27 were extraordinarily lacking in spiritual or moral content. What he said that day made him look, at best, like an uncomfortable apologist for an Italian government which had already and repeatedly shown a scornful disregard for any kind of morality.

One might almost have expected Mussolini to endorse and propagate the Castel Gandolfo speech, not only as a summary of his own reasonable and troubled sentiments about the situation, but also as a public Papal approval of the very thing he intended to do. The Duce, however, was in no mood to tolerate even the most timid questions or qualifications from the Vatican. The Pope would have to be taught a little more humility. As soon as news of the speech reached the government, the Italian ambassador tried to prevent its publication in the official Papal newspaper, *l'Osservatore romano*. When it was published despite the protest, the government-controlled lay press throughout Italy then presented it, including its qualifications, as a Papal endorsement of Mussolini's policies.

Pope Pius, who had apparently considered his statement to be something other than an endorsement, now became sufficiently annoyed at the government to issue a clarification. In the August 30, 1935, *l'Osservatore romano*, he wrote,

> The Pope's thought is clear: The need to expand is not a right per se, but simply a fact of which note must be taken. Self-defense, on the other hand, constitutes a right, but the exercise of this right may be harmful if it does not observe certain limits and a certain moderation.

It appeared now that the Pope was actually preparing to stand up and oppose the Italian government. This short public statement, coupled with the fact that he had refused to bless Italian troop ships embarking for Africa (though he had not forbidden his bishops and priests to do so), made it seem possible that the Pope intended, after all, to exercise his moral and spiritual duty. Even Mussolini seems to have feared such a possibility. The pressures he began applying to the Vatican were so intense that Cardinal Pacelli confided to Charles-Roux, "Oh, how they complain, and with what energy!"

Within a week, the energy of the Fascist complaints bore fruit. On September 7, before celebrating Mass at St. Paul's-Outside-the-Walls for a group of Catholic war veterans, Pope Pius addressed a short statement to them. He was still praying for peace, he said. But at the same time, it was his desire that "the hopes, the demands, the needs of a great and good people, who are [my] people . . . will be recognized and satisfied . . . but with justice and with peace."

In the weeks ahead, while Italian war preparations continued, the Pope was to say not one more public word about Mussolini's intentions, although they were, of course, well known to him. He didn't offer so much as an abstract condemnation of aggression, much less support to the League of Nations and individual nations in their efforts to avert war. While it might be understandable for an ordinary Italian citizen at the time to accept Mussolini's war policies (especially since the ordinary Italian's information was strictly limited by the Italian press), it is difficult to reconcile the acquiescence of the well-informed Pope Pius XI with his Holy Office as God's earthly representative.

In America, as the summer of 1935 progressed through the hot days of July and August, anti-Mussolini sentiment increased rapidly. Newspapers in all parts of the country, reacting against Italy's apparent intentions toward Ethiopia, referred to Il Duce in such terms as "suicidal maniac." One paper called his strutting walk "the approved swagger of military madmen." Another said his behavior was "insane." The Hearst newspapers were among the few who defended him. Hearst columnist Arthur Brisbane couldn't see why people should criticize Italy for doing what France and England had done many times. The Hearst papers had already published a series of articles about the primitive savagery of the Abyssinians.

The attitude of American blacks was exemplified in New York City by a parade and mass meeting in Harlem, August 3, attended by about twenty thousand people, including some white liberals, clergymen, and trade-unionists. Several of the marchers waved Ethiopian flags and many carried posters warning Mussolini to keep his HANDS OFF ETHIOPIA. A large majority of Protestants and Jews in America shared this sentiment. Only the Catholics, out of deference to the Pope and to the Italian-

Americans in their midst, showed any reluctance to speak against the intended Italian aggression. Even intellectual Catholic journals like *Commonweal* and the Jesuit-sponsored *America* remained "neutral" in the matter, though they did not hesitate to criticize England and the League of Nations. The official newspaper of the largely Irish Archdiocese of Boston, *The Pilot*, was one exception among Catholic publications. In its July 13 issue, *The Pilot* said: "Italy wants to expand; she wishes a colony where her interests may be developed. The alleged affront to Italian dignity is little more than a pretext for attacking Ethiopia." Irish Catholics, aware of Ireland's struggle to gain independence, were generally sympathetic to Ethiopia's efforts to preserve it. The American public as a whole sympathized overwhelmingly with Ethiopia.

While the anti-Mussolini sentiment continued to grow in America, however, it could not keep pace with the antiwar sentiment which grew even more rapidly, and which was, ironically, intensified because of Mussolini's aggressiveness. Many Americans disliked him, not so much because of what he might soon do in Africa but because he could conceivably, thereby, force the United States into another war. Their dislike of him inspired them not to resist or prevent what he wanted to do, but to isolate themselves from it as if they could never be harmed by what they refused to touch.

This isolationism had been heightened by the work of a Senate committee investigating the munitions industry. Headed by Senator Gerald P. Nye, it published statistics in 1935 showing the profits of many large American corporations from armament sales during the 1914–1918 war. Senator Nye used these statistics to support a contention that the munitions makers had maneuvered the country into that war simply for their own gain. Because Americans already had good reasons to distrust the methods of many of their wealthiest business leaders, the exaggerated and oversimplified charges of the Nye Committee gained high public acceptance. The Nye Committee report was a major factor in passing a tough neutrality bill during the summer of 1935.

On August 17, before Congress had passed the neutrality bill, but at a time when its passage was already inevitable, the British ambassador in Washington, Sir Ronald Lindsay, acting on telegraphed instructions from Foreign Secretary Sir Samuel Hoare, asked Secretary of State Cordell Hull if he and President Roosevelt would be willing to make some gesture warning the Italians, who were then stalling progress at the tripartite meeting in Paris, that they could not count on American neutrality or indifference to make their way easier in Africa.[30] At the same time, British and French diplomats in Paris were pressing the same plea upon United States Chargé d'Affaires Theodore Marriner, who immediately wired this information to the State Department in Washington. Hull had virtually invited these appeals two days earlier by instructing his embassies in London and Paris to find out whether America could do anything within the limits of its established policy that would "be likely to have a beneficial rather than a disadvantageous effect" on the Paris discussions. When he received Marriner's telegram from Paris, he went immediately to the White House and suggested to the President that they send a message to Mussolini.

Roosevelt having agreed, Hull composed a telegram over his own signature which he sent August 18 to Alexander Kirk, the American Chargé d'Affaires in Rome, for delivery to Mussolini. Unfortunately, it was not a telegram which any man qualified to be Secretary of State should have considered challenging to a person like Mussolini. The telegram said,

> I am asked by the President to communicate to you, in all friendliness and in confidence, a personal message expressing his earnest hope that the controversy between Italy and Ethiopia will be resolved without resort to armed conflict. In this country it is felt both by the Government and by the people that failure to arrive at a peaceful settlement of the present dispute and a subsequent outbreak of hostilities would be a world calamity the consequences of which would adversely affect the interests of all nations.

When Kirk delivered this message in person, on August 19, Mussolini was ready with an oral reply. Though he appreciated the friendliness of the message, it was too late to escape an armed conflict, he said, because Italy had mobilized a million men and had spent two billion lire. He assured Kirk there was no reason to fear the consequences of such a conflict if it was limited to Italy and Ethiopia, but, because of the British attitude, such a limitation might prove impossible. The Anglo-French proposals in Paris were entirely unacceptable. What Italy wanted was the military occupation of Ethiopia, and regardless of League action, Italy would proceed with her plans. If the opposition of other countries developed into actual interference, Italy would take steps accordingly. In that case, the consequences might prove disastrous.

If the diplomatic language of other countries at the time had been half as forceful as that of Italy, Mussolini's opportunity to create the threatened disaster would have been foreclosed. Unfortunately, however, even when Hull showed the President of the United States the rude, blunt words with which Mussolini had told him to mind his own business, Roosevelt reacted not angrily but tepidly, with a follow-up note to Hull which said,

> It would be well in any subsequent note or message by us . . . to point out that it is never too late to avoid an armed conflict. . . . After all these preparations Italian prestige would be enhanced and not harmed if Italy

could take the magnificent position that rather than resort to war she would cancel the military preparations and submit the whole question to peaceful settlement by arbitration.

This was nothing more than Presidential doodling, as Roosevelt must have known. What his note to Hull actually said was that he couldn't cope with Mussolini any better than he could with the isolationists in Congress.

On August 23, these isolationists passed their neutrality bill and sent it to the White House for his signature. The joint resolution made it mandatory for the President, on finding that a state of war existed, to prohibit the sale or export of "arms, ammunition, and implements of war" to all belligerents. American businesses were free under its provisions, however, to sell all other goods to belligerents, including many products which were as essential as guns in waging war. Italy needed many of these secondary war materials, especially oil. What Ethiopia had to have was armament and ammunition. The effect of the embargo would be to give Italy everything she needed while withholding from Ethiopia the things she needed most.

Roosevelt and Hull were disappointed in their hopes for a discretionary embargo which would have allowed the President to block shipment of goods to an aggressor nation (so designated by the League of Nations) without forbidding trade with its victim. Such an embargo provision would have permitted the United States to cooperate with the League in discouraging aggression, and would also have assured the League that if it were to apply sanctions against an aggressor, American firms would not render those sanctions ineffective by supplying what League Members withheld. Secretary of State Hull, in the last frantic days before passage of the neutrality resolution, had done his best to make Congress see the merits of the discretionary embargo, but Hull's best was not good enough.

On August 31, President Roosevelt capitulated to the isolationists. He prepared a public statement which grumbled somewhat about the inflexibility of an embargo that would penalize the innocent at least as much as the guilty. But he assured the American people that he hated war as much as they did, and promised them he would do nothing to get the country involved. Then he meekly signed the neutrality resolution into law.

In Addis Ababa, Emperor Haile Selassie, having failed to secure American support through diplomatic means, had secretly launched a project which he hoped might gain him a measure of United States protection by appealing to the notorious American acquisitive instinct. He and his American financial adviser, Everett Colson, were not unmindful of the possibility that if America had a large enough economic stake in Ethiopia, Washington might look with much more disfavor upon Italy's transgressions there.

The one Ethiopian economic resource most likely to capture the interest of Americans was oil. The secret representative of a huge and politically powerful American oil company had, in fact, explored the possibility of leasing oil rights in a large part of Ethiopia the previous January. Because so few wells had been drilled in the country, no one knew how much oil might be available underground, but this American company had been sufficiently impressed by the prospects to have shown a definite desire for a long-term contract. By granting such a concession, the Emperor would not only be creating an incentive for these powerful Americans to help protect Ethiopian independence; he would also be securing some immediate cash with which to pay for any armaments he could manage to buy. He therefore authorized Colson in early August to invite the company's representative to Addis Ababa immediately.

As it happened, the man who secretly represented the American company was a British subject and flamboyant promoter named Francis W. Rickett. He arrived in Addis Ababa August 23, on the slow, crowded, uncomfortable train from Djibuti.[31] One of his traveling companions, British novelist Evelyn Waugh, who had come to Ethiopia to cover the impending war for a London newspaper, described Rickett as a gay and lighthearted man, "invested with a certain mystery," who spoke openly of being on a "mission" and received lengthy cables in code. When questioned about the mission, he hinted that it had something to do with funds for the Coptic Church. In Djibuti he engaged the only luxury carriage listed as available for the train trip to Addis Ababa and invited Waugh to share it with him, expecting they would have a whole car to themselves with a kitchen and private cook. When they went to the station to board the train August 20, they found no luxury car but a great multitude of people jostling for seats in the hot, crowded coaches. Rickett was undaunted. At least in Addis Ababa he would find a measure of the comfort he liked. He had ordered a suite at the Imperial Hotel there.

When the train reached the capital three days later, there weren't even any rooms available at the Imperial. Both Rickett and Waugh eventually found themselves at a pension, from which the genial and well-dressed but still mysterious Rickett would emerge daily for unexplained destinations.

"He was clearly up to something," Waugh later recalled, "and drove off every now and then to interview such very dissimilar dignitaries as the Abuna [Abuna Kyrillos, primate of the Abyssinian Church] and Mr. Colson, the American financial adviser of the Emperor. I thought it impertinent to enquire further. On the second day of our visit he had promised me an important piece of news on Saturday evening. Saturday came and he admitted, rather ruefully, that he had not been able to arrange anything; it would probably be next Wednesday, he said. It seemed clear that he was involved in the endless postponements of Abyssinian official life."

For five days, Rickett made secret trips to the Imperial Palace, entering through a back door, to negotiate with Everett Colson. On August 29, he signed an agreement with the Ethiopian government which granted a firm called the African Exploration and Development Corporation an exclusive, seventy-five-year mineral concession for half of Ethiopia, including all of the eastern and southeastern sections of the country bordering on Italian Somaliland and Eritrea. When this agreement was made public the next day, the African Exploration and Development Corporation was named but not further identified. It clearly seemed to be a front for some other interest.

News of this transaction caused immediate repercussions in the capitals of Europe. The Italians said it had to be a British deal, Rickett being an Englishman, and that it "throws off the mask of British altruism." In other words, England had been opposing Italian ambitions in Ethiopia only because of her own ambitions.

Publication of the story in the London *Daily Telegraph* August 31 bewildered British Foreign Secretary Sir Samuel Hoare, who knew nothing about it. He sent a "Rush" telegram to Addis Ababa, instructing his minister there, Sir Sidney Barton, to "Please report the facts urgently by telegraph."

Sir Samuel couldn't wait for facts, however, with all the newspapers demanding information. A few hours after the *Daily Telegraph* story appeared, the Foreign Office issued a statement proclaiming British innocence of the matter:

> The British Government have no information about the reported concession granted by the Ethiopian Government to an Anglo-American financial group represented by Mr. Rickett at Addis Ababa, and until official confirmation has been received as to the real facts, they are disinclined to attach undue importance to this information.
>
> No official or unofficial support whatever has been given to Mr. Rickett by the British Government, who have made it clear on several occasions that they have no imperial economic interest in Abyssinia except Lake Tana. . . .

Having dispatched his urgent telegram to Barton, Sir Samuel was inspired by an afterthought to dispatch another a few hours later. This one said:

> . . . While I await confirmation from you of alleged report, it appears evident that concession such as that reported would undoubtedly be matter

of preliminary consultation by His Majesty's Government with French and Italian Governments under article 2 of Tripartite Treaty of 1906. In these circumstances you are authorized, if report is true, to inform the Emperor that His Majesty's Government must for their part advise His Majesty [the Emperor] to withhold the concession.

The British Foreign Secretary was thus making the claim that the sovereign and independent government of Ethiopia had no right to sell or lease its own resources because the governments of three other nations had already got together in 1906 and, without any consent by Ethiopia, had divided the options to its resources among themselves.

In Addis Ababa August 31, Rickett himself stated that no British company was involved in the transaction. He said the company he actually represented (through the dummy African Exploration and Development Corporation) was the American Standard Oil Company.[32]

There were now, as a result of antitrust suits, several Standard Oil companies in America, the corporate connections between which were difficult to trace. Because Rickett did not say which Standard Oil Company he represented, there was a strong tendency to disbelieve his story, especially when a canvas of the Standard Oil companies brought firm denials from every one of them that they had any connection with the Rickett deal.

In Addis Ababa September 1, Emperor Haile Selassie himself announced that he had deliberately given the oil concession to Americans and only to Americans. "What right did Great Britain have," he asked, "to advise withdrawal of the grant, or to object that it violated the Tripartite Treaty of 1906?" A sovereign state, he pointedly observed, had the right to do what it pleased with its own territory. Neither the United States nor Ethiopia had been a party to the Treaty of 1906. "That is one of the reasons," the Emperor concluded, "that I gave the concession to Standard Oil."

When Haile Selassie himself said he was dealing with Standard Oil Company, even the United States State Department began to believe it. Cordell Hull was furious. As he saw the situation, "The impression was now created that all the efforts of the British and American Governments to keep Mussolini from plunging into Ethiopia were dictated by the greedy motive to corner the oil prospects in that country." In Hull's mind, the efforts of the American government had apparently assumed significant proportions. The State Department, having greater resources than the newspapers, was quickly able to ascertain that the Standard Vacuum Oil Company, a subsidiary of Socony Vacuum and Standard Oil Company of New Jersey (both of which had denied connection with Rickett), was the company he actually represented. Two officers of Standard Vacuum, Board Chairman George S. Walden and Vice-President

H. Dundas, were urgently invited to Washington September 3 to discuss the matter.

The first man to see them was Wallace Murray, chief of the State Department's Near East Division.[33] Murray, whom Hull had briefed, told the two oil men rather forcibly that they had made a great mistake. Their procurement of an Ethiopian oil concession at this time, Murray said, was "a matter of grave embarrassment, not only to this Government, but to other Governments who are making strenuous and sincere efforts for the preservation of world peace, which is threatened by the Italo-Ethiopian dispute." Murray also said, "This transaction has come as a most painful surprise and is deeply deplored by the Secretary of State." He referred to "the painful handicap under which certain governments, particularly the British, are now placed in view of the suspicions and recriminations arising out of the oil transactions." (He did not mention any pressure the British might have applied in Washington to get the transaction canceled.) He ended his lecture by saying, "This Government, no less than the British Government, desires to divest itself of any suspicion of self-interest when world peace is at stake, and the oil transaction has created just such a suspicion."

Walden, as if he hadn't yet got the point, asked Murray what the State Department wanted him to do.

Murray said, "Only radical action on the part of your company in the form of an immediate and unconditional withdrawal from the concession would meet the needs of the situation."

The company officials were not initially inclined to acquiesce. Conferences between them and State Department officials, including Hull, went on throughout the day. Walden said the cancellation of such a lease was unparalleled in Standard Oil history. Hull scheduled a noon news conference at which he may have intended to announce the cancellation of the concession, but at noon there was not yet a cancellation to announce. While his aides continued their pressure on the oilmen in another room, Hull issued a statement that the Department still lacked sufficient facts to comment on the reported lease.

In midafternoon, Walden and Dundas left the State Department without agreeing to cancel the lease. They would confer, they said, with other company officials.

In late afternoon, Walden finally called the Department to say that he had talked to his colleagues, and they had agreed to renege on their commitment to the Ethiopian government.

At six p.m., Hull called another press conference in his office to announce this result. He told the reporters that the oil agreement had been made "without this Government having been in any way consulted or informed," and that "the attitude and policy of this Government

135

toward the controversy between Italy and Ethiopia will be maintained hereafter just as it would have been maintained had this reported oil transaction not occurred." He had scored a victory so impressive it made some people wonder if he realized how powerful he actually was. Since he was strong enough to stand up to Standard Oil, might he not also be strong enough to stand up to Italy?

Hull was not worrying about Italy at the moment. Having done yeoman work for Mussolini, he had no reason to expect anything but felicitations from Rome. On the other hand, he might have been feeling somewhat sheepish about Ethiopia after supporting so strongly the British contention that the Ethiopian government was not master of its own resources. He recalled later, "We had next to pacify Emperor Haile Selassie."

The Emperor, as soon as he learned of the Standard Oil Company cancellation and the circumstances under which it took place, lodged a protest with the new American minister to Ethiopia, Cornelius Van H. Engert.[34] He had granted the concession to an American company, Haile Selassie told Engert, not only because he knew the United States was politically disinterested and technically equipped to contribute to the economic development of Ethiopia, but also as a proof of his friendly feeling toward America and his appreciation of the sympathetic interest America was displaying toward Ethiopia's difficulties.

Hull sensed no irony in these remarks. He answered through Engert that the Emperor's sentiments of cordiality and good will were appreciated and reciprocated and that the advice given the oil company by the State Department was no indication of a change in policy. On the contrary, it was intended to be "helpful in the cause of peace," and to "strengthen the hands of those powers, including the United States, which are making strenuous and sincere efforts toward that end."[35]

The Emperor could have let it rest there, but the rains would soon end and the Italians were ready to pounce. Perhaps his growing desperation led him to hope that these latest words of the United States Secretary of State actually had some meaning. On September 10, he instructed his Foreign Office to ask Engert if the United States might possibly change its mind and agree to mediate the dispute with Italy.

Hull quickly let him know how "helpful in the cause of peace" the United States was prepared to be. He replied, on September 12, that the Emperor's suggestion "would not appear to be practicable, coming as it does at a moment when the appropriate agencies of the League of Nations, to which the Ethiopian Government has referred its dispute, are occupied in an endeavor to arrive at a solution."

CHAPTER SEVEN

SIR Samuel Hoare, suffering from an attack of arthritis in one foot, hobbled with the help of a walking stick to the podium of the huge League of Nations General Assembly Hall to make the first major speech of the Assembly's third plenary meeting on the morning of September 11, 1935. After bowing to Dr. Eduard Beneš of Czechoslovakia, who was presiding, he looked down into the faces of the delegates on the overcrowded floor and reflected upon their sophistication. Glancing up into the galleries, he surveyed, with much less admiration, an audience he described as "a grim-looking crowd of hot-gospellers of Geneva." He lacked patience for those unrealistic people who supported the League too staunchly. Many of his most trusted advisers felt the League was virtually dead; while he "clearly realized" that he might be "forced to accept this view," he nevertheless "wished to resist it until the last moment."[1]

Despite such deep reservations about the usefulness and fate of the League, he had come to this General Assembly meeting in Geneva to make what he thought would be an important speech about British policy in the Italian-Ethiopian crisis. He had decided in late August to make "a revivalist appeal to the Assembly," because "there might still, I thought, be a chance of putting new life into its crippled body." He had not been careless or casual in augmenting this decision. With the help of Sir Robert Vansittart in the Foreign Office, and of his friend Neville Chamberlain, the Chancellor of the Exchequer, he had composed an address about which he could later state, "I own that I was pleased with it."

A few days before his departure for Geneva, he had taken his composition to Chequers to show it to Prime Minister Stanley Baldwin, whose indifference to foreign policy was notorious.[2] Hoare and Baldwin talked about the delights of the French countryside, where Baldwin vacationed, and of the English countryside. They walked in the garden and had tea. Finally Baldwin recalled the purpose of Hoare's visit and said, "You have got a speech to make and you have brought me the draft. Let me have a look at it." After giving it what Hoare described as "a quick glance," he

137

handed it back and said, "That's all right. It must have taken you a long time to make it up."

The League Assembly Hall in Geneva was now overflowing with people from all over the world who were much more eager than Stanley Baldwin to learn what Sir Samuel Hoare had to say. Very few League sessions had attracted as much attention as this one. The entire world was waiting to see whether England would now finally assert the leadership which her wealth and power made possible. There had been strong signs recently of an awakening in official London. The British churches, universities, most of the Labour Party, and the rapidly growing League of Nations Union had taken the Ethiopia issue to the people so effectively that even the Baldwin government had felt obliged to ride the public wave. On July 23, a month after publication of the "Peace Ballot" results, Baldwin had reversed his initial scorn of its findings so far as to say that it had shown his government the "large volume of public opinion behind us in the efforts which we are today making to maintain the authority of the League of Nations." On September 5, just a week before the League Assembly meeting, the British Trades Union Congress voted by a majority of 2,962,000 to 177,000 for a resolution demanding the use of "all the necessary measures provided by the Government to resist Italy's unjust and rapacious attack."

It was against this background that Hoare had come to Geneva, drawing with him the foremost statesmen from every other League country. Large crowds had gathered outside the Assembly Hall in the early morning of September 11 to see the international celebrities arrive. The press gallery was jammed. Hoare was impressed by the array of secretaries, interpreters, and microphones surrounding him as he began to speak.

"I do not suppose that in the history of the Assembly," he said,

> there was ever a more difficult moment for a speech and a discussion. When the world is stirred to excitement over the Ethiopian controversy and feeling runs high upon one side or the other, it is easy to say something that will make the situation more critical and the task of the Council more difficult. . . . I will begin by reaffirming the support of the League by the Government that I represent and the interest of the British people in collective security. . . . It is . . . necessary when the League is in a time of real difficulty for the representative of the United Kingdom to state his view and to make it as clear as he can, first, that His Majesty's Government and the British people maintain their support of the League and its ideals as the most effective way of ensuring peace, and, secondly, that this belief in the necessity for preserving the League is our sole interest in the present controversy. No selfish or imperialist motives enter into our minds at all.

As he approached the body of his sixty-four-minute speech, Sir Samuel became conscious of the fact that the house was absolutely silent. He had a firm hold on his audience. He was inclined to credit his precise style, which "often displeased the House of Commons but was in contrast to the rhetoric of most of the Geneva speeches."

"The League is what its Member States make it," he continued.

> If it succeeds it is because its Members have, in combination with each other, the will and the power to apply the principles of the Covenant. If it fails, it is because its Members lack either the will or the power to fulfill their obligations. . . . Collective security . . . is, in its perfect form, not a simple but a complex conception. It means much more than what are commonly called sanctions. It means, not merely Article 16, but the whole Covenant. . . . If the burden [of the Covenant] is to be borne, it must be borne collectively. If risks for peace are to be run, they must be run by all. . . . On behalf of His Majesty's Government in the United Kingdom, I can say that, in spite of these difficulties, that Government will be second to none in its intention to fulfill, within the measure of its capacity, the obligations which the Covenant lays upon it. . . . We believe that small nations are entitled to a life of their own and to such protection as can collectively be afforded to them . . . we believe that backward nations are, without prejudice to their independence and integrity, entitled to expect that assistance will be afforded them by more advanced peoples in the development of their resources and the build-up of their national life. I am not ashamed of our record in this respect. . . .
>
> It has been not only suggested that British national opinion, as well as the attitude of the United Kingdom Government, is animated by some lower motive than fidelity to the League, but also that even this fidelity to the League cannot be relied upon. It is unjust and dangerously mis-leading to hold or encourage such illusions. The attitude of His Majesty's Government has always been one of unswerving fidelity to the League and all that it stands for, and the case now before us is no exception, but, on the contrary, the continuance of that rule. The recent response of public opinion shows how completely the nation supports the Govern-ment in the full acceptance of the obligations of League membership, which is the oft-proclaimed keynote of British policy. . . . The League stands, and my country stands with it, for the collective maintenance of the Covenant in its entirety, and particularly for steady and collective resistance to all acts of unprovoked aggression. . . . There, then, is the British attitude towards the Covenant. I cannot believe that it will be changed so long as the League remains an effective body and the main bridge between the United Kingdom and the Continent remains intact.

The address had commanded complete silence from beginning to end, not once being interrupted even for applause.[3] But the moment Sir Samuel stopped talking, the applause burst like a sudden storm upon the Assembly. For several minutes the cheers and handclaps continued in a show of fervent approval seldom before seen in Geneva. Only Baron

Aloisi and his Italian contingent abstained from the demonstration. Aloisi remained motionless in his seat, pale-faced and solitary. In the French section, everyone applauded, although Pierre Laval showed less enthusiasm than some of the others. Even the Geneva policeman who stood in the gallery above the President's chair, wearing a cocked hat with a black and blue uniform, clapped his gloved hands.

As Sir Samuel descended from the podium, crowds of delegates spontaneously rushed forward to gather around him and shake his hand or pat him on the back. He was amazed at the reaction. Though he felt he had made "a definite impression," he wasn't sure what kind of impression it was. If he needed reassurance as to the enthusiasm of his audience, he had only to await the reaction of the press, which was universally laudatory, except in Italy.

A London *Times* leading article said,

> The speech will rank high as an authoritative and historic declaration of British policy. Without a doubt, Sir Samuel Hoare has succeeded in expressing the views not only of the Government but of the country as a whole.

The *Daily Herald* said,

> Sir Samuel Hoare's speech was a warning to which Signor Mussolini would be well advised to pay heed. This is the voice of Great Britain for the world to hear and to heed.

The *News-Chronicle* said,

> Great Britain for the first time for many years has definitely assumed the initiative and the direction in which her influence is cast is now unequivocally right. . . . Given the obvious need yesterday for the use of diplomatic language, Sir Samuel Hoare could not have hinted much more plainly to France that if the Covenant is upheld on this occasion, then France can look equally to the fullest assistance from Britain under the Covenant in the event of her security being threatened.

In Paris, *Le Temps* said,

> England has now officially taken up her position regarding the question which not only concerns the maintenance of peace in East Africa but upon which the existence of the League of Nations may depend.

And the *Journal des débats* said,

> If the principles invoked yesterday had been strictly applied ever since the end of the war, the world would not be in the state of disorder and trouble in which we see it.

The comments from newsmen and statesmen in every part of the world were similar. To people in the small nations, Sir Samuel Hoare was an

140

overnight hero. He had finally given real meaning to the promise of the League Covenant. Now that Britain had taken the lead, there was no question as to whether the other League Members were ready and willing to do their collective duty. Under such circumstances, even France would be forced to comply, as Pierre Laval reluctantly admitted in his own speech before the Assembly two days later.

Laval did not equivocate. "France is loyal to the Covenant," he said.

> ... The Covenant is our international law. How could we allow such a law to be weakened? To do so would be to deny our whole ideal, and it would be contrary to our very interest to do so. France's policy rests entirely on the League. All our agreements with our friends and with our allies now pass through Geneva or culminate at Geneva. ... Any attack on the League would be an attack on our security. ... We are all united by bonds of solidarity which point the way to duty. Our obligations are inscribed in the Covenant. France will not shirk them.

Laval had supported Hoare's pledge with such firmness that the applause which greeted him was second only to that which Sir Samuel had received. Never before had England and France so forthrightly declared their determination to stand behind the League.

Words were not enough, of course, as David Lloyd George observed in commenting upon Sir Samuel's League address during an address of his own at Plymouth. "This great speech has been delivered," Lloyd George said September 12, "but I want to ask what are the tactical steps to be taken to give effect to it."

As if in answer to this question, large units of the British Home Fleet, including the battle cruisers *Hood* and *Renown*, arrived at Gibraltar that day on the way to the Mediterranean. Units of the Mediterranean Fleet had already sailed eastward from Malta to protect the Suez Canal. By September 20, Ambassador to Italy Sir Eric Drummond was able to point out to Mussolini that 144 British warships, totaling 800,000 tons, were cruising in what the Duce liked to call "Mare Nostrum." There seemed little doubt now that the British had altered their stance and were prepared for a showdown with Italy.

Among the happiest of men at this prospect was Emperor Haile Selassie. He was receiving guests at a Palace function marking the Ethiopian New Year when an Associated Press correspondent showed him the dispatch from Geneva reporting Hoare's speech. After reading the dispatch, the Emperor, obviously delighted, handed it to his Empress and said, "It is a wonderful New Year's present."

Unable to contain his joy at the news, he dispatched messengers to spread it among the populace. Then he said to his assembled guests, "The tide seems to have turned. We face the future with renewed confidence. God, justice and the Great Powers appear to be on our side. . . . Our prayers for peace may yet be answered. We will not be the first to draw blood, but if war must come, we are prepared. We shall yield nothing further in the way of economic, political or territorial possessions to Italy. Our delegation at Geneva is so instructed."

An Ethiopian army general who was among the guests told newsmen, "With our guerrilla tactics, we can wear out the Italians and dissipate their supplies while England is dealing with them elsewhere."

In the streets of Addis Ababa, and throughout the country, the New Year's celebration quickly became a demonstration in praise of England and the League of Nations. Ethiopia's salvation was apparently at hand.

Mussolini, however, did not seem to think so. He responded immediately to the arrival of the British fleet in the Mediterranean by sending two army divisions to Libya to create the impression that he might be planning an attack against Egypt. It appeared to be a ludicrous gesture. He could hardly attack Egypt with such a small contingent and without the necessary sea power to reinforce it. But feeble though this move might be, he thought it would impress the men who governed Great Britain, and his judgment of these men so far had been impeccable.

Besides sending more troops to Libya, he intensified the campaign of threats and dire predictions which had already been so effective in frightening the British. On August 26, he had said, "It should be realized without possibility of misunderstanding that whoever applies sanctions against Italy will be met by the armed hostilities of our country." Two days later, he had told the first meeting of what he called his "war cabinet" that while Britain had nothing to fear from Italian policy, "Italy's colonial question with Ethiopia must not be allowed to influence the European situation unless one wishes to run the risk of unleashing another world war." On August 31, addressing a hundred thousand Italian soldiers at Trento, he had announced his intention to call up another two hundred thousand within a month, increasing the strength of his army to one million men. When the League Council met from September 4 to 6, his representatives had passed around a 217-page memorandum entitled "The Situation in Ethiopia," which described with documents all the worst aspects of Ethiopian life that could be even remotely substantiated. The memorandum contained lurid descriptions of poverty, barbarity, and slavery throughout Ethiopia. "It is known that the Abyssinians have a custom of mutilating their wounded or captured enemies," the memorandum said, "and displaying the genitals of the vanquished as victory trophies."

There was enough truth in the Italian charges to upset the League Members but not enough to convince them that Italy therefore deserved an open license to conquer Ethiopia. The delegates could go no further than to grant Mussolini another delay of Council action, this time by appointing a Committee of Five which was instructed to "find a compromise" between Italy and Ethiopia. On September 14, three days after the Hoare speech, Mussolini issued a statement that the Italian government "feels it is its duty to reconfirm in the most explicit manner that the Italian-Ethiopian problem does not admit of compromise solutions after the enormous efforts made and the sacrifices borne by the Italian people and after the irrefutable documentation contained in the Italian Memorandum [about Ethiopian barbarity]." On September 16, he told correspondent John Munro of the London *Morning Post*, "We have an army in East Africa which has cost us two billion lire. Do you really believe that we have spent such an astronomical sum for nothing? We are on the march." Mussolini's continuing stream of bellicose remarks affected British Ambassador Sir Eric Drummond so profoundly that he had reported in a telegram to London before Hoare's Geneva speech, "In their present mood, both Signor Mussolini and the Italian people are capable of committing suicide if this seems the only alternative to climbing down. Rome today is full of rumours of an impending declaration of war on Great Britain." Nine days after Hoare's speech, on the twentieth, when Drummond visited the Palazzo Venezia, Mussolini opened the conversation by saying, "I note, Mr. Ambassador, that the British Fleet has entered the Mediterranean. I note also that now it will be up to us whether it will be able to leave."

By this time it was evident to the world that despite Sir Samuel Hoare's remarkable speech, and despite the stiffening attitude of the British public, Mussolini had no intention of altering his course. He maintained his defiance of Great Britain and the League so steadily that people began to wonder if he knew something they didn't know. In fact, they had good reason to wonder. Mussolini had better methods than the general public of finding out what was really happening in England and France. The French Foreign Office was in the habit of keeping him informed about private discussions between Laval and the British on the subject of Ethiopia. In addition, he still had his agents at the British Embassy in Rome, through whom he was privy to the secret correspondence between London and Ambassador Drummond. This may have explained the reaction of his Undersecretary of State for Foreign Affairs, Fulvio Suvich, when Baron Aloisi called him from Geneva in a panic directly after Hoare's speech.[4] Suvich assured Aloisi that he, and therefore presumably

Mussolini, were not taking a tragic view of what Hoare had said. Perhaps they already knew the outcome of a meeting between Hoare, Eden, and Laval in Paris September 10, the day before the Hoare speech.

At that Paris meeting, which lasted several hours, Sir Samuel, with his strong, threatening Geneva speech in his pocket, had come to an extraordinary accord with Laval, who later explained it to the French Chamber of Deputies. "We were convinced that our first effort at conciliation had failed and that hostilities were going to begin almost immediately," Laval told the Chamber in December 1935. "We found ourselves instantaneously in agreement upon ruling out military sanctions [against Italy], not adopting any measure of naval blockade, never contemplating the closure of the Suez Canal—in a word, ruling out everything that might lead to war."

Sir Samuel Hoare at no time denied the accuracy of Laval's version of their agreement. The unquestioned evidence shows he made a secret acknowledgment September 10 that there was absolutely no truth or meaning in what he intended to say publicly at Geneva the following day. It cannot be said, however, that Hoare was alone in this deceit. Neville Chamberlain and Sir Robert Vansittart had helped him write the speech, and Stanley Baldwin had approved it. They were carrying out, with dismal consistency, the decisions of the British Cabinet at a meeting August 22. The Cabinet that day discussed for five hours every aspect of the Ethiopian crisis, "including public opinion," which was, to some of the ministers, the most vexing aspect of all. The public, unfortunately, had to be served, or at least it had to appear to be served. The Cabinet therefore agreed that because a war with Italy would be "a grave calamity," the British representatives at Geneva should "reaffirm the statements . . . made in Parliament as to our intention to fulfill our treaty obligations," but that they "should avoid any commitment which France was not equally prepared to assume." What this meant was that the British government, to satisfy public opinion, would support the League only as long as the League followed a safe, innocuous course through the crisis. At the same meeting, the Cabinet voted to continue the embargo of arms to Ethiopia. And in mid-September, when Dr. A. C. W. Martin, the Ethiopian Minister in London, tried to organize an English volunteer force to fight against Italy, the Foreign Office subjected the project to so much pressure it had to be abandoned.

The combination of all these British government signals should have been enough to assure Mussolini that England did not intend to thwart him. In case he needed more assurance, he had a September report from his London ambassador, Dino Grandi, that British generals as well as admirals were opposed to war, and that two of Britain's most powerful newspaper publishers, Lord Beaverbrook and Lord Rothermere, were both sympathetic to Italy, "attracted by the idea that, after having conquered Abyssinia, Italy would become a conservative power." Grandi described a conversation in which Beaverbrook indicated to him that, since the war had to come, it would be better if it came soon. The ambassador quoted Beaverbrook as saying to him, "If the Duce could fire the first cannon shot before the meeting of the fourth of November in Geneva, what a relief for everyone."

With all of these indications in his favor, Mussolini soon became convinced that he could wring from England the ultimate assurance. Toward this end, he authorized Fulvio Suvich, on September 18, to approach the British with an offer so one-sided and insulting that they would be dropping all their pretenses if they accepted it. Suvich asked the friendly French Ambassador Charles de Chambrun, on the eighteenth, to inform the British that, if they and the French would promise to forgo military sanctions against Italy, Mussolini would remove his two divisions from Libya. And if the British wanted a true *détente* with Italy, they should remove their fleet from the Mediterranean. The next day, Baron Aloisi gave the same message to Laval in Geneva, and Laval handed it on to Anthony Eden with the added suggestion that England forswear any intention to close the Suez Canal or impose a blockade.

The British reacted with astonishing alacrity to Mussolini's arrogant proposals. On September 20, Sir Eric Drummond in Rome assured Suvich that the reinforcement of the Mediterranean Fleet was a "purely precautionary measure" resulting from the anti-British campaign in the Italian press, and that the presence of the fleet near Italy was "not intended to imply any aggressive intention." Three days later, on September 23, the British capitulation became almost complete with the arrival in Rome of a personal note to Mussolini from Sir Samuel Hoare, who referred to himself as "an old friend of Italy." He had never intended to humiliate Italy, the note said. On the contrary, he wanted to see Italy strong and prosperous. As for the British naval movements, they were not designed to menace Italy, nor had the British government ever even considered military sanctions or the closing of the Suez Canal. While it was true that Britain planned to take part in the collective action of the League, such action would be limited to economic sanctions.

No one was surprised when, on September 26, the League's Committee of Five, appointed three weeks earlier to seek a solution of the Ethiopian crisis, reported its failure to do so. The Committee of Five (Britain, France, Poland, Spain, and Turkey) had suggested an international protectorate to supervise Ethiopia's development. The protectorate would be sponsored by the League but dominated by Italy, which would also, according to the first though not the final version of the plan, take outright possession of the Danakil desert and much of the Ogaden desert. When the plan was prematurely leaked to the press, Mussolini's ambassadors Grandi in London and Aloisi in Geneva, still frightened of England, suggested he accept it. Knowing more about the English government than they did, he flatly rejected it, in a September 18 interview with a London *Daily Mail* correspondent, even before it became official. "The suggestion apparently is," he said, "that all the two hundred thousand Italian troops in East Africa should be brought home and told they have been sent out there for an excursion trip." Though he didn't say so, he would have had to find jobs for all these troops, and for the hundreds of thousands of others in uniform, if he had canceled the war and returned them to civilian life. He would also have been forced suddenly to convert Italy's war-geared economy back to a peacetime economy. The prospect of war was much more pleasing to him. In any case, the plan offered him far less than he intended to take. "The suggestion is apparently made," he said, "that Italy's need for expansion in East Africa should be met by the cession to her of a couple of deserts—one of salt, the other of stone. . . . It looks as if the Committee of the League thinks I am a collector of deserts."

Mussolini having made his feelings so clear, there was nothing for the League Council to do at its September 26 meeting (which Baron Aloisi did not attend) but to form another committee for the purpose of drafting another report. This was the Committee of Thirteen, which undertook to record a chronology of the successive events in the Italian-Ethiopian crisis in accordance with Article 15 of the Covenant, the section governing mediation of disputes. Presumably this committee's report would lead to some League action, at least economic sanctions, in the event of an Italian thrust into Ethiopia. But as Anthony Eden had just learned in a September 24 telegram from Sir Samuel Hoare, the question of whether Great Britain would support even such a mild measure of disapproval was not yet settled. The telegram from Hoare said,

> I trust that you will not allow any haste on the Council in regard to the discussion of sanctions. The feeling of the Government is that, though the efforts of the Committee of Five have proved unavailing and they rightly remitted the matter to the Council, the latter should make a further effort to find a solution, and that it might not yet prove hopeless in view of the somewhat altered atmosphere produced at Rome by the combination of pressure and friendly message.

Even Sir Samuel Hoare must have had some reservations about the altered atmosphere in Rome. On the same day he sent his reassuring telegram to Eden, September 24, he talked to the French ambassador in London, Charles Corbin. Would France guarantee to help England, Sir

146

Samuel asked, if the British Mediterranean Fleet or its bases were attacked by Italy while Great Britain was preparing to take part in League-sponsored sanctions?

Corbin referred the question to Laval in Paris, from whom no answer was immediately forthcoming, perhaps because the British had been so slow to answer his inquiry of September 10 as to whether they would guarantee to help France in the event of an attack by Germany. Hoare's answer, when it did come, to Corbin orally on the twenty-fourth and to Laval in writing on the twenty-sixth, was so evasive as to be meaningless. The policy of the British Foreign Office during his tenure, he said, was to support the League, but he could not vouch for the policy of succeeding governments. And as for helping France against Germany, he pointedly differentiated between armed aggressions and treaty violations. The implication was clear. It was an armed aggression by Italy that worried England, while it was nothing more than the possibility of a treaty violation by Germany that worried France. England could hardly be expected to stand behind France if Hitler did no more than break a treaty. (England, in the naval pact of June 18, had already given official consent to Germany's abrogation of the Versailles Treaty.)

When Laval received this answer to his plea, he decided it would be stupid to promise the *quid* if England was unwilling to promise the *pro quo*. For the present, at least, he put Hoare's plea in his pocket. And as the days passed, the statesmen of each country became increasingly exasperated at the disloyalty of the other.

Emperor Haile Selassie was now preparing his people for the worst. Almost daily he spoke to them on the country's only radio station, at the Akaki airport in the southwestern suburbs of Addis Ababa, where he also kept the eleven planes in his "air force." (These included four French Potez 25s bought in 1927, two Fokker monoplanes, one trimotor German Fokker, one rebuilt English Moth, one French Farman monoplane, one Italian Breda sport plane, and one twelve-passenger American Beachcraft. Only the Fokkers were in good condition. The Potez planes needed overhauls and none had guns mounted.) On September 15, he said in a broadcast to the small audience of Ethiopians who had access to radios "... Italy, who has been supplied with arms and ammunition by powers that have denied them to our country—which has never manufactured war materials and desperately needs them for self-defense—Italy is seeking to discredit our government and our people in the eyes of the world by asserting that we are savages whom it is her duty to civilize. The attitude that Italy has seen fit to assume will be judged by history."

The Emperor knew how little time he had left before the blow was to fall. Heavy rains were still soaking the whole country with as much as an inch and a half of water per day. Addis Ababa had already absorbed forty-five inches during the season, considerably more than the average for previous years. The Mareb River, which marked part of the northern boundary between Ethiopia and Eritrea, and which Italian troops would have to cross when they began their expected invasion, had overflowed its banks and flooded the countryside around Adowa, about twenty miles south of the border. The rains would stop abruptly on the twenty-seventh, however, if the almost invariable annual weather pattern held true to form. The Italians would then have to give the countryside only a few days to dry before beginning their advance.

The war fever in Addis Ababa intensified daily. Secondhand Mauser rifles were selling in the market place for the equivalent of two hundred American dollars—a price which limited purchasers to wealthy Ethiopians and to Europeans, almost all of whom were arming themselves. Europeans were also buying all the canned goods they could find in the European stores and crowds of them besieged the banks for silver dollars, the one currency expected to retain its value when the war began. An American flier who had arrived to volunteer his services to the Emperor went first to the market where he made a quick profit on fifteen gas masks he had brought with him. There was such a demand for tents, by people who planned to take to the hills, that the tentmakers were getting no sleep. Only the mule-and-donkey market was inactive. Ethiopian farmers, following a shrewd, centuries-old tradition, anticipated the approach of war by withholding these precious beasts until prices reached the optimum level.

Though the Emperor even now refrained from issuing a mobilization order (for fear the Italians would claim it as a provocation), he was training as many soldiers and preparing as many defenses as his limited resources and the skills of his commanders would permit. In August, he had sent north to Adowa a former Russian engineering officer named Colonel Theodore Eugenovitch Konovaloff, with instructions to inspect the defenses and offer his advice toward improving them.[5] After a few days as a guest at the castle of Ras Seyoum, the ruling chief and therefore the military commander of the Adowa area, Konovaloff learned, on his first inspection tour, that defensive warfare was a concept totally foreign to the Ethiopians. The trenches they had dug were so shallow, and so many of them were located in the easily visible lowlands, that they were valueless.

At a meeting with Ras Seyoum's military commanders, Konovaloff tried to explain that trenches should be dug not in the valleys but on the mountain slopes which would provide protection. "You can see how many good places there are," he said, pointing up the mountain sides. "Let's go have a look." When they reached the top of the nearest mountain, he pointed to several ideal places on the slopes below where they could build excellent defenses with a minimum of labor. "These are the positions which God himself has created for you," he said. "You can see everything in front of you, yet you remain unseen and under cover."

The commanders were not so easily convinced. "That is true," one of the older chiefs admitted, "but what do we do with those trenches below which we've built with such cost of energy?"

Konovaloff suggested they leave them as they were. "Let the Italians believe our real positions are there."

After the discussion had continued a while, one of the chiefs finally mentioned the most serious Ethiopian objection to these European ideas. "We always fight in the open field," he said. "What sort of a war is this— fighting behind stones?"

On September 23, some four days earlier than expected, Addis Ababa had its first day without rain since May. On the twenty-fifth, the citizens found reason to forget their war fever temporarily. Several of the Emperor's lions escaped from their casually secured cages and thousands of people in the vicinity of the Palace took cover until the beasts had been either caught or killed.

On September 26, the Emperor sent a telegram to the League Council (which was in session to consider the report of the Committee of Five), asking that the League immediately send impartial observers to Ethiopia, now that an attack by Italy was imminent. The Council did not respond.

On the following day, the first day of the feast of Maskal (a religious holiday commemorating the discovery of what was believed to be the True Cross of Christ, and celebrating the end of the rainy season), the Ethiopian army staged its traditional military parade, which this year took on more significance than ever before. It was not, however, an impressive display. After Mass at St. George's Cathedral, the Emperor reviewed the marchers from a pavilion which had been built for him in the square outside. The closely packed multitude in and around the square was so vast it looked like the entire population of Addis Ababa. Thousands of people held up long poles from which dangled yellow Maskal daisies. Warriors had come from all over Ethiopia, wearing the colorful costumes of an earlier era, to prance and posture, fire their guns, swing their swords, and boast of their exploits in front of their monarch.

Many availed themselves of the privilege which was extended during Maskal to give the Emperor the benefit of their advice. One of the chiefs shouted to him that he "should not meddle any more in the affairs of the outside world, but look after his own country." One after another of the common soldiers, following behind their chiefs, demanded rifles. An old man who already had an ancient, useless-looking rifle, shouted, "What

149

can I kill with this bastard of a *tabanja*?" Whereupon he smashed it so hard upon the ground it broke in two.

After the chiefs and their disorderly troops had passed, the more disciplined Imperial Guard marched by in straight columns, some with new Mauser rifles which had been smuggled into the country despite the arms embargo. They were followed by detachments of lance-bearing cavalry and barefooted infantry. Behind them, filling out the parade, were military academy cadets, Boy Scouts, and some liberated slaves. Three Potez biplanes flew slowly overhead. Then came the few mechanized units—radio vans, trucks with mounted machine guns, and Red Cross ambulances. At the rear appeared Ras Mulugeta, the rough old war minister, wearing a coronet and carrying a long, silver-tipped spear. A body of wild-looking horsemen surrounded him. As he arrived at the Imperial reviewing stand, so did a burst of rainfall; the parade came to a sudden end, with the crowds scattering for cover.

Ras Mulugeta, in recent days, had become increasingly difficult for the Emperor to contain. A veteran of the 1896 Battle of Adowa, deeply conservative, addicted to alcohol, committed to the ancient Ethiopian methods of warfare, and scornful of diplomacy, he hated all foreigners with such passion he believed every one of them should be deported. "They are all spies and friends of Italy," he had once said. In mid-September he had become so exasperated at the Emperor's trust in the League of Nations that he had issued, on his own authority as war minister, orders for a general mobilization. When this came to the attention of the Emperor through Everett Colson, the orders were immediately suppressed. Mulugeta was only one of many Ethiopian chiefs pressing the Emperor to mobilize and fight. Until the last days of September, Haile Selassie had firmly resisted. But on the twenty-sixth, he received a telegram from Tecle Hawariate in Geneva informing him for the first time that within the League virtually everyone now agreed war was inevitable. After the failure of the Committee of Five, no new ideas were forthcoming as to how Mussolini's legions might be stayed.

In his reply to this telegram, the Emperor told his Geneva delegation that if they were thoroughly convinced of their dire prediction, he would have no choice but to order finally the general mobilization he had been resisting.

On the twenty-eighth, the second day of Maskal, Tecle Hawariate wired him again to say the entire delegation considered war not only inevitable but imminent.

Haile Selassie decided he could wait no longer. That night, he signed a mobilization decree, but instead of issuing it, he put it in his desk.[6] Then he dispatched a telegram to the League Council. After reasserting his desire for peace and his reliance on the League, he pointed out once more the desperate situation in which the Italian threat had placed his country:

> Earnestly beg Council to take as soon as possible all precautions against Italian aggression since circumstances have become such that we should fail in our duty if we delayed any longer the general mobilization necessary to ensure defense our country. Our contemplated mobilization will not affect our previous orders to keep our troops at a distance from the frontier and we confirm our resolution to cooperate closely with the League of Nations in all circumstances.

Again there was no response from Geneva.

In Asmara, the Eritreans, who shared the heritage of the Ethiopians, were also celebrating Maskal. Presiding over their parade and military review was General Emilio De Bono, the Supreme Commander of Italian forces in East Africa, who was not, at the moment, a very comfortable man. With only a short time left before Mussolini expected him to launch the invasion of Ethiopia, he was beset by a disturbing conviction that he and his army were not yet ready. His growing concern was reflected in a secret diary he was keeping. If anyone had seen them at the time, several of his entries might have raised questions about his fitness to lead even a platoon of infantry:

> *Sept. 14*—This morning I had a nervous crisis on account of the flies, which made my horse too jumpy. I got off and did six kilometers on foot; this way I calmed down, but my nervous system is beginning to get out of tune.
> This morning a telegram from the Duce: Move within the third ten of the next 30 days! We'll do the best we can. It's necessary that I have at least one division in reserve. This isn't a good day for me. Sometimes I even feel a little pain on the right side of my abdomen, and to tell the truth, I'm thinking it might be appendicitis. May God spare me the knife!

> *Sept. 15*—Yesterday a terrible day all in all. Two airplanes burned at Gura, but without victims. Another airplane here at Asmara ground-looped and ran into some wires. An N.C.O. was injured, seems not too badly. Worst of all, a buluk [platoon] of the Fifth Indigenous has deserted, taking five machine guns with them! The things that happen! Indigenous troops in [such] large units, and for a massive war, I don't know if they'll measure up. Certainly I prefer, when all is said and done, the nationals for this operation, and above all, the army units.
> Complete political disorientation. At times I have the sensation that the Duce has jumped into a blind alley. . . . Will we be putting our head on the block? It could cost us very much. Meanwhile, everybody is advising Abyssinia not to provoke in any way. Here will be the Gordian knot: how to make it look as if we're not the aggressors. Perhaps—but no one

can say for sure—Mussolini puts too much faith in the game of the loud voice. . . .

Sept. 17—An entire buluk of the Fifth Indigenous has deserted, taking with them mules, arms and ammunition. A lack of supervision and respect among the askaris. Ah, that indigenous army corps! Enough, let's not get discouraged. . . .

De Bono was quite convinced that his superiors and colleagues in Rome had no understanding of his difficulties, which he considered desperate. After nine months of preparation, the quartermaster corps still lacked necessary equipment. There were enough mules but not enough mule drivers and pack saddles. Water barrels were in short supply and munitions dumps near the frontier had not been filled.

It was ironic that, as an Italian general, De Bono should be worried about the dependability of the African native troops. Some military commanders might have preferred them because their bravery in battle was traditional and unquestionable. But many Italians in Africa at the time entertained quaint and condescending notions about the blacks. Italian writer Indro Montanelli's 1936 description of the askaris illustrates a fairly typical attitude:

> The askari does not like the white man, he likes the officer. On the other hand, no: he likes his own officer. . . . He loves severity and justice, above all, justice. You can't beat him but you must have him beaten. Woe unto him who would allow a certain tenderness to influence him. . . . The punishment is a solemn rite which has an unalterable procedure: the company drawn up, an ordinance whip measured to the milimeter in thickness and in length, buttocks protected only by trousers. A whistle by the officer. Silence. It begins. A slash to the right, one to the left; a slash to the right, one to the left. From the immobile ranks of the others, at strict attention, rises a low, rhythmic chorus of one, two, three. . . . If the whip-master stops before the ordered ration has been meted out, the penitent himself turns and makes a sign that something is lacking.

It was one of the more insensitive conceits of white colonialists, not solely Italians, that subjugated people actually enjoyed such treatment. But it was a conceit which grew naturally out of the concept of colonialism, based as it was on the belief that the nonwhite races were inferior, and must therefore find comfort and security in being governed firmly, like simple children.

The Maskal military parade in Asmara which De Bono reviewed took place September 28 and was even more frenzied than the Addis Ababa celebration.[7] For the entire day the town was subjected to the racket of war whoops, tom-toms, rifle shots, and shouting crowds. Costumed askaris, their cheeks and foreheads crisscrossed with their battalion colors, waved flaming tree limbs above their heads, and the hot embers rained

152

down upon the crowd. Hundreds of these soldiers walked barefoot over a bed of live coals. Others, armed with spears, performed mock battles against imaginary lions

As in Addis Ababa, the brothels were besieged by eager men on their last holiday before battle. In the native quarters, these were often simply family homes, where wives and daughters made themselves available to augment the pitifully small family incomes. For the Italians, prostitution was better organized.[8] One of their houses, a large, well-kept establishment on a side street, had been supplied with twenty to twenty-five girls from Italy, for whom the white officers, enlisted men, and civilian workers gladly waited in block-long lines. The price was five lire for soldiers and twenty-five lire for the richer civilians. As a man entered, he paid a cashier and received a round, plastic disk called a *marchetta*. If he happened along at the right moment, he might have a choice of girls, most of whom were young and fairly attractive, but with so many men in line, it was not often that more than one girl would be disengaged at any time, especially during the feast of Maskal. None of the girls appeared naked in the parlor, but most of them wore diaphanous gowns or veils which advertised them effectively.

During the Maskal parade, several askaris, bedecked with large red feathers, waved a banner which read FOR ITALY—DEATH OR GLORY. De Bono, standing at attention on the reviewing stand with Coptic clergymen and civil dignitaries of the Italian regime behind him, accepted solemnly the obeisance of the native chiefs who stopped to bow before him and boast of their military prowess. Then, after conferring promotions on a group of native officials, he watched a huge symbolic bonfire in the center of the square. To the Eritreans, the direction in which the central pole of the pyre fell, after everything around it had burned away, was a significant omen. De Bono was relieved when the pole fell to the south, pointing the way toward Ethiopia. In his brief speech, which he himself characterized as "warlike in tone and phrasing," he called upon all his troops to "seize the enemies of Italy by the throat."

The following night, September 29, De Bono received from Mussolini the telegram he had been at the same time awaiting and dreading. "No declaration of war at the beginning," the Duce's message instructed. "Regarding the general mobilization which the Negus has already announced in Geneva, it is absolutely necessary to put an end to all delays. I order you to initiate advance in the early hours of the 3rd, I say, the 3rd of October. I await an immediate confirmation."

In Geneva, on the afternoon of the twenty-eighth, when the fourth meeting of the eighty-ninth session of the League Council adjourned, the delegates hurried to their hotels and packed for home. Perhaps they were feeling disappointed with themselves, but it could not be said that they had accomplished nothing during their nine months of negotiating between Italy and Ethiopia. On September 3, the Commission of Conciliation and Arbitration, investigating the clash at Wal Wal which began the crisis, had submitted its decision to the Council. The verdict of the commission was that neither side could be held responsible for the incident.

PART TWO

CHAPTER EIGHT

As the appointed hour of five a.m. approached on October 3, the sun was still hidden by eastern hills and mountains but the light of dawn had begun to reveal the shallow waters of the Mareb River. Three Italian columns, each composed of an army corps, stood poised on the north bank of the river, at twenty-mile intervals, between Meghec on the west and Barachit on the east, ready to advance in compliance with the order issued the previous night by General De Bono. "You have waited until this day with firm discipline and exemplary patience," the order said. "The day has come. His Majesty the King desires and Benito Mussolini, Minister for the Armed Forces, orders that you shall cross the frontier."[1] At five a.m., native cavalry units, which formed the advance guards of each column, nudged their horses into the muddy water, emerged on the other bank, and rode southward into a largely treeless, broken and difficult countryside, looking for the enemy. The invasion of Ethiopia had begun.

The column on the east at Barachit, the First Army Corps under the command of General Ruggiero Santini, included two white divisions and two battalions of native troops. The column in the center at Debbi, the Third Corps under the command of General Alessandro Pirzio Biroli, was composed entirely of native troops in undisclosed numbers. The column on the west, the Second Army Corps under the command of General Pietro Maravigna, included two white divisions and several detachments of native troops. It was this column which moved in the direction of Adowa, twenty miles south. After the cavalry came the Italian light tanks, then the infantry, many of them blond-haired teen-agers from the northern provinces, singing as they marched. Attached to their Panama-style sun helmets and sticking from the barrels of some of their guns were yellow flowers they had plucked from the "roadside." Behind them came the mule trains of the supply corps—mile after mile of heavily burdened animals carrying food, building materials, ammunition, rifles, machine guns, and even cannon barrels. Occasionally the mule trains

157

were able to rest by the side of the muddy "road" while the trucks of the mechanized transport units rumbled past them.

In the skies ahead, Italian planes searched for some sign of the enemy while the cavalry scouts on the ground did likewise. They discovered no troops, just some emaciated, hungry civilians, dressed in white shammas and waving white flags. The Italian quartermaster corps began immediately to feed them and to question them. Where was the Ethiopian army? They hadn't seen it.

General De Bono, at five a.m., drove from his new field headquarters at Coatit, near Debbi, up a nearby hill to an observation post where his staff and selected members of the press were already assembled in the hope of seeing the center column of native troops emerge into the wide plain of Hasamo across the Mareb to the south. After peering without success through the large telescope provided for him, the General turned to glance at a map his aides were studying on a wooden table. The members of the press, kept at a distance, stared at him curiously. He looked much more calm and composed than he felt. When he arrived at his Coatit headquarters only twenty-four hours earlier, he had been so nervous that only with difficulty could he keep his emotions in check. He felt alone in his little metal barracks with its few comforts. There was a shower, at least, and a toilet. He could be grateful for that. But he was still full of resentment against those men in Rome who failed to understand his problems, failed to give him the support he deserved. "They aren't even thinking about making me a General of the Army," he reflected sourly. "I bet in Rome they all think we're happily dancing the Monferrina here."

Rome, on the morning of the third, was in fact sleeping off a compulsory celebration which had been somewhat disappointing to Mussolini.[2] He had decided not to wait for the invasion before proclaiming it. On the previous evening he had staged a carefully planned *adunata*, or rally, a "Fascist Mobilization" throughout Italy. All Fascist Party organizations and their members had been alerted in advance. Restaurants and shops were ordered closed. The whole population of every community was expected to assemble in the public squares; loudspeakers had been installed to broadcast Mussolini's radio voice. The entire day was planned as an unforgettable fiesta.

The focal point of the fiesta was, of course, the little balcony of the Palazzo Venezia, where Mussolini was to make his expected speech. When Mussolini decided the time had come for this speech, he ordered the prearranged signal—the blowing of steam whistles throughout Rome and the provinces. These steam whistles were not what he had wanted. He had planned to announce his *adunata* by having all the church bells in Italy toll at the same time. Unfortunately for him, the Pope decided it would be inappropriate, so he was forced to use whistles, which were, however, equally effective in luring a crowd. By the time Mussolini was ready to appear on his balcony, in the late afternoon of the second, the square below him, and all the streets leading to it, were "packed to suffocation."

After the cheering stopped, after his jutting jaw and puffing chest had satisfied the cameras, the Italian dictator shouted into the microphones:

> Black Shirts of the Revolution! Men and women of all Italy! Italians scattered the world over, beyond the mountains and beyond the seas, listen!
>
> A solemn hour is about to strike in the history of the Fatherland. Twenty million men at this moment fill the public squares of all Italy. Never was there beheld in the history of mankind a more gigantic spectacle. Twenty million men: one heart, one will, one decision. Their demonstration must show and does show the world that Italy and Fascism are one and a perfect, absolute, unalterable whole. . . . For many months the wheels of destiny, under the impulse of our calm determination, move toward the goal: now their movement becomes swifter and can no longer be stayed!
>
> It is not just an army that strains toward its objectives, but an entire people of forty-four million souls, against whom an attempt is made to perform the most hideous of injustices: that of snatching from us a small place in the sun. . . .
>
> I . . . refuse to believe that the real people of Great Britain, who never had dissensions with Italy, are disposed to take the risk of hurling Europe over the road to disaster to defend an African country universally stigmatized as a country without a shadow of civilization.
>
> To economic sanctions we shall oppose our discipline, our sobriety, our spirit of sacrifice.
>
> To military sanctions we shall reply with military measures.
>
> To acts of war we shall reply with acts of war!
>
> Let no one think of subduing us without a hard fight. . . .
>
> Proletariat and Fascist Italy, Italy of Vittorio Veneto and the Revolution, on your feet! Let the shout of your decision fill the heavens and bear solace to the soldiers waiting in Africa, an incitement to friends, a warning to enemies in every part of the world; a cry of justice, a cry of victory!

For eighteen minutes the Duce shouted, screamed, grimaced, and gesticulated. It was one of his more fiery performances. But he must have noticed as he progressed that it was not igniting the audience of three hundred thousand people below him. When he finished, there was no spontaneous burst of applause, no show of uncontrollable enthusiasm.

The great crowd which was supposedly of "one heart, one will, one decision" began drifting away at the end of the speech, ignoring the rest of the four-hour program their leader had prepared for them. The Italian populace, at this critical moment, was not as enthusiastically united behind Mussolini as he pretended. While his pronouncements about the new Italian valor and military prowess may have impressed the British and French, they did not completely convince the peace-loving Italians. These same Italians had allowed Mussolini to gain absolute power over them, however, and whether they liked his war or not, they were about to find themselves in it.

Since the early hours of October 3, five thousand Ethiopian soldiers had been squatting in the great courtyard of Addis Ababa's old gibbi, the Imperial Palace, built by Emperor Menelik, which was still the official seat of government. These men, resting their guns across the backs of their shoulders as their fathers before them had done, were awaiting the confirmation of a rumor which most of them had begun to believe. Their belief was strengthened when five servants emerged from the Palace carrying the great war drum of the Empire, plus the heavy, crooked club with which it was traditionally struck. The drum was a hemisphere with a tightly stretched lion skin as the striking surface. As soon as it had been installed on its base below the throne chamber, silk national flags attached to tall eucalyptus poles were raised on each side of it by men of prodigious strength. The drummer then began a series of deep, powerful single beats. The sound, loud and resonant, could be heard for miles. The people of Addis Ababa, most of whom knew what it had to mean, put down whatever they were doing and hurried up the hill toward the Palace.

In the Palace, Emperor Haile Selassie produced a copy of the mobilization decree he had written September 28 and handed it to his tall, ferocious-looking court chamberlain, Ligaba Tosso, to read to the gathering. The report of the Mareb River crossings by the Italians had now reached the Emperor, but it was not his first invasion report. At one-fifteen p.m. the day before, as a result of a communication from French Somaliland, he had sent to the League of Nations a telegram announcing that Italy's aggression had begun:

> We inform you ... that Italian troops have violated Ethiopian frontier in region south of Mount Moussa Alli Province of Aussa between that mountain and the frontier of Ethiopia and French Somaliland and have established themselves in Ethiopian territory preparing base for extensive attack. Proximity to sea in this region and its easy access through territory

of French Somaliland make it possible for Council either to send observers or to obtain confirmation of this violation of Ethiopian territory through Government of French Somaliland.

Yesterday's Italian move was of small importance, of course, except as a prelude to today's move. It was apparent now that the main thrust of the invasion would come from Eritrea through the difficult mountain country of northern Ethiopia. Many military experts were puzzled by the Italian decision to drive down from the north, when the southern route from Italian Somaliland, through the fairly flat and vulnerable Ogaden desert, seemed to offer an easier approach. Perhaps Mussolini and De Bono had been influenced in their decision by the greater shipping distances to Somaliland ports. Or perhaps they were influenced by their desire to avenge Adowa, which was in the north. Whatever their reasoning, they were destined to have moments when they would regret it.

At a few minutes before eleven a.m. in Addis Ababa, a selection of court dignitaries and military chiefs appeared in the great courtyard of the Imperial Palace and gathered around the drum.[3] The squatting soldiers obeyed an order to rise to their feet, and as they pressed forward the drumbeats stopped.

The drummer cried out, "Listen, listen, open your ears! The symbol of our liberty wishes words to be said to you! Long may he live, and the enemy within our gates may God destroy!"

Silence descended as Court Chamberlain Tosso stood up on a wooden chair which had been provided for him and began to read the Emperor's proclamation. After a preamble detailing Italy's earlier aggression against Ethiopia, the document quickly brought the situation up to date.

"Italy prepares a second time to violate our territory," the Chamberlain read in a strong, raspy voice.

> The hour is grave. Each of you must rise up, take up his arms and speed to the appeal of the country for defense.
> Warmen, gather round your chiefs, obey them with a single heart and thrust back the invader.
> You shall have lands in Eritrea and Somaliland.
> All who ravage the country or steal food from the peasants will be flogged and shot.
> Those who cannot for weakness or infirmity take an active part in this holy struggle must aid us with their prayers.
> The feeling of the whole world is in revulsion at the aggression aimed against us. God will be with us.
> Out into the field. For the Emperor. For the Fatherland.

The crowd of soldiers plus the civilians behind them, uncontained, began pressing up the steps, waving rifles and shouting out their determination. One of them cried, "We had doubts about our Emperor until now, but now we know he is with us."

Soon a murmur ran through the crowd and its surge shifted around the building to the north tower of the Emperor's lodging, where he was standing, on the top platform, calm and dignified, neat and fresh, in court dress. With him was his second son, the Duke of Harar. Behind them were several cabinet ministers. On the ground in front of the tower, in the shade of an oleander tree, stood the Emperor's American adviser, Everett Colson, who had insisted, despite the pressure of many chiefs, that the general mobilization be held off until the invasion began. The crowd waved swords and guns at the balcony and shouted, "Death to the Italians!" and "Long live the Emperor!"

After holding up his hand to silence them, Haile Selassie said,

> I am happy to see you before me with knives, swords and rifles. But it is not I alone who knows, it is the whole world outside that knows our Ethiopian soldiers will die for their freedom.
>
> Soldiers, I give you this advice, so that we gain the victory over the enemy. Be cunning, be savage, face the enemy one by one, two by two, five by five in the fields and mountains.
>
> Do not take white clothes, do not congregate as you've done now. Hide, strike suddenly, fight the nomad war, snipe and kill singly. Today the war has begun, therefore scatter and advance to victory.

In these very words lay the key to a possible victory. The Emperor knew if he could persuade his Ethiopian warriors and chiefs to concentrate on guerrilla warfare against the Italians, they might have at least a slim chance to win. But it was not easy to tell an Ethiopian warrior he should sneak up behind his enemy and attack him from the cover of a rock or bush. To these proud men, a war was a series of battles or one climactic battle. Each battle should properly be fought in a single day, from dawn to dusk, in an open field, with the winner of the last battle being acknowledged by both sides to be the winner of the war.

In Adowa on the morning of the third, Colonel Theodore Konovaloff, the Russian military adviser to Ras Seyoum, was awakened by his servant boy who rushed into his room shouting, "They're coming! They're coming!"[4]

"Who's coming?" he asked.

"The whites! They're already almost here!"

When Konovaloff went out onto his sunny balcony he saw approaching from the north seven airplanes painted snow-white. People in the streets and courtyards below him were running back and forth in confusion.

Women were screaming and gesturing in despair. A few guns had begun to shoot aimlessly in the general direction of the planes.

Soon Konovaloff saw six more planes. After they had circled the city once, all thirteen began bombardment. Loud explosions ripped the little town, which had a peacetime population of about five thousand but was now partially evacuated. Columns of black smoke arose everywhere as the fires began.

The pilot of one of the airplanes above Adowa was Vittorio Mussolini, the oldest son of the Italian dictator.[5] Vittorio and his brother, Bruno, had volunteered to fly in the Italian 14th Bomber Squadron, while their brother-in-law, Count Galeazzo Ciano, who was married to Mussolini's older daughter, Edda, had taken command of the 15th Squadron. Twenty-two-year-old Vittorio, on his first combat mission, had led his flight across the Eritrean border, swooping so low over the Takazze River he could see the crocodiles and hippopotamuses in the water. Within minutes they were above the conglomeration of houses and huts which constituted Adowa. He looked for the bridge which was to be his first checkpoint. Unable to find it, he decided simply to drop his bombs where they would do the most good—into the midst of the town. But he was quite dissatisfied with his work. He later recalled, "I saw with sorrow, as will happen to me every time I miss a target, that I obtained only meager results, perhaps because I expected huge explosions like the ones you see in American films. These little houses of the Abyssinians gave no satisfaction to a bombardier."

By the end of the first day of war, the Italian armies had penetrated deeply into Ethiopia and De Bono's communiqué covering the day seemed to bespeak satisfaction with their accomplishments:

> At 5 A.M. October 3rd, the army divisions, Black Shirt divisions and divisions of Native Troops, in order to repulse the imminent Ethiopian threat, crossed the border between Barachit and Meghec.
>
> After dispersing enemy covering elements which had not retired—as had been announced at Geneva—the Italian columns advanced . . . to a front about 20 kilometers (12 miles) from the border. . . .

If all of this had been true, De Bono would have had good reason for satisfaction. He had fervently hoped, as the invasion began, that his men would immediately encounter Ethiopian forces of some identifiable description, thus giving the lie to the Emperor's claim that he had withdrawn all troops from border areas. De Bono's hope had been so great that he couldn't resist mentioning imaginary encounters with the Ethiopians in his official communiqué. In his secret diary, he could write more honestly:

163

We had the first news at about 7:30 [a.m.], then more about nine o'clock. All good. Landscape unoccupied. Our march regular and fast. Toward Adigrat, part of the population remained and part, on seeing our airplanes, flew toward the south with their animals. The Makalle road appeared deserted.

De Bono added an afterthought in his diary that day.

The Negus has already protested about the aerial bombardment saying that women and children were killed. Do they expect that we'll drop confetti? . . .

In Rome, Mussolini decided that although his war had not been declared it should, in some way, be made official. He directed Fulvio Suvich to send a telegram to the League of Nations justifying the Italian forward move. Suvich, at one-forty p.m. on the third, sent the following message to the League's Secretary-General:

I have the honor to inform you as follows. The warlike and aggressive spirit fomented in Ethiopia among chiefs and tribesmen who have long been insistently demanding war with Italy and have succeeded in imposing it has found its latest and complete expression in the order for general mobilization announced by the Emperor in his telegram of September 28th. That order represents a direct and immediate threat to the Italian troops, with the aggravating circumstance of the creation of a neutral zone [by the withdrawal of Ethiopian forces from border areas]—announced by Addis Ababa with specious explanations—which is in reality no more than a strategic move intended to facilitate the assembly and the aggressive preparations of the Abyssinian troops. The Italian Government has had the honor to furnish in its memorandum submitted on September 4th documentary evidence of the continual and sanguinary aggression to which Italy has been subjected in recent decades. With the order for general mobilization that aggression has assumed larger proportions and a wider scope manifestly involving grave and immediate dangers against which it is essential for elementary reasons of security to take action without delay. Confronted by this situation, the Italian Government has found itself obligated to authorize the High Command in Eritrea to take the necessary measures of defence. SUVICH

It was not the kind of telegram the Italians would have liked to send. The world might find it difficult to understand why they should complain about Ethiopia's mobilization inasmuch as it did not come until nine months after their own. What Mussolini had counted upon to justify his invasion was a series of border clashes between Italian and Ethiopian troops. He could have established some credibility in blaming the Ethiopians for such incidents. There was a ready inclination, especially among Europeans, to blame the natives for any border incidents which might occur in colonial areas. But when Emperor Haile Selassie pulled his troops back from the borders, he had foreclosed all opportunities to stimulate such "useful" clashes. It was not surprising, therefore, that the Suvich telegram to the League should refer to the Ethiopian troop withdrawal as an "aggravating circumstance."

Anthony Eden, apprised of the Italian thrust when he landed at Le Bourget, Paris, on his way from London to Geneva, hurried to the Quai d'Orsay for a meeting with Pierre Laval and Alexis Léger in the evening of October 3.[6] With Eden were his aide, William Strang, and Britain's ambassador to France, Sir George Clerk. They found Laval quite unperturbed by the news from Africa. He had just received reports from his ambassadors to Italy and the Vatican which encouraged him to believe that the time was now propitious for negotiations with Mussolini. He had even gone so far as to work out a basis for these negotiations. The League, he said, should now offer Italy a mandate over those parts of Ethiopia inhabited by non-Amharic peoples. And for the Amharic areas, which would remain nominally under the Emperor, the League should offer aid and supervision in which Italy would participate. Would England join France in sponsoring such a proposal?

Eden, knowing Sir Samuel Hoare's proclivities, could hardly say England would reject Laval's new plan. Only two days earlier in London, Eden had found the Foreign Office preparing a similar plan which would have added the Ethiopian province of Bale, south of Addis Ababa, to the territorial offers already made to Mussolini. Eden, being personally opposed to any further concessions, told Laval he would refer his idea to London, but he also pointed out that at a moment when they had just received news of an Italian invasion, they could hardly put forward proposals which offered Italy more concessions. "We would then be rewarding the aggressor," he said.

To press his opposition further, Eden examined with Laval a tribal map of Ethiopia published by the Italian government. If this map could be considered accurate, Eden pointed out, three-fourths of the entire country might be regarded as non-Amharic, and might thereby be claimed for Italy under Laval's plan. That was more than even Laval had intended to give Mussolini.

Eden, changing the subject as quickly as possible, registered a complaint against anti-British campaigns then current in many of the French newspapers.

"You can't judge France by its press," Laval replied. "For political and other reasons, it is not a true criterion of French opinion."

Eden surmised that the "other reasons" were Italian lire, then being poured into the coffers of some French newspapers.

It was, of course, true, Laval continued, that French opinion was divided on the subject of Italy. Despite this fact, he was prepared to seek a mandate for economic sanctions, and he wondered what form Eden felt these sanctions should take.

Eden, though well aware of the British Cabinet's reluctance about sanctions, answered that his government thought they should be substantial.

The conversation now took a new turn as Léger, who usually sat "silent and sphinx-like," began to discuss the complications which might result if Mussolini were to declare war formally. Would he then be entitled to claim belligerent rights, which would include the right to stop British or French ships carrying cargoes destined for Ethiopia?

Laval reacted to this possibility with such astonishment that it soon became apparent he had never heard of belligerent rights. The image of Mussolini stopping a French ship affronted his pride. "I have put up with much from Signor Mussolini," he exclaimed, "I would never put up with that."

Eden, who doubted that Mussolini would dare claim belligerent rights at a time when he was violating the League Covenant, nevertheless enjoyed Laval's discomfort at the idea. Perhaps now Laval would begin to realize the scope of the problems they faced as a result of the Italian invasion of Ethiopia.

Laval remained, however, only one source of difficulty for Eden. The next day, from Geneva, he reported the new Laval plan to London and found, as he must have expected, that reaction to it there was not altogether unfavorable. Finally, after an exchange of three telegrams, he convinced Hoare that it would not work. The Foreign Secretary then asked if, instead, Laval might be willing to discuss with Mussolini the similar offer which the Foreign Office staff had developed, adding the province of Bale to the already proffered booty.

Eden, horrified though hardly surprised, replied that

> the whole world is watching to see how the League will acquit itself of its duty. To set M. Laval onto this new tack at this moment (and we could hardly do so without our action becoming public) would, I fear, arouse suspicion in many quarters as to the integrity of our policy at Geneva. M. Laval would be only too glad of a hint from us, if he thought something might be gained by separate contact between himself and Signor Mussolini. He will jump at any chance to delay the functioning of the League machinery, and if we give him any excuse to do so, we may have reason to be sorry for it.

If we had someone less zigzag than M. Laval to deal with, and if the suggestion were likely to bridge the gap between the two parties, the foregoing objections would not apply so strongly, but I have little hope that the suggestion could possibly provide material for a settlement. . . .

Hoare, whose methods and attitudes were not dissimilar to Laval's, must have found Eden a most tiresome nuisance at times. The young fellow's assignment in Geneva had made him such a champion of the League that he failed to see all the practical considerations a foreign secretary had to take into account. But since Eden was Minister for League of Nations Affairs, he could not be ignored completely, so Hoare finally dropped his suggestion, at least for the present. He did not, however, alter his desire to accommodate Mussolini, nor was he encouraged to do so by the influential men around him.

Neville Chamberlain, in a conversation with veteran politician Leopold Amery just a few days before the Italian thrust, indicated it was only for domestic political reasons that the government had been bound to try out the League of Nations, in which he himself did not much believe.[7] As for action against Italy, there was no question in Chamberlain's mind of going beyond the mildest economic sanctions. As for the danger that a successful operation by Mussolini would mean open failure of British policy in the eyes of the world, Chamberlain expressed the hope that Mussolini would be embarrassed even by mild economic sanctions since he was already in hopeless financial difficulties. In any case, if things became too serious, Chamberlain believed, the French would be the first to run out, thus giving the English an opportunity to show that they had at least done their best.

Winston Churchill, though hardly an ally of Hoare and Chamberlain, expressed a view at this time which was not at great variance to theirs. In a letter to Austen Chamberlain he wrote,

> I am very unhappy. It would be a terrible deed to smash up Italy, and it will cost us dear. How strange it is that after all these years of begging France to make it up to Italy, we are now forcing her to choose between Italy and ourselves! I do not think we ought to have taken the lead in such a vehement way. . . .

Perhaps Churchill did not yet know how little vehemence the British government had actually shown. Baldwin and his Cabinet were still publicly pretending full support for the League, in an effort to pacify the British people, who were making their anti-Italian feelings embarrassingly clear. The evening before Mussolini's move against Ethiopia, the British Labour Party voted on a resolution which called for Britain and the League of Nations "to use all necessary measures provided by the Covenant in adopting sanctions" against Italy. The vote in favor of the measure was 2,168,000; the vote against was 102,000.

There was one very famous British socialist, however, who did not stand with the Labour Party majority. Playwright George Bernard Shaw, ever and always ready to take a contrary position, said in an interview which appeared in the London *Daily Mirror* on October 8:

> We simply won't go to war and we will never relax our determination to uphold the League; but the League commits us to collective action which simply can't be taken. It won't be taken. All the pacifists have gone stark staring mad. Sanctions mean war, and the British people won't have it.
>
> Mussolini should have been given a free hand from the start—he has taken it anyway—and he should have been told to go ahead. All the responsibility should have then been put on him.
>
> I am sorry for Abyssinia and its troubles, and it is a pity everything couldn't be managed some other way. However, when it comes to upholding a tribal civilization against ours, the tribal civilization must go.

United States President Franklin D. Roosevelt, on the eve of the Italian-Ethiopian War, arrived in San Diego, California, to begin a three-week vacation trip aboard the Navy cruiser, *Houston*. Though he had not timed his vacation to coincide with the opening of hostilities in Africa, Roosevelt had been aware as he left Washington that the Italians were about to move, and there is some reason to believe he preferred to be on the Pacific Ocean, where he would be peacefully inaccessible, when the fighting began. His itinerary included a leisurely cruise to Cocos Island, then back through Panama to Charleston.

On the afternoon of October 2, he reviewed from the deck of the *Houston* in San Diego harbor a flotilla of 130 United States warships, which was said at the time to be the greatest naval force ever assembled for a tactical maneuver.[8] After the naval review, he went ashore and spoke to a crowd of forty-five thousand people assembled in a San Diego stadium. Like any skilled politician, President Roosevelt did not necessarily say what he was actually thinking, and on this occasion he probably expressed the mood of the American people more than his own beliefs. He quickly won a rousing ovation by proving he had not forgotten the isolationist advice of George Washington, who had strongly cautioned his successors to avoid "foreign entanglements." Speaking directly about the Ethiopian crisis, Roosevelt said, "In the face of this apprehension, the American people can have but one concern and speak but one sentiment. Despite what happens in continents overseas, the United States of America shall and must remain, as, long ago, the Fathers of our country prayed that it might remain, unentangled and free."

Having thus assured America's isolationist majority that he was as

168

parochial as they were, and that he, too, was determined to put a picket fence around the United States, he sailed out of San Diego harbor on the *Houston* at sunset, confident that the truly committed, missionary isolationists like Senators William Borah of Idaho and Gerald Nye of North Dakota would find no excuse to attack him for at least the three weeks he was at sea. Before leaving Washington, he had read and approved a neutrality proclamation the State Department was to issue in his name the moment Mussolini began hostilities. The Neutrality Act made it mandatory that he prohibit the sale of "arms, ammunition and implements of war" to all belligerents as soon as he determined that a state of war existed between them. To put the law in force, Secretary of State Cordell Hull had only to release the presigned proclamation.

As it happened, the Italian attack against Ethiopia at five a.m. October 3 in East Africa began just a few minutes before President Roosevelt's cruiser left. (When it is five a.m. in Ethiopia, it is six p.m. the previous day in California.) Roosevelt was getting out of sight just in time to avoid a lot of embarrassing pleas and troublesome pressures he was not prepared to cope with. It wasn't that he lacked interest in the situation. His loathing for Mussolini and sympathy for Ethiopia were well known among his associates.[9] Given a free choice, or a bit more courage, he might have been prepared to take some effective actions against Italy. It was for him to decide, for instance, what goods were to be classified as "implements of war" and therefore withheld from the belligerents. In the case of several commodities—like oil, which Italy needed but which Ethiopia could not use because she lacked vehicles—the Presidential embargo decision would be critical, especially if that decision came quickly. When news of the fighting reached the *Houston* by radio, however, President Roosevelt did not think in terms of action against the nation he knew to be the aggressor. His first thoughts were of the political importance he attached to his neutrality proclamation. He immediately sent a telegram to Hull instructing him to issue the proclamation as soon as he had official confirmation of the Italian invasion, including battles and casualties well within the Ethiopian border. Because Mussolini had carefully avoided a formal declaration of war, it was up to the President, under the terms of the Neutrality Act, to decide whether a state of war actually did exist. Roosevelt wanted Hull to know that, in his view, if the Italians had actually invaded, then a state of war did exist. In the same telegram, he also suggested the possibility of publicizing the names of American citizens sailing on Italian ships, and the cargo manifests of all vessels carrying goods to either belligerent. Needless to say, there were no Ethiopian ships on which Americans might sail, but Roosevelt's suggestion was not aimed at Italy. It was intended to discourage American citizens or firms from getting involved on either side.

Cordell Hull, who was even more cautious than Roosevelt, decided when he received the first telegram from the *Houston* that he should canvas the opinions of his staff and several ambassadors before issuing the proclamation.[10] It was obvious even to him that "full-scale war had broken out," but should he release the proclamation immediately, thereby recognizing that the state of war did indeed exist, or should he wait until the League of Nations took action? Hull had developed a knack of saving himself from action by waiting for the League to precede him.

On the *Houston*, President Roosevelt was now reading the news dispatches hour by hour as they came over the wire. Each time he saw an item favorable to Ethiopia he would turn to his nearest associate and exclaim, "Good!" But one thing he kept expecting to see on the wire, the release of his neutrality proclamation, did not appear. Unlike Hull, he understood why the United States should act before the League got around to doing something. If the United States waited and then acquiesced in the League action, the isolationist spokesmen in Congress would accuse him of taking his orders from Geneva.

Harry Hopkins, his special assistant, and Harold L. Ickes, secretary of the interior, both of whom were with him, strongly advised that he return to Washington and take charge. He was not ready to go that far. He was quite happy to be away from Washington at the moment. But he did acknowledge their concern by issuing a statement from the ship to the effect that he was "receiving almost hourly bulletins from Washington covering the foreign situation," and that "the complete freedom from a constant stream of callers and telephone messages" allowed him to "give quiet consideration to the nation's foreign and domestic policies."

He also fired off more telegrams to Hull, who continued his ruminations over the matter. It seemed to Hull that the proclamation should be delayed at least until Monday. It seemed to him also that if the United States government were to publish cargo manifests and passenger lists of Italian ships, Italy might consider it a "gratuitous affront in the nature of sanctions."

Finally, Roosevelt lost patience. On Saturday, October 5, he wired Hull: "They are dropping bombs on Ethiopia and that is war. Why wait for Mussolini to say so?" In case Hull might still fail to grasp his meaning, he sent another telegram ten minutes later which said, "It is my judgment that proclamation issue immediately in view of undoubted state of war and without waiting League action."

Even now Hull procrastinated for several hours, but finally, at ten-twenty-three p.m. on the fifth, he released the proclamation, and the United States became the first nation in the world officially to wash its hands of the Italian aggression.

In Geneva, Anthony Eden had gone to work immediately, and with firm resolution. Before the League Council met at five p.m. on the afternoon of October 5, he had already assured his colleagues that Great Britain was now prepared to take some action. While they may have had their suspicions about England's true intentions, most of them were ready to follow whatever lead the British were willing to assume. By the time the Council convened, therefore, another new committee of the League had already been formed—the Committee of Six (Great Britain, Chile, Denmark, France, Portugal, and Rumania) which was to study the Ethiopia situation "and report to the Council not later than Monday afternoon [October 7]."

At this October 5 session, Baron Aloisi, referring to the Italian memorandum of September 4 accusing Ethiopia of widespread barbarism, declared that

> had the League Council given [it] all the attention it deserved, had it made a thorough study of all the factors involved, it would have realized that the situation in Ethiopia was such that there could be no illusion as to the possibility of modifying it by any proposals which failed to take account of the evil itself. . . .
>
> By neglecting to make a detailed and thorough inquiry into this situation, and by causing the discussion to be diverted to theoretical arguments, the facts have been forgotten, and involuntarily the position has arisen where Ethiopia has been enabled to come before the League in the guise of victim, as if the measures which Italy found it necessary to adopt in order to put her colonies in a state of defense had been determined solely by a situation that had arisen suddenly. . . .
>
> So long as the various factors that have led Ethiopia to take up an aggressive attitude toward Italy are not removed, and so long as she is still encouraged by the distortion of the facts relating to the Italo-Ethiopian dispute, no equitable solution can be found for the dispute between Italy and Ethiopia.

Tecle Hawariate, answering for Ethiopia, reviewed the events of the previous ten months, then concluded:

> Despite this threat, the Ethiopian government delayed the general mobilization of its forces until the last moment. Before issuing the final order, the Ethiopian government asked the Council to take the precautionary measures which would dispense it from calling up the whole people to defend the threatened territory. Only when the Italian aggression took place was the mobilization order published with the traditional ceremonies necessary for its execution.
>
> It is therefore without any justification and without being able to invoke any reasonable pretext that the Italian government, applying a program decided upon long in advance, sent its troops across the Ethiopian frontiers,

bombarded defenseless towns and inhabited areas, and massacred an innocent population.

The Ethiopian government respectfully but firmly asks the Council to declare: (1) That these indisputable facts constitute resort to war by Italy within the meaning of Article 16 of the Covenant; (2) That this resort to war has, *ipso facto*, brought about the consequences laid down in Article 16, paragraph 1.

The article Tecle Hawariate thus invoked stated that "should any Member of the League resort to war in disregard of its covenants . . . it shall *ipso facto* be deemed to have committed an act of war against all other Members of the League. . . ."

When Tecle Hawariate finished, Eden arose to say, "Since [the Committee of Six] has much work to do and little time to do it in, I presume it is intended that it should meet almost at once tonight."

There wasn't actually that much work to do. The Italians had already furnished adequate proof of their aggression in their first communiqués from the field and their public pronouncements. General De Bono's proclamation to the people of Eritrea on the eve of war was especially convincing: "In order that your lands may not suffer from war," he had told them, "and in order to bring aid to the numerous peoples of Tigre and other districts which ask for our intervention, I have given orders for the troops to cross the Mareb."

When the Council met on the afternoon of the seventh, its members were in no mood to accept a demand which Baron Aloisi presented to them for a procedural delay. Neither were they impressed by his rather long speech repeating Italy's justifications for war. A short statement by Tecle Hawariate—which he should have made several months earlier— was more compelling. "It is strange," Hawariate said, "that the Italian government has not dared to proclaim before the Council the reasons which it has many times stated at Rome to justify its inflexible determination to annex Ethiopia—namely, its desire to form a great colonial empire, to conquer territory for its surplus population and to impose the superiority of the white race over the colored peoples by force of arms, as well as the necessity to enhance the prestige of the regime by a military victory."

When the Council vote came, after the speeches, only Italy rejected the Committee of Six report, which concluded ". . . that the Italian government has resorted to war in disregard of its covenants under Article 12 of the Covenant of the League of Nations."

The ratification of the Council action by the League Assembly was needed now to brand Italy the official aggressor and make her subject to whatever action the League chose to take. That ratification came October 11 when, with fifty-four Member nations present, the Assembly voted fifty-to-four in condemnation of Italy. The three negative votes in addition to Italy's came from Austria, Hungary, and Albania, one of which nations, Austria, Mussolini would be meekly handing over to Hitler within two years, and another, Albania, he would eventually swallow himself, though with some difficulty.

Emperor Haile Selassie, though he had only an estimated thirty thousand troops in the northern provinces to face the three Italian armies when the war began, was not without a plan for defeating the invaders. He had withdrawn all his forces from the Eritrean border, partly to show the world his peaceful desires, but also to avoid a confrontation with the Italians in an area so close to their source of supplies. It was his intention to draw them into the difficult mountain terrain of northern Ethiopia and make them extend their supply lines before engaging them in battle.[11] His northern forces, under the command of Ras Seyoum in the Adowa sector and Dejasmatch Haile Selassie Gugsa in the Makalle sector to the east, had been instructed to give ground during the early days of the fighting while the bulk of the Ethiopian army completed mobilization and marched to their aid. (Gugsa was the widower of the Emperor's daughter, who died the previous year. He might present a problem. One of the Emperor's confidants had told him Gugsa was taking money from the Italians, but the Emperor had refused to replace him. "Most of my rases take money from the Italians," the Emperor was reported to have said. "It is bribery without corruption. They pocket Italian money and remain steadfast to Ethiopia.") When the Italians penetrated more deeply into Ethiopia, the Emperor hoped to increase guerrilla activity against them, as he had instructed his troops at the Imperial Palace on the first day of the war. He hoped also that a detachment of his troops under Ras Imru of Gojjam, a cousin of the Emperor's, would be able to cross the Takazze River in the northwestern sector and slip behind the Italian lines to wreak havoc in Eritrea.

His plan had some merit. Ethiopian troops, unencumbered by mechanized equipment, could move with astonishing speed on foot through roadless country. While they lacked guns, they were ferocious in hand-to-hand combat with swords and spears. By attacking suddenly, at night whenever possible, they might be able to swarm into the Italian lines, forcing close-quarter battles in which rifles would be no more useful than swords. The principal uncertainty about his plan was whether or not he could convince his commanders that they should adopt it. The traditional Ethiopian concept of a great battle in an open field was stubbornly implanted in the imaginations of most of his chiefs. In 1896, their fathers and grandfathers had defeated the Italians in a single, decisive battle. Why shouldn't they be able to do likewise? Among those who thought they could was the old war minister, Ras Mulugeta, himself a hero of that earlier war.

The possible success of the Emperor's military strategy did not, however, depend entirely upon the willingness of his chiefs to implement it. There was also the problem of finance. He could hope for military victory only if his strategy succeeded in prolonging the war. But the longer it lasted, the more difficult his financial problems would become, especially since he had no prospect of aid from other countries. He had in his treasury only a pitiful sum of gold which had been panned in one of the southeast provinces.[12] Ethiopia's gold-mining operations were meager. The Emperor's principal foreign credit had come from sizable personal accounts his father had established in London banks, but most of this money had already been used to pay for the small consignments of armaments he had been able to acquire in Europe. Though his domestic tax levies were a continuing source of revenue, they would not yield enough to meet the costs of a long war, especially since they would be cut off in parts of the country occupied by the Italian armies. Under these circumstances, the possibility of a prolonged military campaign employing guerrilla tactics, however successful, was almost as worrisome to Haile Selassie as the possibility of military defeat. Disaster was almost inevitable. Yet he continued to call upon his people to enlist, and the streets of Addis Ababa filled up with soldiers from the surrounding southern provinces, assembling for the long march north. On the fifth, he received a telegram from Ras Seyoum, encamped in the mountains someplace south of Adowa. "Casualties heavy near Adigrat," it said. "One Italian and three Eritrean officers killed. Three machine guns captured. My troops are behaving excellently." It might sound encouraging, but the real fighting had not yet begun.

At daybreak on the fourth, the three Italian columns had resumed their southward advance without opposition. Later in the day, General Maravigna's column, approaching Adowa, encountered a few Ethiopian troops on a hill to the west of the town but were able to brush them aside. General Biroli's center column, composed mostly of native troops, moved quickly toward Entiscio, and General Santini's eastern column, on the road to Adigrat, encountered no enemy action until the advance guards reached the outskirts of that town, where they were stopped short by skirmishes which still prevented them, at dusk, from taking their objective.

Adigrat, about fifteen miles within the Ethiopian border, fell to the Italians the next day, after the people who had not evacuated the town raised a white surrender flag to save themselves from continuing bombardment by Italian airplanes. But Maravigna's troops had not yet reached Adowa, and De Bono was becoming impatient. "Nothing is known," he confided to his diary the night of the fifth, "as to whether Maravigna has arrived in Adowa. I don't think so, but he'll certainly be there tomorrow." Despite his slight irritation at the delay, De Bono found reason to be happy. His Duce had telephoned him that evening and said, "*Ciao*, old man. I thank you. The whole nation is enthusiastic about you." Mussolini also imparted another important item of information. The British, he told De Bono, seemed to be easing their pressure against Italy, but this did not surprise him. He reminded De Bono that he had figured them correctly.

Maravigna did reach Adowa on the sixth, and the honor of taking the undefended town, so bitterly remembered by the Italians, was awarded to one of the white divisions, the Gavinana. As De Bono observed, "Adowa, it goes without saying, had to be reconquered by Italian troops."

The reconquering had been done in true Italian style. Assured by black patrols that Adowa was completely clear of Ethiopian troops, the 84th Regiment of the 2nd Battalion of the Gavinana Division had been accompanied and serenaded by its own marching band as it paraded up the deeply rutted main street of the town. There was, indeed, no enemy in sight, Ras Seyoum and his forces having evacuated to the mountains before the invasion began. Those civilians who remained through the three days of bombing now stood with heads bowed in submission as the Italian conquerors marched past.

At the Coptic church near Ras Seyoum's ramshackle "palace," the priests were out, waiting in ceremonial robes to show the conquerors how cooperative they would be. The Italian commander, after bending from his horse to kiss a Coptic cross, said a few words through an interpreter. "Your religion will be respected," he assured the priests. "There will be no more bombing. All who have fled should return. Italy will not violate their property."

Adowa had been revenged, but De Bono was not altogether happy. As he admitted, "We had not had the good fortune to meet the enemy in force." The reasons for this, he acknowledged, were that "the Negus was persisting in his plan of initial retirement," and "the size of our forces, the means at our disposal and our determination had undoubtedly impressed the enemy, who was not yet fully assembled and prepared."

These were rather unguarded admissions for De Bono to make after his claim, in his first communiqué of the war, that the Ethiopian troops had not withdrawn from border regions as the Emperor had stipulated; and after the Italian government's claim that it was Ethiopian aggression which had made the war necessary. The night of Adowa's recapture he received a rewarding telegram from Mussolini:

Announcement reconquest of Adowa fills the souls of Italians with pride. To you and all the troops my highest praise and the gratitude of the nation.

After this message, De Bono's spirits rose. His armies were moving well and his Duce was firmly behind him. Or so it seemed. He might not have been so convinced of it if he had known about a meeting Mussolini had had in his Sala Mappamondo office with Undersecretary of the Colonies Alessandro Lessona.

"I want you to be ready at any time to leave for Eritrea," Mussolini instructed Lessona. "And I want Marshal Badoglio to go with you. It won't please General De Bono, and for that reason you will watch over matters on the spot to prevent any problems. But as the operations continue, it's possible some complications may arise, and I want to have Marshal Badoglio ready for any eventuality."[13]

Neither Lessona nor Badoglio was among De Bono's favorite people. Lessona and De Bono had both developed important financial interests for themselves in Eritrea as a result of their associations there and often complained to Mussolini about each other's corrupt practices. And De Bono felt a special distaste for Army Chief of Staff Badoglio due to the latter's strong reservations about the plans and prospects for the Ethiopian campaign. De Bono was, therefore, properly affronted on the seventh, when he received the following telegram from Mussolini:

> I have decided to send to Eritrea Marshal Badoglio and Undersecretary Lessona to examine together with you on the spot the situation which would result in case of a conflict with a European power, and what Eritrea could do in harmony with other sectors. At the end of the mission Marshal Badoglio will return to report.

De Bono was neither convinced nor comforted by Mussolini's explanation of the mission. He answered by return wire, protesting Badoglio's visit in heated and surprisingly blunt language:

> ... I find it strange that with the possibility of war in other sectors the chief of staff should absent himself from his office for a good number of days. Badoglio, seeing that all of his premature and malignant criticisms were gutted by the facts, probably wanted to raise doubts or something like that about my possibilities and capacities. I tell you now with my usual frankness that if he comes here to stick his nose into what I've done or intend to do, I shall drop everything and leave. Everything has a limit and at a certain point even the sense of discipline becomes supine nonsense. On this I want your frank word. You are the boss and you can do what you please, but I warn you that I'm not in the least disposed to renounce my self-respect and dignity.

Mussolini tried to reassure De Bono in a return wire the same day, October 8:

I beg you not to dramatize. Marshal Badoglio is the chief of the general staff and I have assigned him just what I telegraphed you. No one can take away from you the merit of having captured Adowa; this will go down in history. Badoglio did not offer any criticisms and he is not coming to make any criticism of you. Be absolutely tranquil and Lessona will tell you clearly the rest. . . .

De Bono was not reassured. There was no way to make him happy about a visit from a man he considered an archenemy, and who was probably ambitious to steal his job, now that the Ethiopian campaign looked so pregnant with military honors. "That sickening Badoglio," De Bono wrote in his diary the night of the eighth,

> had to stick his nose in. He's coming with Lessona, with the excuse of seeing what can be done in case of a war in other sectors. I don't believe it. It's the desire to stick his nose in things here. . . I'm sick of it and I'll see it ended. Even Mussolini is a blackbird pulled around by the nose in certain matters by whoever wishes.

At the moment, De Bono seemed to be on better terms with some of the Ethiopian chiefs than with his own.[14] Among those who had accepted money from him was Ras Seyoum, the governor of western Tigre, and perhaps the most powerful ruler in the north. Though Seyoum had declared his loyalty to the Emperor early in the year, he had, at the same time, exchanged friendly greetings with De Bono, and had accepted "a present" De Bono gave him. It appeared now that Seyoum was committing himself to the Emperor, but De Bono, who considered the ras to be weak and indecisive, had not yet abandoned the hope that he might convert to the Italian cause.

De Bono's relationship with Seyoum's colleague and rival, Dejasmatch Haile Selassie Gugsa, the governor of eastern Tigre, had been even more cordial, and now seemed likely to be quite fruitful. Gugsa, in exchange for a gift rumored to be one million lire, had secretly renounced his loyalty to the Emperor (who was no longer his father-in-law since Gugsa's wife had died) and had assured De Bono that his forces would fight on the side of the Italians.[15] The Emperor had given his thirteen-year-old daughter in marriage to Gugsa in 1932 as part of a complicated political arrangement which included the marriage of Ras Seyoum's daughter to the oldest of the Emperor's three sons, Crown Prince Asfou Wossen. It was at this time that the Emperor settled the dangerous rivalry between the two northern leaders by acknowledging Seyoum as governor of western Tigre and Gugsa as governor of eastern Tigre. This settlement did not create any personal friendship between Gugsa and Seyoum or Gugsa and the Emperor, who considered the young man boorish, dissipated, and ignorant. Gugsa was the illegitimate son of Ras Gugsa Araia, for many years the governor of the entire province of Tigrai, who seemed also to lack admiration for the young man. It was not until the old ras was near death, in 1932, and had abandoned hope of having another son, that he officially acknowledged himself the father of Haile Selassie Gugsa. When the Emperor, exercising his traditional option, settled upon Gugsa only half of his father's fief, the young man quickly increased his association with the Italians, who were already, in 1932, politically active throughout Ethiopia. He often visited Eritrea, where he was welcomed and entertained much more sumptuously than in Addis Ababa. When his wife died at the age of fifteen, some of his detractors said it was his mistreatment that had killed her; others said she had died of pneumonia because their palace in Makalle had no glass in the windows. The Emperor wept publicly at her funeral. Afterward, his relationship with Gugsa continued to be correct if not friendly. His refusal to believe the rumors of Gugsa's treason, even in the last days before the war, was a mistake the cost of which he later acknowledged. Gugsa's defection, the Emperor said in retrospect, "lowered the morale of our people" and "produced an adverse effect on the military situation." Some of his military men told him that the loss of Gugsa gave the Italians a two-month advantage over the Ethiopians. An examination of Gugsa's conduct, and his usefulness to the Italians, may raise doubts about this assessment.

During the latter days of September, Gugsa had asked De Bono for specific instructions as to how he should operate when the invasion began. He was becoming nervous about the possibility that Ras Seyoum or the Emperor himself might learn of his defection and move against him before the Italians crossed the border. Though Gugsa claimed an army of several thousand men, neither he nor De Bono was certain that all of them would follow him when they discovered where he was leading them. De Bono had told him, through the Italian consul at Adowa, that he should prepare his army to operate against the flank and rear of whatever forces the Ethiopians sent to meet the invading Italians. After these forces had been beaten, Gugsa and his men would then join the Italians in the move southward. But if, as Gugsa feared, his intentions were discovered before the invasion, he could march his army immediately to a prearranged place on the Eritrean border, where De Bono would meet him in person.

Thanks to the fact that the Emperor had refused to listen to rumors about Gugsa's defection, he had not been molested by his fellow Ethiopians before the invasion, and now, five days later, he was already in contact with General Santini, the commander of the eastern Italian column. Gugsa's confidence in his new role had increased so much by this time that he wanted to attack his own capital, Makalle, which he had previously abandoned, and which he said was now occupied by seven thousand Ethiopian troops under the command of the Emperor's personal

Drumming up enthusiasm for the Ethiopian
war: Mussolini harangues the Roman populace from
the balcony of the Palazzo Venezia

Keystone

Ramsay MacDonald

Keystone

Stanley Baldwin

Keystone

Neville Chamberlain (*right*) with Sir Samuel Hoare

Mr Anthony Eden (*right*) with Sir Robert Vansittart, 1936

Close of the Stresa Conference, 1935: (*left to right*) Laval, Mussolini, Ramsay MacDonald, Pierre Flandin

UPI

The Hoare-Laval Peace Plan: the meeting in Paris, December 8th, 1935, between (*left to right*) Seated: Pierre Laval, Sir Samuel Hoare and Sir Robert Vansittart. Standing: MM. Rochet, René Massigli and Alexis Léger, of the Quai d'Orsay, and Sir George Clerk (British Ambassador)

Mansell

Marshal Badoglio

Keystone

Marshal Graziani

Haile Selassie
planning his campaign
to resist the Italian
invasion, 1935

Keystone

With his personal
bodyguard, the Emperor
Haile Selassie, 1935

Keyston

Ethiopian soldiers guard the royal palace at Addis Ababa

Keystone

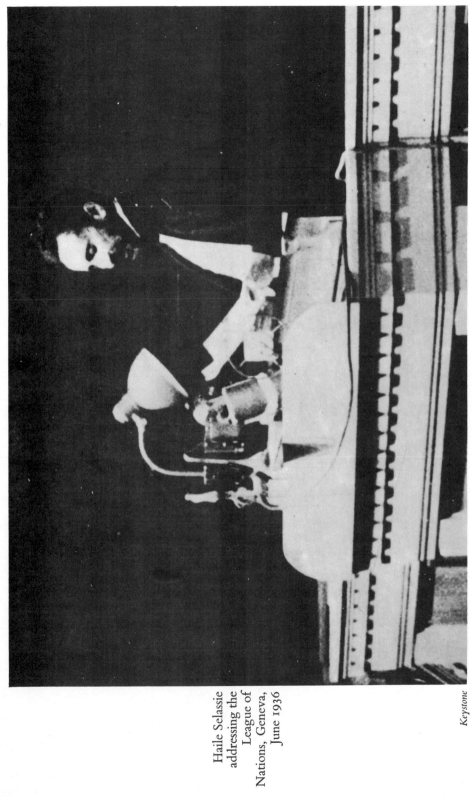

Haile Selassie
addressing the
League of
Nations, Geneva,
June 1936

Keystone

representative in the north, Dejasmatch Wodaju Ali. But Gugsa's confidence had not increased so much that he wanted to attack Makalle with only his own forces. He requested Italian support.

De Bono, before committing himself, sent a reconnaissance plane to examine the situation at Makalle, which was about seventy miles south of the Eritrean border. The reconnaissance pilot, after flying over the town at building-top level, reported that it was virtually evacuated. De Bono decided, nevertheless, against a drive to take it, although "I should not have had much difficulty in sending a detachment of natives to occupy Makalle," he later admitted.

> In all probability this little operation would have been successful, but it would have been difficult to keep troops replenished and impossible to hold the position. ... We can imagine what the foreigners, who were daily fabricating news of an Italian defeat, would have invented if we had had a real setback, however quickly repaired. I was never able to forget (and no calm and qualified judge should forget) the restrictions imposed upon me by logistic necessities.

This concern of De Bono's that he might be trapped by a nonexistent enemy army was the first indication of an embarrassing timidity which would soon give him more trouble in Rome than he was encountering in Ethiopia.

Having rejected Gugsa's offer to move on Makalle, De Bono had no choice but to accept a notice from Gugsa, received the morning of the tenth, that he intended to march his army north and pass through the Italian lines. After turning down Gugsa's offer to fight his way into his own capital, De Bono could hardly prevent him from joining the Italian column, though it was possible that such a move would spoil a carefully conceived Italian plan. De Bono had hoped that Gugsa would maintain his pose of loyalty to the Emperor until such time as the Italians came face to face with the combined forces of Gugsa and Seyoum. If Gugsa were to defect on cue during the ensuing battle, the Italians would then be able virtually to stand by while the Ethiopians destroyed each other, thus eliminating what was still the Emperor's only sizable army in the north.

De Bono did not yet know, though he would soon learn, that Gugsa was marching north to meet the Italians because he had no choice. When he requested Italian help in recapturing Makalle, he was actually either in or very near Makalle and was well aware that the "seven thousand troops" under Wodaju Ali who were supposedly occupying the town did not, in fact, exist. Wodaju Ali, the Emperor's representative, was himself at that time in Addis Ababa, trying in vain to convince the Emperor of Gugsa's intended defection. But on the ninth, Wodaju Ali returned to

Makalle in one of the Emperor's airplanes and quickly sent his own men to inform Gugsa's troops of their leader's treason. Gugsa, who boasted that he had twenty thousand men in his army, and probably did have at least ten thousand, decided to get out of town and join the Italians before he found himself with no army at all.

The afternoon of the ninth, he began gathering his men for the march northward. His orders to them were literally accurate: they would be marching north to meet the invader. Before leaving town, he had the foresight to cut the telephone line which was Ras Seyoum's only direct contact with the Emperor in Addis Ababa. He could not, however, devise a way to prevent Wodaju Ali's men from mingling with his own and spreading their insidious news about him. Throughout the night, even after the march began, Ali's men kept infiltrating Gugsa's undisciplined units, pleading with his troops to desert him. When De Bono's reconnaissance planes flew over the route north from Makalle the next day, the tenth, they saw "a long column, marching in good order, and followed by a fair number of animals," moving toward Adigrat. But Italian pilots flying over the same route a day later were astonished and bewildered to see, in addition to the now-dwindling main column of Ethiopians marching north, several other groups marching away from them to the south, east, and west.

The afternoon of the eleventh, Haile Selassie Gugsa, wearing a tailored European uniform, and followed by twelve hundred men with eight machine guns, met the Italian eastern column at Adigrat. By order of General De Bono, his troops were immediately withdrawn to a location well behind the Italian lines, where General Santini could keep them under surveillance. The Italian communiqué for the eleventh said Gugsa had

> presented himself at our outposts and placed himself and his warriors, numbering several thousand, at the orders of General Santini. Soon after, the Dejasmatch Kassa Araia [a minor Ethiopian chief] with his warriors also passed over to our side. These events are of great importance because they definitely show that Abyssinians of the outlying regions are not willing to fight against the Italians. . . .

Gugsa and some of his retainers drove in two cars from Adigrat the next morning, over a new Italian dirt road which he thought remarkably good, to De Bono's encampment on a high, irregular plateau at Coatit. As Gugsa's automobiles came up the dusty trail leading to the encampment, the old, white-goateed Italian Supreme Commander awaited him at stiff attention in front of the cluster of tents and huts, some wooden, some metal, which formed his headquarters. Farther up the slope beyond these buildings were the round tukuls, now vacated, of a native regiment.

On a steeper slope across a slight divide was the small village of Coatit, with brown, stone, flat-roofed tukuls. Scattered about the headquarters plateau were other huts and tents, some of which housed visiting newsmen. A few automobiles and motorcycles were parked here and there. The place did not look big enough, busy enough, or impressive enough to be the center from which a war was being directed.

As soon as Gugsa's car came to a stop, before the dust it raised had even begun to settle, he alighted and walked toward De Bono. Gugsa was a tall, smiling man, broad-shouldered, but too plump and soft of flesh to appear physically strong. He was wearing his khaki European uniform with large gold shoulder boards and leather boots. His revolver was at his hip. Stopping sharply in front of De Bono, he came to attention and gave an elaborate Fascist salute. After the initial greetings, the two men entered the headquarters hut for a private conversation, while Gugsa's retainers and a few newsmen waited outside.[16]

Gugsa opened the conversation by protesting his devotion to De Bono, who studied him closely, then concluded that he was a "nice" man. No one in Ethiopia, not even Haile Selassie, wanted to make war, Gugsa said, but British agents had talked the Emperor into doing so by assuring him that the Italians would be unable to see the campaign through to the finish. It was important, he said, that De Bono send him and his men back to Makalle immediately, with Italian units to support them. He promised that the Italians would be completely safe there. De Bono, though not convinced, made a tentative promise to send him back with one Eritrean battalion and one battery of artillery, but not until it was possible to travel the route by road.

De Bono then asked Gugsa what he thought of the Italian units he had seen, and Gugsa said he was impressed by their "great strength." He was worried, though, about the maintenance of his own men. De Bono assured him his men would receive the best of care and that he himself would receive "a generous emolument" for his important services.

De Bono then came to a question which was vexing him. "But have you complete trust in your men?" he asked, watching carefully for Gugsa's reaction. Though De Bono believed it was "difficult to read a black man's face," he got the distinct impression that Gugsa "entertained some doubts" about even the small contingent of troops that had stuck with him on the march from Makalle. De Bono was quick to note that Gugsa did not answer his question in the affirmative.

"It will be all right, as I tell you," Gugsa said, nodding his head. "Go to Makalle, as soon as possible."

After lunch, the two men emerged from the hut and De Bono generously introduced Gugsa to an American Associated Press correspondent who had been waiting since the Ethiopian's arrival.[17] Gugsa told the

American he had an army of fifteen thousand men at his disposal, including eight thousand who were still at Makalle but would be arriving soon to join him.

"Do you intend to fight on the side of the Italians?" the American asked through an interpreter.

"At the first opportunity," Gugsa said.

"Will your men fight with you?"

"They will," he quickly answered.

"Why did you come over to the Italian side?"

"Because I have always been friendly to Italy. I want to see the development and modernization of my province."

Though De Bono was still worried about Gugsa as he dismissed him and sent him back to Adigrat, he was considerably more worried about Mussolini, whose messages were a source of increasing annoyance. After Gugsa's departure, De Bono turned his attention to his Roman problems. In his diary on the twelfth he noted:

> Yesterday a telegram from the Duce tells me to move myself and my command into the occupied territory. I'd really like to know who makes him write these stupidities. We have enough trouble here, simply maintaining our communications. What makes him think I'm going to move? Of course I shall move forward, but not until we get our communications arranged; they at least function well enough here. I think by the 16th we'll be able to occupy Axum. [The holy city of Axum was a few miles west of Adowa.]

The next day, while on a short visit to the Eritrean town of Adi Ugri, about twenty miles north of his headquarters, De Bono received a message from Adigrat announcing that Haile Selassie Gugsa now felt he would need more than one battalion of Italian troops to support his return to Makalle. It looked as if Gugsa's ambition was to lead an Italian rather than an Ethiopian army into his capital. De Bono, despite the progress of his invasion forces, was beginning to feel bedeviled by problems he had not anticipated. As if Mussolini's interference were not enough, now he must cope with the demands of an Ethiopian chief who had delivered only twelve hundred men after promising ten thousand. Besides this, in the back of De Bono's mind was the unwelcome impending visit of Badoglio and Lessona.

On the fourteenth, however, he decided to enjoy some of the glory his quick success had earned him and traveled to Adowa for a triumphal ceremony of conquest and submission planned for the next morning. Though he expected the trip from Coatit to include at least six hours on muleback over the rugged mountain trail, he was amazed and gratified to learn that after one week's work, his labor battalions had proven again

182

the renowned skill of Italians in building roads. The trail was already in such excellent condition he was able to make the entire journey by motor-car, arriving in Adowa at eleven a.m., far ahead of schedule.

The squalid little town, now damaged by Italian bombs, was nevertheless bedecked with flags. Flowers lined the streets and several triumphal arches had been erected in accordance with De Bono's instructions. His first official act on the fourteenth was the issuance of a proclamation to the people of Tigre "Concerning the Assumption of Government Beyond the Frontier." The proclamation declared:

> In the name of His Majesty the King of Italy I assume the government of the country.
>
> From today, you, the people of Tigre and Agame, are subject to and under the protection of the Italian Flag.
>
> The Tshikka [local authorities] remain in office and are responsible for the order and discipline of their respective districts. They will present themselves before the nearest military authority together with the clergy of the parish church in order to make the act of submission. Those who do not present themselves within ten days will be considered and treated as enemies. . . .
>
> Let whosoever has suffered injury present himself to my generals and he will receive justice. . . .
>
> Traders, continue to trade; husbandmen, continue to till the soil.

At the same time, De Bono issued another directive—a kind of Fascist Emancipation Proclamation. "You know that where the flag of Italy flies," it declared, "there is liberty. Therefore, in your country, slavery under whatever form is suppressed. The slaves at present in Tigre are free and the sale or purchase of slaves is prohibited." The proclamation might have been slightly more graceful if De Bono had undertaken to eliminate slavery in the Italian colony of Eritrea before he so piously announced its abolition in Ethiopia. A 1935 League of Nations report on slavery, acknowledging its existence in Ethiopia but praising Emperor Haile Selassie's efforts to phase it out, also took notice of the fact that conditions hardly distinguishable from slavery were to be found in Eritrea. And a report from the Italian government to the League of Nations, dated May 1, 1935, included some extraordinary disclosures about what was called "domestic servitude" in Eritrea. "There are some natives whom the people call slaves," the Italian document admitted, "but they are no longer slaves since they live of their own free will in that state of domestic servitude . . . which it would be neither just nor expedient to disturb by an exaggerated and restricted interpretation of the intention of the law."

After issuing his proclamation, General De Bono, accompanied by General Maravigna, commander of the western column, inspected the

Italian defenses around Adowa, then ordered that Axum, which had also been evacuated by the Ethiopians, be occupied the next day. He observed that because of Axum's significance as Ethiopia's Holy City, "its occupation was invested with great political significance for the whole population of the Empire, and also in the eyes of the European nations, even though the fact would only serve still further to envenom them against us." De Bono could not understand why any decent person should oppose Italy's mission in Ethiopia.

At eight a.m. the next morning, he began the great ceremony of conquest and submission to remind Ethiopia and the world that Italy had now avenged her 1896 defeat at Adowa. His own account of the proceedings is a mixture of blunt honesty and boorish insensitivity: "After passing in review the Third Eritrean Brigade, which had not been employed in the occupation of the valley, and after witnessing the inauguration of the monument erected by the Gavinana Division to commemorate the event of the reconquest and vindication, I entered the town on horseback amidst the cheers of the population, who had been told that they must applaud me. I was not so ingenuous as to think this applause sincere."

The reason the Third Eritrean Brigade had not been "employed in the occupation of the valley," after spearheading the drive to capture it, was that they were black, and the honor of the "reconquest" of the area, as soon as it had been rendered safe by the blacks, was reserved for the white Italians. The monument whose unveiling he witnessed was inscribed: TO THE DEAD OF ADOWA, AVENGED AT LAST.

After inspecting Ras Seyoum's palace, which had been devastated ("Nothing was left," De Bono reported, "save a few fowls and a lion cub ... which ... I sent ... to the Duce"), he moved on to Adowa's principal Coptic church, where flocks of Ethiopian priests awaited him, wearing gaudy vestments and holding multicolored silk parasols over their heads.

From here, De Bono and his retinue proceeded to a large field outside town where the entire population had been herded together to hear him talk. His speech to this swarming multitude simply enlarged upon the points contained in his proclamations and explained "the nature of our rights and the mission which Italy had assumed in undertaking the conquest." Because the ranking bishop in Axum had fled south ahead of the invaders, the Italians had been forced to seek out another prelate who would endorse De Bono's speech. They had found an accommodating one—a handsome, eloquent orator who spoke of the Ethiopian civilization's great debt to ancient Rome and promised that the priests would make the people realize "all the privileges and benefits" which would derive from Italian rule.

De Bono, pleased with his reception in Adowa, decided to repeat his success in Adigrat, the headquarters of his eastern column. General Santini, commander in the eastern sector, greeted him there in front of a large tent on a strip of level ground just below the summit of a hill outside the town. Santini's headquarters, unlike De Bono's in Coatit, was an enclosed establishment, near the entrance of which Gugsa's twelve hundred men, with several local chiefs and a contingent of priests in scarlet and magenta vestments, stood waiting patiently to perform their acts of submission. Gugsa himself, the star performer in the planned ceremony, was inside the compound talking to a group of Italian officers when the Supreme Italian Commander arrived.

De Bono and Santini, ignoring Gugsa, went into the tent, where Santini spoke of his uncertainties about the dependability of the Ethiopian chief. He was now becoming almost as much a problem to them as he had been to the Ethiopians. It seemed evident that his insistence on an immediate return to Makalle was dictated by his troops, who feared their homes would be pillaged during their absence. While the two generals were talking, Gugsa came to the tent and, when they admitted him for consultation, repeated his demand that he be allowed to lead a march on Makalle. His impatience was especially exasperating to De Bono because Mussolini was making the same demand for an immediate investiture of Makalle. In a telegram on the thirteenth, Mussolini had said, "When you are ready for Makalle, I prefer as a date the 18th rather than the 20th for general political reasons." The same telegram said, "I think that after Makalle, it will be opportune to nominate Ras [*sic*] Gugsa as the civilian leader—I say civilian—of the conquered regions." De Bono, a cautious man, was no more impressed by Mussolini's orders than by Gugsa's arguments. But he found now that he must also explain to Santini why it would be dangerous to move so quickly toward Makalle. One of his staff officers expounded for him "the reasons why the possible advantage was almost without question inferior to the almost certain risk." From Adigrat, he sent a telegram to Mussolini making the same point.

After assuring Gugsa that his triumphal return to Makalle would soon come, he reviewed with him the Ethiopian troops who had now been drawn up in a line within the compound. Among their weapons were four or five types of rifles, some of which were 1891 models. When De Bono appeared before them, they greeted him with a flourish of trumpets, out of tune. De Bono then took his place on a rock platform, draped with Italian insignia, and Gugsa, under instructions, knelt before him while photographers snapped pictures which would soon prove to the world that Emperor Haile Selassie's former son-in-law had willingly accepted Italian authority. Part of his reward came immediately thereafter when De Bono prematurely fulfilled Mussolini's order to appoint the Ethiopian defector civilian chief of Tigre. "It goes without saying," De Bono noted, "that . . . the Dejasmatch does not exercise any power."

In Rome, Mussolini's impatience at De Bono's exaggerated caution was tempered suddenly by his own growing fears that the League of Nations, inspired by Great Britain, was about to invoke truly substantial sanctions against Italy. His October 17 answer to De Bono's telegram from Adigrat showed a startling change of attitude:

> I agree that you should not march on Makalle before preparing the back roads and before receiving my orders. Intensify the defensive preparations along the Adigrat-Adowa-Axum line, expanding yourself on the right [in the direction of Anglo-Egyptian Sudan]. My orders will come to you when the European situation has been cleared up in regard to the sanctions, and above all in regard to Italo-English relations which have come to a state of extreme tension with prospects of war not far off. In this situation you must hold back, systematize yourself, prepare yourself, and await my orders.

Though Mussolini's brave mention of war with England must be discounted in light of his penchant for drama as well as his total inability to launch such a war, it cannot be doubted that his fear and hatred of England had intensified in the previous ten days. During an interview with an admiring French correspondent October 6, he had made a strong bid for a *rapprochement* with Great Britain. "There is really no common sense in this quarrel England has with us," he said. "Conflict between the two nations is inconceivable. We do not seek, either near or far, directly or indirectly, to harm any British interest. Our consolidating action in East Africa does not menace the prosperity, communications, or security of any imperial territory. I am ready at any moment to prove this and to give indisputable guarantees of our pacific and even cordial disposition."

It must be remembered that Mussolini made these remarks the day before the League of Nations, under Anthony Eden's guidance, officially condemned Italy as an aggressor for its invasion of Ethiopia. Even when it was promulgated there was some doubt as to whether this condemnation would have any significant meaning. But when a new League Committee of Eighteen, meeting for the first time October 11, began to develop specific proposals for sanctions against Italy, Mussolini's early reaction approached panic proportions. The Committee of Eighteen developed four proposals for League approval. Number one would prohibit the sale to Italy by League Members of any arms, ammunition, or implements of war. Numbers two and three suggested financial sanctions which would deny loans and credits to Italian firms and individuals, thus closing all sources of cash. This plan would depend on the prohibition of Italian imports into Member countries. Number four would prohibit the export of certain raw materials to Italy. When this proposal was first developed, oil was not included among these raw materials. On October 19, however, the committee began a discussion of the possibility of an oil embargo. By this time, Mussolini was beginning to think the League and Great Britain might yet foreclose his African enterprise.

Mussolini might have been slightly more relaxed if he had been privy to the polite quarrel still in progress between those two unfriendly allies, England and France, as to the conditions under which they would be willing to come to each other's assistance. But Pierre Laval, who sometimes told Mussolini more than enough about his negotiations with England, had decided to keep this problem to himself. Until October 5, he retained in his pocket Sir Samuel Hoare's question of September 24 as to whether France would side with England if Italy were to attack the British Mediterranean Fleet or its bases. Then, on the fifth, he reiterated, in effect, the conditions he had suggested a month earlier. France might be willing to promise support for England in an attack by Italy if England would promise support for France in case the Germans moved westward. Laval and many other Frenchmen were annoyed at England because, they argued, it was the lack of British support for the League during the past several years that had forced France to seek Italy's friendship. It was intolerable now to find the British driving a wedge between France and her new Italian friends just because young Anthony Eden had become such a rabid convert to the League.

British Ambassador Sir George Clerk, on October 15, saw Laval at Sir Samuel Hoare's insistence and told him pointedly that Britain did not desire or hope for but "expected" French support by land, sea, and air in the event of an Italian attack. Laval was not awed by Britain's expectation. The French government would have to make a reservation, he said, because the British naval force in the Mediterranean was now so large Italy could claim it went beyond the League agreements for the enforcement of the Covenant.

Laval's new argument so frightened Hoare that he sent a message to Anthony Eden the following day instructing him to retard his campaign for strong sanctions. Hoare had met with his Cabinet colleagues and had found them in agreement with him that Eden had been "too much in the lead" at Geneva. There was "a unanimous desire," Hoare wrote, that Eden "should go as slowly as possible and take the initiative as little as possible until Laval had withdrawn his reservation."

At the same time, Hoare sent Sir George Clerk back to the Quai d'Orsay to tell Laval that Britain would withdraw its two battle cruisers from the Mediterranean in exchange for an unqualified assurance of French support against Italy. Laval, after making the British wait two more days, finally and grudgingly gave them their promise on October 18. It was not the kind of settlement which could be said to have cemented the alliance between the two uneasy countries.

CHAPTER NINE

Emperor Haile Selassie, wearing the uniform of Army Commander-in-Chief, took his place in the highest of several elevated chairs within a large open tent just below the old Imperial Palace.[1] The interior lining of the tent was scarlet. Fine carpets covered the dirt floor. The ministers of the Ethiopian Cabinet, holding rifles, squatted on the rugs in front of the Emperor. In front of them was a parade ground and beyond it an open plain where a vast multitude of people waited expectantly. It was ten a.m., October 17, two weeks after the war began, and only now was War Minister Ras Mulugeta ready to march his army of about sixty thousand men (recruited from Shoa, the central section of the country) past His Imperial Majesty on the way north toward the fighting front. It had taken two weeks to muster this largest of Ethiopian fighting forces in Addis Ababa, and the merging of so many men from different tribal origins had created some difficult complications. Two nights earlier there had been bloodshed after a boasting match between tribal contingents. So many men were injured the Red Cross had to be summoned. To separate the antagonists, one faction had been sent north toward the front immediately. At the same time, merchants in Addis Ababa were beginning to complain because some of the men, assuming the traditional prerogative of soldiers, were treating the capital as if it were an occupied city and refusing to pay for the items they took from the shops.

As the first of Mulugeta's troops approached the Emperor's tent at ten-thirty a.m., they announced themselves with thick clouds of dust and fearsome warlike cries. Palace guards, surrounding the tent, brandished swords, rifles, and rhinoceros whips in preparation for the difficult task of maintaining order among the exuberant soldiers. It would take four hours for the vast and straggling army to pass, some running along in a shuffling gait which Ethiopians can maintain for so many hours at a time, some marching in disciplined ranks, some stopping to perform the Ethiopian warrior's boasting routine in front of their ruler. Units of the Imperial Guard were included, barefooted though in European uniforms,

189

with heavy guns carried by pack mules. But the bulk of this army was composed of ordinary men from the Shoa countryside, all wearing cartridge belts, full or empty, though many had no guns. Hundreds of times, as the pass-by continued, the Emperor heard men plead with him for rifles to replace the spears or sticks with which they were armed. Some stopped and begged so persistently that the Palace guards had to flog them on their way. There were those who wore wide sun hats made of dried grass and those who went bareheaded. There were those who had boys to carry their guns and packs; others had mules. Many had wives and children trailing behind them, either pulling mules or carrying the family provisions, including sacks of dried peas and whatever other food they had been able to obtain.

When swordsmen drew their weapons in front of the Emperor to enact for him their techniques of attacking and dismembering an enemy, the Cabinet ministers crouching in front of him were in danger of injury from the flashing blades, but such was the skill of these warriors that no blood was drawn during the entire parade.

About noon, Ras Mulugeta himself approached, preceded by a corps of hornblowers in European dress and followed by another corps of scarlet-turbaned drummers astride the hindquarters of mules to whose backs the drums were fastened. The hard-faced old man, having discarded the silk jodhpurs and lion-trimmed cloak he often wore in Addis Ababa, approached the Emperor's throne in a khaki field uniform, his chest covered with the decorations that had accrued to him during more than fifty years as a warrior. Drawing his newly forged sword, he swaggered boldly up to the tiny man, half his age, who was his ruler, and as he neared the throne, the Emperor rose slowly to salute him. Mulugeta, putting his sword to earth as a gesture of fealty, began without ceremony a soliloquy of boasting and advice, most of which Haile Selassie had heard many times before this day.

"Jan Hoy," he shouted, using the Emperor's Amharic name, "I killed Italians before you were born. I helped preserve the country of which you are now king. I am still a soldier. Our old enemies have forgotten Adowa. I go to battle again, perhaps never to return. I await you in the battle, O King. . . ."

Finally, turning to other matters, he said, "Do not interest yourself overmuch in politics. Your weakness is that you trust the foreigner too much. Kick him out. What are all these foolish newspapermen doing here? I am ready to die for my country and so are you. We know that. War is now the thing. But to conduct it you had better remain in Addis Ababa. Send all the foreigners packing. I swear to you perfect loyalty."

The Emperor made no attempt to reply point by point. How could he answer a man who intended to await him in battle, but at the same time advised him to stay in Addis Ababa? Speaking in measured tones, the

Emperor said that no man placed his money or his confidence with a servant he could not trust, but that fortunately he could trust the Ethiopian people. He then launched a short lesson in his theories of military prudence and tactics, repeating the same ideas, not very popular with Ras Mulugeta, that he had expressed the day the war began. His soldiers, he said, should abandon their white, easily spotted shammas for khaki. They should use guerrilla tactics of hitting and retiring. They should scatter when they saw planes or tanks approaching. They should camp under trees or in caves where they would not be seen from the air.

"Every man who dies for Ethiopia," he concluded, "will be a holy saint and a martyr. I shall be with you on the battlefield, comrades, to shed my blood freely with yours in defense of our common fatherland. We shall accept no such peace terms as those which France now proposes. I shall die with you if necessary rather than submit to such humiliation."

After Mulugeta, several other chiefs, some waving spears and shields, ran to the throne, raising new clouds of dust as they shouted their loyalty to the Emperor and their imprecations upon the enemy.

"We shall drown the baby-killers in their own blood," one of them shouted. "We are going to our death and we are unafraid." (Many Ethiopians had begun calling the Italians "baby-killers" in reference to their bombing of civilians at Adowa and Adigrat.)

Another shouted, "I have a son. If I am killed, call him into the army."

The Emperor wept at one point as he watched the stragglers pass by on their way north. He knew better than any of them the fate to which he had been forced to send them.

In the crowd, also watching, were Colonel Léon Guillon, the French military attaché, and a friend who was a banker in Addis Ababa. "It makes me sick," Colonel Guillon said, "to think how these poor people will be slaughtered." The banker, who was no military expert, disagreed. He spoke of the difficulties the Italians would encounter in the rough terrain of the northern mountain country. Colonel Guillon shook his head. "You have no idea what modern weapons—flame throwers, for instance —will do to the Ethiopians."[2]

By late afternoon, the road winding northward into the mountains toward Dessie was crowded with a procession of soldiers almost twenty miles long. It would take them two weeks to reach Dessie, about two hundred forty miles away, and more than a month to reach Makalle, far enough north to see any Italians.

The French peace proposals to which the Emperor referred in his October 17 exhortation to his troops had grown out of a conversation

October 14 between French Prime Minister Pierre Laval and the Papal Nuncio in Paris, Monsignor Luigi Maglione.[3] Pope Pius XI, who was anxious to see the Ethiopian war end quickly, may have inspired this conversation. As a result of it, Laval summoned Italian Ambassador Vittorio Cerruti on the fifteenth and asked him to find out from Mussolini the minimum Italian demands for a cessation of hostilities. This initiative by Laval delighted Mussolini because it suggested to him that, even though France had participated in the League condemnation of Italy, the French, and therefore perhaps even the British, might yet prove helpful to him in fulfilling his ambitions. He quickly informed Laval of the conditions under which he was prepared to negotiate for peace, and Laval wasted no time in sending out feelers to England and Ethiopia about the possibility of accepting these terms.

On October 20, Mussolini wired De Bono:

> ... As you probably know, the League of Nations has decided to recommend ... various sanctions against Italy. There are some governments which will adopt these League recommendations one hundred per cent; others which will adopt them fifty per cent; still others which won't do anything, not to mention countries outside the League such as Brazil, Germany, Japan and the United States. I don't believe economic sanctions will have any influence on our military operations or on the resistance of the Italian people, formidably unified and resolved. However, a danger does exist, which is that, having seen the inefficiency of the economic sanctions, they might pass to sanctions of a military character. The English and the French have formally excluded it to me, that is, they have declared that they've never thought of blockading, or of closing the Suez, but I have little faith in one or the other. It is possible to suppose, however, that before passing from economic to military sanctions, a certain period of time will elapse. While the sanctionists of Geneva were enclosing Italy in a state of siege, I made known to Laval the minimum demands of Italy. They are, first, the pure and simple annexation to our colonies of the conquered territories. Second, a mandate to Italy ... over all the districts which are not Amharic. Third, rectification of territories in the Danakil and Ogaden. Fourth, participation by Italy in a mandate of several nations over Amharic territories. Fifth, the supervised disarmament of Abyssinia. These requests of Italy will be denied. It is necessary for people to persuade themselves that we surely will keep what we have occupied. To these actual conditions we must adjust our military action in time and method. There will be no complications in Europe before the British elections scheduled for mid-November. So by that time, all of the Tigre, as far as Makalle and beyond, must be ours. In your letter of Oct. 6, you asked me for a month and a month is at your disposition. ... Push forward with the occupation of the territory. ... An occupation of Makalle put off too long can embolden our enemies and cause perplexity among our friends. After speaking with Badoglio and Lessona, answer me.

De Bono's relief from Mussolini's impatience had been short-lived. Once again the Duce was pressing him onward toward Makalle. Worse than that, he was suggesting that De Bono solicit the advice of those two scheming enemies who had now descended upon him. "He wants me to work with Badoglio and Lessona," De Bono exclaimed in his diary October 22. "I don't have to work with anyone." But despite his dislike for Badoglio and Lessona, his first meeting with them, when they arrived at Coatit October 18, had been cordial. Badoglio began by protesting his friendship. After De Bono described the progress and problems in the campaign to date, the problems being mostly logistical, Badoglio agreed with him that under present circumstances Mussolini's suggestion of a possible drive westward into Anglo-Egyptian Sudan (in case of a war with England) was quite impractical. Badoglio had not yet visited the battle-fronts—if they could be called that at a time when no battles had yet taken place. He had seen only Massawa and Asmara, but this was enough to convince him that the supply system was in need of drastic improvement before any large enterprise, such as a move westward, could be safely undertaken. One observer, two weeks earlier, had counted seventy ships lying outside the port of Massawa, waiting to discharge their cargoes. Some of these ships had been there as long as five months. With only five berths along the quays and with a shortage of experienced longshoremen, an appalling congestion had developed.[4] Stores of all kinds lay heaped along the shore, unprotected from the elements or pilferers. The new road from Massawa up to Asmara on the high plateau had been well constructed, but it was wide enough for only a single line of traffic and there were only two passing places on the fifty-mile route. This meant that a schedule had to be fixed for upward and downward traffic.

In his discussion of this situation with De Bono, Badoglio had made no attempt to assess blame for it. At their first meeting, he and Lessona endorsed a De Bono telegram to Mussolini, describing the logistic situation as a reason why the dispatch of two more divisions for Africa should be postponed.

> Accelerated influx of troops in these last two months has necessarily slowed down disembarkation of victuals and materials. After disembarkation of Sila Division and other secondary elements already on the way, provision will be made for rapid clearing of Massawa harbor and subsequent transportation to plateau of victuals, ammunition, and materials which are at the Massawa base. [By] rationing population and troops, it is calculated [we] may have victuals for about six months considering that meat and salt are abundant on the spot. Continual consignments [of] gasoline wanted, of which, notwithstanding recent consignments, there is a deficiency, having two months' supply exclusive of that for aviation. . . .

After this first meeting, Badoglio and Lessona hurried off to the front-line positions, leaving De Bono in Coatit to fend off Mussolini's telegrams from Rome. On the twentieth, De Bono sent the Duce another message complaining about the logistic situation.

> Consider that every step forward means greater consumption [of] barrels of gasoline. You must be confident that your program is mine and that substantially progressive advance is already modestly proceeding. It is a question at most of some difference in time. I will consult with Badoglio and Lessona. What matters to me at the moment is that you should know that I am following your wishes with the utmost activity and pertinacity....

Mussolini's bewilderment and impatience at such telegrams from De Bono was hardly surprising. De Bono had spent almost a year preparing for the invasion of Ethiopia. Then, after an unobstructed advance of twenty-five miles into the country in three or four days, during which time his airplanes hadn't been able to find any enemy armies, he had decided it would be too dangerous to continue, even to a place like Makalle, the Ethiopian "defender" of which was now in his employ. On October 25, more than three weeks after the invasion began, De Bono felt he needed another three weeks before he could safely move farther south to Makalle. When Badoglio and Lessona returned from inspecting the front that day, he secured their approval of his plan "to march in strength on Makalle by the 10th November."

The moment Mussolini received the telegram announcing this further procrastination, he fired back an answer by return wire.

> It is necessary to enlarge and accelerate what you call "progressive advance." . . . See if it is possible for you to move up to the 5th that which you proposed for the 10th. I am sure that calling with great effort on all of your energies you will succeed. . . .

The messages between the two men became more comical with each exchange, perhaps because neither could see the humor in the image of an Italian army being paralyzed even when there was no enemy in sight. De Bono sent a six-hundred-word telegram on the twenty-eighth describing his difficulties—with mules, among other things—and warning his "dear Head of State" to be on guard against "any frivolous statements which may have been reported to you as having been made by Lessona and even Badoglio." After grudgingly agreeing to move forward to November 5 his drive on Makalle, De Bono concluded:

> I have a front that runs from the Sudanese frontier . . . to the sea at Assab, so it is not such an easy matter to safeguard it—knowing for the present nothing definite as to the enemy's intentions. But there is God, there is you, and there is also Fascism, which must triumph.

Mussolini had no intention of waiting for God to demonstrate his support of the Italian armies. He was determined to make De Bono do something. On October 29, he sent him a telegram which he hoped would end the discussion:

> To synchronize the political exigencies with the military, I order you to resume action, objective Makalle-Takazze, the morning of the 3rd November. The 3rd October all went well, now it will go better.

On the twenty-seventh, Badoglio and Lessona had left for home. Though De Bono's conversations with them had been pleasant enough, he was happy to see them go. "They haven't given me too much trouble," he noted in his diary, "but one is better off without them." In another entry, he wrote, "We'll see how sincere they are with the Duce." Their cordiality had done nothing to convince him of their friendship, especially since he had heard secondhand that Badoglio said if it were up to him, he would launch an immediate advance.

While De Bono tried to fight off Mussolini's demands for action on the northern front, General Rodolfo Graziani, the tall, handsome commander of Italian forces on the southern front, based in Italian Somaliland, seemed to show a similar disinclination to do battle. His airplanes had flown bombing missions against several small towns in the Ogaden desert, and his troops had occupied a few others. On October 5, they had taken the little village of Gherlogubi, about thirty miles from Wal Wal, where the Italian-Ethiopian dispute had begun ten months earlier. But there were no indications as yet of an Italian drive up through the desert toward Harar and Addis Ababa. The Italians did not, in fact, envision a serious approach to the Ethiopian capital from the south; the size of Graziani's force proves that: he had sixty thousand men at his disposal. While some other colonial powers might consider this a very persuasive army to send against a collection of poorly armed natives, the Italians, as Mussolini had indicated several times, preferred overwhelming superiority when they made war. Graziani's principal assignment, at least in the early days of the fighting, was to protect the Somaliland border, which was five hundred miles long, and to harass the Ethiopians throughout the Ogaden, especially along the route between Addis Ababa and British Somaliland, from which Mussolini believed vast quantities of war materials were flowing to Haile Selassie' armiess.

The Ethiopian commander in the Ogaden, Ras Nesibu, had accused General Graziani, on October 8, of dropping mustard gas from airplanes as one of his harassment tactics. "Bursting aerial bombs blanketed a wide area with a thick yellow gas," Nesibu reported, "causing soldiers and noncombatants to fall to the ground and suffer painfully."

Emperor Haile Selassie, however, had dissociated himself from this report during an interview October 24. The Emperor also defended the Italians against charges by other Ethiopians that they were using dumdum bullets (which spread on contact, ripping away large sections of flesh) and that they had run tanks into Ogaden towns, crushing some people under the treads and machine-gunning others.

"Let us try if we may," the Emperor said, "to mitigate the inherent horrors of war by being frank and honest, and giving our enemies credit where credit is due. Is not war horrible enough without investing it with such horrors?"

The Emperor was undoubtedly correct that day in defending General Graziani's forces from the charge that they had been using mustard gas. Graziani did not receive authorization to use gas against the Ethiopians until three days later, when Mussolini sent him a secret telegram with the following instructions: "Authorized use gas as last resort in order to defeat enemy resistance and in case of counterattack."

In Washington, D.C., Cordell Hull wrestled with a vexing dilemma as the days of October progressed and the likelihood of League of Nations sanctions against Italy became a certainty. If the Member nations of the League were to become involved in a war against Italy as a result of the sanctions, would the United States Neutrality Act force America to withhold arms from these nations? The resolution gave President Roosevelt a certain amount of discretion in applying embargoes, but no one was quite sure how much discretion. Hull, who might personally have liked to help League Members in their actions against Italy, feared that the isolationists in Congress would further restrict the President's conduct of foreign policy if the State Department were to issue even a hint of support for the League in its punishment of the aggressor. If, on the other hand, the United States refused openly to cooperate with the League in punishing the aggressor, if American companies continued to do business with Italy as usual, or more briskly than usual, while League Members were trying to enforce their sanctions, it might soon appear that the United States was responsible for the failure of sanctions.

Despite President Roosevelt's overwhelming domestic popularity in 1935, there were some strong political reasons for Hull to exercise caution. The isolationist movement was astonishingly powerful and the opening of hostilities in Ethiopia, a country with which Americans sympathized only abstractly since there were virtually no economic or cultural ties between the two nations, had deepened even further the irrational American fear of involvement in foreign wars. The American public, traditionally ignorant of the effects of United States trade practices upon international events, continued to think that if America took no military part in a foreign war, then America was not involved in that war. As long as America was not involved, the average American could enjoy hissing the villain and cheering his victim, even when the villain was white and the victim black. The war was so far away that its racial implications seemed unimportant. The whole affair had reduced itself to a contest between Haile Selassie and Mussolini, David and Goliath. Popular support in such a contest was certain to go to David, whatever color he might be, especially since, besides being the underdog, he was obviously the more civilized of the pair. The public statements of the two men made a mockery of Mussolini's claim that he was entering Ethiopia to civilize the country. But sympathy for Haile Selassie was almost completely divorced in the American mind from political and business considerations.

The isolationists in Congress congratulated themselves for passing the neutrality resolution and warned the public once more of the danger of involvement in a foreign war. They were especially wary of the danger that the United States might again, as in 1917, become the naïve and innocent victim of machinations by England and France, two countries whose statesmen were credited with Machiavellian brilliance in getting other people to do their fighting for them. The lack of brilliance, or even of good sense, among the British and French statesmen of the time was still unknown to most Americans. Senator William Borah, in a nationwide radio address from Boise, in his home state of Idaho, October 7, warned against the "subtle ways of propagandists" in luring America toward war. It would not be difficult for the United States to avoid entanglement in Africa, he said,

> should the war remain a war between the two nations now involved. But should other countries feel their supremacy in the Mediterranean or their territorial interests threatened, then will begin an appeal to the United States to enter the conflict in the name and for the preservation of world peace.

Senator Arthur Vandenberg, on October 26, issued a strong anti-sanction statement from Grand Rapids, in his home state of Michigan.

> The new American neutrality policy . . . is designed . . . to keep us entirely detached from foreign wars. I favor the rigid maintenance of this detachment to the utmost limit. . . . While these programs [of the League] are dedicated in high nobility to peace, it would be absurd to blind ourselves to the patent fact that they are also intimately related to the self-interest of major European powers. . . . We learned in 1917 how easy it is to slip

into external relationships which finally preclude any semblance of neutrality and finally urge us to alien battlefields. . . .

Senator Gerald Nye, on his way to Japan and then Manila as a member of a Congressional delegation to the inauguration of President Manuel Quezon in the Philippine Islands, issued his statement October 27 from aboard the liner *President U.S. Grant*, which was nearing Yokohama. "I have no sympathy with the Italian purpose at this moment," Nye said,

> but I inquire by what process of reasoning can we join in the sanctions program and at the same time maintain strict neutrality? We are blessed these days by two things, the fact that we are not a party to the League and, further, the fact that Congress provided a substantial neutrality policy before it adjourned. But for these we might well expect to be today financing operations against Italy and moving headlong into a repetition of that experience of twenty years ago from which we have not yet recovered. . . . By all means we must keep our hands out of that foreign war and we cannot possibly do that by joining in League sanctions.

With this kind of political thinking in the ascendancy, it was not difficult for American businessmen to maintain piously that they should continue or even increase their exports to Italy. A government spokesman, Howard Welch, chief of the automobile division of the Bureau of Foreign and Domestic Commerce, revealed on October 7 that for the previous two months more American motor trucks were being shipped to Eritrea than to any country in the world. He refused, however, to name the automobile companies supplying these trucks.

Members of the Export Managers' Club of New York, meeting for lunch at the Hotel Pennsylvania October 8, announced that orders placed with their client companies by either Italy or Ethiopia would be accepted in spite of President Roosevelt's October 5 warning that American businessmen dealing with belligerents would have to do so at their own risk. Orders would be filled on a cash basis only,[5] the Export Managers said, which meant that only Italy would be able to buy since Ethiopia had no cash.

The president of Standard Oil Company of New Jersey, Walter C. Teagle, said in New York October 18 that he saw no reason to interfere with his company's regular commercial business with Italy.[6] Teagle enlarged on this view later, in a November 6 letter to Secretary of State Hull. "For more than forty years," Teagle wrote,

> the Standard Oil Company (New Jersey) has owned a substantial majority of the stock of an Italian company (Società Italo-Americana del Petrolio), carrying on a business comparable to that of petroleum marketing companies in the United States. . . . It has come to enjoy the respect and confidence

of the Italian people, represents an investment of close to forty million dollars, and has accumulated a substantial good-will value in addition. In normal conditions this Italian subsidiary has furnished only about one-fourth of the domestic consumption of petroleum, its supplies coming chiefly from subsidiaries of Standard Oil Company (New Jersey). . . .

Thus far we have felt it both our right and our obligation to continue shipments of sufficient supplies to our Italian subsidiary to enable it to maintain its normal trade. . . . On the other hand, we have avoided accepting what President Roosevelt characterizes as "tempting trade opportunities offered to our people to supply materials which would prolong the war." . . . We have not taken on new business involving any war profits or committed any act that might be construed as unneutral. . . . Petroleum has not been included in the sanctions of the League of Nations and, accordingly, there has been no interference on the part of any nation with shipments of oil to either belligerent.

In these circumstances, it has seemed to us that to cut off the normal supplies from our Italian subsidiary, except by reason of conditions of *force majeure*, would be regarded by the Italian government and the Italian people as unfriendly, unneutral, and illegal under international law and the commercial treaty between the United States and Italy. . . .

Since Ethiopia's foreign trade is practically nil, an embargo on American business with the belligerents would be regarded as discriminatory against Italy; and in such event it is to be apprehended that Italy might initiate reprisals against our subsidiary, going even to the point of taking over its property and business. . . .

Perhaps it was possible to sympathize with Standard Oil Company's fear that it might lose a forty-million-dollar enterprise. But Teagle did not explain what good it would do Mussolini to confiscate this Italian subsidiary if the parent company, Standard of New Jersey, were to stop supplying its product. It was also somewhat disingenuous for Teagle to pretend that a company which provided twenty-five per cent ("only about one-fourth," as he put it) of the oil Italy needed for domestic uses was not thereby aiding Italy's war effort. But his most cynical argument was that "since Ethiopia's foreign trade is practically nil, an embargo on American business with the belligerents would be regarded as discriminatory against Italy." It was not by Ethiopia's own choice that its foreign trade was practically nil. There was an endless list of things Ethiopia needed, including even some oil—relatively little, to be sure—for its few vehicles. American businesses which helped fill the needs of Italy while ignoring the needs of Ethiopia were doing their share to bring about an Italian victory.

There was no shortage of American businesses which fitted this description. United States Commerce Department figures disclosed that American oil shipments to Italy had increased roughly six hundred per cent in volume during August and September, as compared with the same two months in the previous year. And on October 19, the Commerce Department announced that American companies were providing "a major part of the large increase in Italian imports of four classes of products easily made into munitions." These included scrap iron and steel, copper, benzol, and cotton waste, which could be converted into gun cotton by a simple chemical process. None of these products was on President Roosevelt's list of materials to be withheld from belligerents under the Neutrality Act provisions.

In addition to the businessmen who were eager to continue or increase their trade with Italy, Mussolini had other powerful supporters in the United States. William Randolph Hearst's large chain of newspapers regaled its millions of readers with its master's logic. An editorial in the New York *Mirror*, October 9, 1935, asked,

> What would happen if Mussolini should say to England, "You are practically declaring war against me for doing in Ethiopia what you have done in a hundred places on the surface of the globe when you have taken by force: stolen the colonies you possess"? One thousand Italian airplanes could make ruins of everything in a few sacred acres around Buckingham Palace and the House of Commons. This may not happen, but if it did, what a lesson in diplomacy it would teach the glib talkers and organizers of Leagues.

Italian-Americans, though not by any means unanimous in praise of Mussolini, gave him enough support to prevent most politicians, including President Roosevelt, from denouncing him or even criticizing him publicly. The Italian Ambassador to the United States, Augusto Rosso, was roundly cheered at the annual convention of the Sons of Italy, in Boston October 14, when he explained the "basic justice" of Italy's crusade against Ethiopia. "We have ignored certain methods of appealing to public imagination, of exploiting popular opinion," he said.

> Why? Perhaps because we have never been good at the game . . . because from the start we set out to be sincere. . . .
> When Mussolini sent our young men to Africa, it was because Italy has there a problem of life and security. . . . And the youth of Italy responded to the call cheerfully and serenely. Why? Because they feel, as the whole nation feels, that the vital interests of the country need their defense. . . . If this conviction be wrong, then it means that not the Italian government alone but forty-four million Italians are mistaken. . . .
> There is still another indictment to the effect that Italy started the war. The aggression is supposed to consist in the fact that the Italian troops were the first to cross the border. But here I ask any man with only an elementary knowledge of military necessities whether the Italian troops, who were thousands of miles from their home base, could have ignored the

order of general mobilization given by the Ethiopian Emperor on October third? . . .

Pro-Italian feeling in America was strong enough so that in Islip, Long Island, Mr. and Mrs. Alfred Ingold almost caused a riot in a local theater when they hissed Mussolini during a newsreel. Cheered by some, they were booed by others. A scuffle ensued and the Ingolds were arrested on a disorderly-conduct charge.

The nationwide isolationist mania, combined with the determination of many businessmen to trade with Italy and the politically potent minority sentiment in favor of Italy, confronted President Roosevelt with a problem which he could not overcome but which, with courage, he might have ameliorated. His almost unparalleled popularity with the American people at the time gave him an opportunity to begin a campaign of public persuasion then which he actually did begin four years later, when the catastrophe that bloomed in Italy was flowering throughout Europe.

The policy Roosevelt and Hull pursued in 1935 can hardly be described as valiant or imaginative. After the President's October 5 statement proclaiming neutrality, embargoing armaments, and warning Americans that their dealings with belligerents would be at their own risk, he said nothing more of importance on the subject until October 30, when he released a statement that mentioned the "tempting trade opportunities . . . to supply materials which would prolong the war." He gave it as his opinion that Americans would not want "abnormally increased profits that temporarily might be secured" by dealing in such materials. Roosevelt would have had to be naïve indeed about his country to have believed these altruistic words. His purpose in this statement could only have been to implant virtue by suggesting it was already there. If he had been determined to stop the trade in "materials which would prolong the war," he could have added them to the list of items already embargoed. The Neutrality Act gave him discretion in the definition of arms and armaments.

Hull, in the meantime, had maintained secret contact with the League's sanction committee in an effort to prevent it from embarrassing the Roosevelt Administration. Hugh R. Wilson, the United States observer at the League, and Prentiss Gilbert, United States consul in Geneva, worked so diligently to this end that the League committee soon abandoned its intention of inviting America to take part in the sanctions. But, on October 15, Gilbert informed Hull of a new danger. The Committee of Eighteen now intended to send a list of its recommendations to Washington and ask the United States government what it might do if the League were to adopt such measures.

Since there was no way for Hull to prevent the League from sending such an embarrassing list, it arrived in Washington October 21, together with a note from committee chairman Augusto Vasconcellos which said, "I am instructed to add that the Governments represented on the Co-ordination Committee would welcome any communication which any non-Member State may deem it proper to make to me or notifications of any action which it may be taking in the circumstances." In an only slightly veiled way he was pleading with the United States to show some kind of approval of League sanctions because the lack of American approval would be a strong boost to Italy. Any indication that the United States planned to ignore the sanctions would be almost enough to defeat them; it would be pointless for League nations to withhold products from Italy if the Italians could get these products from the United States.

After five days of deliberation and consultation, Hull finally answered this note. Beginning with an outline of what he called "the affirmative policy" of the United States in its effort "not to be drawn into the war" and its desire "not to contribute to a prolongation of the war," he went on to say only that the United States "views with sympathetic interest the individual or concerted efforts of other nations to preserve peace or to localize and shorten the duration of war." The message did not mention the word "sanctions," nor did it mention the League of Nations, to which it was addressed. It was the weakest sign of sympathy for the League that Hull, Roosevelt, and all their aides had been able to devise.

When the League's Coordination Committee met in Geneva October 31 to compile and act upon the replies of League countries to its sanction recommendations, the committee members were delighted to learn that forty countries had already signified their readiness to adopt all four of the major proposals. (These were the aforementioned proposals: number one, prohibiting League Members from selling Italy any implements of war; numbers two and three, imposing financial sanctions to deny loans and credits; number four, banning export of certain raw materials to Italy.) There were many factors tempering their satisfaction. The United States' response was so weak no one was sure it had any meaning at all. Germany, one of the other important non-Member nations, had indicated it would not increase its trade with Italy, but Adolf Hitler, after two years in power, had already made sensible men doubt anything he might say. Austria, a League Member which foolishly depended on Italy for protection against Germany, had decided to vote against any sanctions. So had Hungary, another dictatorship which was friendly with Italy. Paraguay seemed likely to follow this example. No one was certain about Brazil, which had indicated an intention to follow its own path. No one was certain about France either. Pierre Laval's personal opposition to sanctions was well known and most of his international efforts now were devoted to working out an accommodation with Italy. Three days earlier he had told United States Ambassador Jesse Straus in Paris that in his opinion the war would not last long, and that it could be settled by granting Italy some form of control over that portion of Ethiopia south of the eighth meridian, which traversed the country along a line about fifty miles south of Addis Ababa.[7] Laval also felt it would be necessary to offer Italy some small parcel of territory in the north, bordering Eritrea and including Adowa. He told Straus it was exceedingly important to sustain the administration of Mussolini in order to prevent the spread of Communism. Despite widespread distrust of Laval, however, it was generally believed in Geneva that France would have to take part in the sanctions, at least officially.

Encouraged by the forty "yes" votes plus the likelihood of several others (out of a possible fifty-six), the Coordination Committee decided to pursue a path even more daring and meaningful. It developed a proposal, to be known as four-A, which would ban the export to Italy of oil, scrap metal, and coal. Here was a proposed sanction which could defeat Italy and end the war in a few weeks. It remained to be seen whether or not Member nations would approve it. The Canadian delegate, Dr. A. W. Riddell, embarrassed many committee members by making a formal motion that proposal four-A be adopted forthwith. But someone— probably in Whitehall—got to the Canadian government in Ottawa and the delegate was repudiated forthwith. The oil-embargo proposal was carried forward, however, and on November 6, the Coordination Committee sent it to the League Members for consideration. Meanwhile, on November 2, the Coordination Committee formally adopted the first four proposals, and since nearly all the governments in the League had declared themselves ready to put the measures into force by mid-November, the committee fixed November 18 as the date when the sanctions would take effect.

The world was now destined to learn whether League of Nations sanctions could force an aggressor nation to abandon a war policy. But before the noble experiment was to begin, many of these League Member nations could spend sixteen days hurrying their ships back and forth between home ports and Italy.

In England, a campaign was in progress for the general election to be held November 14, and Prime Minister Stanley Baldwin's mostly Conservative coalition was appealing to the people on the strength of what it presented as its unfaltering support of the League of Nations.

None of these men seemed to see any humor or irony in the claim. Their campaign manifesto baldly stated, "We shall . . . continue to do all in our power to uphold the Covenant and to maintain and increase the efficiency of the League. In the present unhappy dispute between Italy and Abyssinia there will be no wavering in this policy we have hitherto pursued."

On October 9, two weeks before Baldwin announced his intention to go to the country, his Cabinet decided not to raise the embargo on arms to Ethiopia. At the same time, a large percentage of the oil being used by the Italian navy in the Mediterranean (which at the moment was supposedly threatening British fleet units there) was being supplied by the Royal Dutch Shell Company and the Anglo-Iranian Oil Company. Royal Dutch Shell was owned by British and Dutch interests. Anglo-Iranian was controlled by the British government. These huge corporations were filtering the oil for the Italian navy and for Italian merchant ships through a third company, Consolidated Petroleum, which they owned jointly. Anglo-Iranian was shipping oil directly to Eritrea and Italian Somaliland from its base at Aden.

Prime Minister Baldwin, making a campaign speech to his neighbors and constituents in Bewdley, Worcestershire, on October 19, selected a few reassuring words for that other great supporter of the League—Italy. "It is spread about in some places abroad," Baldwin said, "that one of the main objects in the line of action taken by this country is to fight and overthrow Fascism in Italy. That is a lie of a dangerous kind. What form of government Italy has concerns Italy alone. The day is long past when this country would seek by arms or any other method to overthrow the form of government existing in another country."

Foreign Secretary Sir Samuel Hoare had a few more reassuring words for Italy three days later in the House of Commons. At the prospect of his speech, the House and its galleries had attracted the largest crowd ever gathered there during the four-year regime of the National Coalition government. So many men were jammed into the area around the Treasury bench they overflowed into the Speaker's steps. Some of the members seemed to be sitting on the laps of others. The side galleries were filled to capacity and in the gallery opposite the speaker, reserved for distinguished foreigners, were the ambassadors from France, Italy, Germany, the United States, and virtually every other country, as well as several foreign ministers, plus the high commissioners of Australia, South Africa, and Ireland.

Sir Samuel opened his address in his usual direct, austere, and unrhetorical style by stating that no week had passed during the previous several months without his seeking some solution to the Ethiopian dispute. "There is still breathing space," he said, before economic pressure can be applied. Can it not be used for another attempt at such a settlement? Italy is still a member of the League. I welcome this fact. Cannot this eleventh-hour chance be so used as to make it unnecessary to proceed further along this unattractive road of economic action against a fellow Member, an old friend, and a former ally?

He then went on to assure both Italy and his audience that Britain and the League contemplated nothing stronger than economic actions against the aggressor. "The precondition for the enforcement of military sanctions, namely, collective agreement at Geneva, has never existed," he said, ignoring completely the enthusiasm with which almost all League Members had received his own tough warnings to Italy in his September 11 Geneva speech.

> Military sanctions can only be applied collectively We do not intend to act alone. . . .
> Further, from the beginning of the present deliberations at Geneva until now, there has been no discussion of military sanctions, and no such measures, therefore, have formed any part of our policy. The action that we have been considering, which we believe it to be our solemn obligation to consider, is not military but economic. The distinction is that between a boycott and a war.

Sir Samuel was interrupted only once by his attentive audience. From the Labour Party benches someone shouted, "Close the Suez Canal!"

From the Conservative benches this demand was met with sharp cries of "War monger!"

Hoare quickly passed over the Canal issue. "As there will be no agreement for collective action of this kind," he said, "it is only dangerous and provocative to talk about it."

He did discuss, however, the general lack of action during the eleven months since the crisis began.

> Looking back over the events of the summer, I am convinced that so long as conciliation was possible it was the duty of the League to make every effort to secure a settlement by methods of conciliation. It is all very well to be wise after the event, but up to the month of August there was still the possibility of a peaceful settlement.

Sir Samuel's speech was enthusiastically applauded. It sounded reasonable and forthright. Most of his audience was quite unaware of its untruths, and all but a few of his listeners, all but his Cabinet colleagues, were unaware that, despite his staunch defense of the League, he was now preparing to send the Foreign Office Africa expert, Sir Maurice Peterson, to Paris for conferences with Laval's staff about a new peace plan which would bypass the League.

Rumors of a sellout to Italy circulated during the general-election campaign, but in several speeches Hoare assured his Chelsea constituents that the Baldwin government would never betray the League. These assurances were so effective politically that, on November 14, the government was returned to office by a landslide majority. In the new Parliament, Baldwin's coalition captured 431 seats, to 184 for its combined opponents. One week later, Peterson representing Great Britain, and René Comte de Saint-Quentin representing France, sat down in Paris to work out the final details of this peace plan which Laval had instigated and Hoare had embraced in principle. It was a plan destined soon to startle the entire world and expose the duplicity of Baldwin, Hoare, and company beyond any possibility of credible denial.

In Rome on October 31, several thousand students, smartly uniformed now, formed military ranks at the inaugural ceremony of the new University City about a mile east of the Villa Borghese. The principal speaker, Premier Mussolini, began his remarks as if his mind were devoted entirely to the pleasure of dedicating this new temple of learning. "The present hour may well be termed an historic hour," he said. "The University of Rome is coming again into life. This is an event of extraordinary importance." But after tracing the university's history and explaining why he had decided to build this new campus for it, he soon made it clear that his mind was occupied more with Geneva than Rome. "It must not be ignored that the University of Rome is coming into life again," he said, "when at Geneva a coalition of egotists and plutocrats is trying, without avail, to stop the march of the young Italy of the Black Shirts. Confronting an economic siege, of which the civilized people of the entire world should feel the supreme disgrace, facing an experiment which is being tried for the first time against the Italian people, we must say that we shall oppose to this experiment the most implacable resistance."[8]

Mussolini had good reason to worry about even the timid economic sanctions the League of Nations was preparing for him. His war in Africa, condemned throughout the world, was also unpopular at home. For the first time in several years, Italians were complaining openly about their government. Money was tight. Consumer goods were in short supply. And the moral justification for the invasion of Ethiopia was questionable even to people who could read only Italian newspapers. The government needed some kind of dramatic development to restore its popularity. Pope Pius XI had helped slightly the day before by stating that Italy should be granted a mandate over Ethiopia "to avoid a more dangerous conflagration." But this qualified Papal endorsement was of dubious moral and political value because of the diminishing respect for the Pope.

The regime could still try to make England the scapegoat for difficulties at home. On the night of October 31, Fascist student mobs attacked the British consulate in Rome and several private enterprises associated with the British, including the Majestic Hotel and Roberts Drugstore. But such demonstrations were also losing their efficacy. The anti-British campaign, sustained for several months in the Italian press, was growing tired. What Mussolini needed more than anything else was an impressive military victory in Africa. It was beginning to look, though, as if he would never have one. With a supreme commander who hesitated to march against an absent enemy, even the capture of Makalle, let alone the conquest of Ethiopia, seemed difficult of attainment.

Finally, on November 3, after Mussolini's several demands for action, General De Bono launched his cautious drive toward Makalle, forty-five miles south of Adigrat, which his troops had occupied in force for almost a month. But even as he gave the order to advance, he was filled with misgivings. "Our projected move was certainly known to the enemy," he wrote. "Preparations on as grand a scale as those which were being made could not have escaped even the uninitiated, and we could not be so naïve as not to believe that we were surrounded by numerous spies. However, on the night before the advance, all was perfectly quiet." Though Italian reconnaisance planes had been able to spot "nothing beyond the movement of small bodies of warriors marching northward from Lake Ashangi," De Bono could not overcome the fear that a huge black army was about to descend upon him from nowhere.

The main thrust southward November 3 was by the First Army Corps from Adigrat and the Eritrean Corps from Enticcio. This advance was protected to the east by a column which pursued a parallel course down through the low-lying, hot, dry Danakil desert country. In the west, it was protected by a slower advance of the other Italian army corps in the Adowa-Axum sector. After one day's march, the Makalle columns had moved twenty-four miles without opposition or incident. Native troops were in the vanguard. Progress had been so rapid throughout the day that De Bono was more worried than usual by nightfall. "It was as though the First Army Corps and the Eritrean were running a race," he wrote. "I admired all this dash and it was a real grief to me that I had to check it." But check it he did, after consulting with his supply corps. The two columns, having remained stationary throughout the day of the third, resumed their march at dawn on the fourth in the face of an unusual and very heavy rainstorm, which was the only opposition the Italians encountered that day. Not until the afternoon of the fifth, when the Eritreans were southwest of Hausien, halfway to Makalle, did they encounter any enemy action. There, near Mount Gundi, they met a force of about three hundred Ethiopians whom they easily routed, killing or wounding, according to Italian estimates, about a hundred men. Two white Italian officers were wounded, one of them mortally. This man, Lieutenant Alde Lusardi, was quoted as saying to his colonel just before he died, "I beg you to let the Duce know that I die pronouncing his name. Hurrah for the King! Hurrah for the Duce! Hurrah for Italy!" The Italians did not report how many of their own native Eritrean troops were killed or injured in the action.

To add to General De Bono's worries, his reconnaisance planes reported on the sixth that Makalle was occupied by enemy forces. On the seventh, they reported that the enemy had evacuated. Nevertheless, De Bono made certain his men approached the town with caution. One Eritrean brigade advanced from the northwest on the morning of the eighth, while a white Italian brigade, preceded by Haile Selassie Gugsa's twelve hundred men, advanced from the northeast. When the two columns entered the Makalle basin, the Eritreans were sent to guard the southern end, from which any possible danger was likely to come, while the Italian column, with Gugsa's contingent in front of them, paraded into the city. The way was so clear the commander of the 2nd Division was able to review his troops as they entered the town. They found no enemy forces there.

Mussolini was pleased but not content. In a telegram on the eighth he told De Bono, "News reconquest Makalle makes the hearts of the Italian people vibrate with pride. Take the greetings of the Government and myself to the troops." Three days later, his impatience had returned to crowd his pleasure. On the eleventh, he wired De Bono, "Assign the Maravigna Army Corps [which had advanced from Adowa] to lead on the right toward Takazze [River], and with the indigenous divisions, march on Mount Alagi without delay, while the Italian divisions will wait at Makalle-Scelicot. Answer."

De Bono fumed angrily to himself before answering. He had already noted in his secret diary, "By God, enough with all this pressure to push ahead." After the Duce's latest message he added, "I expected that: incompetence, playing by ear, bad faith." In his reply, he argued for another delay at Makalle. More roads had to be built; communications had to be established. Mussolini, champing with frustration, nevertheless acquiesced for the moment.

Though the Ethiopians were not yet in sight of the Italians, neither were they in terror of them. Their northern forces were slowly organizing behind the western front under the command of Ras Imru and Dejasmatch Ayelu Birru, an able general, whom Imru, however, did not trust. In the center, Ras Seyoum and his forces had withdrawn, in compliance with the Emperor's orders, to the rugged Tembien country west of Makalle, where they awaited the arrival from the south of another army under the command of Ras Kassa, a grandson of Emperor Menelik's brother, and generally considered the most powerful chief in the country. While Seyoum and Kassa moved toward a union of forces, the army of War Minister Ras Mulugeta continued its march northward in the direction of Amba Alagi, the mountain Mussolini wanted De Bono to capture immediately, about forty miles south of Makalle.

Haile Selassie, still in Addis Ababa, was continuing his campaign for outside help while he prepared to move his headquarters north toward the front. At a few minutes past midnight on the morning of November 7, when Italian forces were poised to take Makalle the next day, the Emperor, unguarded and accompanied only by one of his Foreign Office functionaries, drove to Ethiopia's lone radio station at the airport on the western edge of the city for a prearranged broadcast to the American people over the Columbia Broadcasting System. The transmission was remarkably good.

The Emperor's voice was heard throughout the United States with great clarity at five p.m. November 6, New York time. He made his speech in Amharic. Then Josef Israels II, a *New York Times* correspondent, read an English translation:

> The mails to Ethiopia have been laden for months with American letters of sympathy and offers of help or services, a most heartening sort of communication from a distant people. A great many of the writers have asked what they might do to help Ethiopia. Hitherto, we have had no answer to give.
>
> Ethiopia does not desire to involve other peoples and other nations in her distress. But now the time has come—at Geneva the hour for collective action against the aggressor has been solemnly marked by nations in conference assembled. . . . You people of the United States can help. . . .
> I ask no one to take the sword against Italy. Methods of the sword and of force are methods of ancient ignorance. People of the world today are capable of united and thoughtful action through peaceful channels. I give thanks to God that the peoples represented at the League of Nations realized this and have risen in peaceful but mighty strength against Italy.

It was the strongest possible suggestion to President Roosevelt that the

209

United States take part in League sanctions. There was no reply, either direct or indirect, from Washington.

After forty days without any real engagement, the shadow war was now about to end, but not on the high plateau where De Bono, having concentrated his forces, continued nervously to expect an attack. The first significant encounter between Italian and Ethiopian troops took place more than fifty miles northeast of Makalle, on the tortuous route up the steep mountainsides from the hot, low-lying Danakil desert to the towering plateau which stretched north to south almost the entire length of Ethiopia.

The two thousand men under the command of General Oreste Mariotti, who had marched south into the unfriendly desert from Massawa to protect the left flank during the drive on Makalle, were still trudging upward through this rough country on November 12.[9] They had climbed from the salty desert floor almost to the level of the huge plateau, and though the only Ethiopians they had seen were some Danakil tribesmen who probably hadn't even known about the war, Mariotti had insisted that his men maintain fighting formations along the entire route. He was convinced, from information he had received, that a force of Ethiopians under Dejasmatch Kassa Sebat would attack him before he reached the little town of Azbi, which was Kassa Sebat's headquarters. Kassa Sebat would surely have to fight soon, since Makalle was already captured behind him to the southwest and Mariotti's troops were advancing uphill toward him from the northeast.

On the morning of November 12, shortly after nine-thirty, the Mariotti column entered a narrow, east-west ravine about half a mile long, called Ende Gorge. Askaris from Massawa took the lead, followed by Danakil tribesmen recruited in Eritrea. Then came Mariotti, his staff, and two newsmen—Herbert Matthews of *The New York Times* and Luigi Barzini of the *Corriere della Sera* in Milan, all riding mules. Behind them as they moved into the steep, slender gorge was a train of eighty camels and perhaps as many mules, carrying supplies and ammunition. Flanking parties marched along beside the column on both sides, watching for the enemy.

When all but the supply train and rear guard were inside the gorge, Mariotti, noticing a ridge ahead that ran straight across the path his men were treading, called a halt and, without changing the expression on his face, ordered one of his officers to mount their heavy guns. The officer had walked only three steps after taking this order before a burst of rifle fire broke out. The officer fell, his face twisted in pain as he grabbed his groin and his right knee. Matthews' orderly, standing in front of his mule, was hit in the left ankle and grabbed the mule's neck to avoid falling.

Another officer, after looking into the hills whence the fire had come, ordered everyone to take cover. A short time later, when machine-gun fire indicated that the enemy was better armed than anyone had expected, the same officer was still contemptuous enough to say, "Give them a little time. They'll soon exhaust their four rounds of ammunition. Then if they don't run away, we'll counterattack."

This initial confidence was soon replaced by confusion as Mariotti and his staff tried to assess the enemy strength and positions. Because the first shots apparently came from the opposite side of the gorge, it was natural to assume the Ethiopians were concentrated there, but the tree-covered banks on both sides were so steep and close that echoes distorted the direction of the sound. It was impossible to tell where the Ethiopians were installed. The first indication came when heavy firing broke out atop the ridge at the upper end of the gorge, the same ridge which had first alarmed Mariotti. But this rifle and machine-gun barrage was soon augmented by more gunfire from the south wall of the gorge, along its entire length. The Ethiopians had obviously placed themselves in excellent positions from which to bottle up the gorge at both ends and obliterate the Italian column almost at their leisure. Though the Italians were able to mount their four seventy-millimeter guns within twenty minutes, and though their native troops fought back fiercely from their exposed and inferior positions, the Ethiopian gunfire did not abate as expected, and when waves of Ethiopian soldiers began rushing down the hillsides for hand-to-hand attacks, some of the Italian Danakil troops bolted toward the rear, only to be stopped by the drawn pistols of their white Italian officers, who turned them around and forced them to resume fighting. Five times during the full day of battle, waves of Ethiopians charged down upon the Italian troops, pressing their attacks relentlessly even though they sustained greater losses than they inflicted. At the front of the Italian column, their assault was continuous for three and a half hours. At the rear, they shattered the supply train by killing most of the camels and some of the mules. These animals, and many of the Italian troops, suffered exceptionally severe wounds because the soft-nosed lead bullets from some of the old Ethiopian rifles would spread on contact, ripping away large chunks of flesh and bone. Though Matthews reported at the time that the bullets "were 'legitimate,' so to speak, and not dumdums," the Italian government later charged that the Ethiopians made widespread use of dumdums. In fact, the Ethiopians used whatever kind of bullets they could lay their hands on, some of which had been supplied to them by the Italians after the 1928 Treaty of Amity.

By nightfall, when the fighting came to a halt, the Italians had become acutely aware that their prospects were bleak. Escape appeared to be impossible. The Ethiopian force was large—estimated at five thousand men—and was as well disciplined as it was armed. In the morning, the Ethiopians would undoubtedly resume the attack. There was nothing to stop them continuing it until the whole Italian column was wiped out. "We are left without help," Mariotti said. "Let's hope God won't abandon us."

At dawn of the thirteenth, the desperate Italians were braced and ready for the new assault. But as the light of day increased, the stillness within the gorge continued. Only gradually did the Italians come to realize their good fortune. The Ethiopians, with victory in their grasp, had retired during the night. Because the Ethiopians conceived of a battle as a one-day, morning-to-evening event, they had deemed it finished when darkness fell the night of the twelfth. The total destruction of an enemy force, which was a basic concept in European military strategy, had never been part of the Ethiopian military tradition. As the war with Italy progressed, the one-day battle habit of the Ethiopians, exemplified at Ende Gorge, was destined to cost them dearly.

Released from their desperate situation, the Italians moved on up and through the narrow gorge to take Azbi, which had been Dejasmatch Kassa Sebat's stronghold. Kassa Sebat was unable to catch Mariotti in a vulnerable position a second time.

Despite his troubles with the impatient Mussolini, General De Bono was quite pleased with himself by mid-November. He had taken Makalle without mishap and he had forestalled the Duce's efforts to push him on in the dangerous direction of Amba Alagi. He was also conducting an important negotiation which might bring one of Ethiopia's top commanders, plus his ten thousand troops, to the Italian side.

On October 31, De Bono's headquarters, now at Adigrat, received a visit from the nephew of Ayelu Birru, who shared with Ras Imru the command of the western sector of the Ethiopian front against the Italians. The Italian "Political Bureau," whose job it was to suborn prominent Ethiopians, had been at work for some time in an effort to influence Ayelu, who felt a certain dissatisfaction with Emperor Haile Selassie because the latter had not promoted him to ras. Ayelu's nephew had come through the lines to De Bono's headquarters as an envoy, not from Ayelu but from Ayelu's son. The Italians, who understood the subtleties of Ethiopian politics, were quick to see this as a feeler from Ayelu himself, especially when they read a letter the nephew had brought from the son. In it, the son declared his own desire to enter the Italian ranks with all the warriors at his command, and he added, as De Bono reported, that "if he were authorized to tell his father that we approved of his suggestion, and that he would be rewarded, he would guarantee that Ayelu Birru would refrain from any hostile action against us." De Bono then wrote two letters, one to Ayelu's son, the other to Ayelu himself, assuring both that they would be well rewarded if they switched sides.

The outcome of this negotiation was still pending when De Bono traveled to Makalle to inspect his latest conquest. He found it "a wretched place, as are all the towns of the Tigre." His troops were "well off, but certainly not up to advancing." In the evening, he granted an audience to Haile Selassie Gugsa and two associates, who vexed him by suggesting that, having been brought back to Makalle as they had wished, they now felt less than safe there. De Bono indignantly assured them that Makalle was henceforth and for all time Italian.

When De Bono returned to his Adigrat headquarters, he was greeted with a shattering telegram from Mussolini, dated November 14:

> SECRET. PERSONAL. With the reconquest of Makalle I consider your mission in East Africa accomplished. A mission which you carried out in extremely difficult circumstances, and which in the present and in the future will point you out to the gratitude of the nation. Your incontestable and everywhere renowned merits will be explicitly consecrated by the facts. I feel that this message of mine will not bring you excessive surprise because you know from experience that every cycle of activity must be ended at a certain point, that a little rest is needed and that one should not demand too much from fortune when it has been with one for a certain period. I advise you that as your successor I have chosen Marshal Badoglio. Waiting to see you again, I embrace you with unchanged cordiality.

To his private diary, De Bono confided his reaction: "And who's coming to take my place! Badoglio!"[10] The enemy he feared more than the Ethiopians had finally defeated him. All he could hope for now was to win before his eclipse the one honor he had long coveted but had almost despaired of receiving. If he could retire with the title "Marshal of Italy," some of the sting of his dismissal might be removed. He did not hesitate to demand by return wire the title as his price for bowing out cordially and quietly. The notification of its conferral, sent November 16, acknowledged De Bono's insistence upon it. "The communiqué which will make this announcement [of your promotion]," Mussolini wrote, "will be in your terms and to your complete satisfaction." After this message arrived, on the seventeenth, De Bono confided to his diary: "Very good. Badoglio comes on the 26th and I leave on the 26th. I'm happy but my heart cries. I'm a grand animal!" When the notice of his dismissal arrived, he had suggested to Rome the threat that he might return home immediately, before Badoglio's arrival, thus publicly dramatizing Mussolini's organizational

213

problems. In his telegram of October 8 protesting to Mussolini the news of Badoglio's intended visit, he had said, "I tell you with my usual frankness that if he comes here to stick his nose into what I've done or I intend to do, I will drop everything and leave." Mussolini's quick decision to make De Bono a marshal may have been influenced by a fear that the silly old man would actually do such a thing. On the other hand, Mussolini may simply have decided that a title was a cheap gift to confer upon a man at the moment of his dismissal.

It is impossible to determine to what extent De Bono's ouster was due to Mussolini's impatience, and to what extent it was due to intrigues within the regime. The retired Marshal Enrico Caviglia, a friend of De Bono's, blamed Badoglio, Lessona, and Italo Balbo for Mussolini's decision. "Already in July," Caviglia wrote in his diary,

> Badoglio had induced Balbo to support him, then he won Lessona's support. In November he went to visit De Bono in Eritrea with Lessona. There he must have heard that success against the Abyssinians was easy, and then he managed to replace De Bono. He had been against the expedition into Abyssinia in every way; now he was full of enthusiasm for it because it would remunerate him with easy glory.[11]

This entry in Caviglia's diary, made December 12, 1936, after De Bono paid him a visit, included also some private and retrospective remarks by De Bono on the subject. "I am happy to have left," the embittered general insisted,

> but you can't imagine how much effort was made to damage me by my friends and my enemies. Badoglio and Lessona had worked up some infantile pretext to go there, to see whether an operation toward the Sudan was possible, as if I were not capable of assuring [Mussolini] that such was impossible. In order not to have to show them around, I made myself busy, but they must have investigated the question of whether victory over Abyssinia would be easy, and they must have assured themselves that the test would not present any difficulty.

Lessona, in his memoirs, tells the story differently. He has recalled that during one of the meetings he had in Africa with De Bono and Badoglio, De Bono said, "I must think about the war and conduct it as I can. Let him [Mussolini] think of the political problems. After all, that's his job."[12]

Lessona recalled arguing with De Bono that such an attitude would be satisfactory if it were a military impossibility to win the war rapidly, but, since a quick victory seemed certain, it was necessary in this case that arms come to the aid of politics. "Either Italy wins the war in a few months," Lessona claimed to have said, "or it is lost."

De Bono then, according to Lessona, consulted his staff and reaffirmed his opinion that an immediate advance was impossible. "From that moment," Lessona wrote, "I thought it was urgently necessary to replace General De Bono."

When Lessona, the morning after his return from Africa, went to the Palazzo Venezia, Mussolini said to him, according to his recollection, "I have read your report. I have received another one from Marshal Badoglio which arrives at the same conclusions. Then whom are we going to send to assume the command in Africa?"[13]

If Mussolini said this, it means he had already decided, at the beginning of November, to dismiss De Bono. It also means Badoglio joined Lessona in recommending the dismissal. Lessona recalled that he had enumerated the several possible candidates for the job, including, among others, Balbo, Graziani, and Badoglio. "I was about to continue describing the various candidates," he wrote, "and to declare that the only one to consider was Badoglio, when the Duce interrupted me by saying, 'This last one is the solution to adopt. Find Marshal Badoglio, tell him it's my intention to give him the command in Africa, and bring him to me tomorrow.'"

If Mussolini, in his impatience, believed Badoglio was likely to be less cautious than De Bono, he simply didn't know very much about Italian generals. Badoglio's initial report on his return from Africa said that De Bono had "invariably" exaggerated the difficulties and that the drive south presented only a straightforward tactical problem that could easily be solved. A few days later, when Badoglio realized the job of leading the drive would be his, he looked upon it differently. On November 5, he submitted to Mussolini a report which could almost have come from De Bono. "It is evident that our right flank is very exposed," Badoglio wrote.

> The Takazze, which is difficult to cross in large numbers, gives us good protection. But still and all, it will be necessary to take measures to protect our line of operation from any enemy attempt. . . . Furthermore, if we have time, we shall have to create an anchor position at Makalle on which we can lean with certainty in case of an enemy offensive in forces superior to our own. . . . All of the troops available after the occupation of the protective points on the right flank must be sent to Makalle. . . . It will be necessary in addition to bring from their now dispersed positions into Makalle the artillery units. . . . It will be necessary to build in Makalle an airfield with a copious supply of bombs. . . . Everything considered, I hold that from the day of arrival at Makalle, at least a month will be necessary to get ready for another forward leap.

For a plan as cautious as that, De Bono would have sufficed. But Mussolini had no one else to turn to. Graziani, in the south, did not inspire confidence. Though his route through the Ogaden desert toward Harar, and beyond it to Addis Ababa, seemed wide open, being defended by only seven thousand Ethiopians, he was either unable or afraid to take advantage of this situation. And on November 11, his hesitant offensive was stopped completely at a place called Anale, about one hundred miles west of Wal Wal along the northward route toward Harar. In a short battle at Anale, the Ethiopians killed several Somali soldiers and immobilized three Italian tanks, whose crews had got out either to repair them or to breathe some fresh air. After this battle, both the Ethiopian and Italian forces retreated, leaving a vacuum in the desert which Graziani showed no inclination to fill.

In addition to his military frustration, Mussolini also had to face now the League of Nations' economic sanctions which began inauspiciously November 18. Their effectiveness could not be predicted because no one yet knew how rigidly the various League Members would apply their embargoes or whether the war would last long enough for Italy to feel the pinch of shortages, and also because the League had not, so far, added to the sanction list such vital commodities as oil, iron, and steel. Mussolini's immediate reaction to the invocation of sanctions was to turn it into a propaganda weapon for the unification of Italy against the cruel injustice the League was visiting upon it. The streets of Rome were festooned with flags on the eighteenth, and steel-helmeted soldiers stood guard outside the embassies of the sanction countries. Only at the British Consulate near the Piazza di Spagna was there a demonstration (quickly broken up), but newsmen who talked to Italians were finding a marked increase in support of the Fascist regime. Throughout Italy there was a growing resentment against the League, augmented by a resolution which the Fascist Grand Council proclaimed the day before the sanctions began. The eighteenth of November, 1935, the Council declared, was "a date of ignominy and iniquity in the history of the world." It denounced the sanctions as "a plan to suffocate the Italian people and a vain effort to humiliate Italy in order to prevent it from realizing its ideals and defending its *raison d'etre*." The Grand Council concluded by ordering "a stone record of the siege to be sculpted upon the buildings of the Italian communes, so that the enormous injustice perpetrated against Italy, to which the civilization of all countries owes so much, may remain on record down the centuries."

The Italian reticence about plunging southward from Eritrea, or northwestward from Somaliland, after unopposed penetrations of sixty-plus miles into Ethiopia, was an indispensable aid to their victims, who, until the invasion began, had done more talking about it than preparing for it. If the Italians, who had been actively planning their thrust for almost a year, had struck quickly with full speed and power, they might have ended the war before the Ethiopians had even gathered their troops. The

Italian opportunities appeared to be especially good in the south, where the desert offered less formidable obstacles than the northern mountains. But having settled on their northern strategy, and having decided to stop first at Adowa and Adigrat, then at Makalle, they furnished the time and opportunity for Ethiopia's armies to achieve at least rudimentary co-ordination.

By mid-November, the approximately sixty-thousand-man army of Ras Mulugeta was ensconcing itself in the peaks, caves, crevices, and foothills of a mountain called Amba Aradam, about thirty miles south of Makalle. And only a few miles to the west, in the rough mountain and canyon district of the Tembien, at five p.m. on the afternoon of the seventeenth, Ras Seyoum, accompanied by his staff, including the White Russian colonel, Theodore Konovaloff, entered the tree-covered camp of Ras Kassa for a very warm and ceremonial greeting. Henceforth, their combined army of thirty to forty thousand men would act as a unit, under the senior command of Kassa, since he was Ethiopia's premier chieftain. Seyoum accepted Kassa's leadership, as directed by the Emperor, more gracefully than did the older and more stubborn Mulugeta, who felt that, as War Minister, he should hold unquestioned authority.

The two rases met in front of Kassa's large, round tent, Seyoum a heavy-set, burly man whom one reporter described as "a dark-skinned Henry VIII," and Kassa, an older man, gray at the temples, with finer features and deep-set eyes. Kassa was more interested in religion and Coptic theology than war, but he was an accomplished equestrian. He had ridden to war from Gondar, his seat of power, on a thoroughbred horse. Though Kassa liked to study maps, neither he nor Seyoum had ever received more than elementary military training. When Konovaloff showed Seyoum a set of topographical maps of the Tembien area, Seyoum had said to him, "Don't you worry, I can get along without maps. Ras Kassa is the one who's interested in maps. He's capable of studying them for hours on end, but they don't say anything to me. Don't waste your time."

After learning that Kassa was coming north with his army, Seyoum had wanted to march out of the Tembien and meet him, but he had been persuaded otherwise by practical considerations. The Tembien was still free of Italians. It was a difficult region for the Italians to invade. Yet it was an area from which the Ethiopians could attack toward Adowa or Makalle. For these reasons Seyoum had remained hidden in the mountain country to the southwest of Makalle, where he continued his recruitment and awaited the arrival of Kassa. Neither his nor Kassa's army was even as well equipped as Mulugeta's. Each man called to arms had been expected to bring his own rifle and ammunition. Many, having no rifles, reported with sabers or sticks.

217

On the night of the seventeenth, Kassa and Seyoum, with their staffs, gave themselves to feasting in celebration of their union. The next day, they and their armies retired into higher mountains which would provide better cover from Italian airplanes. There, in caves which they furnished as headquarters, they began long and tedious consultations about what they should do next.

CHAPTER TEN

Shortly before eight a.m. on the morning of December 6, Emperor Haile Selassie, having moved his headquarters two hundred forty miles north from Addis Ababa to a mountain town called Dessie near the eastern rim of the high plateau, was hard at work in his quarters, formerly the Italian Consulate, when he heard the hum of distant airplanes. The Italians had not yet bombed Dessie. It was a market town of several thousand people, a sizable cluster of Ethiopian tukuls with an occasional European-style building among them. The crown prince had a palace on one of two hills to the south, and the local chief had a house on the other. An American mission hospital within the town, maintained by the Seventh-Day Adventists, had been converted into a Red Cross dispensary. The former Italian Consulate, now the Emperor's quarters, was undoubtedly Dessie's finest building. When Haile Selassie went to war, he maintained for the most part his peacetime life-style. He still served his guests four courses of European food plus a selection of Ethiopian dishes every night. Wine had been brought north from the cellars of his Addis Ababa palace. He dressed immaculately, as usual, favoring capes of various colors for public appearances and choosing his sun helmets and walking sticks from a large selection kept in the front entrance hall.

If the Italians were coming now to bomb Dessie, it was probably because they had learned he was here. He was a legitimate target, especially since he had with him several thousand of his Imperial Guards, plus a growing army of ordinary soldiers. The mountains around Dessie swarmed with troops awaiting the Emperor's order to continue the march north.

When Haile Selassie heard the approaching airplanes, knowing they were not his, he sprang to his feet, put on a steel helmet he kept nearby, and, after ordering that his fourteen-year-old son, Prince Makonnen, be taken to an air-raid shelter, ran outside into the garden of the establishment where an Oerlikon machine gun had been installed. His entourage, grasping his intention, and seeing the planes which were now overhead, ran after him, pleading with him to take cover.

There were eighteen Italian planes circling the town at medium altitude. The Emperor, who had taken instruction in the use of the gun, took aim and began firing. The planes began dropping their bombs. Within a few minutes, every Ethiopian in Dessie who had a rifle was firing futile bullets into the air. The Emperor, with a more effective weapon, continued his barrage until he noticed that his entourage, having failed in their efforts to make him take cover,[1] were now huddled around him, anxiously watching his performance. For a moment, he transferred to them his anger at the Italians.

"Haven't I told you not to crowd together!" he shouted. "Do you want to make me a target? Take cover! Let me fire!"

By now, the bombs were dropping all over town. Most of them, about a hundred and fifty, were incendiaries, but twenty-one high-explosive bombs were also released, ranging in size from twenty-five to two hundred pounds. Forty of these bombs, mostly incendiaries, hit the Seventh-Day Adventist Red Cross hospital. Five hit the main building in the compound, tearing the roof from the surgery. An instrument tent, contributed by a committee of Ethiopian women under the guidance of Lady Barton, the British minister's wife, was totally destroyed. Whole clusters of Ethiopian tukuls were burned to the ground. No Italian airplanes were shot down.

When the planes retired, fifty-three people were found dead and about two hundred injured. As soon as the hospital was returned to some kind of order, the doctors there performed thirty amputations. Among the dead were a woman and her two small children, caught on the road and wiped out by a single bomb.

As soon as the planes disappeared, the Emperor abandoned his overheated gun to return inside and draft a letter of protest to the League against the bombing of civilians. Then, donning a cloak and selecting a stick, he walked through the town, visiting the wounded. Someone had found a bottle containing a note that had been dropped by an Italian pilot. The note said,

> Long live Italy, long live the Duce, long live the King. We bring, along with our tricolor, the fasces and the civilization of Rome. Greetings to the Negus. Ask him if he has digested his biscuits [bombs].

When the note was brought to Emperor Haile Selassie, he ordered all the unexploded "biscuits" to be piled up in front of his headquarters. There, for the benefit of the news photographers, he posed with his foot on one of the largest of them. The photographers snapped their pictures quickly and asked for no retakes.

* * *

Rumors of a pending Anglo-French peace offer beneficial to Italy were so widespread in early December that Labour Member of Parliament Hugh Dalton, who had once been Parliamentary Undersecretary for Foreign Affairs, addressed himself to the subject December 3 in the House of Commons. "The Foreign Secretary is going to Paris and is going to see Monsieur Laval," Dalton observed. "I trust he will speak what I'm sure is the mind of this country and tell Monsieur Laval that this country is not favorable to, or even interested in, any terms of settlement of this war which will allow the Italian dictator to profit by his aggression."

Dalton's remarks were consistent with those of the newly elected leader of the Labour Party, Clement Attlee, who had spoken in the House of Commons two days earlier, after King George V had officially opened the ninth Parliament of his reign. "The Government has not given firm support to the League hitherto," Attlee had said. "... I find it extraordinarily difficult to see how a settlement acceptable to Italy, Abyssinia and the League can be arrived at. Can we imagine a situation in which the Home Secretary could deplore an outbreak of housebreaking and say he hoped shortly to come to a settlement which would be equally agreeable to the housebreaker, his victim, and the public?"

Prime Minister Stanley Baldwin had arisen to answer Attlee, but not very reassuringly. "The League is on trial," Baldwin observed, "and if the League, on the terms so often quoted, can end this horrible dispute by the methods it is employing, everyone in Europe who is a lover of peace will be grateful and thankful, provided always that the conditions laid down are the conditions obtained."

Unfortunately, no one was quite certain what Baldwin meant when he referred to "terms so often quoted," "methods [the League] is employing," "conditions laid down," or "conditions obtained." Baldwin's recent remarks about the League had been so equivocal as to increase the ambiguity of this latest one. On October 23, when he announced to the House that his government was working with France toward a possible settlement of the war, he had ended with a warning that this settlement might not be a completely satisfactory one. "We must remember," he had said, "that we are not dealing with a League in the plenitude of its strength as envisaged by its founders, but a League which has been left on one side by three of the most important powers in the world, and which has enjoyed, perhaps, a wavering support from some of its members. It is perfectly obvious that what would have been possible with ease in a League constituted as originally contemplated, is not possible in a League as it at present exists."

Baldwin's attitude, coupled with his own, put Foreign Secretary Sir Samuel Hoare at a considerable disadvantage when he arose in the House

December 5 to answer Hugh Dalton. Besides Dalton's general remarks, there was a specific one which could not be ignored. He had charged that the Anglo-Iranian Oil Company, in which the British government was the majority stockholder, had increased its exports to Italy during the first seven months of the year by eighty per cent over the same period in the previous year.

Though the Foreign Secretary could not deny that statement, he did point out that the company's exports to Italy over the first eleven months amounted to less than for the same period in 1934, the decrease having come during the last three months. He was admitting thereby that during the first eight months of the year, for most of which time he and the British Cabinet were totally aware of Mussolini's intentions, they kept sending him oil in ever-increasing amounts, and only when he actually committed the aggression which he had advertised so loudly did the British government get around to decreasing its company's shipments to him.

Having thus lamely answered Dalton's oil charge, Sir Samuel went on to explain what he hoped to accomplish during his pending sojourn in Paris. "The world urgently needs peace," he said. "We and the French, acting on behalf of the League and in the spirit of the League, are determined to make another great effort toward peace. We have no wish to humiliate Italy nor to weaken Italy; indeed we are most anxious to see a strong Italy in the world, an Italy that is strong morally, politically and socially. . . . Let them [the Italians] dismiss from their minds the suspicion that we wish to weaken Signor Mussolini's own position and destroy the Fascist regime. We have not the least desire to interfere in the internal affairs of Italy. . . ."

After reassuring Mussolini, he went on to reassure Dalton and other critics who seemed uneasy about the secret peace plan on which he and Pierre Laval had been at work since late October. The British and French had no intention, he said, of "attempting to sidetrack the League and to impose upon the world a settlement which could not be accepted by the three parties to the dispute."

Sir Samuel spoke as if he were unaware that the matter was no longer a dispute but a war, and that of the three parties to whom he referred, the one he was at greatest pains to reassure had been branded the aggressor by most of the civilized world, including Great Britain. Looking back many years later, he cited ill health in partial explanation of his behavior at this time. Though he no longer suffered from the arthritis in his foot that had plagued him during September, his general health was "very precarious." The doctors, he recalled, "took a serious view and ordered an immediate rest." According to his memory of it, the pending trip Hugh Dalton mentioned was not so much a journey to Paris for negotiation with

Pierre Laval as it was a two-or-three-week holiday in Switzerland, on the way to which he would simply—in the hope of soothing Laval, who had urgently wanted to come to London—"stop in Paris for a few hours" and talk to him.

"It may be that I was so pulled down by overwork," Sir Samuel explained, "that my judgment was out of gear. In any case, I weakly agreed to the invitation, not realizing that it would in every way have been better if I had either let Laval come to London, where I should have had my colleagues around me, or dropped altogether out of the negotiation during the short period of my leave."

A day or two before he left for Paris, he saw Anthony Eden at the top of the Foreign Office staircase and stopped for a few words with him.[2] Eden warned him not only about the wily persuasiveness of Pierre Laval but about the generous inclinations of Sir Robert Vansittart, who was already in Paris. "Don't forget," Eden said to Hoare, "in Paris, Van can be more French than the French."

"Don't worry," Hoare assured him. "I shall not commit you to anything. It wouldn't be fair on my way through to my holiday."

As he was wont to do before departures, Hoare also went to see Prime Minister Stanley Baldwin in his room at the House of Commons. Baldwin's advice to him, as Hoare recalled it, was "very simple." Baldwin was so occupied with the details of launching the new coalition government he had formed after the general election that he "had very little time for discussing with me the implications of my Paris visit."

"Have a good leave and get your health back," Baldwin said to him. "That is the most important thing. By all means stop in Paris, and push Laval as far as you can, but on no account get this country into war."

Sir Samuel, in retrospect, felt that before leaving for Paris he should have insisted on a full Cabinet meeting at which he could come to a clear agreement with his colleagues as to how far he could go in his talks with Laval. "This precaution that has since seemed so elementary," he declared, "I failed to take."

The suggestion here was gentlemanly but not very candid. Sir Samuel would have us believe that the Prime Minister and the rest of the Cabinet knew practically nothing about a set of vitally important negotiations which had been progressing in Paris since late October, and which was now being discussed openly in the press. For what happened in Paris, Sir Samuel seemed to imply, the responsibility was his.

What happened first in Paris, upon Hoare's arrival the afternoon of the seventh, was that he found himself welcomed by Vansittart, who still claimed, several years later, that he was there "in an attempt to counter the Anglophobe press which was more venomous than usual."[3] Vansittart never did explain the function of a British Undersecretary of State in regulating the venom level of the French press. Also on hand at the station was British Ambassador Sir George Clerk and Foreign Office Africa expert Maurice Peterson, who had been the principal British representative in the peace-plan discussions during the previous six weeks. As Vansittart recalled it, "Sam asked me to join him," in the conversations pending with Laval.

Vansittart, looking back, remembered being curious about what instructions Hoare had brought with him from the Cabinet. Home Secretary Sir John Simon, Hoare's predecessor in the Foreign Office, had implied in a conversation with Vansittart that Hoare was coming to Paris only "to take soundings." Vansittart confessed himself puzzled. Peterson and Clerk were able enough to take soundings. During a conversation in their automobile on the way to the Quai d'Orsay, Vansittart asked Hoare about this and learned—for the first time, according to his version—that the Foreign Secretary understood he was authorized and expected to do more. "I warned him that the way of the peacemaker would be hard," Vansittart recalled, "and asked whether the Government meant to fight." Hoare replied that neither the Cabinet nor the nation had any such intention. "Then you will have to compromise," Vansittart advised him. "That will be unpopular but there is no third way."

Vansittart, in explaining his presence in Paris and his concept of Hoare's mission there, conveniently forgot his own role in the development of the new peace plan. He forgot, for instance, his several discussions of the plan's general provisions during the previous months with Italy's Ambassador to Great Britain, Dino Grandi—discussions which led Grandi to say later, "the Laval-Hoare plan of 1935 was nothing more or less than the Grandi-Vansittart plan." Vansittart also forgot that, just before leaving for Paris, he had called in Rex Leeper, head of the Foreign Office news department, and asked him, "How long will it take to alter public opinion on the Abyssinian issue?" When Leeper said it would take at least three weeks, Vansittart had said, "We have only three days."

A swarm of reporters with bulb-popping photographers confronted the British quartet when they arrived at the Quai d'Orsay shortly after five p.m. on the afternoon of December 7. Hoare was astonished at the presence of the newsmen, at their jostling manners and staring faces, and at their barrage of flashbulbs. They made him think of the mob at Versailles in 1789. He did not speak to them. Laval, dressed as usual in his black suit and white tie, greeted the Hoare party in his study. Vansittart considered his appearance grubby. The seating arrangement around his conference table indicated his intention to direct the proceedings. He sat at the very center with a telephone in front of him. To his right were his advisers—Alexis Léger, Vansittart's counterpart as permanent head of the French Ministry of Foreign Affairs; René Comte de Saint-Quentin,

African expert who, with Peterson, had worked out the details of the peace plan; and René Massigli, of the Ministry's political section, subsequently French Ambassador to Great Britain. On his left there were places for Hoare, Vansittart, Clerk, and Peterson, in that order.

The first thing Laval said, after courtesies had been exchanged, was that if the League were to impose an oil embargo against Italy, Mussolini would be driven to a desperate act. France, therefore, was not prepared to agree to any oil embargo until further efforts to compromise had been exhausted. Whether Laval actually believed this or not is difficult to determine. Mussolini was doing everything possible, through his ambassadors all over Europe, and through his own belligerent utterances, to make people think he was capable of the rashest possible conduct, particularly against England. Sir Samuel Hoare claimed then and later that he believed Mussolini's threats, and Vansittart implied the same belief when he told Hoare that unless England was prepared to fight, he would have to compromise. Laval, in a conversation with United States Ambassador Jesse Straus December 9, said Italy was already suffering severely from the economic sanctions and would be completely strangled if deprived of petroleum. He said Mussolini would find himself in civil war if he were to withdraw his army from Ethiopia, but that he could not keep it there unless he could continue to supply it. From this, Laval concluded that application of oil sanctions would force Mussolini into an attack of some sort against England, that France would then get involved, and that Hitler was quietly waiting to see what happened. Oil sanctions would therefore, he said, create a great danger of European war. Mussolini had a rope around his neck, and would be forced to fight.

If Laval, Hoare, and companies believed all this, then Mussolini must have been the only person of importance who did not believe it. Three years later, in the spring of 1938, Mussolini told Adolf Hitler, "If the League of Nations had followed Eden's advice in the Abyssinian dispute and had extended economic sanctions to oil, I would have had to withdraw from Abyssinia within a week. That would have been an incalculable disaster for me." He had always been aware that he didn't dare fight England, and his chief of staff, Badoglio, had reinforced his awareness in the August 1935 study of the military prospects for a war against England.

Hoare's reaction to Laval's opening remark about the inadvisability of an oil embargo was predictable, especially when Laval added that France had no intention of going to war. Sir Samuel, without even momentarily doubting that Mussolini would dare attack England in the Mediterranean, began to worry about French support if such an attack were to take place. He put the question directly to Laval.

Laval's answer was evasive. He would not promise to make military preparations for such a possibility. French cooperation, he indicated, would depend on the outcome of the talks on which they were now embarked. The only definite concession he would make was an agreement to begin military staff talks between the two countries.

The discussion then moved on to the subject of the joint peace plan on which they had been working for six weeks. Laval said the offer to Italy would have to be increased if they wanted Mussolini to accept it. The Italian armies had already occupied a sizable portion of northern Ethiopia, and it was inconceivable that Mussolini would surrender any of this land, especially since it included Adowa, which occupied such a "sensitive spot in every Italian heart." The situation had therefore changed since Peterson and Saint-Quentin had agreed upon the provisional plan.

Sir Samuel "felt there was some force in Laval's argument," especially since he had "been informed that the Emperor would find serious opposition from the rases who had gone over to the Italian side in the occupied districts if their territory was restored to Abyssinia." Sir Samuel did not disclose by whom he had been thus informed. It could hardly have been by the Italians, who were well aware that all of the Ethiopians who had come over to their side had been paid to do so, and that none of them were rases. The highest in rank was Dejasmatch Haile Selassie Gugsa. The Italians made no claim to have converted even one ras. The rases of northern Ethiopia had taken to the field to raise armies against them. Sir Samuel could have learned this by reading the newspapers. Since he chose to be "informed" otherwise, he found it easy to agree with Laval that the Italians should have "some further parts of the Tigre territory," but Ethiopia must be given a port in exchange, and the additional territory for Italy "must be compensated by the lowering of Italian demands in the rest of the country."

What port, or what kind of port should the Ethiopians be offered? It was now too late in the day to go into that. Sir Samuel reluctantly agreed, therefore, to stay in Paris through the next day and continue the talks, which had begun supposedly as discussions but which had now become more akin to negotiations.

When the talks resumed the following morning, a Sunday, Hoare and Laval agreed that the port offered to Ethiopia should be either Zeila in British Somaliland (which Mussolini had already refused to let them have), or Assab in southern Eritrea (which Laval would let them have only if they would promise not to build a railroad to it in competition with the French-owned Addis Ababa–Djibuti line). Vansittart thought the French "niggling" on the railroad issue. Conversely, Laval considered the British "niggardly" in their attitude toward Italy. He felt a necessity, as he told Ambassador Straus, to convince Hoare that England must be more liberal. They would have to offer Italy more than they had intended. Mussolini's back had been stiffened by the obvious weakening of the

English on sanctions. Laval was now totally opposed to sanctions, and, in his view, so were most of the smaller countries because they were losing money by withholding their goods from Italy. He was determined to prevent the imposition of oil sanctions on the grounds that they would lead to a general war. He had already demanded and obtained a postponement, from November 29 to December 12, of a meeting of the League's Committee of Eighteen, at which the practical implementation of the oil embargo was to be considered. By December 12, he hoped, the Anglo-French peace plan would have quelled the demand for any more sanctions. Even though he considered the League of Nations "practically emasculated" insofar as protection against war was concerned, he intended to go to Geneva, after finishing this negotiation with the British, in an effort "to pacify those who might clamor for sanctions."

From the question of the port, Laval, Hoare, and companies passed on to what Hoare called "the form and scope of the economic monopoly that was envisaged for Italy in the non-Amharic provinces to the south." Laval wanted this zone increased. Hoare agreed, but "insisted that any Italian economic monopoly in the province(s) should be subject to League supervision." Laval argued that if this provision were to be included, the plan should be sent for approval to Rome before it went to Geneva or Addis Ababa. He made a great point throughout the negotiations of the danger that Mussolini might reject the plan if it fell short of his expectations. Hoare could scarcely argue with him on that subject. Laval knew very well what Mussolini's expectations were. They talked daily on the telephone. Hoare noticed that during his two days in Paris, Laval "more than once rang up Mussolini, with whom he seemed to have a direct and secret line." Laval disclosed that Mussolini would be more likely to accept the plan if it went first to him, and that when once he had accepted it, and it went to Geneva as an Anglo-French proposal, no one at the League would oppose it. On this point Hoare quickly agreed with Laval. Perhaps it did not occur to either man that there was at least one League member nation very likely to oppose it—Ethiopia. Or perhaps it did occur to them that Ethiopia might oppose it, in which case, with Italy approving it, they could wipe their hands of Ethiopia by blaming that tiresome little country, rather than Italy, for threatening the peace of Europe.

By midafternoon of Sunday, December 8, Hoare and Laval, with their aides bearing witness, had agreed upon and initialed a proposal which would thereafter be known, to their considerable embarrassment, as the Hoare-Laval Plan. If ratified, this plan would give Italy about half of Ethiopia and provide her with the means of swallowing the other half at her leisure. It would cede to Italy most of the northern province of Tigre, which the Italian armies were still timidly probing, the Danakil country as far south as the Sultanate of Aussa, and all of the Ogaden to the east

227

and south of Addis Ababa. It would also establish an economic monopoly for Italy over all of Ethiopia below the eighth parallel (just south of Addis Ababa) and as far west as longitude 35E., which was almost at the Sudanese border. Peterson had wanted to draw the western boundary of this zone at longitude 40E., about seventy-five miles east of Addis Ababa. Saint-Quentin had argued that it should extend to longitude 38E., about seventy-five miles west of the capital. Hoare had settled the argument generously by offering Italy everything as far west as longitude 35E. In exchange for all this, the Hoare-Laval Plan offered Ethiopia the barren, undeveloped port of Assab, with the provision that no railroad was to be built to it. In addition, Ethiopia would be allowed to keep its Coptic religious center at Axum—a tribute to the religious sensitivities of Hoare and Laval.

Before parting, Hoare and Laval agreed on one more thing. It would not be prudent to allow publication of their plan's details at least until after Mussolini approved it. But the reporters outside the door were clamoring for news. Perhaps a joint communiqué would satisfy them. It was quickly prepared:

> Animated by the same spirit of conciliation and inspired by close Anglo-French friendship, we have in the course of our long conversations of today and yesterday sought the formulae for a friendly settlement of the Italo-Ethiopian dispute. There could be no question at present of publishing these formulae. The British Government has not yet been informed of them and once its agreement has been received it will be necessary to submit them to the interested governments and to the decision of the League of Nations.
> We have worked together with the same anxiety to reach as rapidly as possible a pacific and honourable solution. We are both satisfied with the results which have been reached.

As Laval was seeing Hoare to the door, he later recalled saying to the British Foreign Secretary, "Now we have finished with Italy. Together we shall tackle Germany." He also said a new chapter had now opened in Anglo-French cooperation.

These remarks were soon to prove premature. Sir Samuel, on returning to the British Embassy, where he was staying, found another swarm of newsmen pleading for an interview. He saw them for a few minutes, gave them what he considered "a very general idea of what we had been attempting," and pointed out that the plan would have to be approved by all the parties to it. He asked the reporters, therefore, "not to comment upon it in any detail until the two governments released the actual terms." The newsmen, of course, honored this last request for as long as it took them to reach telephones.

Hoare then sent a telegram to Sir Sidney Barton in Addis Ababa urging that he do everything possible to make certain Emperor Haile Selassie would appreciate the benefits of the plan when he was allowed to see it. As Hoare and Laval had agreed, the Emperor was not to see it until after Mussolini had seen it. But, in the meantime, Barton should inform him that the French and British governments were "seeking a solution by conciliation" on the basis of the Committee of Five's September proposals, which Ethiopia had accepted.

Hoare also sent a telegram to Anthony Eden at the Foreign Office in London, asking that a Cabinet be summoned for the next day, but not explaining the need for it. He had already dispatched Peterson to London with the text of the peace plan, which would, he felt, make clear the reason for the meeting. After sending the telegram, he still had time for a short nap before leaving for the Gare de Lyon to catch the night express for Switzerland and his cherished holiday. He hoped to spend two or three weeks with his wife, who had preceded him, resting and ice skating.

Eden, receiving only the bare telegram, and already uneasy about the danger of subjecting Hoare to Laval's persuasiveness, went to see Stanley Baldwin at 10 Downing Street. The Prime Minister said he knew no reason for the Cabinet to meet the next day. After returning to the Foreign Office, Eden telephoned Hoare at the British Embassy in Paris, but was told that the Foreign Secretary was resting. Desperately eager to find out what was happening, Eden sought information from the secretary who had answered the phone. The secretary, excusing himself, returned to the phone a few minutes later to say, "The Secretary of State [Hoare] and Sir Robert Vansittart are well satisfied with the day's work."

As the satisfied Sir Samuel Hoare made himself comfortable on the overnight train to Switzerland, the journalists in Paris were still busy. Unsatisfied by the joint communiqué Laval's office had handed them in the afternoon, they pursued their efforts to learn the details of the Hoare-Laval Plan. Two of them succeeded. Through a leak in the French Foreign Office, which harbored its share of Laval-haters, two Paris newspapers, *Oeuvre* and *Echo de Paris*, were both able the next morning to publish exact copies of the peace plan. At the same time, London and New York papers, thanks partly to Sir Samuel's Embassy press conference, were able to publish, on the ninth, fairly accurate summaries of the plan.

Maurice Peterson, who had arrived in London overnight from Paris, went almost directly to Anthony Eden's home for a breakfast meeting with him. Peterson first handed Eden a short covering letter from Hoare which said it was essential for the Cabinet to make a decision on this matter at once. Every moment counted. Eden would see when he read the proposals that they came "well within the framework of the Committee of Five" (whose peace plan Mussolini had rejected in September), and were "on the basis we had agreed in London."

After reading Hoare's note, Eden turned to the copy Peterson had brought of the plan itself—a four-page typewritten document in French, initialed "S.H." and "P.L." To Eden it looked as if it had been drafted hastily. He was "surprised that Hoare, who was competent rather than fluent in French, had not insisted on a translation." As Eden read the details of the plan, these "mild reflections rapidly turned to astonishment."

"It did not seem to me to be possible," he recalled, "to reconcile these proposals with those of the Committee of Five, nor with the instructions given to Peterson. I knew of no other basis agreed upon in London."

After reading the proposals, Eden looked aghast at Peterson and asked how Hoare had come to sign them.

Peterson, whose views on the final provisions of the plan had not been invited, even though he had been one of the original architects, said to Eden, "I did not suppose that you would like them."

Prime Minister Baldwin was busy elsewhere that morning. As soon as he was free, he went to Eden's office, where the Secretary for League Affairs awaited him. Eden had in hand not only the proposals but a map on which he explained them to Baldwin. After Eden had carefully described these proposals and their implications, the Prime Minister asked him an extraordinary question.

"What do you think of them?" he said. It apparently did not occur to Stanley Baldwin that there was anything wrong with them.

Eden, after elaborating on his objections, said two things were clear: neither the Emperor nor the League of Nations would accept such terms.

Baldwin grunted and looked unhappy. He said, "That lets us out, doesn't it?"[4] He had been acting for months as if he wanted only to cast aside and ignore the inconvenient Ethiopian mess. Now it seemed to him he had the opportunity to do so. He did agree with Eden, though, that the Cabinet would have to meet and discuss the subject that evening.

When the Cabinet met at six p.m. on the ninth, the members were still unaware that the Hoare-Laval Plan had been published verbatim by two Paris newspapers that morning, and that *The New York Times* had published a fairly exact summary of it, cabled from London the night before. Everybody but the British seemed to know what the British were doing. Wrapped in the security of their belief that the whole matter was still a secret and would remain one, some of the ministers began to think and talk in terms of revising the plan slightly in Geneva before it became public, to make it more palatable. Indeed, had it not been for Eden's objections, most of them might have failed to notice there was anything possibly unpalatable about it. Even after listening to Eden and discussing the plan fully, the majority of Cabinet ministers found it satisfactory. They decided not to repudiate the Hoare-Laval Plan (to do so would have indicated disloyalty to their vacationing Foreign Secretary, whom they didn't even disturb with a questioning phone call), but to insist, because Eden was making such a point of it, that both Mussolini and Haile Selassie be informed of the proposal at the same time. Further, the Cabinet instructed Eden that he should press both of them to accept it.

Unable to cope with the cynicism in London, Eden turned his mind to the cynicism in Paris. He was beginning now to suspect Pierre Laval's strategy, which might also have been Samuel Hoare's strategy, in demanding that Mussolini see the plan before Haile Selassie. Perhaps, like Stanley Baldwin, Laval saw in the developing situation a chance to slide out of the whole mess. After the Cabinet meeting, Eden went directly to the Foreign Office and phoned Vansittart at the Ritz Hotel in Paris. The Emperor must be informed of the plan, Eden said, at the same time as Mussolini.

Vansittart saw no reason why the French should object to that change. He agreed to take care of the matter immediately.

After dinner, Eden returned to the Foreign Office just in time to receive Vansittart's return call from Paris. Vansittart had learned in the meantime that he had been too hopeful. Laval had made only a slight concession. He had agreed only that the Emperor might be shown at this time a limited account of the proposals.

Eden decided he had to put the matter as strongly as possible. "This is a Cabinet decision reached after careful consideration," he said to Vansittart. "A partial account will not do, for what is proposed goes beyond the Committee of Five's report." In other words, the Hoare-Laval Plan was offering Mussolini more than the Committee of Five had offered him before he launched his aggression. Vansittart said he would see Laval again, and Eden settled into his office to spend the night if necessary.

Shortly after midnight, a ciphered telegram arrived from Paris. Sir Robert, as a result of another conversation with the French Prime Minister, had a new and startling development to report. If Laval were to agree that the Emperor be informed of the proposals immediately, he would expect in return a definite promise from the British that they would not vote for oil sanctions in Geneva.

Though Laval's strategy was now becoming obvious, Eden didn't respond to it directly. In his answering telegram to Vansittart, he said it was impossible to give such an assurance without the consent of the Prime Minister and the Cabinet. Besides, he didn't see how such a procedure would work.

Though it was sometime after one a.m. when Vansittart received this Eden telegram at the Ritz in Paris, he called Laval once more and made an immediate appointment with him. When Vansittart arrived at the Quai d'Orsay at two a.m., he found Laval wearing a soiled nightgown and looking "bleary-eyed," either from sleep or from lack of it. But while he may have been sleepy, he was not lethargic. After listening patiently while Vansittart enumerated Eden's objections, he produced an answer which apparently caught Vansittart unawares. He didn't want to inform the Ethiopians of the plan right away, Laval said, because he had reason to believe the Emperor would be bound to reject it. Why? Because he would realize that if he accepted it, there would be no oil sanctions. Laval wanted the British to agree that, even if Haile Selassie rejected the plan, there would be no oil sanctions, because, in the event of an Ethiopian rejection, Laval would not be able to persuade his French colleagues to vote for another sanction.

Vansittart thought there was good sense in what Laval said. It didn't occur to him to question Laval's premise that the Emperor would reject the plan simply because an acceptance would foreclose the possibility of an oil embargo against Italy. If Ethiopia were to accept, then a settlement of the war would presumably result and all embargoes could be forgotten. Laval was undoubtedly convinced the Emperor would reject the proposals, but for another reason—because they were an outrageous affront to Ethiopia. Laval did not want the Emperor to reject them, however, until after Mussolini had tentatively approved them, because Mussolini would be unable to approve them once the Emperor had turned them down; and if Mussolini didn't approve them, it would be impossible to make the Frenchman look like a conciliator in the eyes of the world. Laval's plan was an ambitious one. He wanted to arrange a public reversal of roles which would make Mussolini the hero and Haile Selassie the villain. To prevent the English from spoiling this plan, he was demanding of them, in return for his support of the plan, something he knew they could not grant—a definite foreclosure of the oil embargo.

When Vansittart relayed this demand to London, Eden quickly sent the reply Laval must have been expecting. To submit settlement terms to the aggressor while withholding them from the victim would be indefensible. And as for the oil sanction, England could make no undertaking since it was a matter the League must decide.

The question of when Ethiopia would be officially informed of the Hoare-Laval proposals was therefore left in contention, which was agreeable to Laval—since he had already transmitted the proposals to Mussolini. The longer Laval argued with England about when the Emperor should receive them, the more time Mussolini would have to study and at least tentatively approve them as a basis of negotiations.

Laval's plan, though he didn't yet realize it, was already encountering danger not only in England but in Ethiopia. The French Havas News Agency had put on its wire Sunday morning, December 8, a report of the Hoare-Laval meeting and—thanks to the leaks in Laval's own office—

a fairly detailed outline of the proposals under discussion. Because the report was dispatched while the Paris talks were still in progress, Havas could not disclose the final results, but it did give a good general idea of what the results were likely to be.

When Christian Ozanne, the Havas correspondent in Addis Ababa, received this report, he took it immediately to the Emperor's chief adviser, Everett Colson.[5] Though Colson quickly understood the implications of this news, it caught him at a disadvantage. Since the Emperor had moved north to Dessie, it was difficult to get in touch with him. A telephone connection, or a telegram, could take a day or two. The radio closed at noon on Sunday and didn't reopen until Monday morning. There was a question of what the Emperor could do with the Havas information even if he did get it immediately. A head of state could hardly take action, or even make a decision about such a critical matter, on the basis of a speculative press dispatch. In addition, when the Emperor left Addis Ababa November 28, he had empowered his Council, headed by Foreign Minister Blattengeta Herouy Wolde Selassie, to make whatever important decisions might be necessary in his absence. While Colson could advise Herouy and the Council members, it would be improper for him to go over their heads and contact the Emperor directly on the basis of this press dispatch. He could only wait impatiently for the formal notification of the proposals.

Vittorio Mussolini, who had now spent two months bombing defenseless Ethiopians, took off in his CA-133 on the morning of December 9 to attack a cluster of horsemen who had been spotted the previous day moving northward toward Amba Aradam, about thirty miles south of Makalle.[6] The Duce's oldest son was flying with great confidence now. As he later related,

> I was a little bit messed up in the first days. I didn't know anything about military life. I didn't know my colleagues or my superiors. I understood very little about ceilings, altitude, firing, bombs, piloting, etc. I was a novice, like a little bird fallen into the nest of an eagle, but to honor the truth, in the month of waiting [for the war to begin], I managed to make myself, if not equal, at least very close to the others in everything, and with conscience and desire, I was able to avoid being the dead weight of the squadron and to do everything the others could do.

He seemed to be suggesting that in the Italian air force, a novice, after a month of training, could become the approximate equal of a veteran pilot.

Having calculated the probable route and position of the Ethiopian horsemen on the morning of the ninth, Vittorio and his companions decided to approach them from behind in the hope of getting as close as possible before being spotted. Flying a circuitous route toward a town called Corbetta, about ten miles southeast of Amba Aradam, they then banked westward in the direction of the horsemen's route. Vittorio had already discovered the exhilaration with which such a pursuit could fill him. During an earlier mission in which he had dropped five bombs on a cluster of Ethiopian tents, he had experienced an unforgettable delight. "Many tents blew up," he reported.

> I see men and beasts running away toward the edge of the mountains and with pleasure I see little clouds of smoke. They also fired and defended themselves. The joy is so great that I no longer feel disappointed [as he had after an earlier mission]. Oh, if only the whole group were here! What a beautiful chance!

As he and his companions flew west from Corbetta toward the Amba Aradam route, they got the benefit of a broken cloud cover which concealed their approach. After reaching the main north-south route from Dessie to Makalle, they banked again, to the north, and as they passed the second great mountain in the area, Amba Alagi, their search was suddenly rewarded. Below and ahead they saw not only the horsemen they sought but "a few thousand" men on foot. The airplanes dove quickly toward their targets as horses and men scrambled for cover. "In a short time," Vittorio recalled, "the plain was unpopulated." But not before he had his sport. "I still have in mind," he wrote later, "the spectacle of a little group ... blooming like a rose when some of my fragmentation bombs fell in their midst. It was great fun and you could hit them easily. . . ."

Late in the afternoon of December 10, Prime Minister Stanley Baldwin had to face an angry House of Commons. All the London newspapers had now published the full text of the Hoare-Laval Plan, as copied from Paris newspapers of the previous day. A congestion of furious phone calls assailed the Members of Parliament, promising a deluge of furious mail the following morning. Even the Conservative Members were in a mood to lay off some of this anger upon Baldwin and his Cabinet.

Baldwin began with a timid suggestion that if there were any fault to be found it was in the League of Nations. The League's Coordination Committee, he said, "had approved negotiations." As he knew, this was not true. The Coordination Committee had no such authority, but since the Members of Parliament probably didn't know that, he might get away with saying it. In any case, he added, "no suggested basis [of negotiations] has at present been submitted to the views of either Italy or Abyssinia."

This preliminary fib was followed by a large lie. Though he had not yet read the newspaper accounts, Baldwin said, he had been "told by those who had studied the original proposals and the press reports that there were considerable differences in the matter of substance." He could not have been ignorant of the fact that the newspapers had now published the proposals verbatim.

None of this satisfied his audience. It would take something suggestive or mysterious to soothe them. He would have to call upon their faith in him, which, in the case of many, was considerable. What he produced to fill this urgent need was a remark that followed him through the rest of his public life: "I have seldom spoken with greater regret," he said, "for my lips are not yet unsealed. Were these troubles over I would make a case, and I guarantee that not a man would go into the lobby against us."

Anthony Eden, who was also forced by circumstances to say a few words about the Hoare-Laval Plan, tried to perform the feat of disassociation by association. He approved of the negotiations, he said, because they reflected the League's desire "that the search for conciliation be concurrent with the imposition of sanctions." As for the plan itself, opposition was developing. Some said it was contrary to the principles of the Covenant. If so, he said, it was for the League to say so. "If they do say so," he declared, "we shall make no complaint. We shall be ready to accept their judgment just as we have been ready to take our part in this very unwelcome task." Unlike Baldwin, he at least had the intelligence to realize the size of the mess into which the Cabinet had fallen, and to begin looking for a way out of it.

Eden's shame did not, however, induce him to resign from the Cabinet, as some of his associates suggested he should do, nor did it prevent him from carrying out the Cabinet's instructions to try to win approval of the plan by Ethiopia and the League. On the same day he made the above remarks in Commons, Eden initialed and sent to Sir Sidney Barton in Addis Ababa two telegrams, one of which contained the text of the proposals, while the other, prepared for this occasion by Hoare before he went to Paris, urged Barton to vigorous action in support of the proposals. This second telegram, incidentally, left no doubt as to Sir Samuel's intentions in Paris. It said to Barton:

> You should use your utmost influence to induce the Emperor to give careful and favorable consideration to these proposals and on no account lightly to reject them. On the contrary, I feel sure that he will give further

proof of his statesmanship by realizing the advantages of the opportunity of negotiation which they afford, and will avail himself thereof.

At Zuoz, Switzerland, where the air was cold and fresh December snow covered the surrounding Alps, Sir Samuel himself had embarked upon his skating vacation, still blithely unaware of how slippery the ice had become elsewhere. He had learned that there was a bit of a stir at home over the Paris proposals. He had even thought of returning to London when he learned about the publication of the text in the newspapers and the unfavorable early reactions to the plan. But then Stanley Baldwin, in his own good time, had called to assure him that the Cabinet was supporting the plan and that everything was under control.

Baldwin's call was a great relief to Hoare. He loved skating above all other sports and had been looking forward to this holiday for several months. He had even arranged for "one of the best rinks in the Engadine" to be prepared for his private use before it was scheduled to open.

December 10 at Zuoz, the day Baldwin and Eden had to face the House of Commons, was a perfect day for skating. When Sir Samuel looked out of his hotel suite to see the "blue sky, white snow, and black ice," he grabbed his skates and hurried to the rink, "feeling that there was no turn or step that I could not accomplish." He was undeterred by one danger he faced when skating—his tendency to suffer sudden fainting spells. On a recent occasion when he and his wife, Lady Maud, were at the cinema in a party with the Anthony Edens, he had stood up to go out and collapsed in the aisle. Eden and their host, Sir Philip Sassoon, had rushed to his aid and found him unconscious, but Lady Maud had assured them it was nothing unusual and that he would soon recover, which he did within a few minutes. His fainting spells were far from his mind as he glided onto the ice this cold, clear day in Zuoz. Before he had been skating long, however, a sudden and complete blackout overtook him, "even blacker than those that I had had several times in the previous months."

When he regained consciousness, he discovered to his dismay that he had done some painful injury to his face. Tottering back to the hotel, he called his local doctor, who came immediately to examine him and explained that he had expected something like this. Sir Samuel, the doctor found, had broken his nose in two places.

Anthony Eden, after sending his telegrams and addressing the House of Commons December 10, quickly got out of town, hurrying off to Geneva for the December 12 session of the League's Committee of Eighteen, which was scheduled to discuss the projected oil embargo against Italy. If he thought he was escaping the heat by leaving London, he soon learned differently. Salvador de Madariaga, the Spanish delegate to the League, who had earlier made some very obsequious remarks about Italy, told him now that Spain would not support the Paris proposals. Nicolas Politis, the Greek delegate, told him the Balkan countries were confounded. Bozhidar Pouritch of Yugoslavia said the world would regard the proposals as a triumph for Mussolini, who might next decide to attack Albania. Pouritch also raised the possibility that, having taken all he could get from France and England, Mussolini might then turn to Hitler for new friendship.

The attitude of Augusto Vasconcellos of Portugal was even more disturbing to Eden because Vasconcellos was chairman of the Committee of Eighteen. He came to Eden's suite in the Beau Rivage on the morning of the twelfth, just before the Committee was to convene. Members of the committee, he said, were both angered and dismayed. They were asking each other why their countries had been encouraged to apply sanctions, to suffer loss of trade and other inconveniences if France and England intended to offer Italy perhaps more than she would ever have attained by herself, even if the sanctions had never been applied. And what would happen, Vasconcellos wanted to know, if, after Mussolini accepted the proposals, as everyone expected him to do, the Emperor then were to reject them?

Vasconcellos also saw the proposals as a terrible precedent. Was the League telling the world that aggressor countries were to be given the right to seize the territories of other countries? If so, Germany might soon be asking for such privileges in Portuguese colonies. Though he had not yet received instructions from his government, he was confident he would not be allowed to vote for the Hoare-Laval Plan.

By this time, ten of the eighteen member nations represented on the Coordination Committee had already signified their willingness to vote for oil sanctions against Italy, and it was likely that several of the others would do so. There was still speculation as to how England would finally vote. There was no speculation about France. Everyone knew how Laval felt. Three days earlier he had told United States Ambassador Jesse Straus he was going to Geneva to endeavor to pacify those who might clamor for sanctions.

The meeting of the committee opened in a deep gloom which Laval, for one, did not share. The disturbance attendant upon his and Hoare's peace plan had distracted attention from the oil issue, and Laval was determined that the distraction should hold, however exacerbating it might be. With that comfortable insensitivity which infuriated his associates almost as much as his grubby appearance, he stood up as soon as the committee assembled and, ignoring the purpose of the meeting, proposed that the peace plan be examined and acted upon by the League Council. It would be pointless, of course, and not at all conciliatory, to discuss an oil embargo against a country at a time when you were trying to lead it to the negotiation table. Anthony Eden, it must be said, abetted Laval. When he arose, he made it clear that the British government supported the proposals, which he termed "suggestions," and left the impression that he would be very pleased if these "suggestions" (which he privately found appalling) might "make possible the beginning of negotiations."

With Eden thus abandoning them, the pro-sanctionists on the committee surrendered. Titus Komarnicki, the Polish representative, stood and proposed that the group should postpone further consideration of the oil embargo until Ethiopia and Italy expressed their reactions to the Hoare-Laval Plan. The meeting ended as gloomily as it had begun, but at least Laval was happy. The oil embargo appeared to be permanently doomed.

The Takazze River, walled in by a deep gorge along much of its route, and fordable at only a few places, was a natural barrier against any Ethiopian advance northward that might threaten the Italian western sector. For this reason, the Italians had stationed troops to guard the Takazze fords, the most important of which was at a small town called Mai Timchet, about forty-five miles southwest of Adowa. At Mai Timchet, the Italians were keeping about a thousand Eritrean irregulars with white officers. Their armament included a squadron of light tanks.

Within the first ten days of December, the combined forces of Ras Imru and Dejasmatch Ayelu Birru, now numbering about thirty thousand men (of whom Imru felt he could depend upon only his own twenty thousand), had reached the vicinity of the Takazze along its south bank, across from Mai Timchet. Imru, knowing about Ayelu's negotiations with the Italians, distrusted him and his men, but did not intend to be stopped by the danger they represented within his ranks.[7] To get this far, Imru and his army had marched about five hundred miles through the roughest possible country from Debra Markos in the Lake Tana region along a barely visible track up to a height of more than ten thousand feet at one point, then down through a series of deep ravines, up again into another range of mountains, and down once more toward the Takazze. They were ready to fight, whatever might be the plans of Ayelu and his followers, who had joined them along the way. During strategy meetings, Imru found Ayelu "invariably defeatist." The fact that he was talking to the Italians did not, strangely enough, prove that he would be ultimately disloyal to Imru's cousin, the Emperor. Many Ethiopian chiefs engaged in issueless conversations with the Italians, yet Imru was sufficiently distrustful of Ayelu to be cagey about his own plans, which he had already formulated.

Beginning at or just before dawn on December 15, Imru, with five thousand men, began crossing the Takazze as inconspicuously as possible at the Mai Timchet ford. Before they were discovered, enough of them had reached the north bank to overwhelm and rout the Mai Timchet Italian garrison, whose survivors quickly retreated northeastward into the mountains in the direction of the Dembeguina Pass, their only avenue of escape to Selaclaca, Axum, and Adowa. Imru, having foreseen this possibility, had previously sent another contingent, estimated at five thousand men, to cross the river several miles south of Mai Timchet. These men had traveled over ground which Marshal Badoglio later described as "apparently impassable," to reach a defile of the Dembeguina Pass at a point the Italians could not avoid on their way to Selaclaca and Adowa. By midday of the fifteenth, the Italians, pursued by Ethiopians at their rear, were rapidly retiring, though in good order, toward an ambush of Ethiopians in the mountains ahead of them. Ras Imru was now threatening to accomplish exactly what the new Italian supreme commander, Badoglio, feared the Ethiopians might do.

When Badoglio arrived from Rome on November 30 to take over the Italian headquarters in Adigrat, one of the first things he noticed was the danger on his western flank. Recalling later the situation in that sector, he wrote,

> . . . on the right of the line taken up, there remained, more or less open, an inviting way of entry into our colonial territory, the route leading from the Shire by Adi Abo, across Dechi Tesfa, right to the heart of Eritrea. An adversary with no qualms as to his supplies could have taken advantage of that route, as indeed the enemy seemed to contemplate; and this was an anxiety not only, and not so much, on account of the possibility it offered for an invasion of the colony, as for the relative ease with which the enemy could cut our communications between Asmara and Adowa.[8]

Badoglio also found several other military situations which disturbed him upon his arrival. The two main spearheads of the Italian army had penetrated Ethiopia with so little coordination (thanks partly to Mussolini's impatient passion for Makalle) that the eastern column, now at Makalle, was about fifty miles deeper south than the western column at Adowa. The Makalle column was therefore exposed on its right, though protected on its left by the sheer drop-off of the high plateau. The center column, composed mostly of Eritreans, was somewhere between the two, but not far enough south to protect the army corps at Makalle, which Badoglio considered perilously vulnerable, especially since it was eighty miles from its nearest base. Among these three columns, quick communication was almost impossible. Though Badoglio had been named supreme commander because he seemed to promise more rapid action than De Bono, he decided that, until these conditions were rectified, he would be no more eager to advance than was his predecessor.

It is unclear, however, why he failed to send more troops to the Mai Timchet outpost, or at least to Dembeguina Pass, which was the probable Ethiopian route in any attempt to get behind the Italians and drive toward Eritrea. The one thousand Eritrean irregulars at Mai Timchet could not possibly contain a forceful Ethiopian thrust across the Takazze. Apparently they weren't even expected to do so. When their commander withdrew them up the mountains toward the Dembeguina Pass, his eventual goal seems to have been Selaclaca, where the Italians had established a garrison. Why this garrison had not been established at Dembeguina Pass is a question the Italians must have begun asking themselves about noon December 15, when they reached the pass only to find that Imru's second contingent had gotten there ahead of them, and was installed on the surrounding crests.

The day was extremely hot and the Italian troops were already tired from their rapid march up the mountains, a march which had been accelerated by the Ethiopians behind them. As the Ethiopians on the crests ahead of them opened fire, the Italians had only one possible advantage. They had now been joined by their squadron of nine light tanks. There was a possibility, at least, that these rumbling metal monsters might terrify the Ethiopians sufficiently to induce them to flee. The Italian commander decided to force his way through the trap by sending his tanks ahead. But these Ethiopians had heard about tanks and realized there was nothing supernatural about such monsters. In wave after wave, they rushed down the hills, indifferent to their casualties, attacking the tanks with spears, which they thrust into the slits in the armor, and with metal rods, which they used to pry the caterpillar treads from the wheels.

Even when their tanks were put out of action, the black Italian troops did not waver. Hand-to-hand combat was as traditional for them as for the Ethiopians. Fixing their bayonets, they ran past the disabled tanks and engaged the Ethiopians at close quarters. At the end of the day, three hundred seventy of the black Italians were dead or wounded, together with twenty-two white Italian soldiers and nine white officers. But the rest of the party, more than five hundred men, managed to break through and reach Selaclaca.

The Ethiopians, though they had lost more men than the Italians, hurried along behind them. On the following day, Ras Imru and his troops, disregarding the Ethiopian one-day battle tradition, chased the Italians out of their garrison at Selaclaca. They had knocked out nine tanks, captured twenty-eight machine guns and hundreds of rifles, and had found at Selaclaca a sizable supply of ammunition. Most important, they had penetrated the Italian right flank to a depth of forty-five miles, and they were now only ten miles from Axum.

Six European journalists encamped within the compound of the Seventh-Day Adventist hospital in Dessie received a sudden summons December 16 to an Imperial press conference at Haile Selassie's headquarters in what had been the Italian Consulate or commercial agency. (The fact that the Italians had no commerce in Dessie had not prevented them from building a commercial agency there. Such agencies, throughout Ethiopia, had been used as centers for gathering information and cultivating the friendship of local chiefs.) Hurrying up the hill, covered with grass and dotted with eucalyptus trees, the correspondents found a scene outside the gates of the headquarters which reminded them of the usual scene outside the Emperor's gibbi in Addis Ababa. A multitude of Ethiopians, now wearing khaki or ocher-colored shammas instead of white, stood, sat, or squatted on the ground, waiting for a chance either to talk to His Imperial Majesty or simply to catch a glimpse of him. They were willing to wait several days in the hope of petitioning him for something they wanted, or to wave at him as he passed. Against this crowd the gates were kept tightly shut except when the turn came for one of their number to be called inside for his audience. The Emperor liked to see as many as possible of the minor chiefs and common people. They gave him information he was not likely to get from his courtiers and the more powerful chiefs. On both sides of the avenue approaching the headquarters, machine guns had been installed. Near the gates were two tents, one for radio transmission and reception, the other for distribution of communiqués to the press. There was seldom much news in these communiqués because the Emperor seldom had any real news to announce.

Today, the newsmen were quickly brought through the headquarters gate and up to the main building, a handsome stone structure with a porch on its front. One of these correspondents, George Steer of the London *Times*, probably knew more than the others about what to expect because he had been in Addis Ababa when the official text of the Hoare-Laval proposals arrived there in the early morning hours of December 11.[9] A friend and frequent visitor of the Emperor's adviser, Everett Colson, Steer had been informed of everything that happened in Addis Ababa from the moment British Minister Sir Sidney Barton received the notification. The British hope that Barton's influence might persuade the Emperor to accept the plan was thwarted by the fact that the Emperor was in Dessie. Barton had to take the document to Foreign Minister Herouy, who had little practice in making even small decisions and no practice in making large ones. When faced with a critical situation, Herouy looked at it squarely in the hope that it would go away. If it refused to go away, he would think about it silently until it did. He liked to have matters submitted to him on paper because letters could be spindled, and if they remained long enough on the spindle, there was a good likelihood that the reasons for answering them would elapse. Herouy's son, Sirak, was on hand to interpret for his father when Barton arrived to do his distasteful duty. He read the document with what Ethiopian witnesses called "a decent formality," then awaited a reaction. As he might have expected, he got none. Herouy had nothing to say. As Barton knew, it would be pointless to try to influence him. The British minister could do nothing but retire as gracefully as possible.

After Barton's departure, the Emperor's councilors took up the matter. They were angry about it. They wanted to answer it rudely, but Herouy couldn't decide whether that would be the thing to do. Finally the councilors decided to send a copy to the Emperor in Dessie. By this time, Everett Colson had lost patience with them. He himself had sent a four-page telegram to the Emperor, listing reasons why he felt he should fly to Dessie immediately for a conference, and that evening he had left for Dessie in one of the Ethiopian air force's eleven planes. Whatever the Emperor intended to announce now, on the sixteenth, would be the result of his talks with Colson, who was still in Dessie.

The Emperor was already on the porch of his headquarters, awaiting the newsmen when they arrived. He had in hand a piece of paper, from which he read a prepared statement:

> We desire to state, with all the solemnity and firmness which the situation demands today, that our willingness to facilitate any pacific solution of this conflict has not changed, but that the act by us of accepting even in principle the Franco-British proposals would be not only a cowardice toward our people but a betrayal of the League of Nations and of all the States which have shown that they could have confidence up to now in the system of collective security.
>
> These proposals are the negation and the abandonment of the principles upon which the League of Nations is founded. For Ethiopia they would consecrate the amputation of her territory and the disappearance of her independence for the benefit of the State which has attacked her.
>
> They imply the definite interdiction for her own people to participate usefully and freely in the economic development of about a third of the country, and they confide this development to her enemy, which is now

making its second attempt to conquer this people. A settlement on the lines of these proposals would place a premium upon aggression and upon the violation of international engagements.

The vital interest of Ethiopia is in question, and for us this takes precedence over every other consideration, but in reaching our decision we are not unmindful that the security of other peaceful, weak, or small States will be made doubtful if such a recompense should be accorded to a State already condemned as the aggressor and at the expense of the State victim of its aggression.

Having issued this statement, the Emperor did not wait to answer questions. He returned to his office and resumed his work, talking to chiefs, developing strategies, making sure the supply trains were moving northward toward the front, writing to his commanders. One of the many problems he couldn't even hope to solve was his communication with the front. Had he been in direct contact with Ras Imru today, he would have had reason to smile despite the outrageous proposals he had just rejected. But he didn't yet know, and would not learn for another four days, of Imru's victory at Dembeguina Pass.

By early evening of December 12, when Sir Robert Vansittart returned to London from Paris, his aides in the Foreign Office were so alarmed at the growing clamor against the Hoare-Laval Plan that several of them, including the head of the News Department, Rex Leeper, and Vansittart's personal secretary, Clifford Norton, went to Victoria Station to meet him.[10] Leeper had already called Sir Samuel Hoare in Zuoz and advised him, in his own best interest, to come home at once. As soon as Vansittart alighted from his train, his friends gathered around him and, ignoring the crowds rushing back and forth past them, told him how dangerous they considered the political storm which had begun to blow. Sir Samuel Hoare, they agreed, was not the only potential victim.

Vansittart showed no concern over the uproar. "I thought we did a pretty good job in Paris," he said. "Come to dinner and we'll talk it over."

Leeper and Norton, alarmed now not only by the political crisis but by Vansittart's casual attitude about it, continued to impress upon him the violence of the storm.

He was still unperturbed. "We'll have to ride it out," he said.

"It'll bring down the Government," one of them warned him. "You must go and see the Prime Minister."

"When?"

"Now."

At nine p.m. Vansittart, Leeper, and Norton went together to the

House of Commons, where they found Stanley Baldwin in his office. Vansittart entered alone to speak to him. What he should do at this point, Vansittart advised, was to take the press into his confidence. Make it plain that "Sir Samuel's action simply continued the negotiations with France that had been going on for several weeks, and upon which the Cabinet had been informed at every stage." Perhaps Vansittart did not yet know about Baldwin's hope that the public might be convinced of the Cabinet's ignorance of the whole affair. Toward the end of their visit, one of Baldwin's secretaries came in with the latest sheaf of telegrams protesting the Hoare-Laval Plan. When Vansittart had said everything he considered necessary and had opened the door to leave, the Prime Minister, standing at his desk, took hold of the sheaf of unfriendly telegrams and flung them high into the air above his head.

Vansittart, after watching the cloud of telegrams float lazily to the floor, emerged smiling and said to Leeper and Norton, "He's all right."

Baldwin was, in fact, far from "all right," and within the next few days, even he began to realize it. Anthony Eden, when he returned home from Geneva on the fourteenth, found that "Members of Parliament were under severe pressure from their constituents. It might even be that Hoare, who had now decided to return as a result of a firm summons from No. 10 [Downing Street], would have to resign."

The battered and bandaged Sir Samuel himself looked upon his return quite differently. As he recalled, he actually wanted to get back to London, but because of his broken nose, his doctor forbade him to travel, at least "for two or three days, owing to the danger of infecting the two fractures."

It was on the sixteenth that Hoare returned to be met at Croydon Aerodrome, not by any of his Cabinet colleagues, but only by his private secretary, who was wearing "a very long face." Sir Samuel went to bed as soon as he reached his home in Cadogan Gardens, Chelsea, just off Sloane Street. His doctor told him to stay there, not to go outdoors on any account, and to see as few visitors as possible. However, his Cabinet colleagues, while they might not have deemed it politically prudent to welcome him publicly at the airport, were quite certain to want to talk to him as soon as possible. The very next morning, in fact, they sent an emissary—Chancellor of the Exchequer Neville Chamberlain came to talk to him. Hoare had always admired Chamberlain, which was not surprising. They shared the same apparent propriety and the same moral fiber, which looked so inflexible on the outside but was so loosely elastic on the inside. This morning, Hoare didn't much like what Chamberlain had to say because it soon became clear that he had come to get himself and the rest of the Cabinet off the hook on which the foreign minister had hung them.

In the Cabinet meeting on the ninth, Hoare's colleagues had supported the peace proposals, but in a subsequent meeting, as Chamberlain explained, they had come to doubt whether they could continue their support in the face of the outcry against it. What were Hoare's thoughts on that subject? Chamberlain, having made his own thoughts obvious, waited for Hoare to accept the responsibility for the mess in which the government found itself. Hoare, whose mind was even less subtle than Chamberlain's, failed to pick up the cue.

The proposals had "many objectionable features," he admitted, but they were "a great improvement both on the Italian demands and Laval's first attempts to compromise." He didn't explain how the demands of the aggressor had come to be regarded as a proper starting point from which to seek a settlement. He went on to remind Chamberlain that the proposals "did not depart substantially from the conclusions of the Peterson–Saint-Quentin meetings, all of which had been reported to the Cabinet without exciting opposition or criticism." The thing to do now, he concluded, was to "make a full explanation to the House" as to why the government had embraced the proposals.

In Hoare's words, "Chamberlain entirely agreed with me."

If Chamberlain "entirely agreed" with Hoare on the sixteenth, it represented a startling change from the previous day. In his diary for December 15, Chamberlain wrote:

> ... when Sam left for Paris ... we had no idea that he would be invited to consider detailed peace proposals. I believed, and so far as I know, my colleagues believed also, that he was going ... to get the discussions with the French into such a condition that we could say to the League, "don't prejudice the chances of a favorable issue by thrusting in a particularly provocative extra sanction at this moment." Instead of that, a set of proposals was agreed to. ... Nothing could be worse than our position. Our whole prestige in foreign affairs at home and abroad has tumbled to pieces like a house of cards. If we had to fight the election all over again, we should probably be beaten. ... You take some comfort from the thought that, if I had been Premier, the discredit would have fallen on me instead of on S.B. That is true, if the same things had happened. But I affirm, with some confidence, that they would not have happened.

Bitterly ironic though it may be to contemplate Neville Chamberlain criticizing someone else's conduct of British foreign policy, it is even more so to envision him declaring that such grievous mistakes could not happen if he were Premier. Chamberlain proved, in that diary entry, that he was as poor a judge of himself as he had been earlier of Hoare, whom he recommended as foreign minister, and as he would be later of Hitler, at Munich.

Though Hoare didn't yet seem to understand it, the great concern of the Cabinet now, as Chamberlain had indicated in his diary, was to dissociate itself completely from Hoare and his peace proposals, not because they were objectionable but because they were proving so unpopular. Next to visit Hoare came Baldwin, who was, as usual, "uncommunicative." According to Hoare, he did say as he left, "We all stand together," but he didn't say for how long. Later the same day, after another Cabinet meeting, Chamberlain returned.

Once again, Chamberlain was speaking for the Cabinet, whose members had decided, he said, that Hoare's proposed explanation to the House of Commons did not go far enough. The political circumstances were now so explosive it would be necessary to admit that his peace plan was bad and that he had been "mistaken in accepting it." He would have to tell the Commons that "in view of the general opposition I withdraw my support of it."

Hoare was properly indignant and recalcitrant. He was not prepared, he said, to make "any such recantation." He was convinced that "nothing short of the proposals would save Abyssinia and prevent Mussolini's joining the Hitler front." If the Cabinet had deserted him, then the only course open to him was "resignation, not recantation."

Chamberlain's arguments could not prevail against Hoare's stubborn dignity. The two old friends parted again, Hoare to nurse his bandaged nose and Chamberlain to return to the Cabinet with the news that the problem was still unsolved. Something would have to be done soon. Even Stanley Baldwin could see that. Reaction to the Hoare-Laval Plan from abroad was as disturbing as the reaction at home. Several Latin countries were releasing rumors that they might quit the League of Nations. The Scandinavian countries had let it be known that they would fight the plan in Geneva. In Moscow, *Izvestia* criticized the plan. Even in France there was so much opposition that Laval's government was facing a crisis.

Baldwin, alarmed at Hoare's obstinacy, paid him another visit. He found, to his discomfort, that Hoare was facing up to the Cabinet with much more determination than he had ever shown against Mussolini. He would defend his plan, Hoare insisted, and in consequence, he would then resign. Baldwin didn't want him to resign. Not once did he suggest resignation. It wouldn't be necessary to do any more, he said, than to fall in with the Cabinet's wishes in the matter. To Hoare, those wishes spelled recantation. He would have none of it. His resignation, therefore, was settled.

At the Cabinet's behest, Anthony Eden drafted a statement he was to make at Geneva when the League Council met on the eighteenth. Hoare approved the statement reluctantly, the Cabinet eagerly, on the morning of the seventeenth. Baldwin, Chamberlain, and Eden paid another visit to Hoare. The Foreign Secretary looked miserable.

"How do you feel?" Baldwin asked.

"I wish I were dead," Hoare said from behind his facial bandage.

246

Eden, on his way to Victoria Station en route to Geneva, thanked his retiring Cabinet superior and/or colleague for approving the statement to be made to the League Council. Hoare, if not happy, was at least gracious. "Thank you so much for all your loyal help," he said, as Eden bade him good-by. Stanley Baldwin's experiment of allowing two Cabinet ministers to speak for the Foreign Office was now at an end.

In the United States, only the isolationists were pleased with the Hoare-Laval Plan. To Senator Vandenberg, this new indication of "moral bankruptcy" in Europe was added proof that America should avoid all cooperation with the League of Nations and look to a further strengthening of neutrality legislation. Senator Borah pointed to the plan as another example of British chicanery. *Business Week* magazine cited the plan as reason enough for President Roosevelt and Secretary of State Hull to stop "cooperating with the League's sanctions policy under the pretense of neutrality." In a country where the timid vacillations of Roosevelt and Hull could be characterized as "cooperation with the League's sanctions policy," the likelihood of truly effective international cooperation was already slight. The publication of the Hoare-Laval Plan eliminated all possibility. President Roosevelt virtually stipulated this December 12 when the Archbishop of York and British Ambassador Sir Ronald Lindsay came to tea.[11]

The Archbishop, who was touring America, had already been interviewed by members of the press, and the President had been briefed on some of his remarks. Roosevelt was not as polite as one might expect him to be in such a social situation. He was very much interested, he said, in a newspaper quotation of the Archbishop to the effect that the United States, by joining the League of Nations, could be helpful in international matters.

When the Archbishop affirmed that this was, indeed, his belief, the President said Americans might have felt more strongly disposed to join the League a few days ago than they felt now.

The Archbishop, no doubt startled at the tone of the conversation, asked what had brought about this change of feeling.

It was the attempt on the part of Britain and France, the President said, to dismember Ethiopia in order to bring about peace with Italy.

It is at least possible that Roosevelt's remarks about America's attitude were intended to excuse himself and the United States for not doing something which neither he nor the American public had wanted to do anyway. On October 30, both he and Hull had made statements which appeared to discourage United States businesses from trading with belligerents. (Such trade would be almost exclusively with Italy, because Ethiopia had been excluded from the market by poverty and embargo.) It was on this occasion that Roosevelt had mentioned tempting opportunities to supply materials which would prolong the war, and had given it as his opinion that the American people would not want "abnormally increased profits" from trade in such materials. Hull's statement had been similar. But neither had said flatly that such trade with Italy would be abolished. And in subsequent press conferences, they had refused to elaborate. When one correspondent asked Hull what the government would do if American exporters supplied to Italy raw materials which League Members might embargo, he refused to answer. And when Roosevelt was asked a similar question, he answered it coyly and evasively. A shoe manufacturer had inquired, he said, as to whether it would be proper to fill a large order the Italian government had placed. Were they for ladies' slippers, Roosevelt said he had asked. On being informed they were for soldiers' boots, he had told the manufacturer, he said, that if it were his company, he would not take the order. He was careful not to say that the United States government would prevent the shoe company, or any other company, from filling such orders.

There is no doubt that President Roosevelt hated Fascism and wished Americans would desist from trading with Italy. But neither is there any doubt that he understood the power of the profit motive in America. He knew the limits of moral suasion in influencing the policies of American businessmen. Anything less than a government ban on trade with Italy would be considered an encouragement for such trade. By telling cute little stories about his own personal feelings, he was expressing not a policy but a nonpolicy. The result was hardly surprising. The average monthly export of oil products to Italy from 1932 to 1934, for instance, had been $480,000. In the first month of the Ethiopian war, October 1935, American oil companies exported $1,084,000 worth of their products to Italy and Italian Africa; in November, the total rose to $1,684,000; in December it was $2,674,000. Under these circumstances, Members of the League of Nations had good reason to ask whether American trade with Italy would nullify the League sanctions against the aggressor.

In the early evening of December 14, a detail of six hundred New York City policemen, bundled in their heavy winter uniforms, gathered around the entrances of Madison Square Garden on Eighth Avenue between Forty-ninth and Fiftieth Streets, facing a crowd of more than two thousand anti-Fascist demonstrators who had come to protest a rally in the Garden that night for the benefit of the Italian Red Cross in Africa.[12] The demonstrators, one of whom was Socialist leader Norman Thomas, had come to protest the announced attendance at the rally of New York Mayor Fiorello LaGuardia. By the time the Mayor arrived, few of the demonstrators were still on hand to see him enter the building. The New York police had forcefully persuaded the anti-Fascists that they should be elsewhere.

LaGuardia and his wife, occupying a box at the side of the arena, waved at the overflow crowd of twenty thousand people who had jammed the Garden, but he did not intend to speak to them. He was on hand only as a guest of honor. The main speakers were two New York Supreme Court justices, Ferdinand Pecora and Salvatore Cotillo. Both told the audience that Italy's policy of expansion in Africa was justified because it was necessary. Each time a speaker mentioned the name of Mussolini, the crowd broke into loud cheers. At each mention of England or League of Nations sanctions, a rumble of boos arose.

Finally, the crowd began demanding that Mayor LaGuardia leave his spectator's box and take a place on the platform. After he complied with this appeal, they demanded that he make a speech. This was the kind of demand "The Little Flower" always found difficult to resist. After a decent show of reluctance, he approached the microphones.

He did not speak in favor of Fascism or Mussolini. LaGuardia was too intelligent a politician to forget that only a fraction of his constituents were of Italian descent. "I have seen the Italian Red Cross operate," he said, "and I have lived with them for many months during the World War. I can testify that not one penny [of the five-hundred-thousand-dollar collection announced at the rally] is diverted to any other purpose."

When the Mayor sat down, no one could accuse him of having said anything objectionable. He had made no partisan remarks about the war. But he had appeared.

Premier Mussolini, wearing an entirely black military uniform to complement his Fascist black shirt, arrived in the Pontine marsh area between Rome and Terracina early in the morning of December 18. It was to be a busy day for him, beginning with the dedication of the latest in a group of new towns—this one Pontinia—created and developed on lands which had always been malaria-infested marshes. The reclamation of these Pontine marshes, begun in 1931 and still continuing in 1935, was one Mussolini accomplishment which could hardly be criticized. By draining the marshes, unusable through the centuries, he created farms and towns for more than fifty thousand Italians. By 1935, such towns as Littoria and Sabauda were already established. Mussolini had chosen to attend the inauguration of this newest one, Pontinia, partly because he wanted an occasion to make a speech. But the speech would be only perfunctorily about Pontinia. As he looked out over the partially constructed buildings of the new community, his mind was on Ethiopia and Geneva, Pierre Laval and Sir Samuel Hoare.

During the week since he had received his copy of the Hoare-Laval Plan, he had made no public statement about it, but his silence did not indicate indifference to it. The proposals gave him several advantages. First, while under discussion, they would preclude the possibility of the League's applying an oil embargo. And second, they offered him, though not everything he wanted, almost everything he needed, including a basis on which to negotiate for more. In a secret telegram to Badoglio on the twelfth, he had said,

> In the Franco-English proposals, the return of Axum to Ethiopia is contemplated among other things. I shall never accept this return. Since Paris newspapers have published the proposals it is possible that this might come to the attention of the clergy and population of Axum, and it might create negative states of mind. The zone must therefore be closely guarded.

From this telegram, Mussolini's intention to negotiate on the basis of the Hoare-Laval Plan is clear. But he would demand all of the northern province of Tigre and all of eastern Ethiopia. Though he might allow the remaining, truncated Ethiopia to use port facilities in Assab, he would not allow Assab to become an Ethiopian port. The universally negative reaction to the Hoare-Laval Plan outside Italy did not greatly concern him during the first few days after its announcement. However much the British and French people might dislike the plan, their governments had duly and officially submitted it to him, and he had every right to expect that these two governments would stand behind the offer. As the days passed, however, he had come to realize that the British and French governments might be forced by public pressure to renege, or, even if they did maintain the offer, that the League of Nations might reject it. If such were to happen, Italy might look foolish in accepting. Mussolini had therefore maintained silence. But now, on the morning of the eighteenth, he decided to speak up at Pontinia.

> The Italian people are capable of resisting a very long siege, especially when it is certain in the clearness and tranquillity of their conscience that right is on their side while wrong is on the side of the Europe which in present circumstances is dishonoring itself. The war we have begun on African soil is a war of civilization and liberation. . . . It is the war of the poor, disinherited, proletarian Italian people. Against us are arrayed the forces of reaction, of selfishness and hypocrisy. We have embraced a hard struggle against this front. We shall continue this struggle to the end. . . . It will take time, but once a struggle is begun, it is not time that counts but victory.

250

Though Mussolini seemed to say in this speech that he was rejecting the Hoare-Laval proposal, he didn't quite say it. He left the door open in case the French and British might still be able to arrive at acceptance, but he wanted everyone to know the proposal was not his idea, nor was it any favor to him on the part of the British and French. They needn't expect any gratitude for their efforts. He would let them know whether they might hope for any consideration.

He was also warning the League of Nations that Italy would not be toppled, or even swayed, by the sanctions against it. In fact, now that he was fairly certain there would be no oil embargo, he had reason to be almost thankful for the sanctions. The internal discontent which had threatened his regime throughout most of 1935 had been exacerbated first by the economic deprivations connected with the war, and then by the apparent ineptitude of the Italian armies which had been stalled for almost two months in Ethiopia. Private dissatisfaction with Mussolini had reached dangerous levels by the time the League of Nations sanctions went into effect November 18, and he was well aware of it because the one thing even he could not do to Italians was prevent them from talking. Complaints against the government, while never mentioned in the controlled press, were widespread on the streets. Had the sanctions been enforced effectively, Mussolini might soon have been faced by revolt. Because they were poorly conceived and indifferently applied, with some League Member nations almost totally disregarding them, they had the general effect of boosting the nation's morale rather than damaging its economy.

The very fact that Italy, alone among nations, had been singled out for censure and sanction, when she was only doing what all the other great powers had done previously, angered the whole Italian nation so deeply that Mussolini could sense an immediate rise in his popularity. He was quick to take advantage of this unexpected benefit of sanctions. Having already founded and fostered an organization called the Association of War Widows and War Mothers, he put its members to work developing and administering campaigns through which Italy might defeat the sanctions by becoming more self-sufficient. These women helped launch a "Buy Italian" movement, a boycott of foreign businesses, and a massive scrap-metal collection. But their most dramatic enterprise was one which reached its fulfillment December 18.

Mussolini, as soon as he finished dedicating the new town of Pontinia, hurried off to the already populated town of Littoria, also in the Pontine marsh area, where he was scheduled to launch a "Gold for the Fatherland" drive organized by the War Widows and War Mothers in the name of the married women of Italy. When the Duce arrived in Littoria, the married women in the town were already waiting for him. One by one, they came forward to drop their gold wedding rings into a steel helmet, which, when it was full, he held up proudly, like a priest offering to God a consecrated chalice. In exchange for their gold rings, the women received iron ones, each of which bore the inscription, GOLD FOR THE FATHERLAND.

Having collected his helmetful of gold in Littoria, Mussolini hurried back to Rome, where a truly massive surrender of gold wedding rings was soon in progress at the huge monument of Victor Emmanuel II, just a hundred yards from the Palazzo Venezia. At least a quarter of a million Roman wives, led by Italy's elderly Queen Elena and Signora Rachel Mussolini, took part in the ritual, which was also being performed by millions of other women with as much solemnity, though perhaps less majesty and pomp, in every Italian city or town.

The focal point of the Roman ceremony was an installation called the "Altar of the Fatherland," set up directly in front of the tomb of the unknown soldier on the concrete expanse at the top of the rococo monument's wide stairway. In the center of the "altar" was a large crucible from the bottom of which an incense-burning flame arose, suggesting to the naïve that the process of melting down the gold would begin the moment a ring was dropped into the vat. Many of the women must have realized that a showman rather than a goldsmith had inspired the construction of such a crucible, but that was of little importance.

The Queen, who shared with her husband a restrained distaste for Mussolini's vulgarity, began the procession by approaching the receptacle with great dignity and dropping in not only her own but also the King's ring. Then came Signora Mussolini and the wives of other officials. It was rumored that many of them had rushed out to buy inexpensive substitute rings for this ceremony, thus saving their real ones. If so, their cleverness would do them little good for some years to come since it would be embarrassing henceforth to be seen wearing a gold ring. After the more celebrated wives had made their sacrifices, the ordinary wives of Rome, so many of them that they jammed the Piazza Venezia and all the streets leading into it, began their seemingly endless procession up the steps of the monument to the flaming crucible. Mussolini never did announce how much gold he collected that day in the "Gold for the Fatherland" ceremonies all over Italy, but its monetary value, however great, could not approach its value to the Duce in winning the loyalty of Italian women. After making such a sacrificial investment in him, they were truly his. It would be a long time before they could even consider forsaking him. And, as he knew, Italy was one country where you didn't have to worry about the men if you had the women on your side.

* * *

While Mussolini was relieving Italian wives of their wedding rings, the League of Nations Council began an uncomfortable meeting in Geneva. Before the session, Anthony Eden met with Pierre Laval to read him the statement he intended to make. Laval didn't like it. He, for one, had not yet given up on the Hoare-Laval Plan. There was no justification, he insisted, for believing that the terms would not be accepted. In his mind, and for his purposes, acceptance by Mussolini seemed to be the only essential. He expressed no concern over the fact that Emperor Haile Selassie had already rejected the plan in a public statement two days earlier. Former French Premier Edouard Herriot had asked Laval in Paris, "What would you do if the Emperor refused?" France could then, Laval had said, drop all sanctions against Italy. "In which case," Herriot had replied, "you would presumably declare Ethiopia the aggressor."[13] Laval could hardly deny—nor was he likely to deny—the force of Herriot's logic. He would gladly declare Ethiopia the aggressor if he could thereby end the crisis and make Mussolini happy. The notion that Mussolini was a valuable ally against Hitler continued to obsess him.

Eden did not agree with Laval that the Hoare-Laval proposals had any chance of acceptance. World opinion, he said, had already given them "their quietus." Laval argued the point for some time. Eden said his Cabinet colleagues had endorsed his speech and he was not disposed to change it. In apparent despondency, Laval observed that he never seemed to have much luck in his negotiations with the British. On this note they parted.

All the members of the Council, not only Eden and Laval, were in a mood of depression as the meeting began. Eden spoke first and briefly. He began by saying the League's Coordination Committee (Committee of Eighteen) had "welcomed" the suggestion that France and Britain seek a basis for settling the Italian-Ethiopian crisis. "It was, however, recognized," he said, "that any proposals which these two governments put forward must be acceptable to the two parties to the dispute and to the League." Then, after affirming rather apologetically that the principle France and Britain had pursued was right, "even if its application in this instance may not have availed," he solemnly recited the requiem for Hoare-Laval:

> It must be emphasized that the Paris proposals . . . were not advanced as proposals to be insisted on in any event. They were advanced in order to ascertain what the views of the two parties and the League might be upon them, and His Majesty's Government recommended them only for this purpose. If, therefore, it transpires that these proposals which are now before you do not satisfy the essential condition of agreement by the two parties and by the League, His Majesty's Government could not continue to recommend or support them. In its view, this particular

attempt at conciliation could not then be regarded as having achieved its object, and His Majesty's Government for its part would not wish to pursue it further.

Laval, now that his offspring was dead, tried to be gracious about its funeral. But after affirming, as Eden had done, the noble motives attendant upon its birth, he couldn't stop himself from insisting that there might still be some life in the corpse.

> We do not yet know how the parties will welcome our suggestions, and I suppose that, in the meantime, the Council itself will wish to avoid expressing an opinion. In any case, I think it my duty to state forthwith that, if this effort does not secure the consent of all the interested parties, the Council will not be relieved of its duty to explore every avenue . . . with a view to bringing about an honorable and just solution of the present conflict. . . .

In case Laval actually didn't know, as he claimed, how the parties would welcome his plan, Ethiopian representative Wolde Mariam stood up and told him how one of them felt about it. Before addressing himself directly to the Hoare-Laval proposals, Wolde Mariam made some observations embarrassing to certain League Members as well as to Italy. The Ethiopian government "cannot believe," he said,

> that the Ethiopian people will be abandoned and delivered over to its cruel enemy, seeing that the Ethiopian government has always punctiliously conformed to all the procedures of the Treaties and of the Covenant. . . .
> The Italian government, which commands forty-four millions of subjects, does not hesitate to drive to their death tens of thousands of askaris and dubats [Eritrean and Somali native soldiers] in order to exterminate a small nation of ten million people and to destroy their homes.
> The government and people of Ethiopia do not ask any people in the world to come to Africa and shed their blood in defense of Ethiopia. The blood of Ethiopians will suffice for that.
> If they had a larger quantity of arms and ammunition, the Ethiopian warriors, who do not fear death, would not have allowed the Italian aggressor to make even the small advance that has been achieved, after two and a half months of war, by hundreds of thousands of mercenaries, directed by Italian officers and noncommissioned officers, commanded by the best Italian generals, and served by the largest and most perfected armament that has ever been assembled on African soil.
> What Ethiopia asks is that, in mere justice, she should be given facilities to acquire more complete and more up-to-date defensive material than she now possesses.

After this reminder that Italy's huge, well-equipped army had bogged down only a few miles inside Ethiopia, and after noting the cynicism of several nations, including League Members, in supplying war materials to Italy while withholding them from Ethiopia, Wolde Mariam turned to the peace proposals themselves. He didn't intend, he said, to make a statement about them. He wanted only to ask some questions, to wit:

> ... is it consistent with the Covenant that the Convenant-breaking State should be begged by the League of Nations to be good enough to accept a large part of its victim's territory, together with the effective control of the rest under the cloak of the League?
>
> Is the victim of the aggression ... to be invited by the League to submit to the aggressor and, in the interests of world peace, to abandon the defense of its independence and integrity against its powerful enemy on the grounds that the latter's resolve to exterminate its victim is unshakable?
>
> Is the victim to be placed under the implicit threat of abandonment by the League and to be deprived of all hope of succor?

By the time the Council voted to postpone discussion of the peace proposals until a later meeting, even Laval must have known that the Hoare-Laval Plan was totally dead.

While Wolde Mariam was speaking in Geneva of the Ethiopian soldiers' willingness to die, several thousand of them were demonstrating it in the Tembien region of northern Ethiopia. On the morning of the eighteenth, a force of more than four thousand men under Ras Seyoum advanced on the town of Abbi Addi about thirty miles almost directly west of the Italian stronghold of Makalle. Abbi Addi was strategically important not only because of its proximity to Makalle but also because it was the most important town in the Tembien, the junction of caravan routes north, south, east, and west through the rough, canyon-sliced area.

Three days earlier, on the fifteenth, Italian reconnaissance planes had spotted Seyoum's troops crossing the Gheva River about twelve miles south of Abbi Addi. Marshal Badoglio, informed immediately of this alarming Ethiopian move, had ordered that an additional four Eritrean battalions and one battery of artillery be sent immediately to reinforce the town, which was at that moment held by four battalions plus some artillery and light tanks. Italian airplanes, unopposed in the skies over the Tembien, offered further protection to the town's garrison. They harassed the advancing Ethiopians throughout those three days.

Despite the continuous daytime bombing and strafing attacks from the air, the Ethiopian forces under Seyoum were intact and orderly when they established first contact with the Eritrean Italian defenders just south

255

of Abbi Addi on the morning of the eighteenth. From the moment of contact, the battle erupted in full fury, with Italian planes and artillery bombarding the Ethiopians, who rushed forward to get at the enemy in hand-to-hand conflict. Their headlong plunge through the bombs, bullets, and artillery shells procured for them at least one advantage. As soon as they began swarming among the Eritreans, the Italian planes and artillery had to leave them alone for fear of bombarding their own forces. But by this time the Ethiopians had sustained such heavy losses that they needed more than one advantage, especially against the black Italian troops, who were better trained, better armed, and just as courageous. For ten hours, the battle raged, and when dusk fell, it was the Ethiopians rather than the black Italians who were forced to retire. The Ethiopians were not discouraged, however. As a result of this day's battle, Ras Seyoum was convinced that with a few thousand more men, he might yet prevail. Retreating south only a few miles, he set up camp for the night.

Anthony Eden, returning home from Geneva, drove directly from Victoria Station to 10 Downing Street, as the Prime Minister had asked him to come immediately, before communicating with anyone else. When Eden arrived, he did not find the indolent, comfortable-looking, absent-minded Stanley Baldwin to whom he was accustomed. Baldwin was pacing nervously in a small library room overlooking Downing Street. He didn't know, he told his Secretary for League of Nations Affairs, how he could have allowed matters to reach their present pass.

Baldwin had spoken in the Commons the previous day, the nineteenth, along with Sir Samuel Hoare, who had resigned officially the evening of the eighteenth. Hoare had tearfully offered Parliament a long but not very convincing explanation of his policies regarding the Italian-Ethiopian crisis and the circumstances which had brought about the now-defunct Hoare-Laval Plan. Baldwin, who was sacrificing Hoare to save himself, had grudgingly admitted the government's mistake in a peculiar statement which also laid bare, perhaps inadvertently, his own basic cynicism. "I was not expecting," he had said, "that deeper feeling which was manifested by many parts of the country on what I may call the grounds of conscience and honor." In other words, the Hoare-Laval Plan would have been quite acceptable if only the British people could have been as cynical as himself.

Because the British people were so much more decent than the men who governed them, the plan and its coauthor had both been dumped, and here was Stanley Baldwin the next day, having saved his own neck, pacing his library, snapping his fingers nervously as he ruminated about the possibilities for Hoare's replacement. Eden understood, Baldwin presumed, the trouble in which the government now found itself. Did he have any ideas as to who should get the Foreign Office appointment?

Indeed he did have an idea, Eden replied. He knew just the man for the job—Sir Austen Chamberlain.

Austen Chamberlain! Even Baldwin must have been astonished at this suggestion. How could Anthony Eden, presumably England's most ardent supporter of the League of Nations against Mussolini, propose the appointment of a man who was a professed admirer of Mussolini? Chamberlain's wife was at this very moment in Rome speaking out openly in favor of Italy's Ethiopian venture.

"He has the authority and the experience," Eden said. "I've served under him before and would be very happy to do so again in any capacity."

Chamberlain, having been Foreign Secretary for several years in the 1920s, made no secret of his desire to fill the post again. Eden had served under him once as a parliamentary secretary, but his offer now to do so again in the Foreign Office cannot be divorced from the consideration that Eden himself, as he realized, was the foremost candidate for the position. Though he had already insisted privately to a friend that he didn't want the job under present circumstances, he was casting strong doubt upon his own reluctance when he nominated a man like Austen Chamberlain as a presumed alternative to himself.

Baldwin shook his head at the idea. Chamberlain, he said, was too old for the job.

When Eden attempted to disagree, Baldwin interrupted. "Anyway, I saw him yesterday," he said, "and told him so."

Eden was silent for a while, then Baldwin asked him if he had any other names to suggest. On the British political scene of the 1930s, there was no shortage of unsuitable selections one might mention. There was Austen Chamberlain's younger half-brother, Neville, for instance. But Eden passed him up and mentioned instead Lord Halifax, who would one day soon gain lasting fame for helping Neville Chamberlain shape Britain's policy toward Nazi Germany.

Baldwin quickly rejected Halifax. Another silence followed. Eventually, Baldwin turned to Eden and said, "It looks as if it will have to be you."

Eden felt hurt at what he later called "this eliminative method of being appointed." "Six months ago," he said, "I would have been very grateful for the chance to be Foreign Secretary. Now I feel quite differently about it."

By this time, Baldwin had apparently lapsed back into his usual absent-mindedness. Whatever Eden said wasn't really important. To the Prime Minister, the matter was settled. Eden was the new Foreign Secretary.

* * *

The resignation of Sir Samuel Hoare was a severe and unexpected blow to Mussolini. Despite his bellicose assertions at Pontinia on the morning of the eighteenth, he still felt the Hoare-Laval Plan was his to accept or reject whenever he decided to act upon it. The League Council later that day, by tabling the plan rather than vetoing it officially, had left him with some misguided hope that it was still alive. Hoare's dismissal foreclosed that hope and so enraged Mussolini that he issued a statement through his Foreign Office the next day which said the Hoare-Laval proposals as delivered to Italy still held good as far as Italy was concerned. One of his Foreign Office spokesmen at the same time denied to the press that his Pontinia speech was in any way a reply to the plan. The Italian government reply was yet to come.

Mussolini's official reply came the night of December 20, when there was no longer anything left to which he could reply. Through his Grand Council he declared that "after the repudiation by Great Britain of the Paris proposals," Italy would pursue the Ethiopian war "with inflexible decision."

If Mussolini had accepted the plan the moment he read it ten days earlier, it is possible that the people of Europe and the world, pleased at the sudden prospect of re-establishing peace, might have reacted favorably to it. By arrogantly making the world wait for his reply, he had given people time to think about the plan, and to realize how outrageous it was. He had thereby deprived himself of a chance for a cheap victory, and as a result must now be prepared to slug it out with Haile Selassie, who did not offer him the same respect he was accustomed to receiving from men like Hoare and Laval. The Ethiopians, instead of collapsing before his well-advertised legions, were beginning to counterattack. It seemed to Mussolini that Badoglio was sitting down there in the African sun apparently doing no more than De Bono had done. As one of the Duce's generals, Emilio Faldella, wrote about this period, "Mussolini, who cannot bear the slightest setback, thunders that he intends to get rid of Badoglio immediately." Two and a half months after his African adventure had begun, everything seemed to be going sour.

The loss of Sir Samuel Hoare was, to Mussolini, like the loss of a valued ally. Now came the vexing question of who would be Hoare's successor. If Baldwin were to make Eden Foreign Secretary, the League of Nations might yet pull itself together and enact an oil embargo, which would be fatal to Italian chances in Ethiopia. Unable to abide the suspense, Mussolini contacted his ambassador in London, Dino Grandi, and instructed him to find out as quickly as possible who the new British Foreign Secretary would be.

At the same time, misreading the mood of the world and especially of the British, Mussolini decided to take a hand in influencing the choice.

He instructed his Foreign Office to make a statement expressing the hope that Sir Austen Chamberlain would be the new British Foreign Secretary, and to add that if Eden were appointed, "it might almost be considered as a deliberate unfriendly act," which would render automatically more remote "any hope of a conciliatory conclusion of the present crisis."

Meanwhile, in London, Dino Grandi was trying to figure out how the ambassador of an unpopular nation should go about discovering in advance of the announcement who the new British Foreign Secretary would be. Nobody seemed to know whether Baldwin had yet made his choice. When he did so, the Italian Ambassador would hardly be the first person to whom he would confide it. The evening of December 21, having learned nothing as yet, Grandi was listening to the radio and worrying about the wrath of the impatient Duce when the announcer broke in with a special news bulletin. Anthony Eden had been appointed.

Grandi immediately called Mussolini at Villa Torlonia, his home in Rome. "I have just been informed," Grandi said, "that Eden is to be Foreign Secretary."

Though it was not good news, Mussolini took it well. "I congratulate you," he said to Grandi, "on having secured this early intelligence."[14]

On a cold day in England, December 23, Anthony Eden journeyed a hundred miles north of London to King George V's country palace in Sandringham, Norfolk, near the shore of the large inlet called the Wash. A few days earlier, Sir Samuel Hoare had made the same journey to surrender the seals of his office. Today, Eden would receive the seals from the seventy-year-old monarch who had been ailing for some time and was now sick unto death. He looked dreadfully ill. His voice was weak and he was coughing painfully. The ceremony was short, but afterward, the King was talkative despite the congestion he was suffering.

He was always interested in foreign affairs, he said, and in the appointment of ambassadors. He understood the difficulties Eden had inherited, asked to be kept informed, and offered any help he could give. These formalities having been completed, he then turned to the subject which seemed to interest him most—Sir Samuel Hoare.

The King had apparently not spared the retiring Foreign Secretary's feelings. He had told him openly that the Hoare-Laval Plan had been a blunder. You cannot drive a train full steam ahead in one direction, he had said, and then suddenly reverse without somebody falling off.

Eden was still thinking about this when he realized His Majesty had been leading up to a witticism. "I said to your predecessor," the King concluded, "'You know what they're all saying? No more coals to Newcastle, no more Hoares to Paris.' The fellow didn't even laugh."[15]

The black Italian defenders of Abbi Addi in the Tembien region thirty miles west of Makalle had been waiting since the eighteenth for a renewal of the Ethiopian attack against them. At dawn on the twenty-second, the attack began and the Eritrean troops went out to meet it in the hills and ravines south of the town.

They were stronger now than when they had repulsed the Ethiopians on the eighteenth. The four battalions and battery of artillery which Marshal Badoglio had sent to reinforce them had arrived on the evening of the nineteenth. But the Ethiopians had also been reinforced by their commander, Ras Seyoum, who had sent forward all the troops he could spare for today's battle. If he could drive the Italians out of Abbi Addi, he would thereby cut the most direct link between the enemy's eastern and western flanks.

The Ethiopians were stirred to battle pitch by a message from Emperor Haile Selassie, who, having received in Dessie the news of Ras Imru's victory in Dembeguina Pass, had exhorted Ras Kassa and Ras Seyoum to "do likewise." The basic Ethiopian strategy was to force a withdrawal of the bulk of the Italian army concentrated now at Makalle. As the Emperor later explained, "The main object of our maneuver was to isolate Makalle by operating against the enemy's right flank, attacking along the entire length from those positions he held in the extreme south to those on the Eritrean frontier." If the armies of Ras Imru and Ayelu Birru, Ras Kassa and Ras Seyoum, by penetrating the Italian western flanks, could so isolate Makalle as to force a retreat from there, then the largest of all Ethiopian forces, Ras Mulugeta's sixty-thousand-man army encamped in the mountains south of Makalle, could rush north to harass the retiring Italians and perhaps drive them all the way back into Eritrea. Such a repetition of the 1896 victory would certainly humiliate the Italians and might completely defeat them.

The Emperor was not alone in his awareness of this possibility. Marshal Badoglio later wrote:

> The whole theater of war was divided into two distinct and independent sectors. Indeed, the lack of a proper strategic road between western Tigre [the Adowa area] and Agame-Enderta [the Makalle area]—so distant and in such rough country that it took about a fortnight to transfer a division from one to the other—made it difficult, perhaps impossible, and certainly inopportune, to move large units should the necessity arise for rapid reinforcement of a threatened sector. This state of things and the limita-

tion of action which I have outlined created a particularly delicate situation. . . .

Badoglio feared that if the enemy took advantage of "his great mobility and his faculty for quickly varying his own lines of operation," the whole Italian expeditionary army could be in deep trouble. Under the circumstances, he was, as he admitted, "forced to reject the idea of an immediate counteroffensive," however stridently Mussolini might demand it.

Badoglio was keenly aware of the importance of Abbi Addi. He had made it clear to the white officers in charge of the black troops there that he wanted the town held at all costs.

In the fighting which began at dawn, Italian airplanes were of limited value from the start because they could not bomb or strafe the Ethiopians until daylight, by which time the battle was in progress and the hilly ground south of Abbi Addi was a massive confusion of Italian and Ethiopian troops, slaughtering each other under clouds of dust. One Ethiopian column arriving from due south and another from the southwest tried to fight their way toward each other through the six battalions plus artillery the Italians had sent out from the town to oppose them. The artillery, which began by firing at point-blank range, was soon rendered useless by the swarming Ethiopians, and the artillerymen found themselves, like the infantry, battling with rifles and bayonets against Ethiopian rifles, swords, and spears. For several hours the attacks and counterattacks continued, with the Ethiopians sending in wave after wave of men while the black Italians, sometimes charging, sometimes retreating, tried to contain them. By afternoon, the battle had reached the town itself, where the two remaining Italian battalions were entrenched behind barbed wire between the tukuls. Gradually the Italians were dislodged even from these positions, and after nine hours of fighting, with losses in the high hundreds on both sides, the Ethiopians took possession of the town. In the final phases of the battle, they had been assisted by townspeople sabotaging the Italians, who fled northward in late afternoon, chased by Ethiopians as far as Work Amba, a mountain a few miles to the northeast. At Work Amba, the Ethiopians encountered another Italian fortified position, but it was not formidable enough to stop them. After a short struggle, the defenders were routed and the defeated Italians retreated eastward, much to the disgust of Marshal Badoglio, who sharply criticized their commander. The Ethiopians quickly began digging in to protect their newly won positions. They were now only about twenty-five miles from Makalle, and Badoglio had reason to worry about his huge installation there.

* * *

261

About the region to the northwest, also on his right flank, Badoglio had even greater reason to worry. Ras Imru and Ayelu Birru, having forded the Takazze River and captured the Dembeguina Pass as well as Selaclaca just ten miles from Axum, were now in a position either to attack Axum and Adowa or, perhaps even worse, bypass these strongholds and head farther north toward Eritrea, where the supply base of Adi Quala, twenty miles inside the border, lay virtually undefended. If General Pietro Maravigna in Adowa lacked the resources to stop the Ethiopians at Dembeguina Pass, there was no reason to believe he could stop them before they reached Eritrea. Badoglio was now in a crisis. It could be argued that General (now retired Marshal) De Bono was responsible for this situation. When Badoglio arrived three weeks earlier he had decided the supply system was in disorder; the troops were badly deployed; the news correspondents were up near the fighting front, where they might see or learn things it would be militarily indiscreet to publicize; and the Fascist Black Shirt divisions, which De Bono favored because Mussolini favored them, were damaging morale by demanding and receiving better treatment than the regular army and native troops. Black Shirt officers were more political than military and their political influence was strong. When Black Shirt and regular army units disembarked at the same time in Massawa, the regular army troops often found themselves marching away from the docks while the Black Shirts rode away on trucks. Despite their elite treatment, the Black Shirts had not yet proven themselves effective in battle. In the limited action that had taken place so far, most of the fighting had been done by the native blacks, of whom one Italian officer said to an American correspondent, "They're a lot better than the Black Shirts."[16] And the blacks themselves knew they were better than the Black Shirts—they knew it and they said it. Because of their battle experience, the black troops had "adopted a rather superior attitude toward the Italians." And since Italians had long been sensitive about their poor reputation as soldiers, their morale was already beginning to weaken. They were said to feel, "almost to a man," that they would "like nothing better than a transport home."

While Badoglio might privately blame De Bono for the conditions he found on his arrival, it would not suffice to blame his predecessor if he were to suffer a serious defeat three or four weeks later. He was already changing the supply system and redeploying his troops to create an irresistible concentration in the eastern sector. As quickly as possible, he was weeding out inferior Black Shirt officers. And he had also, on arrival, banished the news correspondents to Eritrea, where they would see only the communiqués he chose to issue.

As Badoglio entered the fourth week in December, his strength was increasing daily, but so was the strength of the Ethiopians, who had now arrived in such force on his western flank that he did not have enough conventional resources to cope with them. It would be insane to send infantry into the wild country west of Axum to try to cut off Ras Imru before he reached Eritrea. The trackless terrain there was ideal for the Ethiopians and suicidal for the Italians. Only airplanes could get at the advancing Ethiopians in such country. But since they were now learning to spread out and take cover, the airplanes would have to be armed with something more effective than bombs and bullets.

Because of the foresight of Mussolini and De Bono, Badoglio found that he did have something more effective, and though his country had signed an international agreement never to use it, Mussolini, just a few days previously, on the sixteenth, had reiterated an earlier authorization to use it.[17] Badoglio could congratulate himself now for his foresight in banishing the news correspondents to Eritrea. As long as they didn't actually see what he was about to do, they would probably believe him later when he denied having done it.

On the morning of December 23, Ras Imru himself, with a sizable body of troops, crossed the Takazze River on his way up the mountain to his advance positions at Dembeguina Pass and Selaclaca. He had just reached the north bank near Mai Timchet when he saw several Italian planes overhead. By this time he had been bombed so often, especially on the march north to the front, that he was "not unduly alarmed." He was surprised to see, however, that these planes were not dropping bombs. They were dropping "strange containers that burst open almost as soon as they hit the ground or the water, releasing pools of colorless liquid."

Before Ras Imru had time to ask himself what was happening, a hundred or so of his men who had been splashed by the strange fluid "began to scream in agony as blisters broke out on their bare feet, their hands, their faces."

Some of the men rushed to the river to splash water on their burning skin, or, if they had breathed the ghastly fumes, to drink for the relief of their burning lungs. But since the water had also been polluted by the bursting canisters, these men only aggravated their injuries. Many of them "fell contorted on the banks," where they were destined to writhe "in agony that lasted for hours before they died." A few peasants and villagers who had come to the river for water shared their fate.

Ras Imru's chiefs and lieutenants, totally bewildered by this strange new affliction, rushed to him for advice and help. "But I was completely stunned," he later said. "I didn't know what to tell them. I didn't know how to fight this terrible rain that burned and killed."[18]

On this day, the Ethiopians received their first big dose of Italian mustard gas. As the victims lay twisted upon the ground, without any

263

medical care, unable to breathe the contaminated air, and unable even to wash their wounds, the gas-drenched grass and shrubs around them, as well as the trees above their heads, began to turn a sickly yellow. The barefooted companions of the afflicted men, coming to their aid, soon had to retreat as their own feet began to blister, their own lungs to burn. Marshal Badoglio had found the answer to one of his most acute problems. He needn't worry, for some time at least, about Ras Imru's troops dashing through the back country to raid the vital Adi Quala base in Eritrea.

CHAPTER ELEVEN

Dr. Fride Hylander, chief of the Swedish ambulance unit which had come to Ethiopia under the auspices of the International Red Cross, was able on December 22 to survey with some satisfaction the unit's new encampment on the Ganale River about fifty miles from the town of Dolo in the extreme southeast corner of Ethiopia. Dolo, on the border of Ethiopia and Italian Somaliland, was only a few miles north of the Kenya boundary line. Just the previous day, Dr. Hylander and his group had arrived after an arduous journey through the harsh desert to provide medical care for the now hungry, disease-ridden, dwindling army of Ras Desta, an Ethiopian military commander who was the Emperor's son-in-law, and who had embarked on an overly ambitious campaign to invade Somaliland. Knowing the necessity to keep Red Cross facilities at a distance from military installations,[1] Dr. Hylander had chosen to pitch his camp three miles from Ras Desta's headquarters and twelve miles from Desta's troops. The seventeen Swedish tents had been pitched at the edge of a sparsely wooded palm grove, the only shade within miles, on the south bank of the wide Ganale. The camp was clearly marked by nine Red Cross flags, three on the roofs of tents, and six more, ten to twelve feet wide, on the surrounding ground.

Dr. Hylander's unit had scarcely had time to begin accepting patients on the twenty-second when unexpected visitors arrived. From the southeast, two Italian airplanes approached the camp. Nearing the tents, they veered away separately to fly over the surrounding areas, then each, turning again in the direction of the camp, flew directly toward it. The first, following the river bed, dropped a few bombs before it reached the camp and a few more after passing over it. The second, flying lower than the first, opened machine-gun fire directly above the camp, though apparently not aiming at the camp. This same plane turned after its first pass and made another at a lower altitude, this time aiming a burst of machine-gun bullets at the ground and leaving a trail of them across the entire site. Though bullets came close to three men, no one was hurt, and as the planes flew away, Dr. Hylander could see that no damage had been done. He was puzzled, however, as to the reason for this rude welcome. It was not possible to believe the Italian pilots had been unable to see the nine red crosses displayed on the ground and on the tents.

Dr. Hylander was even more puzzled when more Italian planes flew over his camp the following day and the day after that. Though they did not bomb or strafe, their visits became more alarming as each day passed.

Lieutenant Tito Minniti of the Italian air force was flying a reconnaissance mission in the area of Daggahbur, about a hundred sixty miles south of Harar, the day before Christmas when his plane developed engine trouble. [2] Below him was a fairly flat desert expanse and he was able to land without mishap. His co-pilot, apparently frightened at the prospect of what the much-bombed Ethiopians might do to captured Italian airmen, left the landing site as quickly as possible, disappearing into the desert.

Minniti was still examining his disabled plane, trying to figure out how to repair it, when a group of men arrived and apprehended him. The identity of these men has never been precisely established. The Italians later produced an affidavit that they were Ethiopian soldiers, but so many Italian affidavits were subsequently proven false that others, including this one, were left in doubt.

It is almost certain that the men were Ethiopians. The Ethiopian government later acknowledged Lieutenant Minniti's capture, but stated that he was not taken by Ethiopian troops, that he was seized by "local nomads who were exasperated by the bombing and the machine-gunning of their flocks."

Whoever these men were, they used extreme measures to show their "exasperation." According to the Italian affidavit, taken from an Egyptian named Abdel Mohsein El Wishy who had been an assistant dispenser in his country's medical mission to Ethiopia and who claimed to be an eye-witness, the captors of Lieutenant Minniti "dragged" him along a road near a little town called Bir. Soon they stopped, removed Minniti's coveralls, shackled his legs, and tied him to a tree. They then loosened his hands, which had been held behind his back, and cut off his fingers. Their leader, ignoring his shrieks of pain, reshackled his bloody hands and spat in his face. Subsequently, the men stripped Minniti of his remaining clothes and cut off his genitals.

Abdel Mohsein El Wishy testified in his affidavit that having seen this much, he departed, returning later with a companion. By now, Minniti was dead and had been decapitated, but further indignities were still being visited upon his corpse.

The Egyptian's affidavit was unquestionably correct in one particular: Lieutenant Minniti was definitely killed and decapitated. When word of this outrage reached General Rodolfo Graziani, who was preparing to march against the forces of Ras Desta near Dolo, he was understandably furious. At the same time, he realized the incident might prove useful to him.

On October 27, as noted earlier, Graziani had received permission from Mussolini to use gas against the Ethiopians. In another telegram to Graziani that same day, Mussolini acknowledged the difficulties presented by Europeans in Ethiopia: "I authorize you without doubt to get rid of the Swedish missionaries." In a later telegram to Graziani, December 16, Mussolini renewed his permission concerning gas: "The use of gas is fine in case Your Excellency might hold it necessary for supreme defensive reasons."

Graziani could easily imagine sufficient "defensive reasons" to use gas in his anticipated battle against Ras Desta, but he could see no reason for allowing Europeans to be near the scene where they might observe his use of gas or its effects. This was a problem Graziani shared with Badoglio and Mussolini. In a December 1 telegram, Mussolini had responded firmly to Badoglio's concern about foreign observers. "I give complete and immediate authorization," he had instructed Badoglio, "for the use of the broom against foreigners."

When the Swedish Red Cross unit arrived December 21 to care for the medical needs of Ras Desta's army, Graziani was already aware how inconvenient the unit's presence might soon be. He wasted no time before attempting to scare the Swedish medical men out of the area. The two planes which had dropped bombs outside the Red Cross camp and fired bullets into it on the twenty-second had obviously been sent to intimidate the Swedes, and the daily fly-overs thereafter had been arranged to make them increasingly conscious that they were not welcome. But the Swedes showed no sign of taking the hint. The decapitation of Lieutenant Minniti would provide Graziani with what he considered sufficient reason to send them a more forceful message.

At seven-thirty a.m. December 30, Dr. Fride Hylander and two Ethiopian assistants were in the operating tent of the Swedish ambulance unit. The morning was clear, as was usual in the desert, and the heat was already rising. The sound of airplanes indicated the Italians were about to pay another of their almost daily visits.

Emerging from the tent, Dr. Hylander looked upward in time to see six planes, in two formations of three, fly directly over the center of the camp and begin dropping bombs. Before he could make a move to escape, one of the bombs hit the ground so close to him that he went down with several wounds from steel splinters in his back and both thighs. The operating tent had been riddled and his two assistants killed.

The attack had only begun. Dr. Hylander, unable to get up, remained on the ground in the center of the camp, crawling to whatever cover he could find, as the airplanes returned for pass after pass. They were soon joined by four others. For twenty minutes, the ten Italian planes bombed and machine-gunned the camp. More than one hundred patients in the ward tents, too sick or too bewildered to get up from their cots and escape, absorbed the worst of the bombardment. Many were killed by direct hits. One of the Swedish orderlies, seeking shelter in a truck, was hit in the face by a shell splinter which carried away most of his jaw. He died a short time later. A splinter grazed the skull of another Swedish orderly. One of the medical tents was destroyed by a direct bomb hit. The others were torn to shreds by splinters as the bombs exploded like a succession of thunderclaps. An estimated one hundred bombs fell during the attack. Dr. Hylander, from the spot where he fell, was able to count at least thirty craters.

When the planes finished their work and departed, the survivors found twenty-eight men dead and about fifty wounded, of whom fourteen eventually died, bringing the death toll to forty-two. In addition to the tents, all the motor trucks had been damaged, and much of the medical equipment was destroyed.

Scattered among the debris were several leaflets which the planes had also dropped. Printed in Amharic, the leaflets said:

> You have transgressed the laws of kingdoms and nations by killing a captive airman by beheading him. According to the law, prisoners must be treated with respect. Do not touch them! You will consequently receive the punishment which you deserve.

The leaflet was signed "GRAZIANI," and the Italian government never denied that he was the author. On the same day and again the following day, Graziani's planes also bombed and leafleted an Egyptian ambulance unit 250 miles north at Bulale. Neither he nor the Italian government ever explained why, if these attacks were actually reprisals for the beheading of Lieutenant Minniti, they were directed against foreign medical facilities and not against the Ethiopian troop encampments near each of these facilities.

Mussolini, already unhappy about the apparent stagnation of his armies in Ethiopia, became alarmed when he observed the reaction in Sweden and the rest of the world to the bombing of the Swedish Red Cross unit near Dolo. The Swedish government protested immediately to Italy and to the League of Nations. League Member states hostile to Italy became more so. Though the Duce himself had encouraged Graziani to take action against foreigners, he realized now that the action taken had been as clumsy as it was brutal. Two days after the attack, on New Year's Day, he addressed a secret telegram about it to Graziani's commanding officer, Marshal Badoglio, in Makalle:

> The news of the bombardment of a Swedish Red Cross field hospital unit on the Somali front has raised a great sensation which our enemies are utilizing to the fullest [in Sweden] where the flags have been lowered to half-mast, and in the rest of Europe. After the speculation about Dessie [i.e., the December 6 bombing there] we'll have it about Dolo and the sanctionists will take encouragement from it to invoke measures. This is absolutely damaging. No one is more favorable to hard war than I am, that is, as far as war is concerned, and in such a sense I gave Your Excellency recent instructions, but the game must be worth the candle and the necessary reprisal must be intelligent. If, in order to get rid of ten more Abyssinians we bring upon ourselves the opinion of the world and we constrain our few friends to reservations, we do nothing but render our task more difficult. Give strict orders that Red Cross installations be diligently and everywhere respected.

His mention of "recent instructions" about "hard war" referred to a December 28 telegram to Badoglio which approved, after the fact, the mustard-gas attack against Ras Imru's troops. In that telegram, Mussolini had said, "Given the enemy systems of warfare, in answer to your dispatch No. 630, I authorize Your Excellency to use, even on a vast scale, any kind of gas and flame throwers." But by January 5, Mussolini was so jittery about the international situation and the danger of more sanctions that he decided, temporarily, to rescind that authorization. "Suspend the use of gas," he wired Badoglio that day, "until the Geneva meetings, unless it becomes necessary for supreme offensive or defensive measures. I will give you further instruction with regard to this."

Sitting helplessly at his big rosewood desk in the Palazzo Venezia, the Italian dictator could scarcely contain his anxiety about the peculiar developments in Africa. Since Christmas, newspapers throughout Europe had been publishing stories about Ethiopian victories. The American Associated Press had released a story to the effect that the Italians had suffered a setback near the Takazze River, *The New York Times* had mentioned speculation that four hundred thousand Ethiopians were closing in to attack Makalle. Though these stories were vague, and though Badoglio assured him they were unreliable, he knew there was some truth in the speculation. The story about the defeat at the Takazze,

269

for instance, was gallingly true. He still couldn't imagine what had gone wrong there. On January 6 he sent Badoglio an angry and anguished telegram:

> The missing cooperation of the Command of the Second Army Corps [centered at Adowa and Axum] with its detachments which were surprised and hard-pressed at Mai Timchet and Dembeguina has provoked in me the most painful impression, the more so because of the fact that the news of Dec. 12 showed [the location of] the enemy forces and made known in advance the enemy's intentions. Before proceeding with the publication of the bulletin containing the promotion of General Maravigna, I pray Your Excellency to examine and refer to me information on the responsibilities of the above named general in the grave failure which allowed the Ethiopians to take and keep, even up to now, the initiative in the operations on our right.

Badoglio could make light of Ras Imru's victory at Dembeguina Pass, and he could promise that, as a result of the gas attacks beginning December 23, Imru would not be able to invade Eritrea. But he could not explain satisfactorily the fact that Imru's forces were still in possession of Dembeguina Pass, only ten miles west of Axum, and that the combined forces of Ras Kassa and Ras Seyoum were in possession of Abbi Addi, only thirty miles west of Makalle. During his Roman rages, Mussolini continued his threats to dismiss Badoglio, but both men knew he couldn't do so, partly because it would be an unmistakable sign of panic to relieve two supreme commanders in less than two months, and partly because there was no one with enough stature to replace him.[3] General Graziani, presumably the second man in line, had been passed over when De Bono was relieved. Graziani's record did not inspire great confidence, nor did his current lack of initiative on the southern front. After his capture, November 7, of a town called Gorahai, about one hundred miles inside the Ethiopian border from Somaliland, he had sent a contingent in pursuit of the Ethiopians there, who had escaped up the valley of the Fafan River, on which Gorahai was located. At a placed called Hamanlei, the fleeing Ethiopians had turned on their pursuers and, after a fierce battle, drove them back toward Gorahai. Since then, Graziani had made no significant moves against the Ethiopians. But in Mussolini's desperate need of an immediate victory at least for propaganda purposes, he had to turn to Graziani on the southern front because Badoglio, in the north, refused to move until he was ready. Mussolini therefore sent Graziani a telegram, January 6, encouraging him to action by pointing out to him an excellent opportunity for an easy victory:

> I communicate to you the telegram which I sent to Badoglio and to which I am awaiting an answer: "If Graziani thinks he is able to do it, give him

the order to attack the troops blocking Dolo, who, according to much credible information, are in difficulty."

The Ethiopians at Dolo were the troops of Ras Desta, and the information Mussolini had received about them was entirely accurate. Desta's army, after its march of two hundred fifty miles south through the desert, was afflicted by malaria, dysentery, and hunger. And each day, the condition of the four or five thousand remaining men became more desperate. Until the arrival of the Swedish ambulance unit, they had been getting absolutely no medical care, and even now, the bomb-damaged Swedish dispensary could provide for only a fraction of their acute medical needs. Dr. Marcel Junod, a Swiss citizen and International Red Cross representative who visited Desta's camp on the Ganale River a few days after the bombing of the Swedish Red Cross unit, found conditions there deplorable. "The Abyssinian commissariat was able to give the men only a cup of flour a week," he reported, "and even that was not distributed when the two miserable vans [motor trucks] which were all there was to maintain supplies for the whole army broke down or were plundered en route."

Ras Desta, before marching into the desert from Neghelli, two hundred fifty miles to the northwest, had assembled a sizable herd of cattle to accompany his army on the hoof so his men would have meat, but this herd, as a result of slaughter, hunger, and disease, had now dwindled to a point where only three bullocks a day could be slaughtered. Though his army had also dwindled from the fifteen thousand men with whom he started to less than five thousand, three bullocks a day provided meat for only a pitifully small fraction of them. The others subsisted on wild roots and berries. "The half-starved soldiery," Junod said, "offered little resistance to the scourges which decimated their ranks."

Ras Desta himself, at the same time, managed to maintain in the field a remarkable semblance of the comfort to which, as the husband of the Emperor's older daughter, he had become accustomed. His tent was well attended by servants and his table was not short of food. An elegant young man, small in stature, he wore sometimes a traditional Ethiopian shamma, sometimes an excellently tailored European khaki uniform. Dr. Junod, who had lunch with Ras Desta in his tent after observing the horrible living conditions of his troops, was amazed at the contrast. "The meal he set before us," Junod recalled, "was an excellent one with most savory dishes and a variety of wines. After lunch he opened two bottles of champagne and ceremoniously raised his glass to the health of his guests."

When the toasts were finished, Ras Desta led Junod and the rest of the party to the bank of the Ganale River, quite wide in that area and framed on either side with narrow bands of palm trees and other vegetation, which seemed to cling to the river for protection against the surrounding desert. Servants laid out a carpet on which the ras and his guests could sit, whereupon he offered Dr. Junod his own carbine and pointed out to him a number of crocodiles sunning themselves on the opposite bank. Junod fired three shots, finally prompting the crocodiles to slither into the water. Ras Desta sat back comfortably, fanned by one of his servants as he watched. There was nothing in his manner to indicate that he even suspected what Rodolfo Graziani had in store for him.

General Graziani, at least as well aware as Mussolini of the condition of Ras Desta's men, had been planning for some time to take advantage of the opportunity for glory they offered him. To prepare his intended campaign against them, he had taken a substantial house in the southern Somali town of Lugh Ferandi, about fifty miles southeast of Dolo and the Ethiopian border. In the large, bare central room of this house he had set up his headquarters. On the whitewashed walls were crossed lances and native shields made of hippopotamus leather. Graziani worked at a small table littered with maps and papers which he marked with red or blue pencils as he studied them. His table and chair were the only furniture in the room. An Italian journalist named Sandro Volta, who attended a Graziani press conference in this room, described the general as follows:

> When I entered with other Italian and foreign colleagues, he stood up. He was enormous. He was dressed in a desert jacket, light colored, with dark trousers. His popular heroic image made him appear to us a character created from the fantasy of the masses, an unreal being who gathered together in himself all the characteristics of an ancient race invented by the collective imagination of an entire people. . . . Homer must have imagined heroes like him when he thought of his heroes. Even more, the poets who will create the new myths of Fascist Italy will have to take him into account.

If Graziani was ever to become a hero, it would have to be in myth. In reality, he fell dreadfully short. As a military commander in Italian-held Libya before coming to Somaliland, he had dealt with restless native inhabitants by hanging or shooting several thousand and imprisoning countless others behind the barbed wire of concentration camps. When the Ethiopian war began in October, he had waited only two weeks before asking Mussolini's permission to use mustard gas against the Ethiopians. His subsequent bombing of Red Cross units was characteristic of his military methods. In later years, he once said to a reporter, "At times I search my conscience to see if I can find any justification for the charges of brutality and savagery that have been brought against me, and believe me, never do I sleep as soundly as when I've spent the evening in such

272

self-scrutiny. I know from the history of every era that in order to rebuild, the past, or that part of the past that bears no relation to the present, must be destroyed."[4] Actually, Graziani need not have worried that historians would select brutality as the dominant motif of his career; he was destined to become much more famous for military ineptitude. As Mussolini's North African commander in 1940–1941, he challenged an ill-equipped British force of 31,000 men with a well-equipped Italian army of ten divisions, about 150,000 men. When the campaign ended two months later, the British had advanced five hundred miles; Graziani's entire army had been destroyed; 130,000 of his men were prisoners; 400 of his tanks and 1240 of his big guns had been captured. British losses were 553 killed, 1373 injured.

Nobody yet knew in 1936 that the tall, handsome, and imposing Graziani was so incompetent, though Mussolini had evinced enough reservations to pass over him when he made Badoglio supreme commander. Fortunately for the Italian cause, Ras Desta, the general who faced Graziani at the extreme southeastern border of Ethiopia, was a man of comparable skill and inferior resources, especially since he had dissipated most of his strength in the foolhardy march through the desert from Neghelli. Besides having only enough food for bare subsistence, Desta's men had only enough ammunition for a light skirmish, and there was no possibility of their supplies being replenished. Desta had never burdened his mind with logistical problems. Against him, Graziani had gathered at Lugh Ferandi a force of fourteen thousand men, twenty-six artillery weapons, seven hundred motor vehicles, thirty-seven hundred pack animals, and a few squadrons of armored cars and tanks. He was ready for a long desert campaign which would bring him eventually, he hoped, to Neghelli, three hundred miles northwest of Dolo.

Graziani's troops crossed the border near Dolo in three columns, at dawn January 12, to launch what became known as the battle of Ganale Doria. Aerial reconnaissance had informed them exactly where Desta was encamped. As squadrons of Italian airplanes bombarded the Ethiopian positions, one of Graziani's columns moved up the Ganale valley directly toward them, while the other two swung south in an attempt to get around them and encircle them. Though the battle may not have developed exactly as Graziani hoped, it developed well enough for the Italians. The column on the left, expecting to encircle the enemy, met him in force, while the column on the right, the only mechanized column, encountered slight resistance as it moved up the Ganale valley. But even without mechanized units, the column on the left quickly routed the half-starved Ethiopians, drove them away from their only wells, and began a merciless three-day pursuit which was called a battle but was actually a slaughter. Sandro Volta witnessed it:

The Ethiopians went mad and rushed toward certain death for a gulp of water. It was no longer a question of fighting a war; all they could think of was water, water, water. The machine-gunners had only to aim a few inches above the ground to slaughter them by the hundreds.[5]

It might occur to some that such a crazed need for water, during the height of battle, could hardly be due to thirst alone. Graziani had permission from Mussolini to use mustard gas, and he has been accused of dropping seventeen hundred kilograms of it on the Ethiopians during this battle. The Ethiopian government, however, in its complaints to the League of Nations about the use of gas, did not mention the battle of Ganale Doria. Whether Graziani did or did not use it, there was obviously no need for him to do so. Ras Desta's defenses were shattered on the first day, and while many of his men fought bravely, they lacked resources to fight for very long. Most of them scattered into the desert where they either died of hunger and thirst or surrendered to Italian mop-up squadrons.

Desta himself, in desperation, sent out his cavalry against the advancing tanks, with as much success as one might expect. Finally, with his servants, bodyguard, and a Belgian military adviser, he fled northward in the two trucks which were his only vehicles. When he arrived at Neghelli on the eighteenth, the city was being bombed. He continued his flight to safety while the remainder of his army, and the Swedish Red Cross people who had journeyed south to help them, floundered helplessly in the desert.

Graziani, finding the route to Neghelli wide open, sent his columns northward at full speed. The first Italian troops arrived there January 20. Mussolini at last had a victory about which he could boast.

Everett Colson, who had come to Dessie for consultations, was preparing to fly back to Addis Ababa, the morning of January 18, when he heard airplane engine sounds approaching from a distance. The Italians, who were now bombing the supply route to the northern front almost daily, were apparently preparing to visit Dessie today. If so, the Emperor would no doubt be out in his garden, firing his antiaircraft gun again. It was a sight Colson decided he would like to see. Since he should also say good-by to the Emperor before leaving for the capital, he hurried up the hill to the Imperial headquarters.

Colson should not have hurried. He was the only one of the Emperor's three chief foreign advisers still in Ethiopia (General Eric Virgin having left on the eve of war and Raymonde Auberson in mid-November), and his health was extremely delicate. He suffered from a heart condition which was thought to be aggravated by the altitude of Ethiopia's high plateau. This morning it was further aggravated by his rushing up the hill. When he arrived at the Emperor's headquarters, he did indeed find Haile Selassie firing his gun at a lone Italian plane which seemed to be on a reconnaissance mission over Dessie. But by this time, he didn't feel well enough to appreciate the sight of the diminutive, bearded monarch, standing behind his Oerlikon and filling the air with explosions. When the Italian plane flew away, unharmed, the Emperor turned to find his adviser breathing heavily and looking stricken. Colson had strained his heart. On several occasions already his doctor had told him he would have to leave Ethiopia. This morning's attack was certain to raise again the question of how much longer he could remain.

After regaining his breath, Colson returned down the hill to the concealed airplane which was awaiting him and made his flight as planned. But the Emperor, bidding him good-by, was now faced with another worry. Without Colson, whatever government was still functioning in Addis Ababa might flounder, and Ethiopia's tenuous communications with the League of Nations and other possibly helpful nations were likely to lapse.

The Emperor, with Colson's help, was still bombarding Geneva with protests against Italian methods of war. In a letter December 30 he had informed the League that the Italians had,

> during their recent retreat in Shire and Tembien [the regions from which Ras Seyoum and Ras Imru had routed them], burned the churches and proceeded to the systematic extermination of the civil population. Now, December 23, they have made use against our troops in the Takazze region of asphyxiating and poison gases, which constitutes a new addition to the list, already long, of Italy's breaches of her international undertakings.

This was his first of what would be many protests against the Italian use of gas. Two days later, he had occasion to write once more to Geneva.

> On December 30 again, the Italians, after violently bombing our southern army, made use of poison gas. During the same bombardment, the Italians completely destroyed the Swedish Red Cross ambulance ... plainly marked with treaty symbols. ... After bombing the Adowa hospital, the hospital and ambulances at Dessie and Swedish ambulance, and using gas, Italy proceeds on her barbarous course with impunity and, according to her own professions, in the name of civilization.

These were serious Ethiopian charges, but the Italians, anticipating them, had already found a way to cloud them and confuse the issues. On December 26, the Italian government had sent a letter to the League of Nations charging that the Ethiopians were using dumdum bullets. And on January 16, Italian Undersecretary of State for Foreign Affairs Fulvio

Suvich sent the League a letter reiterating the dumdum charge and adding to it a charge that Ethiopian soldiers were protecting themselves from bombardment by hiding under Red Cross flags. Wasn't that sufficient justification for bombing Red Cross units? It was considered sufficient justification in Geneva, anyway, for allowing the Ethiopian charges and Italian countercharges to balance themselves out.

In Geneva January 20, when the League Council convened ostensibly to discuss once more the possibility (now more remote than ever) of an oil embargo against Italy, the members were embarrassed to find in front of them another letter from Haile Selassie that had just arrived.

"At the beginning of October 1935," the letter reminded the League,

> Ethiopia received the inestimable moral support of a unanimous declaration condemning the aggression committed by the Italian government. Indirect pressure has also been exercised on the aggressor by means of a number of financial and economic prohibitions. . . . But hitherto the Ethiopian government has obtained from the League of Nations neither the indirect assistance of irresistible economic means nor any form of direct assistance. It has never asked and does not ask for armed assistance. But must it forgo the help which would be afforded to it by fresh economic prohibitions and the financial assistance which it has claimed from the outset of hostilities. . . ?

The Emperor was not only demanding the invocation of an oil embargo. He was also pressing seriously a request for material aid. And just as a reminder of the real issue at stake, as far as the League and the principle of collective security were concerned, he added in his letter, "The Ethiopian government is learning the cruel lesson that small peoples must chiefly rely on themselves to defend their independence and their territorial integrity."

Anthony Eden, embarrassed by the letter as he had been a month earlier by the Hoare-Laval Plan, and sincerely in favor of an oil embargo even if his government was not, suggested to Pierre Laval that the League stop wasting time by continuing to discuss the possibility of conciliation. Laval, though he had suffered so much political damage at home as a result of the ill-fated "conciliation" effort of Hoare and himself that he was now reconciled to resigning the French premiership, nevertheless clung stubbornly to his pro-Italian policy. Another attempt at conciliation should be made, he insisted, before oil sanctions were considered. As for the increasing clamor in favor of an oil embargo, he suggested to Eden a plan which might quell it. The League's Committee of Eighteen, which was due to meet on the twenty-second for possible action

276

toward an oil embargo, should instead postpone the matter once more and appoint another committee to study it. Eden, for reasons which he never explained satisfactorily, agreed to this plan.

The next day, January 21, the Council session was disrupted by the news that the ailing King George of England had died. The morning was taken up by condolence calls which the heads of all the delegations paid to Eden in his rooms at the Hotel Beau Rivage. Afterward, feeling distressed perhaps not only by the death of the King but by the knowledge of his own futility in his first assignment as British Foreign Secretary, Eden nevertheless held some meetings with delegates of small nations and found surprising optimism. Nicolas Titulescu of Rumania, for instance, declared that oil sanctions must be applied immediately because Mussolini was bound to fail in Ethiopia, and his failure should be made to look like the result of League action. His suggestion, though not very forthright, might at least save the League, whose very existence was now threatened. Titulescu's remarks were also interesting for another reason. When a man so well informed could conclude that Italy was destined to lose the war, it was an indication of how unimpressive Mussolini's army had been in the first three and a half months since the invasion.

The optimism of men like Titulescu was not sufficient, however, to put any fight into Anthony Eden. When the League Council assembled for its last session, he, like the others, bowed to Laval's wishes and sheepishly voted to reject Ethiopia's plea for financial aid (which would have been difficult to procure, it must be admitted), as well as another Ethiopian request that a committee of inquiry be appointed to investigate methods of warfare on both sides.

The Committee of Eighteen, as completely controlled by France and England as was the Council, met subsequently and appointed what was to be called the Committee of Experts. The purpose of this august body, it was explained, would be to study the practical implications of an oil embargo. If this also delayed the possibility of an oil embargo for another month or two, that simply couldn't be helped. Pierre Laval had prevailed again, even on his last day in Geneva. As soon as the session ended, he returned to Paris and, because of French internal problems, mainly economic, resigned as Premier of France.

On January 19, the Third Army Corps, a sizable part of the main Italian concentration encamped at Makalle, marched southwestward ten miles to Debri-Negaida. At last it appeared that Marshal Badoglio was about to launch his long-awaited offensive against Ethiopia's largest army, the estimated eighty thousand men under Ras Mulugeta who occupied Amba

277

Aradam, the huge mountain about twenty miles south of Makalle which barred the route southward toward Quoram, Dessie, and ultimately Addis Ababa. The advance of the Third Army Corps was, in fact, a feint, the main purpose of which was to isolate Mulugeta's forces from the estimated forty thousand men under Ras Kassa and Ras Seyoum, entrenched now at Abbi Addi in the Tembien region, thirty miles due west of Makalle.

Though Mussolini was impatient to attack Mulugeta, Badoglio had told him in a January 11 telegram that he dared not move south until his right flank was secure against Kassa, whom the Emperor had now appointed commander-in-chief of northern operations, much to the disgust of War Minister Mulugeta. Badoglio's telegram, besides explaining the reasons for not moving south, also addressed itself to Mussolini's demands for immediate victories. Mussolini's answer January 14 said:

> I want first of all to tell you that the Italian people are now anxiously awaiting a great battle. The battle, more or less great, depends not only on us but also on the enemy who, obeying his wise European counselors, will probably do anything to avoid battle. The essential in my opinion is to retake the initiative in operations, which will facilitate the task in case we are attacked or will permit us to attack with success when the circumstances promise to be favorable. Your Excellency has at his disposal in all 15 divisions, and above all, troops which breathe only one thing—to fight.

Having thus reminded Badoglio that he now had an overwhelming force under his command, Mussolini climaxed the telegram by making it clear that his impatience had not subsided:

> A word of order is not to wait placidly for the initiative of the enemy, but to confront him and control him in battles which will be large or small according to the case, but victorious.

It was clear to Badoglio that he must do something immediately to placate the Duce. Since he dared not move south against Mulugeta, he decided to move west against Kassa, whose army, in its present position, threatened to cut off the road from Makalle north to the Eritrean supply bases, and the mule track which linked the Italians in Makalle with those at Adowa and Axum. When Badoglio apprised Mussolini of this plan, he received, on the nineteenth, a telegram of approval: "The maneuver is well conceived and will surely succeed. I authorize Your Excellency to use all the means of war—I say all, both from the air and from the land." Mustard gas had been so effective against Imru at the Takazze that Badoglio fully intended to use it against Kassa and Seyoum. But he was happy to have Mussolini take the responsibility for it.

Whether Ras Kassa actually planned to take advantage of his offensive opportunities was not certain. Kassa owed his appointment not to his military aptitude but to his political eminence as cousin of the Emperor and most powerful ras in Ethiopia. He did not understand the potential effectiveness of small guerrilla groups, or the advantages of very mobile, lightly equipped units operating at night. Only once during the entire war, on January 9 at Doghea Pass below Makalle, did any Ethiopians attempt a night raid against the enemy. It was their tradition to fight in the daytime, and Ras Kassa, a stalwart supporter of one of Ethiopia's most conservative establishments, the Coptic Church, was hardly the kind of man to ignore tradition. Neither was he reconciled to the necessity of facing Italy's new, untraditional weapons. If he were to break out to the north or northeast into the relatively flat country above Makalle, he might subject his men to the Italian tanks, and as he once acknowledged in a message to the Emperor, he had no desire to meet such incomprehensible monsters.

Badoglio, having sent his Third Army Corps south on the nineteenth to try to prevent Mulugeta from reinforcing Kassa, then sent two strong columns of Eritrean troops, on the twentieth, to attack Kassa's right wing, which was encamped on three mountains southeast of Abbi Addi. At the same time, he ordered a Black Shirt division, then garrisoned in the Warieu Pass about five miles north of Abbi Addi, to send a contingent down out of the pass toward Kassa's left wing in the hope of keeping it occupied. These Black Shirt troops were not intended for any heavy fighting. That role, as usual, was reserved for the very dependable Eritrean troops to the southeast of Abbi Addi. The Black Shirt assignment, as Badoglio explained it, was "to engage the enemy, who appeared to be in force in that area, and prevent them from leaving their positions . . . [to make] a rapid concentration with the [Ethiopian] troops distributed to the east."

The Eritreans very quickly established contact with the Ethiopians, who had already been harassed by aerial bombardment, thus beginning the war's first major battle, which would continue for four days and which would eventually be known as the first battle of the Tembien. From morning until dusk on the twentieth, the Eritreans attacked the Ethiopians with rifles and bayonets, slowly pushing them back until, when the sun fell, Kassa's troops had been dislodged from one mountain and from the foothills of another. Ras Kassa, disconsolate at this result, sent the Emperor that night a radio message which, like all other Ethiopian messages, was monitored by the Italians. "The men I sent to cut off the Italians were surrounded," Kassa lamented.

The next day, when the white Italian Black Shirt troops made their thrust south from the Warieu Pass, they did not fare so well as their black Eritrean brethren. Despite the bombs and mustard gas dropped by a hundred Italian planes on Kassa's left-wing positions around Abbi Addi, the Ethiopians swarmed upon the Black Shirts in wave after wave, forcing them to fall back toward the pass and very nearly surrounding them. By sunset, the Black Shirt contingent, having lost 335 men, killed and wounded, during the retreat, finally reached the relative safety of the pass where the rest of their division was garrisoned. Now, however, the pursuing Ethiopians were also at the pass, engaging the garrison's outer defenses. If they were to capture this pass, all roads north would be open to them. As they broke off their attack that evening, they were convinced that a great victory was within their grasp.

The following morning, the twenty-second, waves of Ethiopians braved heavy bombing and gassing as they raced up the approaches to Warieu Pass to take part in a fierce siege of the garrison. This siege was to continue unabated during the next two days. The beleaguered Black Shirts, gradually running short of food, water, and ammunition, found themselves in ever-increasing peril as the barefooted Ethiopians, emitting hideous battle cries and spurred on by the blaring of war bugles behind them, poured forward in such numbers that it was impossible to stop all of them, even with machine-gun fire. Italian gun crews, with mounds of dead Ethiopians in front of their muzzles, found dozens of live ones leaping over their fallen comrades to slash and stab with swords and spears. Gradually the Italians drew back into a tighter and tighter fortified circle as the Ethiopians overran their outer defenses. The Black Shirt division was now completely surrounded.

Marshal Badoglio, informed by radio of the Warieu garrison's plight, sent a relief column immediately to try to free the entrapped Fascists and ordered the Eritreans, who were still advancing southwest of Warieu, to fall back to their original positions in Abaro Pass so they would be able to move on Warieu if they were needed.

Despite the success of the Ethiopians, their casualties were so staggering Ras Kassa began to realize he would need more men if he hoped actually to take and hold Warieu Pass. He couldn't possibly get help from Ras Imru west of Axum because Imru had no radio. He lacked even a receiving set and was therefore unaware that this important battle was in progress. Kassa's only hope was Ras Mulugeta, who was much closer at Amba Aradam, and with whom he was in radio communication. But the old War Minister, still sulking because he had been placed under Kassa's command, showed no inclination to send the help Kassa needed. His forces, he said, were heavily engaged by the Italian Third Army Corps. Actually, there is no record of Mulugeta's having challenged the Third Army Corps, which Badoglio had sent to contain him. Kassa, without any prospect of assistance, nevertheless kept pouring his men into the Warieu battle with the expectation that the Italian garrison must soon collapse.

It was an expectation at least partially shared by Marshal Badoglio, who waited nervously at Makalle for news that the relief column had reached Warieu to free the Black Shirts, or that the Ethiopians had finally run out of men to throw against the garrison's defenders. Rather than sit in his own quarters, where each new message would be brought, he spent hours at the radio tent, listening to the messages directly. As pilots returned from their bombing or gassing missions, he would question them in person about what they had seen taking place on the ground below them.

On the afternoon of the twenty-second, Ras Kassa sent so many waves of men against Warieu that Badoglio could no longer even pretend he had the situation under control.[6] He ordered his staff immediately to make a study "of the possible procedure in the event a retirement from Makalle became necessary." If Kassa took Warieu Pass, such a retirement would be extremely difficult to avert because the Ethiopians would then have completely isolated his western wing at Adowa. They would also be able to cut, wherever they pleased, his supply route from Eritrea. If Badoglio had to retreat, it would mean the evacuation of seventy thousand men, fourteen thousand animals, three hundred artillery pieces, and as much matériel as could be carried back to Eritrea, whence the Italians had launched the war the previous October. It would be a defeat perhaps as devastating as the Italian army had suffered at the hands of the Ethiopians in 1896. It would almost certainly prolong the war a year more than the Italians had anticipated, and it might force the total abandonment of the enterprise. It would undoubtedly end Badoglio's military career and probably end Mussolini's political career. Badoglio had to face all these possibilities as he waited anxiously for good news on the twenty-second and again on the twenty-third.

Italian planes dropped provisions, on the twenty-third, to the besieged division at Warieu, but they could not drop water, of which there was so little left within the ever-shrinking fortification that no one was allowed to drink it. The men could only moisten their lips with dampened pads of cotton, and one of them later wrote a poem about having nothing but boiled urine to drink.

Italian planes that day were also dropping on the Ethiopian rear positions the heaviest concentration of mustard gas Badoglio had used to date. (No Italian commander would drop it into an actual battle zone because it would then injure Italian as well as Ethiopian troops. This might explain why so many Italian soldiers have continued to disbelieve that their commanders used gas.) Ras Kassa afterward described vividly one of these attacks:[7]

> The bombing from the air had reached its height when suddenly a number of my warriors dropped their weapons, screamed with agony, rubbed their

281

eyes with their knuckles, buckled at the knees and collapsed. An invisible rain of lethal gas was splashing down on them. One after another, all those who had survived the bombing succumbed to this new form of attack. I dare not think of how many men I lost on this one day alone. The gas contaminated the fields and woods, and at least 2,000 animals died. Mules, cows, rams and a host of wild creatures, maddened with pain, stampeded to the ravines and threw themselves into the depths below.

In spite of this relentless attack, when night fell on the twenty-third, the Italian relief column had not yet been able to fight its way through to the besieged division, and though Badoglio later tried to minimize the seriousness of his situation, a journalist named Paolo Monelli who was with him that night observed his deep disturbance. "He refused to go to bed," Monelli later wrote.

> Fully dressed, still wearing his cap, with his cape spread over his knees like a blanket, he sat on a stool in his tent beside the telephone. On the few occasions when it rang, he lifted the receiver and listened in silence, his face a mask of stone in the crude light of the acetylene lamp. The sun was beginning to rise when it rang once more, and at last he heard the news for which he had been so anxiously waiting. His set expression relaxed, the shadow of a smile played about his lips. He rose, went outside and took his customary morning exercise, pacing to and fro among the sleeping tents.[8]

The relief column had finally reached the men at Warieu. Ras Kassa, who might have continued his assault against the exhausted Black Shirts trapped there, had now lost so many of his own men to gunfire, bombs, and gas that he could not sustain the attack against fresh, well-armed replacements. Gradually, in the words of Marshal Badoglio, he "relaxed his pressure and withdrew."

As the Ethiopian survivors gathered up the weapons and ammunition of the fallen Italians, they loudly boasted of victory. It was true that the Italians suffered severe casualties—almost eleven hundred men killed or injured, including sixty officers. It was also true that the only ground which exchanged hands in this first battle of the Tembien, the territory north of Abbi Addi on the approaches to the Warieu Pass, had been taken from the Italians by the Ethiopians. And it was true that Badoglio's first attempt at an offensive had failed. But the cost to the Ethiopians had been almost prohibitive. Ras Kassa had suffered an estimated eight thousand casualties, dead and wounded. And he had fallen short of what would have constituted an overwhelming victory, the capture of Warieu Pass. Considering the costs on both sides, the first battle of Tembien would have to be assessed as a stalemate.

CHAPTER TWELVE

THE entire corps of war correspondents, Italian and foreign, gathered at ten a.m. February 9, in the mess tent of Marshal Badoglio's hillside head-quarters at Enda Jesus near Makalle, where he had finally brought them after isolating them in Asmara since December.[1] Many of the newsmen were getting their first glimpse of Ethiopia. Badoglio's headquarters, built into the bleak hills above an ancient walled fortress, was a random scattering of about fifty buildings and tents connected by roads which were now rivers of mud since the "little rains," as the Ethiopians called them, had begun. The newsmen, who had been brought to the mess tent to hear their first words of welcome from the Supreme Italian Com-mander, puzzled over an aerial reconnaissance map of northern Ethiopia as they awaited his arrival.

Badoglio walked in looking tired and red-eyed. He wore a broadcloth desert jacket and waved in his hand the white horsehair Ethiopian fly whisk he used as an officer's baton. As he stood before them they studied his wide, wrinkled forehead, his flat, pugilist's nose, his trim, solid physique maintained, despite his sixty-five years, by daily exercise.

Most of the newsmen had notebooks. "You can put them in your pockets," he said. From this day until further notice, no one would be allowed to send a word to his newspaper. Each man would be expected to maintain military discipline. "I consider you as soldiers," he said.

It was evident now that they had not been brought to the front lines simply because so many of them had been demanding it. Having kept them in Eritrea for two months, Badoglio had now brought them to Makalle for a reason.

"Two months ago in Asmara," he said, "I promised you that when something interesting to see happened, I would bring you here. Now I am keeping that promise."

He paused to indicate a momentous message was forthcoming. Then he resumed in the same even, monotonous voice in which he had begun. As one newsman observed, he separated each of his words with the same interval and spoke just so many per minute, so precisely he seemed to be counting them.

"I have decided," he said, "to attack Ras Mulugeta. I shall proceed as follows: Tomorrow, Monday, the tenth, the First Army Corps will transfer to positions farther forward than those it now occupies. On the eleventh, the First Army Corps and the Third Army Corps will advance in two columns toward Antalo, south of Amba Aradam, where they will converge. I do not expect any enemy reaction on the first day, but this will be an action on a very large scale. I shall be directing the movements of seventy thousand men. You will observe the battle from an observation post near mine. Therefore, you shall see what I see. Good day, gentlemen."

After waving his hand in a friendly salute, he walked out of the mess tent and returned to his own quarters about a hundred yards farther up the hill. His days of preparation were now at an end. Tomorrow he would be attacking Ethiopia's largest army, the estimated eighty thousand men of Ras Mulugeta encamped in the caves, crevices, and foothills of the great Amba Aradam massif less than twenty miles below Makalle. If he could defeat and destroy Mulugeta, as he fully expected to do, the route southward would lie open. The entire Ethiopian strategy in the north would be shattered and only the armies of the Emperor himself, now at Waldia about a hundred fifty miles below Makalle, would stand between him and Addis Ababa. On January 31, a week after the indecisive battle in the Tembien, Badoglio had issued all the orders for what he referred to as "the battle of annihilation." He had decided by then that, even though he hadn't been victorious in the Tembien, he had succeeded in neutralizing the Ethiopian forces there. Ras Kassa had lost so many men and had so thoroughly depleted his meager ammunition supplies that he could no longer threaten the Italian rear lines.

In a message to Mussolini January 31, Badoglio said,

> I shall concentrate the troops available here into one mobile body; with it I shall march on Antalo and Debra Aila [south of Amba Aradam]. Ras Mulugeta will either accept battle or will have to retire southward, thus uncovering Ras Kassa's lines of communication and abandoning his strong position on Mount Aradam. I hope he will decide to fight, in which case there will be an important battle. . . .

Badoglio's basic strategy was to attack Amba Aradam in a four-pronged operation, with two small columns converging from the northeast and northwest, while the other two columns, constituting his main strength, would encircle the mountain on each side to link up south of it, thus trapping Mulugeta's entire army and preventing his escape. This plan was dictated not only by the desire to surround the Ethiopians but also by the fact that there were five easy routes up the mountain from the south and none from the north. Badoglio fervently hoped Mulugeta had been so thoughtless as to leave his flanks and rear undefended.

Mussolini, on February 4, wired back to Badoglio: "I approve the preparation and I confirm my certainty of victory. I authorize you to use any means." Once again, Badoglio had the Duce's permission to use mustard gas.

Shortly before eight o'clock in the morning of February 10, Marshal Badoglio, in a closed automobile, drove up the slope of Amba Gheden, a mountain on which his observation post had been prepared, only a few miles east of Amba Aradam. Several silver-colored tents had been pitched to house radio equipment, mess, etc. The newsmen, kept at a distance, watched the marshal through binoculars as he got out of his car. There was very little else for them to watch. On one of the roads in an arid valley to the south they could see a column of trucks. And to the east, on the Plain of Scefta, some troops were moving forward in parallel lines. To the west, on Mount Aradam, there was no sign of life. It seemed that, though three Italian army corps were moving forward to encircle and attack them, Mulugeta and his men stuck to their caves, clefts, and trenches as if nothing were happening.

Badoglio, after talking to his staff and looking out over the scene, eventually paid a visit to the press. "Well, gentlemen, are you satisfied?" he asked. "Have you a good view of what's going on? You are watching a drama that will unfold itself in several acts. This is the prologue. Our troops have made excellent progress."

For the newsmen, the prologue was tediously dull because they could see almost nothing of it except the distant bursts of the bombs and shells the Italian planes and big guns kept bestowing upon the near side of the great mountain. But for Badoglio, it was completely satisfying. All his plans seemed to be working on schedule.

During the first two days, the First Army Corps to the east of Amba Aradam, and the Third Army Corps to the west of it, moved southward without incident. Not until the third day did either of these formidable forces, each composed of about three divisions, encounter any opposition.

On the afternoon of the twelfth, the First Corps, arriving near Afgol at the southeastern foot of the mountain, met the advance guard of a twenty-thousand-man force under the command of Dejasmatch Wodaju, Governor of Dessie. Though Wodaju was staunchly loyal to the Emperor, some of the chieftains under him were less so. A battle of wills developed in the upper echelons of command as to whether this army should stand or retreat. Wodaju seemed to prevail. His army advanced to meet the Italian 3rd-of-January Division (which commemorated the day in 1925 when Mussolini assumed dictatorial powers) and the battle of Amba Aradam finally began. This first phase, though bloody, did not last long.

285

With two other divisions coming up on the flanks to help the 3rd-of-January, the Italian strength quickly began to tell and the Ethiopian chieftains, who had not wanted to fight in the first place, led their men in pell-mell retreat. Wodaju, wounded in the action, barely managed to disengage himself and the remnants of his army.

While the First Corps was routing Wodaju's troops on the afternoon of the twelfth, only one mishap overtook the Third Corps advancing southward on the west side of the mountain. Its Sila Division was right below an Italian airplane when a lever broke and five incendiary bombs were accidentally dropped. A hundred men and forty animals in the middle of the sanitary section were killed or wounded.

The morning of the thirteenth, with the two Italian army corps still advancing toward each other south of Amba Aradam, the wounded Dejasmatch Wodaju had himself carried up the mountain to Ras Mulugeta's well-stocked headquarters cave to warn the old man of his imminent danger. Though Mulugeta was aware that the Italian armies were on the move—and in a message to one of his commanders the previous day had mentioned the possibility of defeat—he was apparently so shell-shocked and bomb-shocked by now that he could not quite comprehend what Wodaju tried to tell him.

Italian planes had been bombing Mulugeta and his men ever since they moved into their nine-thousand-foot, plateau-shaped mountain retreat in December. Badoglio had estimated there were eighty thousand of them. There were actually only about twenty thousand in the caves and crevices of the mountain itself, with fewer than forty thousand more encamped in its southern foothills. Badoglio also believed that, in addition to some ancient cannons, Mulugeta possessed some modern artillery. Actually, he had nothing but a few field pieces captured from the Italians at Adowa in 1896—pieces whose range Mulugeta didn't even know. His principal military concern during the two months on the mountain had been not offensive strategy but simply defense against the infernal bombs, or "pomps," as the Ethiopians pronounced it. And now, with 280 Italian artillery pieces plus a sharply increased number of airplanes (about 170) blasting him all day long, every day, he could think of nothing but burrowing into his cave to escape the incessant explosions. When he met with his staff nothing was ever decided because there didn't seem to be any need for decision. He continued to believe his mountain was impregnable. He could not imagine the Italians surrounding it or sending an army up to storm it.

At seven a.m. on the fifteenth, while Mulugeta was putting on his field boots, Italian artillery and planes began saturating the mountain with the fiercest attack to date. (During the battle, Badoglio's big guns fired 23,000 shells and his planes dropped 396 tons of high explosives on Amba Aradam. Badoglio believed in using clubs to swat mosquitoes.) Mulugeta, instead of being galvanized into action by this obviously significant increase in the tempo of the bombardment, simply moved deeper into his cave to escape it, while outside his men ran for shelter in their own caves or holes. They fired no return salvos. With the guns they had it would have been useless. They didn't even send out scouting parties to look for advancing Italian troops. They were totally unaware that the Third Army Corps, arriving from the west under cover of heavy clouds, had reached the southern foothills of the mountain and had begun the ascent in force.

Finally, at ten a.m., a great wind cleared away the clouds. When the Ethiopians looked down from behind their rocks and crevices they saw thousands of Italians and Eritreans rushing up the hills toward them with rifles and machine guns ready. As the firing began, Mulugeta, hearing it, came out of his cave, and saw for the first time the proportions of the disaster facing him. Drawing his sword, he called for his commanders and his hornblowers to sound the alarm. There was no time for planning or organization, nor was there any prearranged line of defense to be manned. Mulugeta's only possible answer to the well-executed Italian advance was to send wave after wave of Ethiopians downhill toward the storm of gunfire.

Fortunately for Mulugeta, one of his commanders, Bidwoded Makonnen from Wollega province in western Ethiopia, had his men organized that afternoon. Encamped near Antalo in the southern foothills, Makonnen was the first to realize the Italians were pursuing a strategy of encirclement, with the intention of trapping every Ethiopian on the mountain. Choosing four thousand of his men, including his own sons, Makonnen marched against the First Army Corps approaching from the northeast. Throughout the afternoon, even after Makonnen himself was killed, his small band held back two Italian divisions, preventing a link-up of Italian forces and thus holding open an avenue of escape for Ras Mulugeta.

By the end of the afternoon, even Mulugeta realized that escape was the only hope of survival. The 23rd-of-March Division (named for the day the Fascist Party was founded in 1919), which had approached unseen from the west, raised its flag on the summit at five-thirty p.m. Only the approaching darkness could save the remaining Ethiopians now. Abandoning all their equipment, and led by their half-crazed old commander, they stumbled down the mountain and fled southward through the gap Makonnen and his men had held open for them.

At two o'clock the next morning, Mulugeta, unencumbered by baggage and accompanied by only fifty armed men, reached Enda Medani Alem, a little village about twenty-five miles south of Amba Aradam near the foot of another imposing flat-topped mountain, Amba Alagi.[2] Here he met the remnants of Bidwoded Makonnen's staff escaping with his body, which they had cut into two pieces and hidden inside two war drums— the severing process having been simplified for them by an Italian machine gun. Before Makonnen died, a sixty-two-year-old retired British army officer and now a Red Cross volunteer, Major Gerald Burgoyne, had tried to treat his wounds but found him perforated at the waistline. His men were determined now to get him back to his Wollega home for burial. Mulugeta had greater worries on his mind. He sent the men on ahead up the endless hairpin trails of Mount Alagi while he prepared a message for the Emperor, explaining his defeat.

A short time later, a runner arrived from the south with an urgent message from the Emperor addressed to Ras Kassa and Ras Seyoum. How could this message be delivered now? Kassa and Seyoum were isolated. The Italians controlled all the roads into the Tembien region. A native of the area stepped forward and volunteered to try to reach Kassa's camp through the back country. Though the possibility seemed remote, Mulugeta, weary and resigned, accepted the man's offer. Then he flopped down for a few hours of sleep before the long climb up and over Alagi.

The Battle of Amba Aradam (sometimes called the Battle of Enderta after the region in which it was fought) was now at an end. But the slaughter of the Ethiopians, who had already lost about six thousand men, had hardly begun.

At dawn the morning of February 16, the Italian airplanes found Ras Mulugeta's more than fifty thousand defeated troops plodding southward along the routes toward Quoram and Dessie. Today, the planes were not loaded with bombs. Now that there was no danger of contaminating Italian troops, they were carrying mustard gas, which they sprayed mercilessly upon the barefooted men below them.

Vittorio Mussolini, who took part in this exercise though he did not admit dropping gas, bragged later about the fun he had:

> ... whoever refueled and reloaded first took off first. It was a continuing contest. The Abyssinians run fast and you can't let them disappear in smoke as they have done in the past. So, on the day of the 16th, I made two attacks. ... Over the radio we kept getting information, almost like hunting bulletins: "There's a beautiful covey of fat doves at Castel Porciano," or, "I advise you to go to Samra and see how full it is." To make sure, I ignored no one. I went everywhere.[3]

Along the roadsides south from Amba Aradam, the dead and the gassed-but-still-living lay side by side, equally unattended by their panicky, fleeing comrades. As the planes roared in low overhead, they spurted an oily-looking fluid which fell like light rain, causing screams of pain within moments of contacting the skin of the Ethiopians. Those who absorbed heavy or even moderate doses fell quickly by the wayside, clutching their limbs or their faces, gasping for breath as the lethal gas entered their lungs. Those who were sprayed by only a few drops cried out like the others but kept moving in the hope that they might avoid the next shower as more planes approached.

For three more days, Italian planes sprayed mustard gas and machine-gun bullets on the fleeing Ethiopians until the bodies lay in sprawling piles along the route and an estimated fifteen thousand men had been added to the six thousand casualties of the Aradam battle. By evening of the nineteenth, the army of Ras Mulugeta no longer existed.

The old Ras himself was now at the summit of Amba Alagi where he had remained for three days, watching the survivors arrive and trying to stop their flight so he could make one more stand against the Italians on this huge massif, which was a better defensive position than the one from which he had been driven. By now he realized his efforts to control his men were hopeless. Once the most feared commander in Ethiopia, merciless and cruel in his punishments, the scourge of all who disobeyed him, he had become simply a weak, pathetic old man with barely enough followers to insure his own safety. On the night of the nineteenth he sent a message to another chief, Ras Kebede, who had agreed to help him make another stand. There was no way to hold the mountain, the message said. Amba Alagi would have to be abandoned.

Having come to this decision, Ras Mulugeta and his small party began descending the mountain southward in the direction of Mai Chew, about twenty miles away, on the warm, sunny morning of the twentieth. To avoid bombing and gassing, they took a circuitous, westerly trail, even though they knew it was infested with *shiftas* (Ethiopian bandits) who lived off passing travelers. Mulugeta still had enough men, he decided, to ward off bandits. Five days later, on the twenty-fourth, his party arrived at Mai Chew, where he was met by Ras Kebede and by Major Burgoyne, who was moving south with as many wounded men as he could accommodate on the few mules he had left. Burgoyne had come north with a full mule train of medical supplies for Mulugeta's troops, and had just unloaded these supplies when the Battle of Amba Aradam began. Now he was part of the general retreat. He decided to join Ras Mulugeta's party.

The main road from Mai Chew south, however, offered not only the danger of aerial bombing but the threats of growing shifta gangs, plus the warrior mobs of a rebellious tribe called the Azebu Gallas, who had been paid by the Italians to harass the Ethiopians. As Marshal Badoglio phrased it, the Gallas had been "attracted to and armed by us." They operated like small armies, living off farmers and travelers. The morning of the twenty-sixth, a few miles above the beautiful Lake Ashangi, half-way between Mai Chew and Quoram, Mulugeta's party encountered at the same time a band of Gallas or shiftas and a flight of three Italian Caproni bombers.

The old ras was at the front of the party with his bodyguard. At a distance behind, walking with Major Burgoyne, was his son, Major Tadessa Mulugeta. An Italian bomb landed between these two men, killing both of them.

By the time Ras Mulugeta learned of his son's death, the snipers in the surrounding hills had opened fire. Disregarding the danger, Mulugeta hurried back to where his son's body lay. As he was leaning over the remains, he was killed by a bullet. Whether it came from a sniper's rifle or from the machine gun of one of the planes was never determined. Fleeing the gunfire, the rest of his party hurried onward toward Quoram.

Emperor Haile Selassie, installed now in a temporary "palace" on top of a small knoll at Waldia, about 150 miles south of Amba Aradam, did not learn of Ras Mulugeta's defeat until February 19. He immediately sent another message to Ras Kassa and one to Ras Imru, instructing them to fall back from Tembien and Shire and install themselves on Amba Alagi, perhaps the best defensive position in all of northern Ethiopia, and one which Mulugeta should have occupied with at least a part of his army before the Battle of Amba Aradam. Unless Kassa and Imru could stop the Italians there, only the Emperor's own army would stand between them and Addis Ababa.

The Emperor had demonstrated good military judgment on the twelfth in a message he sent Ras Kassa after learning that the Italians were attacking Mulugeta. The message had ordered Kassa to help the ras "by sending very powerful forces to the rear of the Italians, who are outside their fortified positions and engaged well forward, thus forcing them to detach part of the troops employed against Ras Mulugeta." The message also suggested, alternatively, that Kassa might help "by occupying Makalle with a large army, if that place is empty." These were sound enough strategies which might have been effective if Kassa had launched them on time, and if he had possessed the men and ammunition to sustain them. But he didn't even receive the message until the fifteenth, the day the Battle of Amba Aradam ended. Ethiopian communications were such that he may not even have known the battle was in progress until shortly before that.

The Emperor, realizing the possibility that his February 19 message might not get through at all, decided he had better move his own army forward to be ready to meet the Italians as far north as possible. This questionable strategy was perhaps the only one open to him, given the nature of his Ethiopian followers, who had not abandoned their belief that wars should be decided in great, pitched battles. It would be beneath an Emperor's dignity to hide in the mountains and resort to guerrilla warfare. He must meet his enemy openly in the field. Consequently, he issued an immediate order that his Imperial Guard should march north to Quoram and prepare a headquarters for him there.

On the twentieth, perhaps after receiving further information about the extent of Mulugeta's defeat, the Emperor sent more messages north, instructing Imru to remain in a defensive attitude and Kassa either to attack the enemy, if possible, or to pull back and join Mulugeta, wherever he might be. As the enormity of Mulugeta's disaster became more evident, the Emperor's compulsion to march north became more urgent.

But he was still weighted down with matters which should have been delegated to others. He still felt it necessary to handle all the details of government. He supervised personally the supply system to the northern armies. In the northwest province of Gojjam, a sizable revolt had developed among peoples who had never quite accepted rule from Addis Ababa. With Gojjam's ruler, Ras Imru, off to war, the Emperor himself had to make sure this revolt was contained. He had also to write, or at least approve Everett Colson's drafts of, letters to other nations and the League of Nations. He even had to worry about the maintenance of his Paris-Geneva legation. In mid-January, Tecle Hawariate, distressed because he hadn't received operating funds, had sent a telegram saying, "I ask you to tell us if we must close the legation, abandon the League of Nations and come back home." Mussolini, who intercepted this evidence of Ethiopia's financial distress, was delighted with it, although a month later he seemed equally delighted with a rumor which would have disproved it if it were true. In a message to Badoglio February 18, Mussolini said, "Spread the news among the people of Gojjam—and it is authentic —that the Negus has had all his gold taken to Egyptian banks." Could Mussolini have failed to observe that if the Emperor had to scratch for funds to keep his Paris-Geneva legation open, it was unlikely that he had much gold to deposit in Egyptian banks? Finance was a continuing source of distress to Haile Selassie throughout the war, particularly since neither the League of Nations nor any individual nation would even extend him credit.

Despite these problems, the Emperor struck camp at Waldia February 27 and moved north, about forty miles to Cobbo. By March 1, he had reached Alamata, about fifteen miles below his destination at Quoram.

All along his route he had been passing his own troops marching north-ward. Now he began passing Mulugeta's bombed, gassed, and benumbed men straggling southward. The reports of Red Cross doctors in the area indicate some of the scenes he had to witness.

Dr. George Dassios, a Greek volunteer, had seen his first gas patient in January, at Waldia. The man had been brought from Quoram, where he was a victim of an air raid. "Seeing this first victim," Dr. Dassios recalled,

> I could not believe it, though the signs were there—difficult breathing due to gas in the lungs, blisters on the skin. Because it had taken a considerable time to get the man from Quoram to Waldia, I thought he might be suffering from something else. But within a few days, more victims came and I realized the Italians were actually using mustard gas. From that time on, there was a continuous increase in the flow of victims. During January, I treated more than fifty.[4]

In February, Dr. Dassios moved north toward the front. Here is his description of the trip:

> Going to Quoram, one passes a small lake, beautiful and picturesque. The water was yellowish and all around the shore lay bodies of men and animals—more animals than men. During that period I was so hungry and had so many things on my mind I can't remember exact dates, but it was after the battle of Amba Aradam. After that battle, thousands of men came our way. There were so many we could do nothing for them. There were so many we couldn't count them. We couldn't even put up tents at treatment centers during the daytime. The planes were still attacking. After five p.m. we would put up our tents and do what we could. I asked one patient if he had seen the plane [which attacked him]. He said, "No, I think it was the devil pulling someone by a string." The gas victims I saw [after Amba Aradam] must have numbered around two thousand.

Dr. John W. S. Macfie of the British Red Cross unit, who had also treated "a few cases of gas burns" in Waldia, arrived at Alamata February 29, the day before the Emperor passed through en route to Quoram. Dr. Macfie and the other men in his unit were "not fully prepared" for "the sight that greeted us" on driving into the camp which other members of the unit had built at Alamata.

"In a corner on our right under a tree," Dr. Macfie wrote,

> we saw the outpatients collected, scores of them, and Chandler [Warrant Officer E. D. Chandler, another member of the unit] and his dressers feverishly covering them with bright yellow pieces of gauze and rolls and rolls of bandages. Somewhere in the middle of the group stood a great pail of yellow fluid—picric acid solution [the only medication available for treating the burns]. On closer inspection, the patients were a shocking

sight. The first I examined, an old man, sat moaning on the ground, rocking himself to and fro, completely wrapped in a cloth. When I approached he slowly rose and drew aside his cloak. He looked as if someone had tried to skin him, clumsily; he had been horribly burned by mustard gas all over the face, the back and the arms. There were many others like him: some more, some less severely affected; some newly burned, others older, their sores already caked with thick, brown scabs. Men and women alike, all horribly disfigured, and little children, too. And many blinded by the stuff, with blurred, crimson apologies for eyes. I could cover pages recounting horrors, but what would be the use?

Early the next morning, a Sunday, the Emperor arrived in Alamata with his entourage just as the Italian airplanes began the day's bombings.[5] Like the thousands of his soldiers encamped along the road and on the surrounding plains, he retired into the hills for safety during the day. When bombing time came, the Ethiopian troops, accustomed to it now, swarmed up the hillsides to find shelter, leaving their folded tents and personal effects hidden from the planes under trees.

In the afternoon, when the bombing receded, the Emperor, again like all his soldiers, emerged from shelter and resumed his journey to Quoram. Though it was only a little more than fifteen miles north of Alamata, the road, which followed a winding, hilly trail, was only partly finished. It was also overcrowded with troops going both ways, arriving from the south and retreating from the north. The daily bombings were almost constant. It took Haile Selassie three days to reach Quoram, a small village within a circle of big hills about five miles south of Lake Ashangi.

Captain John Meade, the American military attaché, who was at Quoram when he arrived, found him obviously much depressed but quite pleasant in his manner. By this time, the remnants of Mulugeta's army had circulated fearsome rumors about the strength of the Italian forces and the speed with which they were driving southward. The Emperor immediately sent a party of men northward on a reconnaissance mission to determine the exact location of the enemy. Then he settled into one of the three large caves which had been set aside as his headquarters and began the tedious details of molding his rabble-like followers into a battle-ready army.

Marshal Badoglio, having routed Ras Mulugeta and destroyed his army, was now able to turn his two hundred thousand well-equipped and battle-seasoned men upon the sixty to seventy thousand Ethiopians left in the north under the commands of Kassa, Seyoum, and Imru. He gave his attention first to Kassa and Seyoum, whose combined forces, about thirty thousand men, were still encamped near Abbi Addi and Warieu Pass, where the first battle of Tembien had taken place, about thirty miles west of Makalle.

On February 16 and 18, determined to give the Ethiopians no respite, Badoglio issued orders disposing his troops for a second battle in Tembien. He sent his First Army Corps from Amba Aradam to Amba Alagi, which mountain this force captured without opposition February 28, thus closing the best and one of the few possible routes of retreat for Kassa and Seyoum. He then sent his Third Army Corps from Amba Aradam southwest into the Tembien, whence this force could advance northward toward Abbi Addi as one prong of a pincers movement. The other prong would be the large Eritrean Corps, which he had already concentrated just north of the Kassa-Seyoum positions, in the area of the Warieu Pass.

Badoglio was feeling much more confident now. When he addressed the war correspondents at his Amba Gedem observation post after the Battle of Amba Aradam, he was, in the words of one reporter, "extremely animated, in high good humor, and looking twenty years younger." He had become so certain of the ascendancy as a result of his great victory that when Mussolini suggested to him the possible use of "bacteriological war," he had advised against it. He must have felt that as long as he had enough mustard gas, he could afford to show how humane he was by forgoing even more hideous weapons. In a February 20 telegram, Mussolini acceded to his advice. "I agree with what Your Excellency observes about the use of bacteriological war," the Duce wrote. No other references to the subject have been found.

Badoglio launched his drive to annihilate Kassa and Seyoum in the early hours of February 27 by sending his Eritrean Corps against their strongest position, Amba Work, the western sentinel above Warieu Pass and the highest point overlooking it. If he could dislodge the Ethiopians from Mount Work, he would open the road to Abbi Addi south of it, where the Eritrean Corps and the Third Corps intended to meet, crushing the whole Ethiopian army between them. But Amba Work was fully garrisoned by hundreds of Ethiopians, better armed than most and equipped even with a cannon. A frontal assault against it would be very costly. To avoid this the Italians used their increasing knowledge of Ethiopian habits, which were regular to a fault. The Ethiopians fought only in the daytime. At night they slept, and they slept deeply, like children. Instead of sending an army against them at dawn on the twenty-seventh, Badoglio sent 150 of his best Alpine, askari, and Black Shirt mountain-climbing troops in the middle of the night, so that they had scaled the heights to the Ethiopian positions two or three hours before dawn. When they arrived, they spread out and distributed hand grenades so liberally among the sleeping Ethiopians that scores of them died on the ground without even waking. Those who did awaken before being hit by any of the metal fragments were so shocked and terrified by this unprecedented intrusion that their resistance was uncoordinated. Though they fought on for most of the day, they couldn't regain the advantage. Badoglio, at small cost, had captured the key stronghold in the second battle of Tembien almost before it started. As the sun began to rise, two fast Eritrean columns marched down through the Warieu Pass unmolested and wheeled south toward Abbi Addi.

Though the Ethiopians, under the command of Ras Seyoum, were ready for battle now, they had lost their superior strategical position and were forced to abandon their entire plan of defense. They could only fall back on their usual *modus operandi*. Wave after wave of screaming, barefooted men, as many with spears and cudgels as with rifles, descended against the Italian machine guns, tanks, artillery, rifles, and bayonets. From eight a.m. until four p.m., the waves of Ethiopians kept coming and falling, but at the end of the day, the Italian spearhead was undaunted and still on the move.

At the more vulnerable rear of this spearhead, however, near the heights of Warieu, some difficulties had developed; the Ethiopians there were attacking in equal force and with greater effect. As Badoglio later admitted, the situation in Warieu Pass was "delicate" until the commander in the field, General Pirzio Biroli, threw in his reserves. By this time, the Italian planes and the 195 tons of bombs they dropped on the Ethiopians had also taken their toll. As dusk approached and Ras Seyoum realized his drive to encircle the Italians might soon end in his own encirclement, he drew back his troops in a westerly direction. With the Italian spearhead now between him and Kassa's forces east of Abbi Addi, he could not retreat southward. His only hope was to retire in the direction of the Takazze River, which flowed south in this area and offered him at least a possible avenue of escape. For all practical purposes, Seyoum's army, decimated by the day's fighting and almost devoid of ammunition, was now out of the battle. An Italian reporter who was in one of the bombers overhead described the flight of Seyoum's men:

> The Ethiopians straggled along in disorder. There was only one road open to them and the fords were so narrow, the rocky walls of the ravines so precipitous that they were soon jammed together in a solid mass. Even though we were flying at 3,500 feet, we could see them quite plainly. Our plane swooped down, zigzagged along the defile, sowed its seeds of death and zoomed upward.

The seeds of death at the Takazze fords were mustard gas. Many years later, an Italian soldier who had settled in Ethiopia, who did not want to admit the use of gas, said, nevertheless,

When the Ethiopians were escaping from Takazze, it's possible they [the Italians] used gas. In Takazze [afterward] the trees were yellow.[6]

On the night of the twenty-seventh, a few hours after Ras Seyoum's retreat, Ras Kassa, encamped on a mountain called Debra Amba just above Abbi Addi to the northeast, and not yet engaged by the Italians, sent a telegram to the Emperor which, like all other Ethiopian telegrams, was intercepted by the Italians. Kassa was so ill-informed he asked the Emperor if Ethiopian troops at Amba Alagi might "make a demonstration with artillery fire in order to prevent the Makalle [Italian] troops from coming up in motor lorries to reinforce the enemy." Though Kassa must have known by now that Mulugeta had been defeated, he obviously did not yet know the extent of the defeat, nor did he know that Amba Alagi was in Italian hands. He told the Emperor he was ready to march into the Seloa region (about twenty-five miles due south of Abbi Addi) and that he might "camp in the Seloa region," which "would assist our retirement, preventing any determined advance by the enemy" and thereby making it possible "to remain where we are four or five days longer." Not only was he unaware of the fall of Amba Alagi and the immediate threat of Badoglio's Third Army Corps directly south of him, between his army and the Seloa region; he didn't even know, when he sent this telegram, of the beating Ras Seyoum had taken that very day, just six or eight miles to the northwest of him. Later in the evening of the twenty-seventh, he apparently learned about Seyoum's defeat. Finally aware that he was trapped between two Italian armies, each bigger than his own, Kassa began to evacuate without further delay. But his evacuation could be more accurately described as a disintegration. His army simply broke up overnight into small groups and individuals, with every man seeking his own route of escape.

The second battle of Tembien ended without a major confrontation, but with a flight as disastrous as any battle could have been. In the southern Tembien and Seloa regions during the following days, the Italians found a wealth of targets for their mustard gas as the bewildered Ethiopian soldiers struggled southward through forests, rivers, plains, canyons, and mountains, trying to escape the burning rains which fell upon them from the airplanes' bomb racks.

Colonel Theodore Konovaloff visited Ras Kassa on Debra Amba that night. Konovaloff had not seen Kassa since January 26, when he was still being congratulated for the Ethiopian showing in the first battle of Tembien. He had said to Konovaloff then, "The cannons, the airplanes are nothing but toys; strength is shown in the last phases of the fight when the attackers enter into direct contact with the enemy. Only in this moment can one judge who is the stronger." Kassa was at that time studying a plan to cut the Italian lines of retreat by occupying positions behind the Italian lines. Now, without having fired a shot in the second battle of Tembien, he had abandoned all offensive plans. Though he smiled as usual in welcome, he warned that Konovaloff and the other two Europeans in camp (both technicians) should leave as soon as possible because his army was surrounded. "I advise you to go to Quoram," he said, "where you'll be under the protection of the Emperor, who has a large army in perfect order."

"And you?" Konovaloff asked.

"For the moment I'll stay here, defending Debra Amba."

That moment was a short one. With his men disappearing into the wild countryside, Kassa soon did likewise. Two weeks later, when he and Ras Seyoum reached Quoram, they had with them only their personal bodyguards. Their armies no longer existed. Their surviving troops, bewildered by bombs and mustard gas, were still trudging southward toward their homes, weary, hungry, disillusioned, and resigned.

The concentrated power of the Italians was now about to descend upon Ras Imru, who had defeated them in his first engagement against them and had posed such a danger in late December as to prompt Badoglio's first use of mustard gas. Imru and Ayelu Birru, with a combined army of twenty to thirty thousand men, were encamped about fifteen miles west of Axum in the hills around Selaclaca, from which location they had driven the Italians just before Christmas. Imru, the only Ethiopian commander in the north with significant military skill, had not been challenged during the intervening two months by General Pietro Maravigna's Second Italian Army Corps centered at Axum. Small parties of Imru's men had, in fact, forced the Italians to retire from several outposts between Axum and Selaclaca.

Imru had used the time to develop a crude intelligence network between himself and Ethiopian friends in Axum; to build more supply roads from the Takazze fords north to his encampments; and to fortify his positions with trenches and tank traps. In compliance with the Emperor's orders, he had adopted a defensive attitude, but this did not preclude his sending sizable parties of men on a series of raids behind enemy lines. No other Ethiopian commander had shown the imagination to conduct such raids, which Imru found very productive of arms and supplies.

On February 11, a thousand of his men had traveled as far north as the Eritrean boundary (the Mareb River) to take cattle from Ethiopians who were cooperating with the Italians. The next night, when these men were returning, they attacked an Italian blockhouse seven miles south of the

Mareb on the road to Adowa. They claimed later to have killed 412 Italians during the battle while losing about 100 of their own men. Though their figures might be questioned, no one can doubt that they carried off great quantities of food, ammunition, rifles, and machine guns.

Another raiding party of five hundred, on the twelfth, was able to ambush a truck convoy between the border and Adowa, either killing or routing all the Italians and bringing back to Imru's camp "over 100,000 cartridges." On the thirteenth, Imru raiders made an attack against an Italian work crew near the border and killed sixty-eight laborers, for which they were severely condemned by the Italian government and Italian newspapers. Ras Imru did not deny this attack; on the contrary, he defended it. "Yes, I gave . . . the order to fall on their camp at Mai Lahla," he said later. "I felt and still feel that this was a legitimate act of war because all these men [the Italian laborers] were armed with rifles. Indeed, they defended themselves fiercely and inflicted heavy casualties on us. At least they had the means of defense whereas our people were unable to strike back when they were bombed and decimated by the Fascist air force."[7] Emperor Haile Selassie, however, condemned this raid when he learned of it.

Either from one of his raiding and scouting parties or through his friends behind the Italian lines, Imru learned in February that the Italians were building a road across Eritrea, which would allow them to send an army against him from the northwest, thus threatening his left flank. Such a thrust, coupled with a frontal assault by Maravigna's Second Army Corps from Axum, would be difficult if not impossible for him to contain. He decided to prepare an offensive before this road could be completed. But in the last days of February, before he was ready to make a move, he received a long letter from the Emperor ordering him to retire. Since he didn't yet know about the battle then progressing in the Tembien, and hadn't even been informed of Mulugeta's defeat at Amba Aradam, he could only accept on faith the Emperor's judgment that he must retreat southward.

He couldn't even seek the advice of his fellow commander, Ayelu Birru, because he still suspected, with good reason, that Ayelu was too friendly with the Italians. (Badoglio, referring later to Ayelu, said he had "shown in various ways that he was not averse from submitting to our rule.") The Emperor's letter, carried by messengers on foot, warned Imru that the enemy was about to spring a trap on him. Isolated as Imru was from action in other sectors, he decided the Emperor knew more about the demands of the situation than he did. He prepared, therefore, to execute the withdrawal, but only after sending a strong rearguard force to occupy the hills between Selaclaca and Axum. If the Italians should decide to chase him, he wanted to be able to slow their advance. This move on his part proved to be remarkably astute and timely.

Marshal Badoglio, who transferred his field headquarters from Makalle back to Adi Quala in Eritrea February 27, was indeed planning what Ras Imru anticipated. The Italian Second Army Corps (three divisions plus artillery and other smaller units) would move straight west from its Axum-Adowa base and attack Imru's Selaclaca positions frontally. Meanwhile, a new army group, the Fourth Corps (two white divisions plus one Eritrean battalion), having traversed Eritrea on the newly built road above the border, would strike southwest fifty miles through largely unfamiliar country to attack Imru's left flank and rear at the same time as the Second Corps attacked his front. The thrust against Imru's rear was designed to prevent him from escaping in the direction of the Takazze fords. Badoglio never explained publicly how he expected his Fourth Corps to make its journey through the difficult, uncharted northwestern corner of Ethiopia on such a precise schedule that its attack could be coordinated with that of the Second Corps.

At dawn February 29, the two corps began their moves, one from fifty miles northwest of Imru through difficult country; the other from about fifteen miles due east of him through an easy, familiar landscape. The Fourth Corps, with its long journey ahead, could soon be forgotten by everyone except Badoglio, who was unable to understand its delays. Before long, the peculiar antics of the Second Corps gave him something else about which to worry. The sky was so blue and the day so pleasant that General Maravigna decided to move his three divisions west like a long caterpillar, on the only motor road available to him. The countryside was so quiet he didn't even bother to send scouting parties out on his flanks. By midday his elongated column was within a few miles of Selaclaca, at a crossroad where one division (the 21st-of-April Black Shirts) was to go left, another (the Gran Sasso) was to go right, and the third (the Gavinana) was to proceed straight ahead. No Ethiopian move disturbed this plan. As the other two divisions split off to the north and south, the Gavinana marched straight into hilly country in the direction of Selaclaca, still without any patrols on its flanks. As one of Maravigna's officers said later, "We advanced as if we were on an exercise."

As the division passed through the hilly country and began its descent into a valley near Selaclaca, Imru's rearguard, hidden behind bushes and rocks, began spraying it with an amazingly accurate crossfire. This began a battle which for once did not end at dusk, but continued until almost midnight. The Ethiopians' rifles were ancient but their marksmanship was good. And thanks to their raids against Italian supply sources, they even had a few machine guns, with enough ammunition to keep them firing. Under cover of the machine-gun fire, they rushed down the surrounding slopes and battered the stretched-out division, which was now desperately trying to form itself into a defensive square. When the Italian artillery pieces were finally set up, they had to be fired at point-blank range, killing Italians as well as Ethiopians. In an effort to get at the division's motor trucks, which they saw as a source of guns and ammunition, hordes of Ethiopians rushed headlong into the fire, some of them being cut in half by machine-gun bullets. One wounded Italian officer said later,

> They threw themselves on the guns as though they could silence them. Their courage was unbelievable. They were utterly oblivious of danger. I saw a shell explode in the midst of a group of fifteen. Ten men fell, but the remaining five never even noticed and rushed on frenziedly.[8]

General Maravigna, unable to believe this was only a rearguard action, ordered his entire First Corps to halt and assume a defensive attitude. In the morning, when he surveyed the damage to the Gavinana, he petitioned Badoglio for permission to delay his advance for another day. Badoglio, though he was furious at this disruption of his schedule, and would later accuse Maravigna of "overestimating the potentialities of the enemy," nevertheless had no choice but to accept the judgment of the commander in the field. Badoglio must have known that with a force as overwhelming as the one at Maravigna's disposal, damage to one division should not halt the entire corps. The other two divisions, completely undamaged, could have been used for an immediate pursuit of the Ethiopians, who had sustained at least as many and perhaps more losses than the Italians. By stopping for a full day while he prepared for a new attack, Maravigna also gave the Ethiopians an opportunity to re-form, reorganize, and prepare for a new defense in the next group of hills.

At dawn March 2, when the Second Corps resumed its march, Ras Imru's rearguard was again waiting for it. This time, the Ethiopians did not show themselves until shortly after midday, but when they did come out from behind their rocks and bushes, they fought as fiercely as they had done the previous day. Because the Italians were better prepared on this day, the battle lasted only four hours before the Ethiopians retired, but this was long enough so that, in Badoglio's words, "the corps again failed to reach its assigned objectives, and in the evening, after slow progress, it consolidated its position on the heights a little to the west of Acab Saat. . . ." It was at Acab Saat that Maravigna's divisions had divided to go their separate ways shortly before noon two days earlier. Imru's rearguard had been able to stop for two and a half days an Italian army corps of three divisions plus artillery plus several special units. Badoglio's fury at Maravigna's delay was intensified late in the day when his air arm reported seeing "sure signs of a general retirement" by Ras Imru's main force. Badoglio knew now what he had suspected—that Maravigna had been duped into mistaking a rearguard action for an attack in force.

When Maravigna's Second Corps moved forward the morning of the third, it quickly became apparent that Badoglio's strategy of entrapment could not be fulfilled. The only Ethiopians the Italians found were the dead ones littering the ground, and a few live ones who had been trapped in caves or on hilltops the day before but still refused to surrender. Ras Imru's force had retired in good order toward the Takazze fords. But the failure of Badoglio's basic strategy was not completely the fault of General Maravigna. It was a strategy which depended on the timely arrival of the Fourth Corps to prevent Imru's retreat. As of March 3, and as of the fourth and fifth also, the Fourth Corps was nowhere to be seen. It was still hacking its way through the hot, waterless, uncharted country northwest of Selaclaca which, as Badoglio later tried to explain, "though apparently flat, was in reality cut up by numerous deep furrows lying across the line of march." These inconvenient geographical features had been unknown to Badoglio, yet he had not hesitated to send such a large force into it. Though Badoglio pretended later that this corps had played an important role in the battle, it actually represented a wasted resource. It was patently foolish of him to think the Fourth Corps could travel fifty miles across unfamiliar terrain while the Second Corps was traveling fifteen miles over well-known terrain which even offered a motor road.

Fortunately for Badoglio, he did have the means at his disposal to cover up his mistakes in battle strategy. Once again at the end of this battle, which was to become known as the Battle of Shire, he sent his airplanes against the Ethiopians, whose retirement, he later reported, "very quickly turned into a disorderly rout."

> On reaching the [Takazze] fords, difficult enough in themselves because [they were] sunk between high, steep and thickly wooded banks, his [the enemy's] passage was rendered even more critical by continued air activity. In addition to the usual effective bombing and machine-gun fire, small incendiary bombs had been used to set on fire the whole region about the fords, rendering utterly tragic the plight of the fleeing enemy. . . . Our aerial activity may be summed up in the following figures: 80 tons of explosives were dropped, and 25,000 rounds of machine-gun ammunition were fired.

Once again Badoglio failed to credit his most useful ally—mustard gas. Italian pilots who bombed, strafed, gassed, and burned the area of the fords between the third and the sixth of March later reported seeing "vast numbers of Ethiopian dead on the north bank of the Takazze and countless bodies of men and beasts floating on the river." Later, when Italian ground troops crossed the Takazze, they found the area "littered with thousands of corpses in an advanced state of putrefaction."

Ras Imru, describing his flight many years later, said,

> I succeeded in leading some ten thousand of my men across the river to safety, but they were so demoralized that I could no longer hold them together. It had been my intention to carry on a guerrilla war in the mountainous regions of Tsellemti and Semien, ideally suited to such tactics, but when I told Dejasmatch Ayelu Birru . . . of my plan, he would have nothing to do with it and, with his brother Admasu, made his way to Begemder [a northwestern province]. Day by day my ranks thinned out; many were killed in the course of air attacks, many deserted. When at last I reached Dashan [about fifty miles south of the Takazze], all that remained of my army was my personal bodyguard of 300 men.

Only one Ethiopian fighting force now stood between the Italians and Addis Ababa—the Emperor's army at Quoram, less than thirty miles south of Badoglio's First Army Corps at Amba Alagi.

When Anthony Eden arrived in Geneva at the beginning of March for a renewal of the League of Nations' running conversation about oil sanctions against Italy, he already had his instructions from his Cabinet colleagues. They were the same instructions he had been using so effectively for several months to avert oil sanctions—Great Britain would adopt the embargo, he had been told to say again, if other League members would do likewise. There was one valid excuse for this evasive British attitude. As long as the United States continued to sell oil to Italy, a League embargo would be ineffective. And a new extension of the American Neutrality Resolution, which President Roosevelt signed February 29, served notice that America had no intention of penalizing Italy for her aggression. The British Cabinet appreciated the excuse the United States was providing. Yet with the British people becoming more impatient and the opposition more inquisitive, Baldwin's government was conscious of the need to keep its public image at a high gloss, so Eden, the Cabinet's most absorbent chamois, was dispatched to polish it once more in Geneva.

As soon as he arrived there, Eden began by replaying with the new French Foreign Minister, Pierre-Etienne Flandin, the same charade he had so often played with Pierre Laval. Though Flandin might have been expected to react with amusement or even boredom to Eden's restatement of the British equivocation, he reacted instead with a show of indignation. Mussolini, he said, had told the French ambassador in Rome that if there were any further extensions of sanctions, Italy would leave the League. Though he didn't say so to Eden, Flandin was also told by the secretary of the Italian delegation in Geneva that in the event of an oil embargo, Italy would, in addition, denounce its Rome agreements with France. Eden repeated all of his old arguments about not wishing to reward the aggressor. Flandin listened impatiently, perhaps wondering why the British, unlike the French, found it so necessary to season their cynicism with unpalatable ideals. Finally, after he had heard enough, Flandin closed the discussion by making it clear to Eden that the French would not let the British down, that he would express before the League the policy on which both governments agreed but which the British did not wish to enunciate, and that Eden could then, after ratifying the policy, express again the ideals he so dearly loved to repeat.

Accordingly, when the League's Committee of Eighteen met March 2, Flandin arose with a proposal. "Another urgent appeal" should be made to Italy and Ethiopia "to make an end of the war," he declared. And until the results of this appeal were obtained, all discussion of additional sanctions against Italy should be postponed.

Eden popped up to second this suggestion. And only after he had thus stated the British government's actual policy did he give voice to its pious pronouncement that Great Britain would join in an oil sanction if other League members would do likewise. Once again Mussolini had his way. Once again he had demonstrated to the world, and especially to Adolf Hitler in Berlin, the most effective way to deal with the Western democracies.

In Berlin March 1, Hitler summoned his Minister of Defense, General Werner von Blomberg, and told him that although Germany had only begun to rebuild her military power, and the German army would make a pitiful showing against the French, he had decided to prove his utter defiance of the Versailles Treaty by reoccupying the demilitarized left bank of the Rhineland. Acutely aware, however, that the French had the power to stop him if they decided to march into the Rhineland, he reserved the right in such an event "to decide on any military countermeasures."[9] As several German generals testified many years later at Nuremberg, the only countermeasure Hitler contemplated in case the French resisted was an immediate German retreat. But Hitler had already learned so much about France and England by studying Mussolini's methods of bluffing, bullying, and manipulating them that he did not believe the French would make any move which might bring on a war.

At dawn March 7, while German generals quaked in fear, a skeleton force of three German battalions marched timidly across the Rhine River bridges into the demilitarized zone. In the days that followed, the French and British filled the air with querulous complaints, but not one French soldier set foot in the Rhineland to resist this first aggressive move the German army had made since 1918, this first military foray of Adolf Hitler's career.

CHAPTER THIRTEEN

Dr. John Melly, the commanding officer of a British Red Cross unit newly situated on an open plain near Quoram, was preparing for a busy workday when, between seven-thirty and eight a.m. March 4, he heard an airplane approach. Like most of the men in the thirty-one-tent camp, he glanced up at the plane and noticed, not surprisingly, that it was Italian. Its visit was no cause for alarm. The camp was marked with two Red Cross ground flags, one forty-six feet and the other thirty-six feet square. Flying from poles were another Red Cross flag and a British Union Jack. In addition to being well marked, the camp was at least two miles from the nearest Ethiopian troops, who avoided the level ground and clung to the hillsides for protection against the ever-increasing air attacks. Though the British camp was new, Melly himself having arrived only the previous day, several Italian planes had flown over it since the first tent was pitched a few days earlier. One of the staff members waved a towel at this one as it flew away toward a woody hillside two miles distant, where it dropped some bombs. Dr. Melly didn't give the incident much thought. He and his associates had twenty-one surgical operations to perform that day and more than a hundred patients to treat, mostly gassing and bombing victims.[1]

At noon, Dr. Melly was in the camp's operating tent with Dr. Macfie and two assistants, beginning his first surgery, "a rather hopeless case of peritonitis." After making his initial incision, he was complaining about the bluntness of the knife when engine sounds indicated another plane was approaching, very low. A moment later, an alarm whistle blew, people outside the tent began to run and shout, and a loud explosion shattered the quiet atmosphere. Dr. Macfie, looking out through the gauze wall of the tent, saw the smoke of a bomb which had fallen dangerously near. It still seemed unbelievable that they were being attacked. Dr. Melly was sufficiently calm to make a joke. That particular flier, he said, was sailing a bit too close to the wind. Despite his lighthearted remark, he stopped operating and plugged the incision with a dressing.

One of their associates shouted from the door of the tent, "He's bombing us!" Two more bombs exploded, followed by others. Melly and his two assistants ran outside to see what was happening while Macfie tried to decide what should be done with the patient, who was under deep anesthesia. Melly came back into the tent and the two doctors discussed what they should do as the airplane again dived toward the camp. The first thing they did was to hit the ground, sheltering themselves behind some boxes. The next bomb fell so close it dumped clods of earth upon them.

"We'd better go," Melly shouted. Since the nearest possible hiding place was a river some distance away, they could hardly carry the anesthetized patient. Deciding to run for their lives, they raced out of the tent toward the river, Melly still wearing his long white operating gown, which made such an inviting target that the plane went for them on its next pass, dropping a bomb between them as they neared the riverbank. Macfie dove into a shallow mule track at just the right moment, receiving only a scratch wound on his knee. Melly was picked up by the force of the bomb and dumped into the water, where he remained for the duration of the air raid, even though he knew the river was infested with leeches.

For about half an hour, the plane continued dropping explosive and incendiary bombs on the Red Cross camp. When it finally exhausted its load and departed, the two doctors returned to the camp which was now a jumble of littered wreckage in which dead and wounded men were strewn. Macfie came first upon one of the patients on the ground, pleading for help, having crawled from a shattered ward tent "dragging behind him a mangled mass of bleeding flesh, almost severed from his body, that was once his leg." Five Ethiopians had been killed and several others wounded, including the anesthetized man Melly and Macfie had been forced to leave behind. He had suffered a leg wound as he lay, unconscious, on the operating table. One of their assistants was able to stitch and dress it before he even awoke from his anesthetic. The operation tent and two ward tents were wrecked; a third ward tent was burned. Five other tents were also destroyed and with them a great quantity of medical equipment. Among the forty large and small bombs the plane had dropped, one scored a direct hit on the huge Red Cross flag.

It was said later that the Italian airplane's number, which would be easily readable at such a low altitude, was "S62," and that Vittorio Mussolini was its pilot. The statement has not been substantiated. The Italian government, while admitting the bombardment, claimed it had been authorized because Italian planes, on previous passes over the Red Cross camp, had drawn gunfire. On February 28, the Italian government had submitted to the League of Nations a long memorandum charging the Ethiopians with such atrocities as torture and mutilation, and claiming again, with affidavits, that they were concealing military operations beneath Red Cross flags. If this were the case, European Red Cross officials and doctors in Ethiopia at the time should have protested against it to the Emperor, especially since their units were so often the targets of Italian "reprisals." Yet no European Red Cross officers on the scene in Ethiopia ever substantiated the Italian charge that the Ethiopians were misusing the Red Cross symbol. British author-journalist Evelyn Waugh suggested in an Italian affidavit that they might be doing so, but Waugh's entire account of the war as he saw it was so provably inaccurate and so openly biased in favor of Italy that his testimony could not be taken as any more factual than his very entertaining novels. (After the war, Waugh summed it up as follows: "The Italian occupation of Ethiopia is the expansion of a race. It began with fighting, but it is not a military movement, like the French occupation of Morocco. It began with the annexation of potential sources of wealth but it is not a capitalistic movement like the British occupation of the South African gold-fields. It is being attended by the spread of order and decency, education and medicine, in a disgraceful place. . . .") The most likely reason for the March 4 raid against the British Red Cross unit at Quoram, and against other Red Cross hospital units, was to encourage European medical men to get out of Ethiopia. Red Cross doctors were becoming a nuisance to Italy with their increasingly frequent reports about the treatment of Ethiopians for mustard-gas burns. If these doctors were already complaining, what would they tell the world when the concentrated gassing began in areas where they were located?

Dr. Marcel Junod, the thirty-two-year-old Swiss surgeon and traveling inspector for the International Red Cross, took off from Addis Ababa at two p.m. March 16 in a plane piloted by Count Carl von Rosen, a handsome, fair-haired Swedish nobleman who had flown his own plane to Ethiopia to offer his services to the Emperor. His plane, a small Swedish model, was so unsuitable to the high altitude of the Ethiopian plateau it crashed on its first take-off from Addis Ababa's Akaki airfield. The Emperor had subsequently assigned one of the Fokkers in his eleven-plane air force to Rosen for Red Cross use, and it was in this plane, clearly marked with Red Cross symbols, that he and Dr. Junod took off on the sixteenth, flying north to Quoram, where two Red Cross units, as well as the Emperor and his army, were now located. Junod and Rosen were making the trip to take a cargo of badly needed medical equipment to the units, especially to the bombed-out British group, whose damage Junod wished also to inspect.[2]

After a stop in Dessie and a near encounter with two Italian planes which, fortunately, did not spot them, they landed on the flat Quoram plain at 6:05 p.m., just as night was falling, and parked next to another of the Emperor's aircraft which had arrived half an hour earlier. When they came to a stop, they found that Haile Selassie had sent an officer with two mules to carry them up the mountainside to the caves which had been converted into the Imperial field headquarters. As they rode the mules up the narrow path, Dr. Junod noticed "a certain persistent smell, something like horse-radish." He asked the Ethiopian officer what it was.

"What! You don't know!" the officer exclaimed. "That's mustard gas. Every day Italian planes sprinkle it over the whole sector."

This was Dr. Junod's first personal observation that the Italians were using the hideous, internationally banned gas, just as so many of his Red Cross medical officers had claimed in reports.

They were using it in two ways, the Ethiopian officer explained. Sometimes they dropped it in bombs which scattered it over an area of two hundred yards or more. Sometimes they sprayed it from low-flying planes so it fell like rain. "They know our soldiers go barefoot," he said, "and in that way contract terrible burns. In addition, our mules die from nibbling grass and leaves contaminated with the liquid."

After about a two-hour trip up the dark pathway, the Junod party rounded the shoulder of a hill and came upon the sight of thousands of campfires glowing among the trees ahead of them. Here were the tents of the Imperial Guard, bivouacked in front of the Emperor's caves. Dismounting from their mules, Dr. Junod and Count Rosen walked up an increasingly steep and narrow path to a terrace in front of what looked like a wall of rock. On this terrace Junod could see the Emperor's now famous Oerlikon antiaircraft gun. A general officer escorted Junod into one of the caves, which was divided into several chambers by heavy hangings. The floor was covered with a thick carpet. A curtain was raised, admitting Junod into a large area furnished only with two small garden chairs facing each other. The Emperor, sitting in one of them, motioned for Junod to take the other. Junod noticed a sadness in Haile Selassie's expression. He seemed depressed.

"Have you any news?" he asked. "Is there any message from the League of Nations?"

Even now he retained some flicker of hope that the League would finally come to his aid. Junod had nothing to support that hope. He was a delegate of the International Red Cross, he pointed out, not of the League of Nations.

"Yes, I know," the Emperor replied, "but I thought you might nevertheless have a message for me."

The only message Junod had was about the acute needs of his Red Cross units and the terrible conditions under which they were laboring. None of this was news to the Emperor, who had been right here in Quoram when the British unit was attacked twelve days earlier. This unit had now moved into a cave he had provided on a mountain a few miles north, overlooking Lake Ashangi. There was little more he could do. Dr. Junod had one other request. Could he have a company of soldiers to help camouflage the Red Cross airplane before the Italian bombers arrived over Quoram in the morning? The Emperor assured him the soldiers would be at his disposal, and they were, at four a.m.

When Dr. Junod and Count von Rosen emerged, still sleepy, from their tents in the predawn light, they found two hundred Ethiopians lined up in silence, each carrying a big leafy tree limb. The procession of this moving forest down the mountain took an hour and a half. After both planes were draped with leaves, Dr. Junod and Count von Rosen thanked their company of *camoufleurs*, then went up the mountain to the north where the British Red Cross unit was now located. Halfway up the mountain, they looked back to see how well the two aircraft were hidden by the camouflage. Alas, the carefully arranged greenery stood out clearly on the treeless landscape—in the precise shape of two airplanes.

Before they could figure out what to do about this, three Italian Caproni bombers, the first of the day, arrived overhead. Their pilots, sharing the same sight, knew exactly what to do about it. Heading directly toward the leaf-covered planes, they began to drop their loads. One of their first bombs scored a direct hit on the Emperor's plane, which burst into flames. But the Red Cross plane seemed miraculously to have been preserved from damage. Junod and von Rosen decided there was only one hope of saving it from further attacks. They ran down the mountain with the intention of stripping off the ineffectual camouflage so the Italian pilots would be able to see the Red Cross markings.

When they reached level ground and began running fearfully across it toward the aircraft, keeping their eyes on the three bombers which were still circling and bombing the surrounding hills, Dr. Junod became aware of "an acrid odor," and at the same time his eyes began to smart. The Italians were now seasoning their menu of high explosives with mustard gas. They had done no damage, however, to the Red Cross plane. Junod and van Rosen had just finished stripping the camouflage from it when they looked up to see three Fiat fighter planes approaching. The two men sheltered themselves behind a rock and waited to see whether the pilots would respect their plane's Red Cross symbols. They found out quickly enough. The three fighters, one after another, poured machine-gun bullets into the plane. Yet once again it seemed to escape damage. Not until Junod and von Rosen returned to it did they learn that the reserve gas tanks had been riddled by bullets and almost all their gasoline was on the ground. Before they had time to confront this problem, more planes arrived, with incendiaries, but they, too, failed to hit the standing Fokker. Junod decided now to hurry up the hill to the Emperor's headquarters in the hope either of finding someone who might be able to repair the gas tanks, or of phoning Red Cross headquarters in Geneva to see if someone there could get the Italians to call off their planes. These were vain hopes. When he reached the brow of the last hill which gave him a view of the airfield, he saw "with a sinking heart" that the plane was now a smoking mass of charred wreckage. After dumping what von Rosen estimated to be about two hundred bombs on the ground around the plane, the strafing Italians had finally set it afire.

Several hours and several narrow bomb-burst escapes later, Dr. Junod approached the Emperor's mountain camp with the intention of asking him for some means of conveyance back to Addis Ababa, more than four hundred miles away by existing "roads." Trudging along the narrow path, he kept meeting Ethiopian soldiers, "their faces bloodless under their color, their features drawn and suffering." The bombing and gassing of the entire area had continued now for several hours. There was nothing Junod could do for these men.

As he came to the last hill before reaching the Emperor's caves, he began to hear "a strange, chant-like plaint in the distance, an uncanny sound. . . . It was a heart-rending chant that came and went in a slow but persistent rhythm."

A few minutes later, walking quickly in his anxiety to investigate the sound, he rounded the curve of the last hill in front of the Emperor's camp and came upon the hideous sight of men in agony stretched out everywhere beneath the trees. He estimated there were thousands of them.

The sound he had first heard, and which he now heard in a rising chorus, was the common Ethiopian cry for help, pity, mercy. "*Abeit! Abeit! Abeit!*"

As he approached these men, he could see "horrible, suppurating burns on their feet and on their emaciated limbs." The gas could not, of course, be blamed for their "emaciated" limbs. Most Ethiopian soldiers were thin and underweight because of the chronic food shortage. As Dr. Junod walked through this writhing, piteous mass of men, he had to endure his frustration at being unable to relieve their pain. The two Red Cross units under his supervision in the area, the Dutch and the damaged British, were already treating as many gas cases as they could handle. But if Junod expected this suffering multitude at his feet to make impossible demands upon him, he soon learned otherwise. It was not the white medical men, whose skills they scarcely knew, that they begged for help.

Their voices were raised toward the cave of their Emperor, who was their only hope, but who could do no more than pace the floor, as helpless as they, listening to their cries.

After hearing these cries until he could scarcely endure them, Haile Selassie wrote his wife, Empress Menen, in Addis Ababa, the first letter in which he had showed any indication of despair. It was horrible, he said, to hear the screaming of his men during the night. Old friends had come to see him whom he no longer recognized because of the terrible burns on their faces. He could bear it no longer, he told her.

He continued to bear it, however, because he was acutely conscious of his role and duty as Emperor of Ethiopia. No matter how hopeless the military situation might appear to be, he must, as the supreme leader of the Ethiopian people, lead them in an ultimate battle against the invading enemy. Though he had constantly advised his men to adopt guerrilla warfare methods against the Italians, he knew now he could not follow his own advice. The Lion of Judah must confront his enemy in the open field. He hastened to do so, ordering his chiefs to prepare their men for battle. He now had at his disposal about thirty thousand men, including his own Imperial Guard, who were Ethiopia's best soldiers. But the Guard was comprised of only six infantry battalions plus a brigade of artillery. Most of the thirty thousand in this last-ditch Imperial army were untrained and nondescript.

On March 20, Ras Kassa and Ras Seyoum reached Quoram after a three-week flight from the Tembien. Their remaining troops, more a rabble than an army, dressed in rags and followed by their surviving mules, women, and children, all of whom served the function of pack animals, shuffled down the mountains above Quoram with no other thought than to get home and forget this dreadful war. Most of their number had already died or deserted. Some of these who were still following the two great chiefs did so only to procure the safety of traveling south in a group. Kassa and Seyoum, when they reached the Emperor's headquarters, were immediately ushered into his cave for a private reception, which included, in addition to personal welcomes, a certain amount of military questioning and criticism.

In the evening, the Emperor summoned Colonel Konovaloff and two European technicians who had arrived with the defeated generals. The Emperor, wearing a khaki uniform, received all three graciously but concentrated his questions upon the trained military tactician, Konovaloff. Why had the retreat been necessary? What conditions had they encountered on the march south?

"Are you convinced," he asked finally, "that Ras Kassa could not hold on to the Tembien any longer? Was he really forced to retire?"

Konovaloff, before answering, allowed his mind to dwell momentarily on his own assessment of what he had seen in recent weeks—the absence on the part of Kassa and his chiefs of the slightest initiative or forethought. It seemed to him they knew nothing at all about modern warfare.

"We allowed every moment to escape," Konovaloff told the Emperor, "when we could do anything to remedy the evil. And so the Italians by a neat maneuver encircled us on all sides."

The Emperor made no comment. Finally Konovaloff asked, "What do you think of the situation, sire?"

The Emperor's answer made him sound either dreadfully ill-informed or somewhat distrustful of his audience. "It's all going normally," he said. "Up to now we have resisted as best we might and kept them back. I see nothing very dangerous in the situation." Beyond that, he offered no details. Instead he served apples and wine. "I suppose it's a long time," he said, "since you have eaten fruit."

After ordering one of his aides to procure new outfits for the three shabbily dressed Europeans, he dismissed them. But the next day, he again summoned Konovaloff to a field position he was surveying about fifteen miles north of Quoram, above Lake Ashangi.

"I have decided," he said, "to attack the Italians at their camp near Mai Chew [another twenty miles farther north] before they have gathered in force." He asked Konovaloff to accompany three Ethiopian officers who had been trained at St. Cyr, the French military academy, on a reconnaissance tour of the area.

Konovaloff and the three Ethiopian officers made the tour, and when they returned southward to the Ethiopian ranks, March 22, they found that the Emperor had moved his headquarters to a new cave on Mount Aia, twelve miles above Lake Ashangi. He was not intimidated by the news that the Italians had already occupied the mountains just a few miles north, that they had installed observation posts and perhaps artillery batteries on the highest peaks, that they were gathering in force to the northeast at what might be a take-off point for an encircling movement, and that they were also advancing toward the town of Sokota to the west of Lake Ashangi. When Colonel Konovaloff advised an attack before the Italians completed their preparations and became even stronger, the Emperor agreed and decided the time to march was that very night.

Toward evening, he ordered an Ethiopian warrior's feast of raw meat in his new forty-foot-long, rectangular cave. The usual carpets had been laid on the floor, and a white silk drape covered the door. Seated on an improvised throne, with Ras Kassa on one side of him and Ras Seyoum on the other, he greeted his lesser chiefs and their aides as they took their places in descending order at basket tables. Young Imperial household servants moved from table to table offering chunks of freshly butchered raw flesh, while others followed offering cups of *tej*, the Ethiopian honey wine.

After the meal, the Emperor announced his intention to attack that night and explained his plan, which he had already discussed with Kono-valoff. He concluded his exhortation by saying, "Don't destroy the enemy who come over to us, but make them prisoners and send them to the rear."

It soon became apparent, however, that the Emperor's desire and decision to attack that night did not settle the matter. The older and more powerful chiefs wished to discuss it first, and many of them argued for postponement. Their soldiers, they said, were not yet ready to attack. Some of them hadn't even reached Aia. Many necessary items of supply were missing. It soon became apparent that some of the chiefs didn't want to attack at all. They thought it would be better to let the Italians take the initiative.

The Emperor, showing his displeasure at their timidity, continued to argue for an immediate advance, but he was no absolute monarch. Like his predecessors he derived his power from the support of the chiefs, and when he found that too many of them opposed his plan, he had to agree to a short postponement.

The mood in which this enforced delay left the Emperor was illustrated by a letter he wrote the following day, March 23, to Ras Imru, a letter which fell into Italian hands when its carrier was intercepted on the way to Dabat, 120 miles west, toward which Imru was believed to be moving. The letter said:

> How are you? We, thanks be to God, are well. . . . As you will certainly have understood, an army [that of Kassa and Seyoum] so numerous that it had already thrust back and intimidated the enemy . . . went to pieces without having suffered serious losses and without any attempt whatever at resistance.
> This is a grievous matter.
> Our army, famous throughout Europe for its valor, has lost its name; brought to ruin by a few traitors, to this pass is it reduced. . . .
> In order to push forward our front, we have arrived in the neighborhood of Aia; since the enemy has been the first to occupy the position of Dubbar [a mountain pass about ten miles north of Mai Chew], we have placed ourselves where we, in our turn, can watch him. Within a week we shall certainly know what is going to happen.
> Ras Kassa and Ras Seyoum are with us, but have not a single armed man with them. For yourself, if you think that with your troops you can do anything where you are, do it; if, on the other hand, your position is difficult and you are convinced of the impossibility of fighting, having

lost all hope on your front, and if you think it better to come here and die with us, let us know of your decision by telephone from Dabat.

From the League we have so far derived no hope and no benefit.

(In Geneva that same day, as it happened, the League's Committee of Thirteen adopted another resolution similar to the one it had adopted March 3. This latest one requested the committee's chairman "to get in touch with the two parties and to take such steps as may be called for in order that the Committee may be able, as soon as possible, to bring the two parties together and, within the framework of the League of Nations and in the spirit of the Covenant, to bring about the prompt cessation of hostilities.")

The days of argument, indecision, and prayer among the Emperor and his chiefs continued. Their councils of war stretched on endlessly as Italian planes continued bombing their men. When the day's air attack began on the twenty-sixth, Konovaloff and the Emperor stood side by side watching it. At one point the Emperor turned and, speaking of the low-flying Italian pilots, said, "They are really very brave."

The following day, at four-thirty in the afternoon, he sent his Empress a telegram which, of course, was intercepted by the Italians, saying,

> We are drawn up opposite the enemy and are observing each other through field glasses. We are informed that the enemy troops assembled against us number, up till now, not more than approximately ten thousand men. Our troops amount to exactly thirty-one thousand. . . . Since our trust is in our Creator and in the hope of His help, and as we have decided to advance and enter the fortifications [of the enemy], and since God is our only help, confide this decision of ours in secret to the Abuna [his Church Primate], to the ministers and dignitaries; and offer up to God your fervent prayers.

If it was Konovaloff who had informed him that there were only ten thousand Italians facing him, then Konovaloff had badly misled him. Konovaloff, whose version of the war was published in Italy only a few months after it ended, was very vivid and convincing about many of the details of what he had seen but strangely silent, obscure, or baffling about others. His admiration for the Italians, against whom he had aligned himself, was greater than for their victims, on whose side he had enlisted. He was fulsome in his praise of Italian aviators but failed to mention the fact that they sprayed tons of mustard gas on the Ethiopians. During his March 21 reconnaissance trip into the mountains north of the Ethiopian camp, he is believed to have passed through the Italian lines disguised as an Ethiopian priest. It would be difficult for a Russian to make do with such a disguise unless the Italians were either quite accommodating or remarkably oblivious. If he did indeed pass through the Italian lines, and was as skilled a military observer as he appears to have been, he must surely have returned to the Ethiopians with the conviction that they faced more than ten thousand men. In his memoirs, Konovaloff did not say exactly what he told the Emperor when he returned, although he admitted that, on March 29, he said he thought there were "five-to-eight thousand" Italians at Mai Chew.

The Emperor's March 27 telegram to his wife also said his attack against the Italians would begin either the next day, Saturday the twenty-eighth, or Monday the thirtieth. Ethiopians never fought on Sunday. The Saturday attack plan was canceled because negotiations were then under way to buy off the rebellious Azebu Galla tribesmen, who were already in the pay of the Italians, as Marshal Badoglio noted, and who had probably been responsible for the death of Ras Mulugeta. The Emperor, conscious of the danger that these savages might attack his flanks, was offering each of their chiefs silk shirts and satin capes, plus arms and money, to adopt the Ethiopian cause. The usual stipend was ten or fifteen Ethiopian dollars, enough to make a man feel wealthy. Many of the Gallas arrived at the Emperor's camp carrying new Italian rifles. They left wearing their new silk garments over their old ragged ones. They had agreed to attack the Italians from behind as soon as the battle began.

On Sunday the twenty-ninth, the Emperor prayed, then made an inspection tour of the forward positions. The advance against the Italians seemed finally to be set for the following morning. But late Sunday afternoon, several of the great chiefs arrived again at the Emperor's cave. Their forces were not yet assembled, they said, nor had they properly studied the terrain on which the battle would be fought. Was it not possible and advisable to postpone the advance one more day?

The Emperor promptly called another council of war at which "it was almost impossible to speak and utterly impossible to hear," according to Colonel Konovaloff. "The soldiers, strung up by waiting so long for the offensive, kept firing their guns in the air. Some of the nearer ones were arrested and beaten soundly, but that did not stop the row." While all of this commotion continued outside, the Emperor tried to listen once again to the fears and objections his chiefs were voicing. It didn't actually matter whether or not he could hear what they were saying. He had heard it all before. But he still couldn't cope with it. Once again the battle was postponed, this time until Tuesday, March 31, at dawn.

Thanks to the Italian Communication Corps's blanket interception of all Ethiopian telephone and telegraph messages, and thanks also to the continuing availability of information from the Azebu Gallas and other rebellious Ethiopian tribesmen, Marshal Badoglio, at his Makalle head-quarters, grew more confident every day. Until the middle of March, he had worried that the Emperor, instead of advancing northward for a climactic battle, might withdraw to Dessie or even farther south, "thus compelling me to organize a large-scale battle hundreds of miles from our bases." Badoglio's fears had been fed by his knowledge of Haile Selassie's earlier advocacy of guerrilla warfare. When, on March 21, Italian head-quarters learned that Ethiopians were beginning to appear in Agumberta Pass, five miles above Lake Ashangi, Badoglio was suddenly relieved. He sent a telegram to Mussolini assuring him that whether "the Negus" attacked, or whether he waited to be attacked, his fate was now decided. He would be completely defeated.

This telegram enabled the Duce to appear on his Palazzo Venezia balcony March 23 and tell a cheering multitude, "The sky is not yet absolutely clear, but no matter: I say to you here and now that the few remaining clouds must be and will be rapidly dispersed."

By this time, even Mussolini was beginning to relax about the war. His crony, Achille Starace, Secretary-General of the Fascist Party, who had gone to Ethiopia determined to harvest some easy military glory for him-self, was now more than halfway from Asmara to Gondar with his own 3400-man, 450-vehicle caravan on a junket which was advertised as a "march of conquest," even though it was carefully routed through a territory where there were no Ethiopian troops to oppose it. Much closer to the battle zone, other Italian forces were on their way to Sokota, directly through the mountains west of Mai Chew. On the twenty-eighth, the day Sokota fell, Mussolini answered Badoglio's confident telegram: "I am certain that, old but always vigorous and faithful, the marshal will give the Italians new reasons for pride, and to the world, reasons for admiration. I am even more certain that the battle will be decisive."

The same day, Mussolini sent Badoglio another telegram for relay to Starace: "Any Red Cross unit which might be found at Gondar and any flag which might be pulled out at the last moment, Your Excellency should go ahead and shoot at it, but avoid damaging the British Red Cross if any exists there."

Aware that he had already tried British patience beyond reasonable limits, and that they could still thwart him at the edge of victory by closing the Suez Canal, he apparently felt the time had come to begin handling them with at least a small degree of prudence. But there was still no need for prudence in his treatment of anyone else, especially the Ethiopians. On the twenty-ninth, he sent Badoglio the familiar endorsement: "Given the enemy methods of war, I renew the authorization for the use of gas at any time and in any measure."

* * *

316

The use of mustard gas by the Italians was now being so widely and authoritatively reported in England that the British people were becoming restive about it. On March 19 and again on the twenty-second, the London *Times* published dispatches detailing the effects of the gas upon the Ethiopians. On March 24, Dr. T.A.Lambie, an American who was General Secretary of the Red Cross in Ethiopia, said in a telegram to *The Times*: "The bombing of country villages around Quoram and Waldia, the permanent blinding and maiming of hundreds of helpless women and children, as well as the infliction of similar injuries on soldiers with that most dreadful of all dreadful agencies, yperite, or so-called mustard gas, should cause us to ask ourselves the question—whither?"

In addition to all this unofficial information, the British government had an official report from its minister in Addis Ababa, Sir Sidney Barton, with affidavits from several doctors describing the gas-burn cases they had treated. Dr. Macfie, for instance, signed a statement that he himself had "seen and treated several hundreds of patients, men, women, and children, suffering from burns caused by mustard gas."

On March 30, Lord Hugh Cecil arose in the House of Lords and addressed an inquiry to the government about the alleged Italian use of gas.

Lord Halifax, answering for the government, said he wished it were in his power to give the assurance that there was no foundation for these reports, but he had no information. "It would be quite wrong and quite unjust," he continued, "to prejudge a matter so grave and so vitally affecting the honor of a great country [Italy]. . . . The first step must be to obtain the observations and comments of the Italian government."

Emperor Haile Selassie watched the shadowy figures of his soldiers moving tentatively in the darkness as they formed themselves into three columns of about three thousand men each. These were assault troops who would be moving north across the Mecan plain before dawn to attack the Italians in the hills and mountains above it at sunrise. The time was now four o'clock in the morning of March 31. Before the men moved off to their pre-battle positions, the Emperor addressed those who could hear him. He began by reminding them that, the previous evening, Italian bombers had spread mustard gas on the plain they now had to cross. "If you smell it," he said, "change direction immediately. If you are contaminated by it, wash yourselves at once."[3]

With this warning he sent forth the three columns, led by Ras Kassa, Ras Seyoum, and the third most powerful chief in his camp, plump, pince-nez'd Ras Getachu from the southwestern province of Kaffa. None of the three was young. None had military credentials. The first two had already proven their ineptitude in the Tembien. But all three held such impeccable positions in Ethiopian society that command could not be denied them. In any case, their lack of military skill was unlikely to be decisive in this battle, because the Emperor himself would be directing it and he had chosen a plan so simple all three could grasp it.

A small force of a few hundred men would begin the engagement with a diversionary attack against the center of the Italian position directly north of the Mecan plain. As this attack proceeded, the bulk of the three columns would move silently up the Mecan Pass to the east and attack the Italian left flank. If this larger force could break through to Mai Chew, just north of the Mecan Pass, it would be able to belabor the Italians from the rear, while at the same time the Emperor would send a second large force against their front lines. The pincers movement envisioned by this strategy, while simple in design, was ambitious in execution. It was based on the hope that the Italians had anchored most of their strength in the center, thus leaving the mountain pass to the east less heavily defended.

As the three columns crossed the plain, the men could smell mustard gas on the grass, but since its strength had dissipated during the night, they were able to disregard it. The darkness allowed them to cross the plain apparently undetected and by five-thirty a.m., or shortly thereafter, the troops in the diversionary force were crouched and waiting, with their machine guns installed, only a few hundred yards from the Italian center positions.

In the Italian camps, the night had passed quietly but expectantly. Everyone knew the attack was coming at dawn, because the Azebu Gallas, after accepting the Emperor's bribes, had gone immediately to the Italians and disclosed his plans. Having been bribed now by both sides, the Gallas knew that the Italians, besides being stronger, were wealthier and more generous.

As an Italian front-line reporter described it, one tried to imagine, during the hours of waiting, how the thing would begin. One listened for the slightest sound but heard only the animal-like cries of the askari observation scouts, who had been instructed to make their usual sounds and pretend they did not see the approaching Ethiopians.[4]

At five-forty-five a.m., as the first light of dawn began to reveal the outlines of the hills and mountains, two Mauser shots fired from the Ethiopian side broke the silence. It was the Emperor's signal for the battle to begin.

The Ethiopian machine guns opened fire immediately against the advance units of the white Italian Pusteria and Sabauda divisions, and from the rear, the Emperor's few 75-millimeter guns opened up to support them. Though the Italians were ready, their initial casualties were heavy and they were forced to fall back in several places when the Ethiopians—shouting, "Makalle!" and "Alagi!" to remind themselves of previous Italian conquests—came charging up the mountainsides against them. Italian General Negri Cesi described the scene:

> Two companies are more gravely exposed than the others—the 24th and the 7th. . . . While the artillery [Ethiopian] drops its precise shots on the two redoubts, the enemy, coming out of the brush land which marks the southeast boundary of Mount Bohora, collides with them.
>
> The commander of the 24th, while he was launching signal flames to ask for artillery, fell with a bullet in the forehead. A little later the commander of the 7th was seriously wounded and had to leave the battle. A corporal in the act of firing fell forward on his machine gun, killed by a burst from the enemy. Quickly the Alpinist closest to him substituted for him, only to fall himself after a few minutes. A third Alpinist had just managed to take the post and begin firing when he was hit in the head and the shoulder. But a machine gun must not be silenced. A fourth Alpinist took the place of the fallen man and the gun resumed firing. The enemy fire became more and more precise and homicidal. It could be seen that they had purposely directed their bullets against officers and gunners. Another machine gun lost, in succession, its weapon leader, its gunner, its squad leader and its first reloader, all mortally wounded.
>
> But the courage of the defenders grew with the increase in the danger. Sub-lieutenant Toni, wounded in one arm, quickly had himself medicated and returned to the lines. Wounded again, he refused to abandon his post until he was wounded a third time in the chest by numerous pieces of shrapnel. To avoid taking men from the line, he ordered the stretcher-bearers not to accompany him; alone, losing blood, he started out laboriously toward the medication post, under fire, turning back from time to time to shout encouragement to his men.

Subjected to such determined Ethiopian attacks, the Italians lost some ground, and were even routed from one mountaintop, but their strategic situation was not threatened. The few hundred men in the Ethiopian diversionary force, despite their fierce and continuous advances, lacked the strength even to reach the main defenses of the Italian center.

As the attack on the center continued, the eight thousand or more Ethiopians embarked hopefully under the three rases on the flanking movement toward the east, succeeded in rounding the corner of the Italian center defenses, and were swarming up the Mecan Pass when, at seven a.m., they encountered the black troops of the 2nd Eritrean Division.

The area was now in full daylight, which exposed the spectacular beauty of the battleground. This was green, fertile country, the grassy plains dotted with eucalyptus and juniper, the gently rising foothills below the mountains half covered with cactus-like euphorbia trees whose thickly bunched arms curved gracefully upward. Even the mountains, with the exception of Bohora to the west, showed more vegetation than rock.

As the advance guard of the main Ethiopian force engaged the Eritrean shock troops in their forward posts, the Ethiopian artillery pieces across the plain to the south, and even their eight Oerlikon antiaircraft guns, concentrated all their fire power, meager as it was, against the Eritrean strong points farther up the pass. The Emperor himself, at the foot of the euphorbia-covered Mount Ugu on the southern edge of the Mecan plain, took part in this bombardment, firing his own antiaircraft gun as fast as it could be loaded.

After several sharp exchanges of gunfire, the Eritreans gradually withdrew from their forward posts to their entrenched positions farther up the pass. Ras Seyoum's men now attacked them in force and with some success on the western side of the pass, while Kassa's men advanced slowly against heavier opposition on the eastern side, driving the Eritreans from a small hillside village, which was soon in flames. The Imperial Guard and other units, under the command of Ras Getachu, made only tentative advances up the center of the pass while awaiting the Emperor's order to hurl themselves into the battle.

By this time, the Emperor found himself trying to cope with scores of his men who were returning from the initial attack against the Italian center positions.[5] These men, instead of holding the ground they had taken, were now making the traditional Ethiopian mistake of returning with whatever booty they could carry to advertise their bravery and boast about their victory. They had pushed the Italians farther up the hill. Was that not a victory? Apparently unaware that they had only dented the Italian defenses, they presented their booty to the Emperor and leaped back and forth around him, improvising victory dances and songs for his benefit. Haile Selassie tried to ignore them. He was already busy enough, issuing orders and firing his gun at the same time.

At about eight a.m., the Emperor heard a droning sound above the battle and looked up to see what he had been expecting for an hour—large formations of Italian planes arriving from the north. From this moment onward, the Ethiopian troops fighting their way up the mountain pass on the other side of the plain could no longer depend on the "artillery" support of the antiaircraft Oerlikons. At the Emperor's command, all these guns were turned skyward against the fighters and bombers diving toward them. The Emperor could derive only one small comfort as he saw the planes approach: they would not be dropping gas, because the Ethiopians were contaminatingly close to the Italians.

At nine a.m., as the progress of Kassa's and Seyoum's men seemed to be diminishing, the Emperor ordered his best-trained troops, the Imperial Guard, into the battle across the valley from him. Now he had committed the full force of the three columns designated to capture Mecan Pass and open the road to Mai Chew just beyond it. The Imperial Guard quickly penetrated the lower Italian posts, but, on reaching higher ground near the saddle of the pass, had to face well-prepared defenses—stone walls, trenches, bunkered gun emplacements. These defenses were manned mostly by Eritreans but also by some white Italians. During the next two hours, four successive waves of Ethiopians raced across the open ground in front of these redoubts, absorbing what Badoglio later referred to as a "veritable avalanche of fire" in an effort to get to them. Before long, there were so many fallen Ethiopians on the ground that their comrades who came after them could take cover behind their bodies. They were so close now, and such accurate marksmen, that they almost knocked out of action a whole battalion, the 10th Eritrean, which lost nearly all of its officers as well as hundreds of men. By eleven a.m., the 10th was in desperate condition and sent an urgent plea for artillery support. A few minutes later, the commanding officer of the 10th and his second in command were both killed by an Ethiopian artillery blast. The officer who replaced them sent a message to division headquarters: "Even the wounded are fighting here. Soon we shall all be dead but we shall continue to fire."

While the entrenched Italians sustained heavy casualties, the exposed Ethiopians were absorbing even greater losses. After four brutal charges, they lacked the strength to mount a fifth. Those who managed to reach the Italian redoubts were either shot, bayoneted, or hurled back. The survivors, finally abandoning their frontal strategy, swung eastward where the ground was more broken and offered better cover. Here they made so much progress that the Eritreans were forced to emerge from their fortifications with bayonets fixed and mount a counterattack. When the Ethiopians were finally driven back, they moved even farther east, but now they encountered the 1st Eritrean Division, which had been in reserve and was still fresh.

By four p.m., rain had begun to fall. The Emperor, realizing that if he could not pierce the Italian lines today, he wouldn't have the strength to do so tomorrow, sent all the reinforcements he could spare to augment the badly diminished forces in Mecan Pass. Committing their full strength, the Ethiopians launched one more general attack across the width of the pass, concentrating especially on an effort to drive a wedge into the junction between the 1st and 2nd Eritrean divisions. For a short time, they actually created a breach, but they were unable to widen it. By six p.m., with darkness approaching, the Emperor ordered his men to fall back "to a hill not far from Mai Chew, from whose summit we could see the entire plain [around Mai Chew] and the enemy positions."

Unfortunately for the Ethiopians, their retirement was not destined to be as easy or as orderly as the Emperor envisioned it. Before the battle, Marshal Badoglio had stationed on the eastern flank the three thousand Azebu Gallas who had taken money from both sides but had manifested their loyalty to the Italians. As soon as the exhausted Ethiopians began their retirement for the night, Badoglio turned these fresh Gallas loose upon them. Riding into the Ethiopian ranks on horseback, or sniping at them from the hillsides, the Gallas created so much bewilderment and disruption that the Ethiopian retirement became a disorderly retreat all the way back to their encampment of the previous night.

The Emperor, at his headquarters on Mount Aia that night, sent a telegram to his wife:

> From five in the morning until seven in the evening our troops attacked the enemy's strong positions, fighting without pause. We also took part in the action, and by the grace of God, remain unharmed. Our chief and trusted soldiers are dead or wounded. Although our losses are heavy, the enemy too has been injured. The Guard fought magnificently and deserves every praise. The Amharic troops also did their best. Our troops, even though they are not adapted for fighting of the European type, were able to bear comparison throughout the day with the Italian troops.

This message shed further light on his compulsion to engage in a battle he knew he could not win. The following day he said to Colonel Konovaloff, "I'm glad we attacked the enemy. It was a question in which our honor was involved."

Konovaloff, who viewed the battle from the rear encampment, was not so convinced the Ethiopians had fought well. In his later assessment, he said only about nine hundred of them had been brave enough to storm the Italian redoubts while "the rest lacked the courage to advance and crown their efforts with the capture of the Italian works." He said also that the Imperial Guard "had not justified the hopes reposed in it." But even the Italians disagreed with Konovaloff's evaluation of the Ethiopian performance. Badoglio said of the Imperial Guard that they "moved against our positions, advancing in rushes and making good use of the ground, giving proof of a solidity and a remarkable degree of training combined with a superb contempt of danger." Konovaloff said only a thousand Ethiopians were killed in this battle of Mai Chew. Badoglio, who had the opportunity to count the bodies, said there were eight thousand, but he may have included those killed in the days that followed. An Italian reporter set the figure at about five thousand.[6] The Ethiopians made no estimate. Statistics meant very little to them. They knew only that their ranks had been woefully depleted. Their camp was full of wounded men who had dragged themselves back from the battleground. Their ammunition supply was virtually exhausted. And their morale, when they realized their failure to dent the Italian defenses, was dismally low. The renewed treachery of the Azebu Gallas further depressed them.

The Emperor spent the morning after the battle, April 1, arguing with the surviving chiefs about the possibilities of another attack. In the afternoon, he said to Konovaloff, "I feel that we ought to renew the offensive."

Konovaloff, when asked for his opinion, said, "There is nothing for Your Majesty to do but retire."

The Ethiopian chiefs, who could see, even if they didn't bother to count, their losses, were in full agreement with him. A timid bishop in the Emperor's camp added his voice to theirs. He would not give his blessing, he said, to another advance. Late that afternoon, the Emperor acquiesced and the Ethiopian retreat began.

On April 2, as the evacuation proceeded, the Italians, aware now that they had exhausted the Ethiopian offensive, launched a full-scale counter-attack. Their reserve divisions ventured, carefully at first, across the Mecan plain and engaged the Ethiopian rear guard, while those planes which had survived the previous day's battle (the Emperor and his fellow antiaircraft gunners had shot down seventeen of them) began pouring bombs on the almost twenty thousand men cluttering the route through the mountains southward.

The Emperor, after watching from his observation post the bombing and machine-gunning of his troops on the roads below, said to Colonel Konovaloff, "I fail to understand the role of the League of Nations. It seems quite impotent."

In the evening, he made a speech to his assembled chiefs, a much smaller group than he had addressed before the battle. "We should not lose courage," he said. "The Ethiopian army is at this moment in a very dangerous position. We ought to retire beyond Quoram into the mountains and there give the Italians a new battle."

The Italian air attack against the retreating Ethiopians and the ground attack against their rear guard intensified the next day, April 3, creating such confusion that when the Emperor saw the swarming, shoving mass of men near the mouth of his cave on Mount Aia, he exclaimed, "What disgraceful disorder, when we ought to be ready to stop the Italians!"

There was no way now to stop the Italians and the Emperor knew it. That evening, near nightfall, he began distributing to his men all the supplies he had left. Then, at nine-thirty p.m., under cover of darkness, he left Mount Aia, escorted by his personal bodyguard in a small caravan

323

of vehicles, and headed south over a road now congested with men, donkeys, and corpses. By morning, his party had reached the cave near Quoram which he had assigned to the British Red Cross unit after it was bombed March 4. Like all other Red Cross units, it had since been evacuated, leaving the defeated Ethiopian army with absolutely no medical care. Before dawn, the Emperor moved into this cave for protection against the intense air attacks he expected that day.

His melancholy expectations were more than fulfilled. At dawn on the fourth, Badoglio sent every available airplane against the retreating Ethiopians in a bombing, strafing, and gassing campaign which was to last for the next fortnight. "From that moment," one Italian newsman reported, "a tornado of fire was unleashed. Wave after wave of bombers with full loads hammered their main objective, the Ethiopian column making for the east shore [of Lake Ashangi] ... the bombs exploded among the dense mass of fugitives who bent double and clapped their hands over their ears as if they had been caught in a heavy hailstorm."[7]

The Emperor himself later described the hideous scene enacted and re-enacted day after day along the entire route southward until his army simply dissolved into nothingness, leaving only a trail of corpses and equipment beside the roads:

> Of all the massacres of the terrible and pitiless war, this was the worst. Men, women, pack-animals were blown to bits or were fatally burned by the mustard gas. The dying, the wounded screamed with agony. Those who escaped the bombs fell victim to the deadly rain. The gas finished off the carnage that the bombs had begun. We could do nothing to protect ourselves against it. Our thin, cotton shammas were soaked with yperite.[8]

In Geneva, April 8, while these scenes were being enacted in Africa, the League's Committee of Thirteen met to discuss its progress toward bringing about peace between Italy and Ethiopia. When a question was raised about Italy's use of gas, most of the delegates agreed that efforts should be made to collect reliable information on the subject. But Pierre-Etienne Flandin, the French Foreign Minister, objected. He asked if any inquiries had been made into atrocities committed by Abyssinians, including the use of dumdum bullets.

At a private meeting after the committee's first morning session, British Foreign Secretary Anthony Eden attacked the implications of Flandin's remarks. There was, Eden insisted, "a distinction between the irresponsible atrocities of undisciplined military forces and the use of poison gas which could not be other than a governmental act."

Flandin agreed. He said the Italians were "very stupid" to use this form of warfare, but he doubted "the wisdom of issuing a formal condemnation at a moment when an attempt was being made to bring hostilities to an end, for this might disturb the negotiations."

The Committee of Thirteen decided at a meeting later that day not to inquire into the Italian use of poison gas.

CHAPTER FOURTEEN

IMPORTANT as it was for Marshal Badoglio to destroy the Ethiopian army, he now faced another task perhaps equally important—the capture or elimination of Emperor Haile Selassie, who was fleeing south, presumably on the main road, the quickest route, toward Dessie and then Addis Ababa. If he were to escape the Italians and reach the safety of some hospitable country, he might be an embarrassment and a nuisance to Italy for many years, telling the world his version of the war.

Badoglio, on April 5, ordered his fast-moving Eritrean Corps to make haste for Dessie, where they might possibly overtake the Emperor, especially if the Azebu Gallas, meanwhile, managed to slow his flight by harassment. The Eritreans were not ready to travel until April 9, but when they began speeding southward, in echelon formation, they moved with remarkable speed over the primitive road, averaging more than twenty-five miles per day. To enable them to travel light, with a minimum of rations, Badoglio ordered his air arm to drop them a continuous flow of supplies, as much as twenty-five tons per day, along the entire route. This remarkable operation was the first large-scale airlift of supplies in military history, and it gave the Eritrean Corps so much mobility that the Emperor, though he didn't know it, was now in danger of losing his freedom or his life, as well as his empire.

Haile Selassie, traveling toward Dessie as the Italians anticipated, was now making his way laboriously over cold, wind-swept trails between the mountain towns of Marawa and Mugia. In an attempt to escape the incessant air attacks, he had chosen not the main road but an even more primitive route through the scenic, rough, high country to the west of Lake Ashangi. Though this route did attract fewer Italian planes than the main road, it was also slower, and it attracted enough planes, as well as Azebu Galla snipers, to make daytime travel prohibitively hazardous. The

Emperor's party, moving only at night, had to find caves in which to hide each morning at dawn.

From one of these caves, on April 8, the Emperor issued a pathetically useless document entitled: "Imperial Order for General Mobilization." It said, "Thanks to the help of Almighty God, we are still able to defend ourselves. We call upon all who are fit to take up arms and come to the aid of their heroic countrymen. . . ." Though the Emperor had overcome his immediate post-battle shock, under the influence of which he had said to Konovaloff, "I don't know what to do . . . my brain no longer works," he was still so isolated from the reality of his situation that he could entertain delusions of organizing a new army when he reached Dessie.

On April 11, which was the Coptic Easter Saturday, his party reached a mountain town called Bohaie, a few miles north of Mugia.[1] Ever and always mindful of religious occasions, he celebrated this one somberly in "a small and filthy tukul," eating the traditional raw meat and drinking tej. That night, he traveled through Mugia and crossed the Takazze River, a much less formidable stream at this point, near its headwaters, than in the lower-lying country to the north, where so many of Ras Imru's men had been killed trying to cross it.

On the south bank of the Takazze, the Emperor found at his disposal the huge home of the governor of that region. Here, he took a short rest, and, thanks to the offers of food and meat from the people of the surrounding countryside, was able to provide for his men a proper Easter celebration. One hundred at a time, his soldiers crowded into a large, round tukul where they ate their fill and each received, in addition, an Ethiopian dollar.

Haile Selassie, in the meantime, had made an extraordinary decision about his own immediate course of action. Though he knew the Italians must now be pursuing him with all possible speed, he resolved to detour westward about twenty-five miles and visit the city of Lalibela, renowned for its ancient churches carved from solid rock. In one of these churches, he would seek Divine guidance through prayer and meditation. All the arguments of his chiefs and advisers failed to sway him from this decision.

Reaching Lalibela at dusk with only a small group of his closest followers, he went directly to the most imposing of the rock churches (all hewn in the thirteenth century at the command of an emperor named Lalibela) and spent the next forty-eight hours there, on his knees, refusing food or water. Finally, feeling sufficiently nourished by this intense communion with his God, he emerged from the church, to the great relief of his retinue, and, on April 15, made his way eastward again, resuming his journey toward Dessie.

* * *

Black cavalry units, comprising the vanguard of the Eritrean Corps, rode unmolested up the mountainside to the town of Berumieda on the afternoon of April 14. From this vantage point, almost eighty-five hundred feet high, they could see for the first time, only six or seven miles farther south, the town of Dessie, which was their destination.[2] Though these native Italian soldiers may not have known it, Ethiopian Crown Prince Asfa Wossen, who served also as Dessie's governor, was at that moment evacuating the town, having learned, just in time, that the Italians were almost upon him.

Fortunately for Asfa Wossen, the Eritrean vanguard had not been instructed to take the city. These men dismounted and settled down for one more night in the mountains, awaiting the main body of the Eritrean Corps.

On the morning of the fifteenth, the corps commander, General Alessandro Pirzio Biroli, took official possession of Dessie, hoisting the Italian tricolor above the onetime Italian Consulate now also the onetime headquarters of Emperor Haile Selassie. The Eritreans, having searched in vain for the Emperor on their rapid sweep south from Quoram, had reason to believe, nevertheless, that they had reached Dessie ahead of him, that he was probably hiding someplace behind them, and that he might yet fall into their trap.

Mussolini, no longer concerned about progress on the northern front, had now begun to wonder what was stopping General Graziani in the south. In a March 31 telegram, he had said to his southern commander,

> I am beginning to have the feeling that Nesibu [Ethiopia's southern commander, Ras Nesibu] is ready to receive the sound thrashing he deserves. I'd like to know Your Excellency's opinion.

Graziani's opinion, as expressed in numerous letters to Rome, had long been that he needed more men. He resented Badoglio's monopoly both of power and of glory. It did not improve his mood when, in an April 2 telegram, Mussolini reminded him of Badoglio's accomplishments:

> Given the quick movement of events on the northern front, I ask Your Excellency if—with a forcefulness of which Your Excellency is always capable—it wouldn't be possible to move up your schedule by a few days?

Finally, Graziani had resigned himself to the fact that he was not going to get any more men to command, that his forces were already, as everyone knew, overwhelmingly superior to those he faced, and that he must soon

328

launch an attack in the direction of Harar, south of which Nesibu's army was concentrated.

On April 14, Mussolini sent him a telegram which was nothing short of an ultimatum:

> Today, the 14th, our advance troops are about to reach Dessie. Even from the international point of view, things are moving faster. Dear Graziani, it is necessary not to delay any longer. I am awaiting an announcement of the initiation of the march on Harar.

Finally, that day, Graziani began to move against Ras Nesibu's forces in the Ogaden desert, hitting first a "fortified" line which had been prepared near the town of Sasa Baneh, about 130 miles southeast of Harar. A retired Turkish general named Wehib Pasha, who supervised the construction of this fortification, had shown a nice sense of defensive strategy but he had not figured out how to get from Addis Ababa such necessary materials as barbed wire and bullets. Consequently, the trench system he had built was impressive enough to frighten the reluctant Graziani, but not formidable enough to stop Graziani's troops. When Pasha's defensive line was attacked, April 16, it was strong enough to endure for only three hours. After it fell, there was nothing to stop Graziani's army except the caution of Graziani. He managed to make the battle of the Ogaden last another nine days before eking out an inevitable victory.

Emperor Haile Selassie and his bedraggled company of soldiers, chiefs, advisers, and hangers-on, still traveling the back-country route which ran roughly parallel to but west of the main route, reached the Bashilo River near Magdala in the Dalanta region April 18. Here the altitude was low enough and the temperature high enough to support fields of cotton and big shade trees. It was lovely, peaceful-looking agricultural country, but the river itself provided a gruesome reminder of the war. On its banks and in the water were countless decomposing corpses of Ethiopian soldiers. These men had not, however, been killed by the Italians. They were stragglers who had tried to support themselves by looting on their southward retreat and had been killed by the hastily organized villagers in the area. The same villagers, on guard against any further attempts at looting, began to fire at the Emperor's party along the hilly route eastward from the river to Magdala. After the Emperor's soldiers had silenced this assault with their rifles and machine guns, his party continued the trek to Magdala, arriving there late in the day.

The Emperor did not find the townspeople friendly or even respectful.

The retreating soldiers who came before him had done too much looting. On the twentieth, he was told that the people in the district were planning to attack him. To avoid having to fight his own people, he decided on an immediate departure for Dessie.

The warning he received had not been unfounded. For several miles his men had to fight their way southeast from Magdala, as people in the hills sniped at them or swooped down to attack them. Colonel Konovaloff, still traveling in the party, saw some of the Emperor's servants killed at his side. The battle became so fierce at times that hundreds of houses were burned and the road was "covered by the bodies of the dead, the fresh dead and the dead long since." But finally the path was cleared and the Emperor's party climbed again toward the high plateau and toward Dessie, where even greater dangers lurked.

The march across the high country on the twenty-first was uneventful and the progress so rapid that the Emperor was now only twenty-five miles from Dessie. But at about this time, he learned, perhaps from people fleeing toward him, that Dessie was in Italian control. The warning came none too soon. Another day's march eastward would have put him in Italian hands. Turning southward, he and his men now headed for a town called Warra Hailu, in the mountains about forty miles southwest of Dessie. Here there were telephone lines, and perhaps he would be able to call Addis Ababa and get at least some information as to what was happening all around him. His flight was becoming more desperate by the hour. Even his own personal troops had begun to loot and pillage. His authority had diminished so sharply that he had only a tenuous hold upon them.

When his party was twenty miles from Warra Hailu, more bad news overtook him. The Italians had also captured that town and held it, he was told, with two hundred cavalry troops. His first instinct was to march against them and attack. The chiefs who were still with him, including Ras Kassa, soon banished this idea from his head. There was only one chance of escaping the Italians now. The Emperor and his advisers decided they would have to travel the hidden camel paths of the back country to the town of Fiche, about a hundred twenty miles southwest. From Fiche there was a road, primitive but at least passable, to Addis Ababa, which was another sixty-five miles farther south. It would take perhaps a week, however, to reach Fiche through the rough, almost uninhabited mountain country. By that time the Italians would have advanced much farther south. The road from Dessie to the capital lay wide open to them now, as did every other road. There were no Ethiopian forces anywhere to resist them.

* * *

In Geneva April 20, the League of Nations Council met to discuss the efforts of its Committee of Thirteen to end the "dispute" between Italy and Ethiopia by inducing the two parties to negotiate. After three sessions lasting from ten-thirty a.m. to almost ten-thirty p.m., sessions in which the entire committee report was read and assessed by each member and the representatives of both Italy and Ethiopia, the Council forged a new resolution to be addressed to the two countries. This resolution, while noting several obvious facts and regretting several others, stated that "the Council ... approves and renews the appeal addressed by the committee to the two parties for the prompt cessation of hostilities and the restoration of peace in the framework of the League of Nations and in the spirit of the Covenant. . . ."

Twelve large Caproni bombers carried Marshal Pietro Badoglio and his staff to Dessie on April 20. Before the day ended, they had established a new Supreme Italian Headquarters where Emperor Haile Selassie's headquarters had been only two months earlier and Badoglio was at work expediting the passage of a vast and fast motorized column in the direction of Addis Ababa.

Anticipating the need of such a caravan, he had ordered Quartermaster General Fidenzio Dall'Ora, on March 8, to assemble at least 1,000 lorries and hold them in readiness behind the Italian lines. Actually, Dall'Ora was able to gather 1725 vehicles of all kinds, carrying, in addition to troops, guns, and supplies, a contingent of newsmen who would thus be able to see for themselves the great speed, cleverness, and power of Mussolini's new Fascist army. Never before had a motorized column this large attempted such a move through potentially hostile territory.

Starting from Quoram April 18, the first trucks in this huge caravan reached Dessie on the twenty-first, only one day after Badoglio arrived there by air. During his plane journey from Makalle, he could look down and see the endless stream of vehicles below him, moving steadily, despite difficulties, over the endless miles of bad road. When the trucks arrived in Dessie, his staff was ready to supervise their servicing so they could be rushed southward on the second half of their journey.

Badoglio still did not know where the Emperor was. He heard new rumors every day about Haile Selassie's whereabouts and his plans, about Ethiopian efforts to reorganize and continue their resistance. But Italian planes, searching as far south as the capital (which they had bombed in early April), had not yet spotted the fleeing monarch. Badoglio felt it was unlikely that he had passed through Dessie before the Eritrean Corps arrived there. No one in Dessie, not even the most cooperative Ethiopian residents, reported seeing him come or go. He must still be on the road someplace, which meant there was still a possibility of intercepting him.

On April 24, Badoglio dispatched eight thousand Eritrean troops toward Addis Ababa as a vanguard for his otherwise vulnerable motorized column. Two days later, on the twenty-sixth, his great mechanized caravan left Dessie for the capital, carrying more than twelve thousand white Italian troops, plus two hundred horses for their officers to ride during the triumphal parade into the city. Though the Eritrean troops were destined to reach Addis Ababa before their white comrades, they would not take part in the initial entry of the city. An April 23 telegram from Mussolini to Badoglio stipulated that. "For obvious reasons," the Duce wrote, "it is necessary to reserve precedence for the national troops in the occupation of Addis Ababa."

Haile Selassie, on his eight-day hike through mountains, woods, and rivers to Fiche, had sent runners ahead with messages and instructions so that when his party reached there April 29, five trucks and five cars had arrived from Addis Ababa to carry him and fifty to a hundred members of his party the remaining sixty-five miles. It was still possible to reach the capital ahead of the Italians. After a rapid meal for his men, he ordered an immediate departure. Colonel Konovaloff, who fought his way onto one of the crowded trucks, watched the Emperor walk to his car as the ten-vehicle caravan prepared to leave. His face was thin and tired.

Rumor-ridden Addis Ababa, which was now visited daily by threatening Italian airplanes (Mussolini had ordered these flights in the hope of "straining the nerves of the Abyssinians"), had already begun, on April 30, to show signs of panic. The streets were full of cars, mules, and men, "all mixed up in indescribable confusion." The foreign legations were barricading their compounds and stocking up on food for an expected siege. The railroad station was jammed with people, many of them high government officials, trying to get on the next train to Djibuti. Demobilized soldiers, with guns but without leaders, wandered every place looking for food. There was talk that the Italians were now at Debre Berhan, about eighty miles northeast. There was talk that a great Ethiopian army was on the way to stop them. There was talk that Ethiopia no longer had any armies to stop them. There was talk that the Emperor had fled, or that he was dead.

At midday, a new rumor began to mingle with the others: the Emperor was returning to the capital, and would drive down Entoto Mountain on the road from Fiche sometime that afternoon.[3] This rumor was at least partially substantiated by the fact that many elderly aristocrats, the kind of men who ought to know what was happening, began riding up the Entoto road on their mules, as if to meet someone. Addis Ababa police were also hurrying up the road. The crowd began to follow.

In midafternoon, the curious were rewarded by the sight of a car speeding down the mountain with several policemen clinging to the running boards. Behind this car came three or four others. The Emperor had indeed come home, accompanied by Ras Kassa and Ras Getachu. The few soldiers he had left were still several miles behind, on the five trucks which had left Fiche with him. His only guards, as he rode to the Great Palace of Menelik, were the Addis Ababa police. Dressed in a khaki general's uniform which was uncharacteristically soiled, he seemed unable to conceal his fatigue and misery. His face looked haunted; his step and carriage lacked resilience.

When he entered the Palace, he summoned his councilors, and then he listened to a plan, submitted by one of his secretaries, suggesting that he remove himself and his government to the town of Gore, in the mountains about two hundred miles west of Addis Ababa. There he could direct a guerrilla war against the invaders. Since Gore was not easily accessible, the Italians would have difficulty finding him. And even if they did manage to reach Gore, he would be able to slip away, across the nearby Sudanese border, before they could capture him. The plan so completely suited Haile Selassie's mood that he quickly approved it, despite the obvious certainty that, even if he and his government could reach Gore, there was no reason to suppose the Italians would be unable to do likewise. And that when they came, they would be unlikely to approach only from the east— they would surely send troops at the same time around the mountains to the west, where they could block every possible escape route into the Sudan.

The Emperor, choosing to ignore these considerations, called in several foreign diplomats, including, first of all, Sir Sidney Barton of Great Britain. On the assumption that the war was to continue, he asked Barton if he thought the British government would maintain its support of sanctions against Italy now that the Italians had taken most of Ethiopia.

Barton said he could not honestly give any such assurances.

The Emperor, undeterred, announced to Barton that, whatever the British might do, he intended to go on defending his country.

He made the same announcement a short time later to French Minister Albert Bodard, and then to the United States Consul General, Cornelius Van H. Engert. The latter found in him "remarkable *sang-froid*," under the circumstances, and "the same gracious, unhurried suavity which had always impressed me on previous occasions." Engert decided that while Haile Selassie's "thoughtful, deep-set eyes showed a profoundly perturbed soul, . . . his inscrutable features were lit up by the same winsome smile."

333

After their formal business, the Emperor spoke approvingly of President Roosevelt's public utterances against dictatorships. "Convey my greetings to your President," he said, "and tell him the fate of my country may serve as a warning that words are of no avail against a determined aggressor who will tear up any peace pacts whose terms no longer serve his purpose."

That afternoon the Emperor also issued a short statement to the press. "Ethiopia is not defeated," he said. "It will carry on its fight to the last man." He indicated, however, that it was not part of his strategy to make a stand inside the capital. To the great relief of all foreigners there, he disclosed that "Addis Ababa will continue to be an open city." He did not divulge to newsmen his military plans.

He did divulge them to his councilors when they met in the evening. At first they seemed subdued, with little to say. They knelt and kissed his feet. He served them vermouth. When he outlined his plan to move the government into the western mountains, a majority of them—excluding Ras Kassa, however—seemed mildly in favor of it. They discussed it for several hours, but the meeting ended without any decision being taken.

After this long and tedious session, the exhausted Emperor rode up the hill to his personal palace, the Little Gibbi, where he spent his first night in several months with the Empress. She reacted much more negatively to his plan of continued resistance. A deeply religious woman, she surrounded herself with attentive clergymen, who had developed a strong influence over her. She agreed with their consensus that the war had now ended and Ethiopia had lost. When the Emperor told her that she and the rest of the royal family were to be sent out of the country while he continued his efforts at defending it, she tried to persuade him that he should go with her, that he could accomplish more for Ethiopia through a life of prayer in the holy city of Jerusalem, where she wanted to go, than he could in the mountains around Gore.

The next morning, May 1, brought definite news that the Italians were at Debre Berhan, only eighty miles away. (They might now have reached Addis Ababa had it not been for a delaying rock slide, arranged by saboteurs, on the steep, winding mountain road near Debre Sina, about twenty-five miles farther north.) Despite the fact that Badoglio's Eritrean vanguard was close enough to reach him within a day, Haile Selassie still refused to flee. Around noon, he ordered his aides to carry the huge war drum of Menelik out onto the hillside in front of the Great Palace, and with it to summon his people.

To the multitude which assembled he issued an appeal for a last effort to keep the Italians from Addis Ababa. He asked every able-bodied man to take up whatever arms he possessed, supply himself with enough food for five days, and march north the next morning against the invader.

The people responded with cries of obedience. "We shall go!" they shouted in chorus.

The Emperor met again that afternoon with twenty-three members of his Council of Ministers while his aides were gathering important documents and loading trucks for the difficult trek into the western mountains. Having considered the plan overnight, the councilors had now developed stronger views about it. Ras Getachu, who was to command the new army on the march north against the Italians, said the men he would have at his disposal were too demoralized to continue the fight. Ras Kassa argued that if the Emperor and his weakened government went west, they would be subjected to attacks not only by the Italians, but also by the rebellious Galla tribesmen. The Emperor should go to Europe, Kassa said, and continue his appeal for help from the great nations which had promised him help under the League Covenant. These nations, despite their disappointing performances to date, were still Ethiopia's only hope for liberation.

Against this viewpoint, Haile Selassie could muster the support of only three councilors. It soon became apparent that the overwhelming majority of the men in front of him, the country's most powerful and influential aristocrats, were not simply advising him; they were telling him his plan was unworkable and they were unwilling to commit either themselves or their supporters to it. By the time this meeting ended, the Emperor realized he had no alternatives. The packing continued, both at the Great Palace and the Little Gibbi, but the destination now changed. The loaded trucks, instead of moving out of the city westward, carried their cargoes of government papers and personal belongings to the railway station.

By two a.m. May 2, Haile Selassie, bowing finally to the pressure not only of the Italians but also of his own wife, his chiefs, and his religious advisers, was ready to take one last look at his home. Surveying all the personal items he must leave behind, he turned to whoever might hear and said, "Take what you please. Sack this ill-fated city, but do not burn the gebbi or a curse will fall on you. I give you all my possessions. Leave nothing for the Italians."[4]

Shortly after this, he and his Empress got into their car, accompanied by their sons and daughters and followed by about thirty high court dignitaries who intended to share their exile. At four a.m., their train, with several cars added to accommodate the Imperial party, pulled out of the station in the direction of Djibuti.

Already, the sack of Addis Ababa had begun. For the next three and a half days, the drunken pillage was to continue as thousands of people, many of them ex-soldiers, took advantage of the absence of authority in a spontaneous attempt to work off the tragedy and frustration of their nation's defeat. Though most foreigners barricaded themselves in their

335

homes, some were caught up in the carnage and fourteen of them died, including Dr. John Melly, the British Red Cross commander, who was shot while trying to care for wounded men in the street. The deaths of these fourteen whites were apparently not the result of any special animosity toward foreigners. Red Cross representative Dr. Marcel Junod estimated that five hundred Ethiopians were also killed during the pillage of the capital. For the duration of this thieving, drinking festival, the random gunfire was so general it endangered everyone in the city.

In the midmorning of May 3, after a thirty-hour journey through the hot desert of eastern Ethiopia and French Somaliland, the Emperor's train reached the safety of Djibuti, where three ranks of French soldiers were waiting to fire a royal salute as he emerged onto the station platform. He was bareheaded and, like the rest of his party, he looked "travel-stained, weary, haggard, and dejected." The Empress wore a heavy veil and appeared to be "overcome by emotion." The French governor general, who was at the station to meet the Emperor and his party, drove with them to his executive mansion, where a luncheon had been prepared.

The following day, May 4, at four-fifteen p.m., Haile Selassie sailed for Jerusalem on the British cruiser *Enterprise*, which had been sent to help him escape at least the ultimate indignity of capture by his nation's conquerors.

After Haile Selassie's escape to Djibuti, Mussolini, on May 3, sent Badoglio a message outlining his formula for restoration of law and order in the ravished capital:

> When Addis Ababa is occupied, Your Excellency will give orders that,
> 1. all those in the city or its surroundings who are caught with arms in hand will be summarily shot; 2. all of the so-called Young Ethiopians [a group of the Emperor's protégés, many of whom had been educated in Europe at his expense], cruel and pretentious barbarians and the moral authors of the sacking of the city, be shot summarily; 3. anyone who participated in violence, sacking, or fires be shot; 4. all those who within 24 hours have not given up their arms and munitions be summarily shot. I await word which will confirm that these orders will be—as always—carried out.

At four p.m. May 5, under heavy rain, Marshal Badoglio made his triumphal entrance into Addis Ababa, which was then already occupied by enough of his troops to make it safe. In front of the Italian Legation, he raised the flag of Italy to signify that Ethiopia was now Italian.

Mussolini that day sent another indication (this one to Graziani) of what life would be like for the Ethiopians now that they were suddenly

Italian: "A foreigner points out to me," Mussolini wrote, "that he saw on April 15 in Massawa a noncommissioned officer of the Royal Navy playing a friendly game of cards with a native. I deplore in the most grave manner these familiarities, and I order that they be avoided. Humanity, yes; promiscuity, no."

On May 9, after Graziani and Badoglio had met at Dire Dawa (a few miles north of Harar) to celebrate the victorious union of Italy's northern and southern armies, Mussolini staged a much bigger celebration in Rome. From his Palazzo Venezia balcony he shouted through amplifiers to the hushed crowd below him:

> Officers! Noncommissioned officers! Soldiers of all the armed forces of the State in Africa and Italy! Black Shirts of the Revolution! Italians at home and throughout the world! Listen to me! . . . Today, May 9, of the fourteenth year of the Fascist era, the fate of Ethiopia is sealed. . . . At last Italy has her empire. A Fascist empire because it bears the indestructible signs of the will and might of the Roman Lictor. . . . An Empire at peace, because Italy wants peace for herself and for everyone. . . . A civilizing empire, humanitarian toward all the peoples of Ethiopia.

Then, after proclaiming two decrees, one of which placed Ethiopia under the sovereignty of the Kingdom of Italy while the other named Italian King Victor Emmanuel III the new Emperor of Ethiopia, he closed his peroration by invoking the memory of ancient Rome.

"Legionnaires! . . . raise high your insignia, your weapons, and your hearts to salute, after fifteen centuries, the reappearance of the empire on the fated hills of Rome. Will you be worthy of it?"

A sibilant chorus of "*Si! Si! Si!*" arose from the crowd.

"Your cry," he concluded, "is a sacred oath that binds you before God and men, for life and death!"

A staccato chorus of "*Duce! Duce! Duce!*" now burst from the frenzied multitude. Mussolini stood silent for some time on his balcony, savoring the greatest moment his career had yet produced, unaware that it was also his last great moment, that he would now begin a steady decline. Though he saw the African victory as the first in a long series which would restore Rome to its ancient pre-eminence, it had actually done nothing for Rome or Italy except temporarily boost Italian egos, including his own. At an exorbitant cost he had conquered an undeveloped country into which he must now continue pouring vast sums of money for development—money badly needed at home—money that would never bring Italy any return.

Mussolini's most notable accomplishment in his Ethiopian venture was his success in exposing and exploiting the weakness and corruption throughout Europe, especially in the governments of England and France, as well as the indifference and cynicism of the United States. The real beneficiary of this accomplishment, however, was not Mussolini but Adolf Hitler, who also gained Mussolini as a sacrificial ally, having learned from him precisely how to handle the moribund governments of the Western democracies. For the next three years, Hitler was to treat England and France exactly the way Mussolini, during the Ethiopian crisis, had taught him to treat them. The whole world knows the result.

At midday May 12, Italy's League of Nations representative Baron Pompeo Aloisi called upon Secretary-General Joseph Avenol in Geneva to state, "with his usual courtesy," that his government had ordered him to withdraw the Italian delegation from the League.

When Avenol asked him exactly what this meant, Aloisi said he was not in a position to explain. His instructions had been brief and he was merely complying with them. As both men knew, Italy's withdrawal was only a protest against Ethiopia's continuing membership.

The League Council, meeting at five p.m. that afternoon, decided that Italy's action provided the occasion for adopting a new resolution, to wit: "The Council, having met to consider the dispute between Italy and Ethiopia . . . is of opinion that further time is necessary to permit its Members to consider the situation created by the grave new steps taken by the Italian Government; [and] decides to resume its deliberations on this subject on June 15th. . . ."

It was Anthony Eden, presiding, who offered this resolution. Among the British and French statesmen who took active parts in Italy's conquest of Ethiopia, he was undoubtedly the most reluctant. Yet he had continued speaking to the very end for those others with whom he later professed strong disagreement. On May 3, the day Emperor Haile Selassie fled the borders of his defeated country, Eden had said in a speech to his constituents at Leamington:

> Many of you tonight, like myself, have your thoughts in Africa. I have only one observation to make about the events of the last seven months in connection with that dispute.
> We had an obligation—a signed covenant obligation—to play our part. We have sought to play that part to the full, and so far as we have done this we have nothing to reproach ourselves with, nothing to apologize for.

In Rome on May 12, Pope Pius XI made clear to the world his feelings about Italy's victory in Ethiopia. During a Catholic press exhibition, he

338

proclaimed the Vatican's satisfaction at "the triumphal happiness of a great and good people in a peace which it hopes and confidently expects will be a prelude to ... new European and world peace."[5]

Haile Selassie arrived in England at Southampton, aboard the liner S.S. *Orford*, June 3, to an embarrassed and minimal reception. No high government officials greeted him. Some would have been content to see him go elsewhere, but he had chosen England as the base from which he would be best able to campaign for his country's liberation. He had already, since leaving Ethiopia, sent the League of Nations two new demands for help (one on May 6, the other on the tenth, from the cruiser *Enterprise* en route to Jerusalem) and he intended to follow these messages with an invocation of his right as a Member to speak before the League Assembly, in a personal appeal to the decency of the other Members.

The British government, to prevent any possible kidnap attempt against him by the Italians, had provided him safe passage from Jerusalem to Gibraltar on the British cruiser *Capetown*, which was coming home from the Orient. At Gibraltar, he had been transferred to the *Orford*, a merchant passenger ship, as a signification that his arrival in England was not under official British auspices. When he reached London, he did not receive the courtesy customarily offered to a visiting monarch. As in Southampton, there was no reception. The people of London, again showing their disagreement with the government over the handling of the Ethiopian crisis, turned out by the thousands to cheer him on his anticipated route to the Ethiopian Embassy at Prince's Gate near Hyde Park. The police shielded him from these supporters by conducting his motorcade along a different route.

Two days after Haile Selassie's arrival in England, Sir Samuel Hoare returned to Prime Minister Stanley Baldwin's Cabinet as First Lord of the Admiralty. As he later recalled, he was "conscious of a feeling" among some of his colleagues that his reinstatement was "premature."[6] He decided, therefore, that he should pick his steps very delicately, "and on no account point to the way in which all my prophecies of the previous December, the conquest of Abyssinia, the consolidation of the Axis and the occupation of the Rhineland had unfortunately come true."

At a dinner in London June 10, honoring Neville Chamberlain, still Chancellor of the Exchequer in the Baldwin Cabinet, one of the speakers remarked that it was time for the sanctions against Italy to be dropped by the League of Nations. "When there is a corpse in your midst," he said, "it is better to bury it."

Chamberlain, rising in agreement, observed that to his way of thinking the continuation—or, even worse, the intensification—of sanctions was "the very midsummer of madness." Chamberlain was, at that time, already the most influential man in the Cabinet and the heir-presumptive to Baldwin's position as Prime Minister.

Foreign Secretary Eden, in a June 18 speech to the House of Commons, clarified for the world the British Cabinet's new public position about sanctions and about Ethiopian independence: "It cannot be expected by anyone," he said, "that the continuance of existing sanctions will restore in Abyssinia the position which had been destroyed; nobody expects that. That position can only be restored by military action. So far as I am aware, no other government, certainly not this government, is prepared to take such military action."

Though Marshal Badoglio had been named Governor General and Viceroy of Ethiopia as soon as he reached Addis Ababa, he had quickly tired of the job and, on May 22, returned to Italy, where he could better enjoy the glory he had accumulated. General (now Marshal) Graziani, who replaced him, received, in early June, two telegrams from Mussolini which reflected the fact that the Italian celebration of peace and victory in May had been premature.

Mussolini decreed, in a June 5 message, "All of the rebels taken prisoners must be shot." On June 8, he wrote, "In order to get finished with the rebels . . . use the gases." But even these measures were ineffective against the growing number of Ethiopians who were finally learning what the Emperor had meant when he pleaded with them, early in the war, to adopt guerrilla methods. On July 8, Mussolini sent Graziani a much stronger prescription against rebellion: "I authorize Your Excellency once again to begin conducting systematically the policy of terror and extermination against the rebels and the accomplice populations. Without the law of tenfold retaliation the wound will not heal quickly enough."

Mussolini was beginning to find out that the Ethiopian people were more difficult to conquer than the Ethiopian armies. The Italian terror was destined to continue, and so was the Ethiopian resistance, which Emperor Haile Selassie, in exile, never ceased to support and encourage.

A crowd described as what seemed like "half the population of Geneva" had gathered around the League of Nations Assembly Hall when, shortly before five p.m. June 30, Emperor Haile Selassie's automobile arrived. He was greeted with a great cheer, which continued until he had followed his official escort into the building. By the time he was led into the large assembly chamber by a member of the Secretariat, the eighteenth plenary meeting of the Assembly had begun, and Anthony Eden, as temporary chairman, was making preliminary announcements. The Emperor took his seat with the Ethiopian delegation almost unobserved. No demonstration greeted his arrival.[7]

The early minutes of the session were devoted to the resignation of Czechoslovakia's Eduard Beneš as Assembly president and the election of Belgium's Paul van Zeeland to succeed him. When van Zeeland took the chair, he read a long communication from Count Galeazzo Ciano, Mussolini's son-in-law and newly appointed Foreign Minister, which was designed to answer in advance any charges Emperor Haile Selassie might make in the speech he was scheduled to deliver that day.

Italy and several other countries had tried but failed to prevent the Emperor from speaking. In the credentials committee, the question was raised of Ethiopia's right to League Membership, now that the country had been conquered by Italy. At the insistence of Yugoslavia, this question, more embarrassing to the League than to Ethiopia, had been quickly dropped. Thereafter, at a steering-committee meeting, Switzerland and Hungary had insisted it would be unwise to permit the Emperor to speak. Britain and France, though perhaps no more eager than any of the Members to hear him, had nevertheless ended the debate by pointing out that it would be even more unwise to try to silence him. His bid to speak had therefore been accepted, and the delegates of all the League Members must now sit listening to him in embarrassment.

After the Italian letter was read, the Argentine representative made a few remarks about the principles of the League, then President van Zeeland turned finally to the day's unpleasant duty. Tacitly acknowledging Italy's claim that its King Victor Emmanuel was now Emperor of Ethiopia, van Zeeland announced, "His Majesty, the Negus Haile Selassie, first delegate of Ethiopia, will address the Assembly."

Dressed in a black cloak over a white tunic, Haile Selassie walked up to the rostrum from his seat on the floor, and with the spotlights turned upon him, began unfolding the pages of his address as the delegates and the people in the galleries applauded mildly.

As the applause died, a great, jeering racket arose from the section of the press gallery reserved for Italian journalists. About a dozen of them, leaping to their feet in unison, shouted and shrieked in the direction of the rostrum. One of them, "a red-faced man with a bull voice," led the others in "execration and abuse" of the little man in front of the microphones. Shaking their fists and setting off mechanical whistles, the

Italians continued their protest despite efforts by colleagues from other countries to silence them. One of the delegates on the floor, Nicolas Titulescu of Rumania, stood up and shouted, "*À la porte les sauvages!*" But the police were slow to react because they were concentrated in the spectators' gallery, where the danger of a demonstration had seemed greater.

When the police did arrive at the press gallery, they handled the offenders "without ceremony." Ten Italian newsmen were grabbed by the collars and escorted outside, where they were promptly arrested. They included the editor of the Turin *Stampa*, the press attaché of the Italian Embassy in Vienna, the general secretary of the Fascist Journalists' Association, the diplomatic correspondent of Mussolini's newspaper, *Il Popolo d'Italia*, and two correspondents for Milan's *Corriere della Sera*. Given the notorious obedience of Italian newsmen to Mussolini, it seemed unlikely that they would have staged such a scene without his authorization.

Emperor Haile Selassie, who had waited impassively for the noise to stop, now spoke in Amharic, while simultaneous interpreters translated his speech into French and English. His listeners, wearing earphones, could select either language by turning a dial.

> I, Haile Selassie the First, Emperor of Ethiopia, am here today to claim that justice that is due to my people, and the assistance promised to it eight months ago by fifty-two nations who asserted that an act of aggression had been committed in violation of international treaties. . . . There is perhaps no precedent for a Head of State himself speaking in this Assembly. But there is certainly no precedent for a people being the victim of such wrongs and being threatened with abandonment to its aggressor. . . . It is to defend a people struggling for its age-old independence that the Head of the Ethiopian Empire has come to Geneva to fulfill this supreme duty, after having himself fought at the head of his armies.
>
> I pray Almighty God that He may spare nations the terrible sufferings that have just been inflicted on my people, and of which the chiefs who have accompanied me here have been the horrified witnesses.
>
> It is my duty to inform the Governments assembled in Geneva, responsible as they are for the lives of millions of men, women and children, of the deadly peril which threatens them, by describing to them the fate which has been suffered by Ethiopia.
>
> It is not only upon warriors that the Italian government has made war. It has, above all, attacked populations far removed from hostilities, in order to terrorize and exterminate them.
>
> At the outset, toward the end of 1935, Italian aircraft hurled tear-gas bombs upon my armies. They had but slight effect. The soldiers learned to scatter, waiting until the wind had rapidly dispersed the poisonous gases.

The Italian aircraft then resorted to mustard gas. Barrels of liquid were hurled upon armed groups. But this means too was ineffective; the liquid affected only a few soldiers, and the barrels upon the ground themselves gave warning of the danger to the troops and to the population.

It was at the time when the operations for the encirclement of Makalle were taking place that the Italian command, fearing a rout, applied the procedure which it is now my duty to denounce to the world.

Sprayers were installed on board aircraft so that they could vaporize, over vast areas of territory, a fine, death-dealing rain. Groups of nine, fifteen, eighteen aircraft followed one another so that the fog issuing from them formed a continuous sheet. It was thus that, from the end of January 1936, soldiers, women, children, cattle, rivers, lakes and fields were constantly drenched with the deadly rain. In order to kill off systematically all living creatures, in order the more surely to poison waters and pastures, the Italian command made its aircraft pass over and over again. That was its chief method of warfare. . . .

These fearful tactics succeeded. Men and animals succumbed. The deadly rain that fell from the aircraft made all those whom it touched fly shrieking with pain. All who drank the poisoned water or ate the infected food succumbed too, in dreadful suffering. In tens of thousands the victims of the Italian mustard gas fell. It was to denounce to the civilized world the tortures inflicted upon the Ethiopian people that I resolved to come to Geneva. None other than myself and my gallant companions in arms could bring the League of Nations undeniable proof. The appeals of my delegates to the League of Nations had remained unanswered; my delegates had not been eyewitnesses. That is why I decided to come myself to testify against the crime perpetrated against my people and to give Europe warning of the doom that awaits it if it bows before the accomplished fact.

After outlining the events which led to the war, he reminded the delegates again of their solemn commitment.

In October 1935, the fifty-two nations who are listening to me today gave me an assurance that the aggressor would not triumph. . . . I ask the fifty-two nations not to forget today the policy upon which they embarked eight months ago, and on the faith of which I directed the resistance of my people against the aggressor. . . . Despite the inferiority of my weapons, the complete lack of aircraft, artillery, munitions and hospital services, my trust in the League was absolute. I thought it impossible that fifty-two nations, including the most powerful in the world, could be successfully held in check by a single aggressor. Relying on the faith due to treaties, I had made no preparation for war, and that is the case with a number of small countries in Europe. When the danger became more urgent, conscious of my responsibilities towards my people, I tried, during the first six months of 1935, to acquire armaments. Many governments proclaimed an embargo to prevent my doing so, whereas the Italian

343

government, through the Suez Canal, was given all facilities for transporting, without cessation and without protest, troops, arms and munitions. ... What real assistance was given to Ethiopia by the fifty-two nations who had declared the Rome government guilty of a breach of the Covenant and had undertaken to prevent the triumph of the aggressor? ... The Ethiopian government never expected other governments to shed their soldiers' blood to defend the Covenant when their own immediately personal interests were not at stake. Ethiopian warriors asked only for means to defend themselves. On many occasions I asked for financial assistance for the purchase of arms. That assistance was constantly denied me. What then, in practice, is the meaning of Article 16 of the Covenant and of collective security? ...

I assert that the issue before the Assembly today is ... not merely a question of a settlement in the matter of Italian aggression. It is a question of collective security; of the very existence of the League; of the trust placed by States in international treaties; of the value of promises made to small States that their integrity and their independence shall be respected and assured. It is a choice between the principle of the equality of States and the imposition upon small Powers of the bonds of vassalage. In a word, it is international morality that is at stake. ...

No subtle reasoning can change the nature of the problem or shift the grounds of the discussion. ... If a strong government finds that it can, with impunity, destroy a weak people, then the hour has struck for that weak people to appeal to the League of Nations to give its judgment in all freedom. God and history will remember your judgment. ...

In presence of the numerous violations by the Italian government of all international treaties prohibiting resort to arms and recourse to barbarous methods of warfare, the initiative has today been taken—it is with pain that I record the fact—to raise sanctions. What does this initiative mean in practice but the abandonment of Ethiopia to the aggressor? ... Is that the guidance that the League of Nations and each of the State Members are entitled to expect from the great Powers when they assert their right and their duty to guide the action of the League? ...

On behalf of the Ethiopian people, a Member of the League of Nations, I ask the Assembly to take all measures proper to secure respect for the Covenant. ... I declare before the whole world that the Emperor, the government and the people of Ethiopia will not bow before force, that they uphold their claims, that they will use all means in their power to insure the triumph of right and respect for the Covenant.

I ask the fifty-two nations who have given the Ethiopian people a promise to help them in their resistance to the aggressor: What are they willing to do for Ethiopia?

I ask the great Powers, who have promised the guarantee of collective security to small States over whom hangs the threat that they must one day suffer the fate of Ethiopia: What measures do they intend to take?

Representatives of the world, I have come to Geneva to discharge in your midst the most painful of the duties of the Head of a State. What answer am I to take back to my people?[8]

On July 6, 1936, a week after Emperor Haile Selassie delivered this final plea for help, the League of Nations voted to suspend all sanctions against Italy.

EPILOGUE

In 1939, three years after Haile Selassie appeared before the Assembly, the arrival of World War II fulfilled his warning against "the deadly peril" which threatened the nations of the League if they abandoned the principle of collective security. In early 1941, after Italy had entered the war on the side of Germany, Haile Selassie returned to his country with a small British expeditionary force. He found that, despite Mussolini's terrorizing methods and the execution of thousands of Ethiopians, there were thousands of others still resisting the Italians. With help from these eager but poorly armed men, the British, though vastly outnumbered by the Italians, were able quickly to defeat them.

On May 5, 1941, five years to the day after the Italians took Addis Ababa, Haile Selassie returned to his capital and resumed his long reign as Emperor of Ethiopia.

NOTES

PART ONE

CHAPTER ONE
1 Cimmaruta, 79 *et seq.*
2 **League of Nations,** *Official Journal,* February 1935, 252 *et seq.* June 1935, 750–59.
3 Cimmaruta, 110 *et seq.*
4 Yilma, 269.
5 A written protest against the continuing Italian presence at Wal Wal, delivered to the Italian Ministry in Addis Ababa on the afternoon of December 6, does not mention the previous day's fighting there, which could only mean the Emperor did not yet know about the battle.
6 Telegram, Barton to Simon, December 6, 1934.
7 Virgin, 139.
8 Telegram, Simon to Barton, December 8, 1934.

CHAPTER TWO
1 Schuschnigg, 115, 220, 238.
2 Lessona, 165–71. De Bono, 116.
3 Herriot, 402–403.
4 "Procès du Maréchal Pétain," 184.
5 Cameron in *The Diplomats . . .,* 384.
6 *Il Popolo d'Italia,* January 7, 1935.
7 Tissier, 29–58.
8 Mallet, I, 69.
9 **France,** Chambre des Députés débats, December 29, 1935, 2863–66.
10 Cameron in *The Diplomats . . .,* 385.
11 Carmine Senise, "Quando ero capo della polizia," 37.
12 De Bono, *Anno XIII,* 56 *et seq.*
13 *Ibid.,* 13.

CHAPTER THREE
1 Hoare, 124.
2 Earl of Avon, 193.
3 Kathleen Simon, *Slavery,* Hodder & Stoughton, London, 1929.
4 Telegram, Drummond to Simon, January 14, 1935.
5 Telegram, Barton to Simon, January 17, 1935.
6 Eden, 197.
7 **League of Nations,** "Report on Slavery in Ethiopia," May 22, 1935.
8 Farago, *Abyssinia on the Eve,* 31 *et seq.*

9 *The New York Times*, March 4, 1935.
10 Farago, *Abyssinia on the Eve*, 86 *et seq.*

CHAPTER FOUR
 1 Guariglia, 226–27.
 2 Thompson, 96 *et seq.*
 3 *Ibid.*, 97–98.
 4 Guariglia, 781–82.
 5 Colvin, 60–61.
 6 Flandin, 178.
 7 Aloisi, 266.
 8 Mussolini, *Opera omnia*, XXVII 140.

CHAPTER FIVE
 1 Guariglia, 230–32.
 2 *Ibid.*, 232–34.
 3 *Ibid.*, 236 *et seq.*
 4 "Documents on German Foreign Policy, 1918–1945," United States Government Printing Office, 1959–1962, IV, 209, 231–32.
 5 Hoare, 108. Feiling, 264.
 6 Hoare, 150–52.
 7 *Ibid.*, 154.
 8 Vansittart, *The Mist Procession*, 530–31.
 9 Aloisi, 280. Eden, 231.
10 Aloisi, 280. Toscano, 126 *et seq.*
11 Collier quoting Mario Panza, 121 *et seq.* Eden, 221 *et seq.*
12 Toscano, 129.
13 Collier quoting Mario Panza, 122.
14 Aloisi, 282.
15 Toscano, 146 *et seq.*
16 Eden, 230 *et seq.*
17 Telegrams 385–86, Moreno Pignatti to Mussolini, June 28, 1935.

CHAPTER SIX
 1 Telegrams, George to Hull, July 4 and 15, 1935.
 2 Telegram, George to Hull, December 19, 1935.
 3 Telegram, Hull to George, December 21, 1935.
 4 Hull, 419–20.
 5 Telegram, George to Hull, July 15, 1935.
 6 Hull, 420–21.
 7 Telegram, Hull to Robert Bingham, United States Ambassador to Great Britain July 11, 1935.
 8 Hull, 420.
 9 Salvamini, 237.
10 De Bono, 181.
11 Dall'Ora, 217.
12 Hoare, 160.
13 *The New York Times*, July 19, 1935.
14 Steer, 43.
15 Hoare to Bingham, "United States Diplomatic Papers, 1935," I, 613.
16 United States, Department of Defense, G-2 report, London, July 17, 1935.
17 Charles-Roux, 135. *Le Temps*, Paris, July 12, 1935.

18 Eden, 245.
19 *Ibid.*, 247.
20 Potter, 16.
21 *Paris-Soir*, September 4, 1935.
22 Guariglia, 250.
23 Salvemini, 255–56.
24 *Corriere d'informazione*, Milan, January 14–17, 1946.
25 Chambrun, 218–19.
26 Aloisi, 292–94.
27 Vansittart, *The Mist Procession*, 531.
28 Eden, 253.
29 *The New York Times*, August 29, 1935. Charles-Roux, 139–40.
30 Telegram, Hoare to Lindsay, August 17, 1935. Hull, 421–22.
31 Waugh, 56–58.
32 *The New York Times*, September 1, 1935.
33 Hull, 423–25.
34 Telegram, Engert to Hull, September 4, 1935.
35 Hull, 424–25.

CHAPTER SEVEN
1 Hoare, 169.
2 *Ibid.*, 167.
3 *The New York Times*, September 12, 1935.
4 Aloisi, 303.
5 Konovaloff, *History of Ethiopia*, 307.
6 Steer, 130.
7 De Bono, 216.
8 Interview, February 9, 1972 in Addis Ababa, with a former Italian soldier who insisted that he remain anonymous.

PART TWO

CHAPTER EIGHT
1 De Bono, 228.
2 London *Daily Mirror*, October 3, 1935.
3 Steer, 135.
4 Konovaloff, *Con le armate . . .*, 51.
5 Vittorio Mussolini, 26.
6 Eden, 273.
7 Amery, III, 174.
8 *The New York Times*, October 3, 1935.
9 Ickes, 450.
10 Hull, 428–31.
11 Steer, 63.
12 Fred Abel, interviewed in Addis Ababa, February 16, 1972
13 Lessona, 184–85.
14 De Bono, 92.
15 De Bono, *Confidential Diary*, October 10, 11, 12, 1935.
16 De Bono, 262.
17 *The New York Times*, October 13, 1935.

CHAPTER NINE
1 *The New York Times*, October 18, 1935. Steer, 153.
2 Fred Abel, interviewed in Addis Ababa, February 16, 1972.
3 *The New York Times*, October 16, 1935.
4 *Ibid.*, October 14, 1935.
5 *Ibid.*, October 9, 1935.
6 *Ibid.*, October 19, 1935.
7 Telegram, Straus to State Department, October 29, 1935.
8 United States, Department of Defense, report from Rome, November 1, 1935.
9 *The New York Times*, November 17, 1935. Matthews, 123–48.
10 De Bono, *Confidential Diary*, November 16, 1935.
11 Caviglia, 135.
12 Lessona, 190.
13 *Ibid.*, 221.

CHAPTER TEN
1 Stuart Emeny in Farago, *Abyssinia Stop Press*, 189.
2 Eden, 298.
3 Vansittart, *The Mist Procession*, 538–40.
4 Eden, 302.
5 Steer, 207.
6 Vittorio Mussolini, 47 *et seq.*
7 Imru to Angelo Del Boca, in interview, April 13, 1965.
8 Badoglio, 23.
9 Steer, 207.
10 Colvin, 74 *et seq.*
11 Ickes, 483–84.
12 *The New York Times*, December 15, 1935.
13 *Manchester Guardian*, December 11, 1935.
14 Kirkpatrick, 329.
15 Eden, 317.
16 United States, Department of Defense, report from United States Military Attaché, Rome, January 3, 1936.
17 Telegram, Mussolini to Graziani, December 16, 1935.
18 Imru to Angelo Del Boca, interview, April 13, 1965.

CHAPTER ELEVEN
1 League of Nations, Document c. 207.M.129, May 7, 1936. Junod, 33–36.
2 League of Nations, *Official Journal*, April 1936, 406 *et seq.*
3 General Emilio Faldella in "Storia Illustrata," May 1963, 633.
4 Orano, 16.
5 Sandro Volta in *Con l'esercito . . .*, I, 269.
6 Badoglio, 56.
7 Haile Selassie I, "Une victoire de la civilisation," 37.
8 Paolo Monelli in "Storia Illustrata," May 1963, 651.

CHAPTER TWELVE
1 Tomaselli, 127.
2 Clarissa Burgoyne in *Ethiopia Observer*, XI, No. 4, 322.
3 Vittorio Mussolini, 73.
4 Dr. George Dassios, interviewed, Addis Ababa, February 17, 1972.
5 Macfie, 79.

6 *Corriere della Sera*, Milan, March 3, 1936.
7 Imru to Angelo Del Boca, April 13, 1965.
8 *Con l'esercito . . .*, II, 406–407.
9 Shirer, 358–66.

CHAPTER THIRTEEN
1 Melly in Nelson and Sullivan, 217–18, 223, 243. Macfie, 86–92, plus photos 19–22.
  League of Nations, Document C.201.M.126, May 9, 1936, photos 1–25, Appendix
  9.
2 League of Nations, Document C.201.M.126, May 9, 1936, 22–23. Junod, 41–47.
3 Colonel Kosrof Boghossian to Angelo Del Boca, April 15, 1965.
4 Tomaselli, 201.
5 Haile Selassie I, *La vérité sur la guerre . . .*, 40–43.
6 Tomaselli, 211.
7 *Ibid.*, 218–19.
8 Haile Selassie I, *La vérité sur la guerre . . .*, 45–48.

CHAPTER FOURTEEN
1 Konovaloff, *Con le armate . . .*, 188 *et seq.*
2 Report from United States Military Attaché, Rome, May 4, 1936.
3 Steer, 356.
4 Pierre Itchac in *l'Illustration*, July 1936, 200. Konovaloff, *Con le armate . . .*, 210.
5 *Il Giornale d'Italia*, May 13, 1936.
6 Hoare, 202.
7 *The New York Times*, July 1, 1936.
8 League of Nations, Records of the Eighteenth Plenary Meeting of the Assembly,
  June 30, 1936, Special Supplement 151, 22–25.

BIBLIOGRAPHY

BOOKS

Allen, W. E. D. *Guerrilla War in Abyssinia*. London: Penguin, 1943.
Aloisi, Pompeo. *Journal, 25 juillet 1932–14 juin 1936*. Translated by M. Vaussard. Paris: Librairie Plon, 1957.
Amery, Leopold S. *My Political Life*. 3 vols. London: Hutchinson, 1953–5.
Attlee, Clement R. *As It Happened*. New York: Viking, 1954; London: Heinemann, 1954.
Avon, Earl of. *The Eden Memoirs: Facing the Dictators*. Boston: Houghton, 1962; London: Cassell, 1962.
Badoglio, Pietro. *The War in Abyssinia*. New York: Putnam, 1937; London: Methuen, 1937.
Baer, George W. *The Coming of the Italian-Ethiopian War*. Cambridge: Harvard, 1967; London: Oxford, 1967.
Baldini, Mario. *Italiani in Africa*. Milan: Longanesi, 1972.
Baldwin, A. W. *My Father: The True Story*. Fair Lawn, New Jersey: Essential Books, 1955; London: George Allen & Unwin, 1955.
Baldwin, Stanley. *This Torch of Freedom*. London: Hodder and Stoughton, 1935.
Baraduc, Jacques. *Pierre Laval devant la mort*. Paris: Librairie Plon, 1970.
Bardens, Dennis. *Portrait of a Statesman* [Anthony Eden]. New York: Philosophical Library, 1956; London: Muller, 1956.
Barker, A. J. *The Civilizing Mission*. New York: Dial, 1968; London: Cassell, 1968.
Barnes, James S. *Half a Life Left*. London: Eyre, 1933; New York: Coward-McCann, 1937.
Barros, James. *Betrayal from Within—Joseph Avenol*. New Haven and London: Yale, 1969.
Baskerville, Beatrice. *What Next, O Duce?* London: Longmans, Green, 1937.
Bastico, Ettore. *Il ferreo Terzo Corpo in Africa Orientale*. Milan: Mondadori, 1937.
Bastin, Jean. *L'affaire d'Ethiopie et les diplomates (1934–1937)*. Brussels: L'Edition universelle, 1938.
Beard, Charles A. *American Foreign Policy in the Making, 1932–40: A Study in Responsibilities*. New Haven: Yale, 1946; London: Oxford, 1947.
Benelli, Sem. *Io in Africa*. Milan: Mondadori, 1936.
Beonio-Brocchieri, Vittorio. *Cieli d'Etiopia*. Milan: Mondadori, 1936.

Berhanu Denge. *Kawalwal Eska Maychew*. ["From Wal Wal to Mai Chew"]. Addis Ababa: Ethiopian Government Publication, 1942.

Bianchi, Gianfranco. *Rivelazioni sul conflitto italo-etiopico*. Milan: CEIS, 1967.

Binchy, Daniel A. *Church and State in Fascist Italy*. London: Oxford, 1941.

Borchard, Edwin, and Lage, William P. *Neutrality for the United States*. New Haven: Yale, 1940.

Bottai, Giuseppe. *Vent'anni e un gioron*. Rome: Garzanti, 1949.

Broad, Lewis. *Sir Anthony Eden*. New York: Crowell, 1955; London: Hutchinson, 1955.

Burns, James MacGregor. *Roosevelt—The Lion and the Fox*. New York: Harcourt, Brace, 1956.

Caioli, Aldo. *L'Italia di fronte a Ginevra*. Rome: Volpe, 1965.

Campbell-Johnson, Alan. *Eden: The Making of a Statesman*. New York: Washburn, 1955.

Cameron, E. R. "Alexis Saint-Léger Léger," in *The Diplomats, 1919–1939*. Princeton, N.J.: Princeton University Press, 1953; London: Oxford.

Castelli, Giulio. *Il Vaticano nci tentacoli del fascismo*. Rome: DeLuigi, 1946.

Caviglia, Enrico. *Diario, aprile 1925–marzo 1945*. Rome: Casini, 1952.

Cecil, Lord Robert. *A Great Experiment*. New York: Oxford, 1941; London: Cape, 1941.

Chaplin, William W. *Blood and Ink*. New York: Telegraph Press, 1936.

Charles-Roux, François. *Huit ans au Vatican, 1932–1940*. Paris: Flammarion, 1947.

Ciasca, Raffaele. *Storia coloniale dell'Italia contemporanea*. Milan: Hoepli, 1940.

Cimmaruta, Roberto. *Ual Ual*. Milan: Mondadori, 1936.

Clonmore, Lord. *Pope Pius XI and World Peace*. London: Hale, 1937; New York: Dutton, 1938.

Collier, Richard. *Duce!* New York: Viking, 1971.

Colvin, Ian. *Vansittart in Office*. London: Gollancz, 1965.

Con l'esercito Italiano in Africa Orientale. 2 vols. Milan: Mondadori, 1936–7.

Currey, Muriel Innes. *A Woman at the Abyssinian War*. London: Hutchinson, 1936.

Dall'Ora, Fidenzio. *Intendenza in Africa Orientale*. Rome: Istituto nazionale fascista di cultura, 1937.

Deakin, Frederick W. *Brutal Friendship*. New York: Harper, 1963.

De Bono, Emilio. *Anno XIII*. Translated by B. Miall. London: Cresset, 1937.

de Chambrun. *Traditions et souvenirs*. Paris: Flammarion, 1952.

de la Pradelle, A. *Le conflit Italo-Ethiopien*. Paris: Editions Internationales, 1936.

Del Boca, Angelo. *The Ethiopian War*. Chicago: University of Chicago Press, 1969.

Dell, Robert, *The Geneva Racket, 1920–1939*. London: Hale, 1940; New York: Transatlantic, 1943.

Del Valle, Pedro Augusto. *Roman Eagles over Ethiopia*. Harrisburg, Pa.: Military Service Publishing Company, 1940.

de Sanctis, Gino. *La Mia Africa*. Milan: Mondadori, 1938.

Durand, Mortimer. *Crazy Campaign*. London: Routledge, 1936.

Eden, Anthony. See Avon, Earl of.

Farago, Ladislas. *Abyssinia on the Eve*. New York: Putnam, 1935.
———. *Abyssinia Stop Press*. London: Hale, 1936.
Feiling, Keith. *The Life of Neville Chamberlain*. London: Macmillan, 1946.
Feis, Herbert. *Three International Episodes*. New York: Norton, 1936.
Fermi, Laura. *Mussolini*. Chicago: University of Chicago Press, 1961.
Flandin, Pierre-Etienne. *Politique française, 1919–1940*. Paris: Nouvelles, 1947.
Fuller, John F. C. *The First of the League Wars*. London: Eyre & Spottiswoode, 1936.
Gamelin, Maurice. *Servir: Le Prologue du drame 1930–août 1939*. Paris: Librairie Plon, 1946.
Garratt, G. T. *Mussolini's Roman Empire*. Indianapolis, Ind.: Bobbs, 1938; London: Penguin, 1938.
Gentizon, Paul. *La Conquête de l'Ethiopie*. Paris: Berger-Levrault, 1936.
———. *La Revanche d'Adoua*. Paris: Berger-Levrault, 1936.
Gingold-Duprey, A. *De l'invasion à la libération de l'Ethiopie*. Paris: Dupont, 1955.
Goiffon, Paul. *Les clauses coloniales dans les accords franco-italiens de 7 janvier 1935*. Lyons: Rion, 1936.
Gorham, Charles. *The Lion of Judah*. New York: Farrar, Straus & Giroux, 1966; Rexdale, Ontario: Ambassador, 1966.
Graham, Robert A. *Vatican Diplomacy: A Study of the Church and State on the International Plane*. Princeton, N.J.: Princeton University Press, 1959; London: Oxford, 1960.
Graziani, Rodolfo. *Il Fronte Sud*. Milan: Mondadori, 1938.
Griaule, Marcel. *La peau de l'ours*. Paris: Gallimard, 1936.
Guariglia, Raffaele. *Ricordi, 1922–1946*. Naples: Edizioni Scientifiche Italiane, 1950
Haile Selassie I. *La vérité sur la guerre Italo-Ethiopienne*. Translated from the Amharic by Marcel Griaule. Paris: Impr. Française, 1936. Published also as a supplement to *Vu*, Paris, 1936, under the title "Une victoire de la civilisation."
Hamilton, Edward. *The War in Abyssinia*. London: John Heritage, 1936.
Harris, Brice, Jr. *United States and the Italo-Ethiopian Crisis*. Palo Alto, Calif.: Stanford University Press, 1964.
Haskell, Daniel C. *Ethiopia and the Italo-Ethiopian Conflict*. New York: Bull (New York Public Library), 1936.
Henson, Herbert H. *Abyssinia: Reflections of an Onlooker*. London: Hugh Rees, 1936.
Herriot, Edouard. *Jadis, II: D'une guerre à l'autre, 1914–1936*. Paris: Flammarion, 1952.
Highley, Albert E. *Actions of State Members of League in Application of Sanctions*. Geneva: Imprimature du Journal du Genève, 1938.
Hoare, Sir Samuel (Viscount Templewood). *Nine Troubled Years*. London: Collins, 1954.
Hubbard, Wynant D. *Fiasco in Ethiopia*. New York: Harper, 1936.
Hull, Cordell. *Memoirs*. New York: Macmillan, 1948; London: Hodder, 1948.

Ickes, Harold L. *The Secret Diary of . . .* , Vol. I: *The First Thousand Days, 1933–1936.* New York: Simon and Schuster, 1953; London: Weidenfeld, 1955.

Jemolo, Arturo Carlo. *Chiesa e stato in Italia dalla unificazione a Giovanni XXIII.* Turin: Einaudi, 1965.

Johnson, A. G. C. *Anthony Eden.* London: Hale, 1938.

Jones, A. H. M., and Monroe, Elizabeth. *History of Abyssinia.* London: Oxford, 1935.

Julian, Hubert Fauntleroy. *The Black Eagle.* London: Jarrolds, 1964

Junod, Dr. Marcel. *Warrior Without Weapons.* New York: Macmillan, 1951; London: Cape, 1951.

Kabadda Tasamma. *Yatarik Mastawasha* ["Historical Memoirs"]. Translated by Makonnen Terere. Addis Ababa, 1962.

Kirkpatrick, Ivone. *Mussolini: A Study in Power.* New York: Hawthorn, 1964; London: Odhams, 1964 (under the title *Mussolini: Study of a Demagogue*).

Konovaloff, Theodore E. *Con le armate del negus.* Bologna: Zanichellie, 1936.

———. *History of Ethiopia.* Unpublished. Typescript in Hoover Library, Palo Alto, Calif.

Koren, William. *The Italian-Ethiopian Dispute.* (In cooperation with the Foreign Policy Association.) Geneva Special Studies, VI, 4. Geneva Research Council, 1935.

Laurens, Franklin D. *France and the Italo-Ethiopian Crisis.* Paris: Mouton, 1967.

Laval, Pierre. *Diary with a Preface by Josée Laval.* New York: Scribner, 1948; London: Falcon Press, 1948 (under the title *Unpublished Diary of . . .*).

Lessona, Allessandro. *Memorie.* Florence: Sansoni, 1958.

Macfie, John W. S. *An Ethiopian Diary.* Liverpool: Liverpool University Press, 1936

MacLean, Robinson. *John Hoy of Ethiopia.* New York: Farrar & Rinehart, 1936.

Makin, William J. *War Over Ethiopia.* London: Jarrolds, 1935.

Mallet, Alfred. *Pierre Laval.* 2 vols. Paris: Dumont, 1955.

Mariotti, Delio. *In armi sulle Ambe.* Milan: La Prora, 1937.

Martelli, George. *Italy Against the World.* London: Chatto & Windus, 1937; New York: Harcourt, Brace, 1938.

Matthews, Herbert. *Eyewitness in Abyssinia.* London: Martin, Secker & Warburg, 1937.

McCormick, Anne O'Hare. *Vatican Journal, 1921–1954.* New York: Farrar, Straus and Cudahy, 1957.

Millis, Walter. *Why Europe Fights.* New York: Morrow, 1940.

Monfried, Henri de. *Le Drame Etiopien.* Paris: B. Grasset, 1935.

Montanelli, Indro. *XX Battaglione Eritreo.* Milan: Panorama, 1936.

Mosley, Leonard. *Haile Selassie: The Conquering Lion.* London: Weidenfeld & Nicholson, 1964; Englewood Cliffs, N.J.: Prentice-Hall, 1965.

Mussolini, Benito. *My Autobiography.* Translated by Richard Washburn Child. New York: Scribner, 1928; London: Hutchinson, 1928.

———. *Opera omnia.* Edited by E. and D. Susmel. 36 vols. Florence: Casa Editrice La Fenice, 1951–63.

Mussolini, Vittorio. *Voli sulle Ambe.* Florence: Sansoni, 1937.

Nelson, Kathleen, and Sullivan, Alan. *John Melly of Ethiopia*. London: Faber and Faber, 1937.

Nesbitt, L. M. *Desert and Forest: The Exploration of Abyssinian Danakil*. London: Cape, 1934; New York: Knopf, 1935 (under the title *Hell-hole of Creation*).

Newman, E. W. Polson. *Italy's Conquest of Abyssinia*. London: Thornton Butterworth, 1937.

Orano, Paolo. *Rodolfo Graziani, generale scipione*. Rome: Pinciana, 1936.

Pankhurst, E. Sylvia. *Ex-Italian Somaliland*. New York: Philosophical Library, 1951; London: Watts, 1951.

———. *Ethiopia: A Cultural History*. Essex, England: Woodford Green, 1955.

Pavolini, Alessandro. *Disperata*. Florence: Vallecchi, 1937.

Pesenti, Gustavo. *La Prima Divisione Eritrea alla battaglia dell'Ascianghi*. Milan: L'Eroica, 1937.

Peterson, Maurice. *Both Sides of the Curtain*. London: Constable, 1950; New York: Macmillan, 1951.

Pigli, Mario. *Etiopia, l'incognita africana*. Padua: Cedam, 1935.

Pignatelli, Luigi. *La Guerra dei sette mesi*. Naples: Mezzogiorno, 1961.

Pobers, Michel. *L'Ethiopie et des puissances* (Textes Diplomatiques). Geneva: Genève-Informations, 1935.

Potter, Pitman B. *The Wal Wal Arbitration*. Washington, D.C.: Carnegie Endowment for International Peace, 1938; New York: Columbia University Press, 1938.

Puglisi, Guiseppe. *Chi è dell'Eritrea?* Asmara: Regina Agency, 1952.

Ridley, Francis A. *Mussolini Over Africa*. London: Wishart, 1935.

Rochat, Giorgio. *Militari e politici nella preparazione della campagna d'Etiopia*. Milan: Franco Angeli, 1971.

Roghi, Bruno. *Tessere verde in Africa Orientale*. Milan: Ed. Elettra, 1936.

Rossi, Francesco. *Mussolini e lo stato maggiore*. Rome: Tipografia Regionale, 1951.

Ruggero, Zangrandi. *Il lungo viaggio attraverso il fascismo*. Milan: Feltrinelli, 1962.

Salvemini, Gaetano. *Prelude to World War II*. London: Gollancz, 1953; New York: Doubleday, 1954.

Sandford, Christine. *Ethiopia Under Haile Selassie*. London: Dent, 1946.

———. *The Lion of Judah Hath Prevailed*. London: Dent, 1955.

Sandri, Sandro. *Sei mesi di guerra sul Fronte Somalo*. Anconia, Italy: Bertarelli, 1936.

Schaefer, Ludwig F. *The Ethiopian Crisis: Touchstone of Appeasement?* Boston: Heath, 1961; London: Harrap, 1961.

Schuschnigg, Kurt von. *Ein Requiem in Rot-Weiss-Rot*. Zurich: Amstutz, Herdeg, 1946.

Shirer, William L. *The Rise and Fall of the Third Reich*. New York: Simon and Schuster, 1960; London: Secker & Warburg, 1960.

Simon, Sir John. *Retrospect*. London: Hutchinson, 1952.

Slocombe, George. *A Mirror to Geneva*. London: Cape, 1937; New York: Holt, 1938.

Stanco, Francesco. *Epitome di cultura fascista*. Turin, 1936.

Starace, Achille. *La marcia su Gondar*. Milan: Mondadori, 1936.

Starhemberg, Prince Ernst. *Between Hitler and Mussolini*. New York: Harper, 1942; London: Hodder & Stoughton, 1942.

Steer, George. *Caesar in Abyssinia*. London: Hodder & Stoughton, 1936; Boston: Little, Brown, 1937.

Stevenson, Frances. *Lloyd George*. New York: Harper & Row, 1972.

Taylor, A. J. P. *The Origins of the Second World War*. London: Hamish Hamilton, 1961; New York: Atheneum, 1962.

Teeling, L. William. *The Pope in Politics*. London: Dickson, 1937.

Thompson, Geoffrey. *Front-Line Diplomat*. London: Hutchinson, 1959.

Tissier, Pierre. *I Worked with Laval*. London: Harrap, 1942.

Tomaselli, Cesco. *Con le colonne celeri dal Mareb allo Scioa*. Milan: Mondadori, 1936.

Toynbee, Arnold J. *Survey of International Affairs, 1935*. Vol. II. London: Oxford, 1936.

Ullendorff, Edward. *The Ethiopians*. London: Oxford, 1960.

Vansittart, Sir Robert. *Lessons of My Life*. New York: Knopf, 1943; London: Hutchinson, 1943.

————. *The Mist Procession*. London: Hutchinson, 1958.

Vecchi, B. V. *Il crollo dell impero del leone di Guida*. Milan: Bietti, 1936.

Villari, Luigi. *Italy, Abyssinia and the League*. Rome: Dante Alighieri Society, 1936.

————. *Storia diplomatica del conflitto Italo-Etiopico*. Bologna: Zanichellie, 1943.

Virgin, Eric. *The Abyssinia I Knew*. Translated by N. Walford. London: Macmillan, 1936.

Vitali, Giovanni. *Le guerre Italiane in Africa*. Milan: Sonzogno, 1936.

Volta, Sandro. *Graziani a Neghelli*. Florence: Vallecchi, 1936.

Warner, Geoffrey. *Pierre Laval and the Eclipse of France*. London: Eyre & Spottiswoode, 1968; New York: Macmillan, 1969.

Waugh, Evelyn. *Waugh in Abyssinia*. London: Longmans, Green, 1936.

Whitaker, John T. *And Fear Came*. New York: Macmillan, 1936; London: Hamish Hamilton, 1937 (under the title *Fear Came on Europe*).

Wienholt, Arnold. *The African's Last Stronghold*. London: John Long, 1938.

Wilson, Hugh R., Jr. *For Want of a Nail: The Failure of the League of Nations in Ethiopia*. New York: Vantage, 1960.

Woolf, Leonard. *The League and Abyssinia*. London: Hogarth Press, 1936.

Work, Ernest. *Ethiopia: A Pawn in European Diplomacy*. New Concord, Ohio: privately printed, 1935.

Wrench, John Evelyn. *Geoffrey Dawson and Our Times*. London: Hutchinson, 1955.

Xylander, Rudolf. *La conquista dell'Abissinia*. Milan: Treves, 1937.

Yilma, Princess Asfa. *Haile Selassie, Emperor of Ethiopia*. New York: Appleton-Century-Crofts, 1936; London: Sampson, Low & Marston, 1936.

Zoli, Corrado. *La conquista dell'impero*. Bologna: Zanichellie, 1937.

Ethiopia

Documents on Italian War Crimes. 2 vols. Ministry of Justice, Addis Ababa, 1949–50.

Liberation Silver Jubilee. 2 vols. Edited by David A. Talbot. Ministry of Information, Addis Ababa, 1964–6.

France

Chambre des Députés. *Journal officiel, débats parliamentaires.* Paris, 1935–6.

Haute Cour de Justice. Procès du Maréchal Pétain. Paris, 1945.

Ministère des Affaires Etrangères. Documents diplomatiques français, 1932–1939, 2nd series.

Great Britain

Documents Relating to the Dispute between Ethiopia and Italy. His Majesty's Stationery Office, London, 1935.

Documents on British Foreign Policy, 1919–1939. Edited by E. L. Woodward, R. Butler, *et al.* London, 1950–7.

Foreign Office. Correspondence and documents relating to the dispute between Ethiopia and Italy. Located in the Foreign Office file, Public Records Office, London.

House of Commons. Parliamentary Debates: Official Report for 1935–6.

Italy

Annali dell'Africa Italiana. March 1939, Vol. II, No. 1. Mondadori, Rome.

La Campagne 1935–1936 in Africa Orientale. Vol. I. Rome.

Comando del Forze della Somalia. *La Guerra italo-etiopico : Fronte sud.* 4 vols. Rome.

Ministero degli Affari Esteri. *Documenti diplomatici.* 7th series (1922–35), I–IV, R. Moscati, ed., Rome, 1953–62.

Istituto per gli Studi di Politica Internazionale. *Il Conflitto italo-etiopica : Documenti.* 2 vols. Milan, 1936.

League of Nations

Official Journal, February 1935 through June 1936. Debates and documents relating to the dispute between Ethiopia and Italy.

Special Supplements 138 and 145 through 151. Sections dealing with the dispute between Ethiopia and Italy.

Records of the Eighteenth Plenary Meeting of the Assembly, June 30, 1936. Special Supplement 151, beginning page 17.

"Report on Slavery in Ethiopia." Published May 22, 1935, Geneva.

United States

Department of Defense. Military Attaché reports and G-2 reports from Rome, London, and Addis Ababa, 1935–6. Located in National Archives, Washington.

Department of State. Diplomatic Correspondence pertaining to Italo-Ethiopian Conflict. With special emphasis on File 765.84. National Archives, Washington.

Department of State. Foreign Relations of the United States: Diplomatic Papers. The Near East, Africa, 1935. The British Commonwealth, Europe, 1935. Washington, 1951–3.

Department of State. Peace and War: United States Foreign Policy, 1931–41. Washington, 1943.

De Bono, Marshal Emilio. *Confidential Diary*. Notebook 39. Beginning 14 September, 1935. (As published in Gianfranco Bianchi, *Rivelazioni . . .*, 95 *et seq.*)

Mussolini, Benito. Telegrams to military commanders in East Africa between February 26, 1935, and July 8, 1936, as published in *Il Giorno*, Milan, November 11–21, 1968.

ARTICLES

Angell, Norman. "The Politics and Morals of Mustard Gas, Today and Tomorrow," *Time and Tide*, London, 1936.

Arnold, A. C. "Italo-Abyssinian Campaign." *Royal United Service Institution Journal*, London, February 1937, 71–88.

Askew, William C. "The Secret Agreement between France and Italy on Ethiopia, January 1935," *Journal of Modern History*, 25: 47–8, March 1953.

Bidou, Henry. "La Conquête de l'Ethiopie," *Revue des deux Mondes*, Paris, 1936. Period 8, Tome 33, 880–913.

Braddick, H. "A New Look at American Policy during the Italo-Ethiopian Crisis, 1935–1936," *Journal of Modern History*, March 1962, 34: 64–73.

Castellani, Sir Aldo. "Hygienic Measures and Hospital Organization of the Ethiopian Expeditionary Forces," *Journal of the Royal Society of Arts*, London, May 27, 1938. Vol. 86, 675–89.

Clifford, E. H. M. "The British Somaliland–Ethiopia Boundary," *Geographical Journal*, April 1936. 87: 289–302.

Fredo, Michael A. "Observations of an Italo-American in Connection with the Italo–Ethiopian Conflict," *Boston Sunday Globe*, January 26, 1936.

Lloyd, H. P. "The Italo-Abyssinian War, the Operations: Massawa–Addis Ababa," *R.A.F. Quarterly*, London, 1937. Vol. VIII, 357–67.

Melly, John M. "Ethiopia and the War from the Ethiopian Point of View," *International Affairs*, January–February 1936. 15: 103–21.

Pankhurst, Richard. "The Ethiopian Army of Former Times," *Ethiopia Observer*, 1963. 7: 118–43.

Toscano, Mario. "Eden's Mission to Rome on the Eve of the Italo-Ethiopian Conflict," *Studies in Diplomatic History*, London, 1961. 126–52.

Watteville, H. de. "Italy and Abyssinia," *Army Quarterly*, London, 1936.

NEWSPAPERS AND MAGAZINES

The New York Times
New York *Mirror*
Boston Globe
The Times (London)
London *Daily Telegraph*
London *News-Chronicle*
London *Daily Mail*

London *Morning Post*
London *Daily Express*
London *Daily Herald*
Ethiopia Observer, Addis Ababa
Il Giornale d'Italia, Rome
Il Popolo d'Italia, Rome
Corriere della Sera, Milan
London *Daily Mirror*
London *Evening Standard*
Manchester *Guardian*
Le Temps, Paris
Paris-Soir
L'Osservatore romano, Vatican City
L'Illustration, Paris, Special edition on Italo-Ethiopian War, July 1936.

PUBLIC ADDRESSES

Meriwether, Lee. "Italy's Seizure of Ethiopia: Does It Merit Censure or Approval?" Delivered at Church of the Messiah, St. Louis, and published by Domus Italica, St. Louis, 1935.

Varè, Daniele. "Italy, Great Britain and the League in the Italian-Ethiopian Conflict." Delivered over NBC September 16, 1935, and published by Unione Italiana d'America, New York, 1935.

INDEX

Abaro Pass, 280
Abbi Addi, 255, 270, 278, 279, 294, 295; battle of, 260-1
Abdel Mohsein El Wishy, 266
Acab Saat, 300
Addis Ababa, *passim*: description of, 45-50; foreign press corps in, 51-5; Imperial Guard parades, 107-8, 150, 189; special session of Parliament (July 1935), 109-10; heavy rains, 148, 149; war fever in, 148-50, 189-91; army leaves for front, 189-91; Emperor leaves, 219, 233; Emperor re-enters, 332-4; he leaves again, 335; sack of, 335-6; Italian occupation, 336-337; Emperor's victorious return, 346
Addis Ababa-Djibuti railroad, 29, 30, 93, 226
Adi Quala, 262, 264, 299
Adi Ugri, 182
Adigrat, 164, 174, 180, 185, 191, 212, 213, 239
Ado, 6, 7, 9, 11
Adowa, 148, 203, 226, 262, 281; Italian advance on, 157, 162-3; bombing of, 163, 191, 275; capture of, 175-6, 177, 182-4
Adowa, battle of (1896), 11, 16, 22, 31, 73, 92, 103, 112, 161, 184, 286
Aeizanas, King, 47
Afdub, 43
Afgol, 285
African Exploration and Development Corporation, 133, 134
Agumberta Pass, 316
Aia, Mount, Emperor's headquarters at, 312-15, 322, 323

Akaki airport, 50, 147, 307
Ala, plain of, 105
Alamata, 291, 292-3
Alemayehu, Fitaurari, 8, 9
Aloisi, Baron Pompeo, 19, 28, 64, 66, 67, 78, 79, 87, 88, 118-19, 140, 143, 145, 146, 171, 172, 338; hard line at League meetings, 36, 37-8, 40, 72-4; softer attitude, 40, 41; plan to relieve League of blame for not stopping Italy, 92-3; panic over British memorandum, 122-123, 124; rejects British and French plans, 125
Amba Alagi, 208, 209, 212, 234, 288, 289, 290, 302; Italian capture of, 294, 296
Amba Aradam, 217, 233, 234, 278, 284, 294; battle of, 285-90, 292, 298
Amba Gheden, 285, 294
Amba Work, 261, 294
Anale, 216
Anglo-German Naval Treaty (1935), 85-86, 88-9, 147
Anglo-Iranian Oil Company, 204, 222
Antalo, 284, 287
Aras, Rustu, 65, 66
Asfou Wossen, Crown Prince, 177, 328
Ashangi, Lake, 290, 293, 309, 326
Asmara, 105, 151-3, 193
Assab, Hoare-Laval plan for, 226, 228, 250
Attlee, Clement, 82-3, 221
Auberson, Raymonde, 10, 17, 18, 274
Avenol, Joseph, 18, 55, 122, 338
Axum, 182, 184, 228, 250, 262, 270, 297, 298
Ayelu Birru, Dejasmatch, 209, 212-13, 238-9, 260, 262, 297, 298

30–3; earlier career, 31; builds up Eritrea as military base, 32, 70; hopes for border incident, 42, 43, 45; Mussolini's messages to, 45, 70, 153, 176–7, 186, 192, 194–5, 208, 213; concern over unreadiness, 151–3; invades Ethiopia, 157–8, 163–4, 175–86; aggrieved at Badoglio's visit, 176–7, 182, 193; dealings with Gugsa, 177–82; excessive caution, 179, 182, 186, 193–195; triumphal ceremonies in Adowa and Adigrat, 182–6; delays action on northern front, 193–5; at last launches drive on Makalle, 207–8, 212; replaced by Badoglio, 213–15

De Jacobis, Giustino, 115
Debbi, 157
Debra Aila, 274
Debra Amba, 296–7
Debra Markos, 238
Debre Berhan, 332, 334
Debri-Negaida, 277
Dembeguina Pass, Imru's victory at, 235–240, 243, 260, 262, 263, 270
Dessie, 191, 241–3, 274–5; Emperor moves headquarters to, 219, 233; bombing of, 219–20, 269, 275; Emperor flees towards, 326–7, 329–30; Italians occupy, 328, 330, 331
Desta, Ras, 265, 267, 271–2, 273–4
Dire Dawa, 337
Djibuti, 93, 132, 335, 336
Doghea Pass, 279
Dolo, 271; Swedish Red Cross unit bombed near, 265, 267–9
Drummond, Sir Eric, 37, 38–9, 44, 60, 74–5, 77, 84–5, 87, 88, 141, 143, 145
Dubbar, 313
Dundas, H., 135

Eboli, 103–4
Eden, Anthony, 41, 57, 58, 70, 100, 121–122, 144, 145, 146, 171–2, 186, 187, 223, 244, 324, 338, 341; as League delegate, 35, 36–8, 39–40; sympathy with Ethiopians, 36, 37–8, 125–6; tries to delay Emperor's complaint to League, 37, 39–40; tries to restrain Italy, 69, 72–3, 75–6, 77–9, 85–95; expects to become Foreign Secretary, 79–80; becomes Minister for League of

Nations Affairs, 81; answers opposition attacks on policy, 82–3; explains Anglo-German Naval Treaty to Laval, 85–6; brings unilateral British offer to Italy, 87–93; talks with Mussolini, 88–93; talks with Laval, 116–18, 165–6; suggests tripartite talks, 119; opposes Laval's plan for concessions to Italy, 165–7; and Hoare-Laval Plan, 229–32, 235, 236–8, 246–7, 253; abandons pro-sanctionists, 238, 276–7, 302–3, 340; becomes Foreign Secretary, 256–7, 259; justifies British action, 338
Elena, Queen of Italy, 252
Enda Jesus, 283
Enda Medani Alem, 288
Ende Gorge, battle of, 210–12
Engert, Cornelius Van H., 136, 333
Enterprise, HMS, 336, 339
Eritrea: part of French Somaliland transferred to, 25, 30; build-up as military base, 32, 69, 97, 104–5, 151–2, 198; Ethiopian troops withdraw from border, 173; Badoglio mission to, 176–7, 193–5, 214; slavery in, 183; Ethiopian threat to, 262–3, 270; Italians build road across, 298, 299
Ethiopian Imperial Guard, 107–8, 308, 311, 321, 322
Ethiopian Orthodox Church, 47–8

Fafan River, 270
Faldella, Emilio, 258
Farago, Ladislas, 50, 52–5
Fiche, 330, 332
Flandin, Pierre-Etienne, 57, 62, 85, 302–303, 324
French Somaliland, 93, 160–1; part transferred to Eritrea, 25, 30
Frumentius, Saint, 47

Ganale Doria, battle of, 273–4
Ganale River, 265, 271
George V, 44, 259, 277
George, W. Perry, 97–8, 100–1
Gerlogubi, 24, 195
Getachu, Ras, 317, 320, 333, 335
Gheva River, 255
Gilbert, Prentiss, 201
Giornale d'Italia, Il, 87, 88
Gojjam, 291

randum pointing to subjugation of Ethiopia, 31; aim to forestall British and French action, 22; seeks entente with France, 22–3, 24, 26–30; meeting with Laval, 26–9, 36; appoints De Bono High Commissioner for East Africa, 31–3, 70; aggressive audience with Drummond, 38–9; begins mobilization, 42–3, 44–5, 69–70; at Stresa conference, 57–8, 61–62; appoints arbitrators for League, 69, 72; secret instructions to De Bono, 70, 104; British statesmen's admiration of, 71; determination to go ahead, 73, 74–75, 79; threatens to leave League, 75, 76, 91, 93; *rapprochement* with Hitler, 77; gains new League delay, 78–9; rejects Zeila proposal, 89–93; publicly states plans for Ethiopia, 103, 120, 123–124; warns Britain against meddling, 113–14, 132–4, 125, 142; seeks Vatican compliance, 114, 127–8; agrees to three-power meeting, 119; announces war as inevitable, 125, 130; American feeling against, 128–9; rejects American conciliation, 130; maintains defiance of Britain and League, 142–6; sends troops to Libya, 142; rejects idea of international protectorate for Ethiopia, 146, 229; orders De Bono to advance, 153; proclaims invasion, 158–160; protests to League at Ethiopian mobilization, 164; plans to replace De Bono, 176–7, 215; urges him to press north, 185, 192–5, 208; concern over prospect of sanctions, 186–7, 192, 206–207, 216, 225; authorizes use of gas, 196, 263, 269, 272, 274, 278, 316; need for impressive victory, 207, 270, 278; replaces De Bono by Badoglio, 213–16; and Hoare-Laval Plan, 226–7, 232, 250–1, 258; speech at dedication of Pontinia, 249–51; popularity increased by sanctions, 251; launches 'Gold for the Fatherland' drive, 251–2; tries to influence choice of new British Foreign Secretary, 258–9; alarm at reaction to bombing of Red Cross unit, 268–9; suspends use of gas, 269; urges march on Harar, 328–9; celebrates victory, 336–8; orders strong measures against rebels, 340

Mussolini, Bruno, 163
Mussolini, Rachel, 252
Mussolini, Vittorio, 163, 233–4, 288, 306

Naples, 42
Neghelli, 271, 273, 274
Negradas, Yesus, 27, 43
Nesibu, Ras, 195
New York Times, The, 230, 269
News-Chronicle, 140
Norton, Clifford, 243, 244
Nur, Ali, 9
Nye, Gerald P., 129, 198

Ogaden desert, 52, 84, 110, 146, 161, 192, 195, 215; Italian bombing of, 195–6; Hoare-Laval plan for, 227; battle of, 329
Orford, s.s., 339
Osservatore romano, l', 127
Ozanne, Christian, 233

Pacelli, Eugenio Cardinal (later Pope Pius XII), 114, 116, 128
Panza, Mario, 92
Paris-Soir, 122
'Peace Ballot', 95–6, 138
Pecora, Ferdinand, 249
Pemberton, Harold, 51–2
Peterson, Sir Maurice, 205, 206, 224, 225, 226, 229–30
Pignatti, Moreno, 94
Pilot, The, 129
Pius XI, Pope, 114–16, 126–8, 206, 338
Politis, Nicolas, 237
Pontinia, 249–51, 258
Popolo d'Italia, Il, Mussolini's article in, 120
Potter, Pitman B., 69
Pouritch, Bozhidar, 237

Quoram, 290, 291, 292, 297, 302; Emperor's headquarters at, 293, 308–12; Red Cross unit bombed at, 305–7, 309–311

Red Cross units, bombing of, 265–6, 267–9, 305–7, 309–11
Ribbentrop, Joachim von, 76
Rickett, Francis W., 132–4
Riddell, Dr. A. W., 203

367

Roosevelt, Franklin D., 196, 302, 334; reluctance to intervene, 97, 98–101, 129–31, 168–70, 247–8; signs neutrality bill, 131; approves neutrality proclamation, 169–70, 201; evasiveness over trade embargo, 247–8
Rosen, Count Carl von, 307, 308–9
Rosso, Augusto, 102, 200
Rothermere, Lord, 112, 144
Royal Dutch Shell Company, 204

Saint-Quentin, René Comte de, 28, 206, 224, 226, 228
San Diego, 168
Santini, General Ruggiero, 157, 174, 178, 180, 185
Sasa Baneh, 329
Schuschnigg, Kurt von, 21
Selaclaca, 239, 240–1, 262, 263, 297, 298, 299, 301
Seloa region, 296
Seyoum, Ras, 148, 180, 209, 260, 288, 317; commands in Adowa sector, 173, 174; evacuates Adowa, 175; accepts money from De Bono, 177; union with Kassa, 217–18; battle of Abbi Addi, 255–6, 270; second battle of Tembien, 293–5; retreat to Takazze River, 295–296; reaches Quoram, 297, 311, 312; at Mecan Pass, 320–1
Shaw, George Bernard, 168
Shiferra, Fitaurari Balchi, 4, 7, 8–9
Shire, battle of, 301
Simon, Sir John, 16, 63, 68, 71–2, 78, 96, 224; presses Ethiopia for concessions, 36–7, 38, 39, 40–1, 60–1; tacit approval of Mussolini's plans, 43–4, 68; at Stresa, 57, 58, 60–1; seeks to delay League intervention, 64, 66; annoys Italy, 66–7; seeks pact with Germany, 76
Sokota, 316
Standard Oil Company, 134, 136, 198–9
Starace, Achille, 316
Steer, George, 241
Strang, William, 87, 88, 93, 165
Straus, Jesse, 203, 225, 226, 237
Stresa conference (1935), 57–62, 72, 75, 77, 85
Suez Canal, 22, 70, 82, 101, 111, 124, 141, 144, 145

Suvich, Fulvio, 23, 26, 28, 58, 59, 62, 63, 84–5, 86, 87, 88, 93, 143, 145, 164, 276

Taezaz, Dr. Lorenzo, 5
Tafari Makonnen, Ras — see Haile Selassie
Takazze River, 173, 208, 215, 327; Ethiopian crossing of, 238–9, 262, 269; mustard gas used on troops at, 295–6, 301–2
Tana, Lake, 87, 113
Teagle, Walter C., 198–9
Tecle Hawariate, P., 36–7, 39–40, 41, 55, 64–6, 68, 72, 120, 125–6, 150, 171–172, 291
Tembien, 209, 217–18, 255–6; first battle of, 279–82, 296; second battle of, 294–297, 311, 312
Temple, William, Archbishop of York, 247
Temps, Le, 140
Thomas, J. H., 35
Thompson, Geoffrey, 43, 58–60, 61, 68, 87
Tigre, 177, 192; Hoare-Laval Plan for, 227, 250
Times, The, 96, 140, 317
Titulescu, Nicolas, 277, 342
Tosso, Ligaba, 160, 161
Trades Union Congress, 138
Trento, 142
Tunisia, Italian claims on, 25, 30, 91

Uelie, Ali, 3–4
Ugu, Mount, 320

Vandenberg, Arthur, 197, 247
Vansittart, Sir Robert, 57, 59, 60, 62, 71, 76, 83, 96, 125; and Zeila offer, 84; helps Hoare write speech on Covenant, 137, 144; and Hoare-Laval Plan, 223–225, 226, 231–2, 243–4
Vasconcellos, Augusto, 202, 237
Victor Emmanuel III, 20, 27
Vinci-Gigliucci, Count Luigi, 15, 67
Virgin, General Eric, 10, 17, 53, 274
Vitetti, Leonardo, 59, 60
Volta, Sandro, 272, 273–4

Wal Wal: dispute over occupation and

ownership, 3–7, 9–11, 14–15, 18, 19, 35, 67–8, 78–9, 104, 119–20; battle at, 8–9, 11, 13–14, 17, 18, 23, 33, 67, 80–1, 119, 154

Walden, George S., 134, 135

Waldia, 290, 291, 292

War Widows and War Mothers, Association of, 251

Wardair, 4, 7, 14

Warieu Pass, 279, 280–2, 294, 295

Warra Hailu, 330

Waugh, Evelyn, 132–3, 307

Welch, Howard, 198

Wilson, Hugh R., 201

Wilson, Woodrow, 34, 98

Wodaju, Dejasmatch, 285–6

Wodaju Ali, Dejasmatch, 179–80

Young Ethiopians, 336

Zauditu, Empress, 12, 13

Zeeland, Paul van, 341

Zeila, 7; British plan to offer to Ethiopia, 84, 89, 110, 226; Mussolini's objection to plan, 89–93

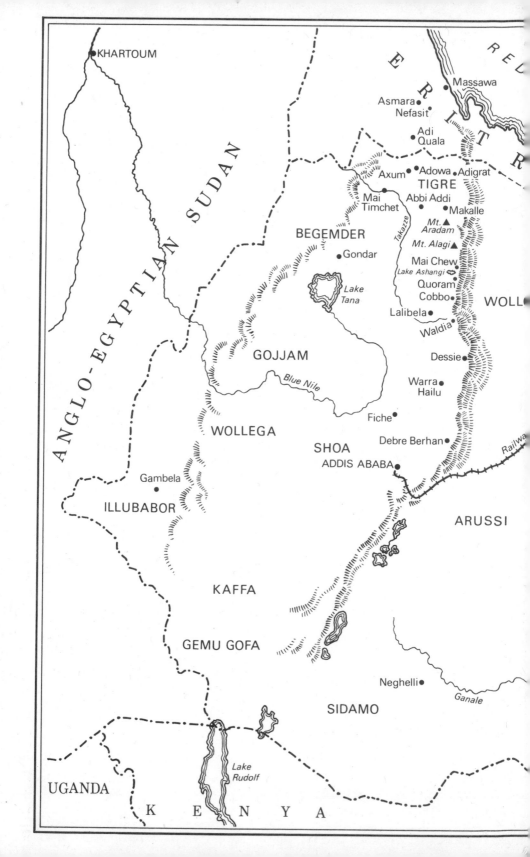